THE PANDEMIC PARADOX

The Pandemic Paradox

HOW THE COVID CRISIS MADE AMERICANS MORE FINANCIALLY SECURE

SCOTT FULFORD

PRINCETON UNIVERSITY PRESS

PRINCETON & OXFORD

The views expressed here are those of the author and do not necessarily represent the views of the CFPB or the United States.

Data from "Insights from the Making Ends Meet Survey," CFPB Office of Research, Research Brief No 2020-1, Consumer Financial Protection Bureau, July 2020, https://www.consumerfinance. gov.

Published by Princeton University Press
41 William Street, Princeton, New Jersey 08540
99 Banbury Road, Oxford OX2 6JX

press.princeton.edu

First paperback printing, 2025
Paperback ISBN 9780691245331
Cloth ISBN 9780691245324
ISBN (e-book) 9780691245348

Library of Congress Control Number: 2022946260

British Library Cataloging-in-Publication Data is available

Editorial: Joe Jackson, Josh Drake, Whitney Rauenhorst
Jacket/Cover Design: Karl Spurzem
Production: Erin Suydam, Lauren Reese
Publicity: James Schneider, Kate Farquhar-Thomson
Copyeditor: Ashley Moore

THis book has been composed in Arno Pro

For my wife, who encouraged me to write this book.
We survived two young kids, two full-time jobs,
and a pandemic together.

CONTENTS

THE PANDEMIC PARADOX

1

Introduction

THE BAD NEWS kept coming for Sofia. In March 2020, Sofia's workplace closed to help prevent the spread of COVID-19. In addition to losing her job, she suffered a death in her family. The associated costs were around $2,000. Because her income had gone down, Sofia could not pay all of the funeral expenses initially and charged some to a credit card. Her family also delayed paying some utility bills, reduced their food spending, and made a mortgage payment late. Because of the pandemic, their financial situation was spiraling out of control.

Even before the pandemic, Sofia's family had been having financial difficulties. Sofia, a Hispanic woman in her late twenties, lived with her husband and their two kids in a big Texas city. Before the pandemic, she worked a part-time job in an office and her husband had a full-time job. Between them, they earned about $30,000 a year. Their income was pretty stable from month to month, unlike about one-quarter of American households.

The expenses just kept adding up, leaving them with little ability to adjust. Some expenses were regular. The mortgage on the house they owned cost about $700 a month. With two kids, food was a big part of the budget. There were also the unexpected expenses. In the year before the pandemic, Sofia's family had had to find ways to cover a major house repair, a mobile phone replacement, and an increase in child care expenses. The regular expenses plus the unexpected ones made it difficult to save regularly. Sofia's family had less than $100 in checking and savings accounts in 2019.

And then there were all of the expenses that came from not having much money. Because they had so little in checking and savings, Sofia and her husband had had several overdrafts in the past year. Sofia's family was not intentionally overdrafting, but it was often difficult to know how much money was in the account before paying for groceries. Combined, the overdraft fees were more than they typically kept in savings.

Although some areas of Sofia's life—the kids, the house, the job— seemed to be going well, Sofia felt that her finances often controlled her life. Among her problems, she had an auto loan and at least one credit card bill that had been sent to collections agencies. She also had some student loan debt. She attended college briefly but did not get her degree; the experience left her with more than $6,000 in outstanding student loans. Those unpaid debts left Sofia's credit score in tatters. Although they had mostly managed to make ends meet in the past by borrowing, cutting back, and occasionally not paying a bill, they were unprepared for a major shock.

When she lost her job at the beginning of the pandemic and faced the unexpected funeral expenses, Sofia's family was already on the edge, and their finances started to deteriorate rapidly. They missed a mortgage payment. Perhaps they would lose the house. They cut back food spending, the one expense they could readily control. Perhaps they would have to start skipping meals. Or their electricity might get cut off because they had skipped paying a utility bill.

———

Everything changed in March 2020. For the first several months of 2020, COVID-19, a disease caused by a new virus that had been slowly spreading, looked like it might be contained. Something to be worried about, but with so much else to be worried about it was not most people's primary focus. The first confirmed U.S. deaths occurred around Seattle at the end of February. The first confirmed case in New York City was on March 1. But it soon became clear that these deaths and cases were just the beginning. Because testing was so limited, the virus had been spreading everywhere. By April, New York City briefly reached 800 deaths per day.

As it became clear that the virus was everywhere, suddenly everything stopped. Schools closed across the country. In the third week of March, businesses everywhere sent their employees home. Some employees continued to work from home, figuring it out as best they could. Others were soon fired or furloughed. From mid-March to mid-April, 22 million people lost their jobs. People whose jobs were deemed "essential" for society's functioning—from physicians and nurses to grocery checkout clerks and meat packers—were asked to still report to work in person but faced terrifying new risks.

"This is a huge, unprecedented, devastating hit," former Federal Reserve Board chairwoman Janet Yellen told CNBC on April 6, 2020.[1] As the bad news continued, the headlines captured just how terrifying the economic collapse was. The April unemployment rate was "the worst since the Depression era," the *Washington Post* headline told us.[2] GDP fell faster in the second quarter than at any time since we started calculating it officially in 1947, leading Reuters to declare, "COVID-19 crushes U.S. economy in second quarter."[3] It was impossible to escape the grim economic news.

Most Americans were not prepared for an economic collapse of this magnitude. Even before the pandemic, many Americans found it difficult to make ends meet. High housing costs left many families with little left over every month. Frequent unexpected expenses and variable incomes often left families facing difficult financial choices. In 2019, 40 percent of families had difficulty paying at least one bill or expense in the previous year. Black and Hispanic families were particularly likely to have had difficulty; two-thirds of Black families and nearly half of Hispanic families had difficulty paying at least one bill.

These problems left many families with little financial cushion. Two out of every five families could not cover their expenses for more than a month if they lost their main source of income. One out of five could not cover expenses for more than two weeks.

As it became clear that the pandemic was going to last longer than two weeks, suddenly many families were staring at a financial cliff.

Because of their limited financial cushion, within two weeks, one-fifth of families would need to start making hard cuts, and within a month another fifth would need to make cuts. Before the pandemic, families that faced difficulty paying bills often cut back on food, medical expenses, and other bills, leading to cascading problems. What cuts would families be forced to make this time?

The response to the 2008 financial crisis and Great Recession suggested that the government would not be there to help. Following the 2008 crisis, millions lost their homes and millions more suffered through years of unemployment and a weak labor market. The wealth of the bottom half of the population—150 million people—had only reached its precrisis peak in 2019. Black employment had also just recovered. While the bankers had quickly moved on, most people were only recovering from the 2008 financial crisis a decade later, just in time for the pandemic.

As the bottom fell out of the economy in March and April 2020, it looked as if widespread financial suffering was imminent.

Then something remarkable happened. Despite the economic collapse starting in March 2020, the pandemic did not bring about widespread financial suffering. In fact, by June 2020 most Americans were better off financially than they had been a year earlier. Even the unemployed, like Sofia, were doing better.

In May, Sofia received money from the CARES Act, a large pandemic relief bill. She and her husband received a total of $3,400, $1,200 for each adult and $500 for each of their two kids. That amount was around 10 percent of their prepandemic income and covered their mortgage for a couple of months plus the unexpected funeral expenses. In addition, Sofia applied for unemployment insurance and started receiving it after three weeks. The benefit included an extra $600 per week from the CARES Act in addition to about $100 in regular unemployment benefits.[4]

Until that aid arrived sometime in May, Sofia's financial situation looked dire: unpaid bills, a missed mortgage payment, reduced food expenditure. But after she started receiving unemployment insurance, Sofia's family's income increased by about $400 a week. As a result, she felt that her financial situation was somewhat better in June 2020 than it had been a year earlier, despite the period of unemployment and the big unexpected expenses.

These improvements for Sofia and many others continued through 2021 and into 2022, despite the many changes in the economy. Fewer people had difficulty paying bills or expenses. Unlike in 2008, few people lost their homes to foreclosure. Half as many people were evicted during the pandemic compared with the previous years. The average American's savings went up and credit card debt went down. Somehow, a pandemic that would eventually kill over a million Americans and take away so many opportunities left most Americans better off financially.

What explains this paradox? Three massive pandemic relief bills, starting with the CARES Act on March 27, 2020, transformed the pandemic economy. These bills collectively budgeted more than five trillion dollars, although not all of it was spent immediately. This pandemic relief was more than five times the relief in response to the 2008 financial crisis. The aid increased unemployment insurance benefits, extended them to new people, and provided them for longer. It sent direct payments worth several thousand dollars to most Americans. The relief bills gave nearly a trillion dollars to small businesses. The bills and other policies helped struggling homeowners and kept many people from being evicted. The aid kept struggling families from being pulled over the financial cliff, as Sofia's story illustrates.

Part I of this book tells the story of the pandemic's initial months. The story of a terrifying economic collapse. The story of what that meant for already financially precarious families. And the story of how pandemic policy protected so many families.

As the pandemic settled in, in Part II we'll turn to the many ways Americans changed their lives to adapt to the new reality in sometimes creative and sometimes tragic ways. To help slow the virus's spread, many people stopped going out to restaurants and bars, stopped traveling for vacation or to visit grandma. And most people's spending declined sharply. The government aid kept most people's incomes from declining, even if they were unemployed. With incomes the same or up and spending down, the average American's savings increased sharply.

Many paid long-standing debts. With the newfound financial freedom, many Americans started new businesses and, as the economy roared back, others became choosier about jobs. The pandemic gave many Americans a rare opportunity to reset their financial lives.

The pandemic was also just weird. Often stuck at home, we had to learn to muddle through new and suddenly stressful situations. We often had to come up with new ways of doing things to avoid contact. What activities are safe? Where can we get toilet paper? How do we make bread? How do we date or buy houses in a pandemic? Should we go to the dentist? As the pandemic unwound, we had to figure out how to do things again.

And even as the CARES Act distributed near-unprecedented aid, some people were left behind. Even as poverty fell, food insecurity increased. Renters and their landlords were left out of direct assistance until December 2020, and even then, rental assistance took months to go out. And while government aid kept many families from financial catastrophe, inequality increased as wealth became more concentrated. Life expectancy fell sharply for everyone, but especially for Black and Hispanic households. Drug overdoses increased and many Americans drank more.

Finally, in Part III we will examine the pandemic's aftermath. The pandemic fundamentally changed many Americans' lives, effectively pausing them in place for more than a year, with long-term consequences. Education was severely disrupted, harming our children's long-term ability to earn and thrive. The millennial generation faced the second economic catastrophe of their working lives, disrupting their march toward paying down student debt, buying a house, and saving for retirement. Millions of women left the workforce to take care of children whose schools and daycares shut their doors, setting back or permanently derailing their careers. Millions of people retired early, leaving the workforce before they planned and wondering whether they have enough for retirement.

The nature of work changed, as suddenly and for nearly two years, more than a third of the labor force worked from home and began to reconsider where work needed to occur and whether crushing commutes were really necessary. The massive work-from-home transformation may unleash new productivity gains and revive declining cities and towns across the country. Businesses had to rethink the nature of work. And the pandemic forced many people to become creative about how and when they work, juggling child care, cats, work calls, and emotional well-being.

As the pandemic wound down, new troubles emerged. The surge in demand for physical goods created shortages of different kinds as supply chains struggled to keep up. Labor markets did not always align as employers tried to hire under their old approaches and fed-up employees rethought their priorities. Inflation picked up and new economic worries emerged as well as new opportunities.

As we'll see, the pandemic experience shows that it is possible for American society to rapidly change direction. America and the world faced a new threat with massive economic and health implications. And American society responded to that threat in innovative ways. Individually, we learned to navigate a new, sometimes stressful and scary world. Collectively, we found ways to protect each other from the financial collapse. In the process, we learned we do not have to repeat past mistakes. We learned that targeted programs can relieve suffering. But we did not protect everyone. And against these benefits, there are also the costs of increased debt and inflation as the pandemic wound down. As we'll see, we also learned that not all policy was effective, not all spending worth the costs.

By understanding America's response to the pandemic, we can find a better way forward. A path that takes what worked in the pandemic and avoids the blunders. A path that protects the most vulnerable, without the pandemic's suffering. A path that makes us less financially fragile. A path that shows we can still accomplish big things, if we decide to. A path that leads to a fairer and more productive society.

———

Between chapters, I introduce other families like Sofia's. Sofia responded to a survey—aptly called the Making Ends Meet survey—which

I helped design for the Consumer Financial Protection Bureau (CFPB), where I am a senior economist. Sofia is not her real name. The survey carefully protects its respondents' identities, and we do not have information that would directly identify them, such as their names or addresses. Sofia and others responded to the survey before the pandemic in June 2019, again in June 2020, and again in February 2021. The respondents' credit bureau records are also associated with the survey. Together with their credit records, the three survey waves tell a richly detailed story of the ups and downs in Americans' financial lives before, during, and after the pandemic.[5]

The COVID-19 pandemic had a profound financial impact on people across the country. For some, like Sofia, the impact was immediate and financial. For others, it presented new opportunities or difficult choices. Not all of the families I introduce are having financial problems. But all of them have to think about their finances, have had ups and downs, and are trying to balance the competing demands of expenses and saving for the future. And all of them lived through a pandemic and had to make decisions affected by it. I approach telling their stories as a social scientist. I want to understand their choices and financial constraints, not judge them. These families' financial stories illustrate how the big economic and policy changes affect individuals. I chose families whose unique experiences echo some of the broader trends and families whose age, gender, race, and ethnicity reflect American society's complexity. But Sofia does not represent all Hispanic women any more than John— introduced after Chapter 3—represents all white men; their stories are their own even as many Americans faced similar struggles.

The survey helps understand the financial ups and downs faced by Americans and how they try to make ends meet in the middle. In addition to telling individual stories, I use the survey to describe the broader situation American households faced during the pandemic. It is common in news stories about the pandemic to learn about one family's difficulties. The difficulties these families recount to journalists are real, but they may not be common or representative of others' experiences. By drawing on a national survey, I can give broader context to individual stories and examine what experiences were common. At the same time, economists often forget that economic statistics are composed of millions of individual stories. Hiding behind dry statistics, we miss diverse experiences for the boring average and often focus on our own frequently limited and privileged experiences. The sometimes messy individual financial stories like Sofia's and John's are a reminder to look beyond the average.

This book draws from many other sources as well. I use research and data collected by a range of research organizations, inside and outside government, to paint a full picture of the pandemic economy. I spent the months after the pandemic hit looking at the CFPB's data sources, reading the evolving research, and briefing policy makers to help them understand what was going on. This book draws from my experience as a research economist at the CFPB during this tumultuous time.

Not many people have heard of the CFPB. As we wrote on the survey, "The Consumer Financial Protection Bureau is a federal agency created in 2010 to make mortgage, credit card, automobile, and other consumer loans work better and ensure that the markets are fair, transparent, and competitive." The CFPB was created by the Dodd-Frank Wall Street Reform and Consumer Protection Act after the 2008 financial crisis exposed deep problems in consumer financial markets. The Dodd-Frank Act consolidated consumer financial protection, which previously had been distributed across the federal government, into one agency whose primary focus would be consumers.[6] The first thing the act instructed the agency's director to do was to set up a research unit— the part of the CFPB where I work—to research, analyze, and report on emerging issues in consumer finance.[7] The Making Ends Meet survey I draw from is part of that research mission. But good research also requires independence, so this book does not necessarily represent the views of the CFPB or the U.S. government.

This book is about how the pandemic and pandemic policies affected Americans, not about politics.[8] Most of the major policies were broadly bipartisan, although they were certainly subject to many compromises. There is ample blame for bad policy, poor administration, and missed deadlines during the pandemic at all government levels. And there is ample praise for civil servants throughout government who worked through the pandemic to keep necessary services running and for politicians, their staff, and their appointees who championed effective and rapid policy in a quickly changing and uncertain time. Throughout, I focus on the evidence for what happened and why rather than attempt to assign blame or praise.

The pandemic also caused a research boom. New research papers came out more rapidly than ever before. Many research groups were able to use their knowledge and data to speak to current problems, including the JPMorgan Chase Institute, Opportunity Insights, the Census Bureau, and many others. In addition, the investments many newspapers and websites had made in data and economics journalism suddenly paid off. As so much changed so rapidly, good data and economics journalists were at the front analyzing and decrypting it. FiveThirtyEight, the *New York Times*, the *Washington Post*, Vox, and many other publications and sites put together original research based on data and interviews. I draw on this exciting research to explain how and why the often surprising pandemic economy evolved.

Sometimes the research I discuss conflicts; different teams using different methods reach different conclusions. To someone outside the research community, these different messages can be confusing. But good researchers know that we learn more about the world by challenging our assumptions and not relying too much on any individual study. And we will surely learn more about the pandemic's effects. While I present what we currently understand, good research refines and builds, and there is more to come on this massive economic and social event.

During the pandemic, we were often operating through uncertainty. Just as the pandemic brought new challenges for many Americans, it brought new economic conditions that evolved in unexpected ways. While individual families were trying to navigate a newly complicated world, government statistics offices, economists, and journalists were trying to puzzle through what was happening, and policy makers were trying to make decisions. Throughout the book, I try to highlight how our understanding evolved as the pandemic went on.

Like many parents, I spent the pandemic balancing work and being a parent, getting up early and staying up late so I could help take care of my two young kids, whose school and daycare had closed. Trying to be a teacher, economist, and dad at the same time. My wife and I sewed (bad and uncomfortable) cloth masks in early April 2020 and baked (delicious) bread in June when we could not buy sandwich bread. I cut my own hair for more than a year. Because I wasn't commuting, I spent a lot more time with my kids. While we have each had our own journey through pandemic, from wondering what was safe, to unemployment, to loneliness, to shortages, to juggling work and child care, we all shared the experience of living through the defining event of our time. I hope this book helps give you perspective on your own experiences and helps you understand others' experiences.

For most of us, the pandemic's primary impact has been social and economic rather than viral. But we should not forget the virus's direct impact. By June 2022, more than a million Americans had died of COVID-19, around one-quarter of worldwide deaths at the time. Grandparents, parents, friends, and loved ones who are no longer with us. At the same time, around three quarters of Americans had COVID-19 by July 2022.[9] Most cases were so mild that they went unreported. But millions had severe cases, suffering through weeks of breathing difficulty, and some experienced debilitating long-term symptoms. While this book is not primarily about the virus's path through society, these losses are the grim reality that shaped the COVID economy.

————

The financial ups and downs of families like Sofia's often followed the start, stop, and effectiveness of pandemic policies. The CARES Act policies that had done so much to support Sofia's family largely ended in July 2020. The next six months were hard. When she took the next round of the survey in February 2021, Sofia reported having difficulty paying some bills several times, the most recent in December 2020. They had to cut back on food spending again. And they paid some utility bills late, reduced other household expenses, used a credit card, and borrowed from family and friends. But all of that was not quite enough, so Sofia took out a payday loan that she rolled over at least once. For a fee, a payday lender advanced money before Sofia's next paycheck. Perhaps Sofia was worried that the skipped utility bills might cause their power to be turned off. But payday loans can be expensive and often get rolled over so many times that borrowers pay more in fees and interest than the amount of the original loan.

Around September 2020, Sofia stopped working so that she could take care of her children. This decision must have been hard for her, as it was for millions of other women. It is likely that the reduced income is one of the reasons they were continuing to have financial problems. But their family's school or daycare was closed because of the pandemic and someone had to look after the kids. Sofia's husband continued to work full time.

The pandemic affected them in other ways. Even though everyone in Sofia's household was covered by health insurance, they delayed some medical treatments because all nonessential medical care was shut down for a while during the pandemic. They could not buy enough of a necessity because it was not available in stores. The tightened finances meant that they looked for ways to cut back on expenses. For example, Sofia reported that although they had enough to eat, it was not always the kinds of food they wanted to eat. Despite this financial tightening, Sofia felt their expenses had increased, while their income had decreased after the expanded unemployment benefits expired. For a family without a large financial cushion, such changes could be dangerous.

The constant expenses that had always been part of their life continued during the pandemic. Part of being in a family network whose members support each other financially is the give and take. Sofia faced a significant unexpected expense when she loaned money to a family member. They also had some large home repairs and expensive phone replacements.

Once again, government support seems to have helped give them a buffer against disaster. Two large pandemic relief bills, one in December 2020 and one in March 2021, sent new cash payments and added to unemployment benefits. Sofia's credit card debt dropped several hundred dollars to nearly zero between January and March 2021 after these payments.

Despite all of the problems she faced during the pandemic, by June 2021 Sofia's debts were down and her credit score was up. They had not missed any more mortgage payments. Unlike millions of families following the 2008 crisis, they had not lost their home. Maybe this financial reset wouldn't last, but it gave her some financial space she had never had before. Like many Americans, Sofia had weathered the ups and downs of the pandemic economy. And despite it all, she was in a better position financially than before the pandemic.

As we'll see in Part I, Sofia's experience before and during the pandemic was common. Many families struggled to make ends meet before the pandemic. So when the bottom fell out of the economy starting in March 2020, it looked like painful cutbacks were just weeks away.

PART I

The Pandemic Economic Collapse

2

The Bottom Falls Out

THE PANDEMIC suddenly became real for most Americans on March 11, 2020.[1] Early that day, the World Health Organization finally declared that the spread of COVID-19 had become a pandemic.[2] Compared with Italy or China, the U.S. had yet to experience many deaths. There were about one thousand reported cases in the U.S. at the time, although the actual number of cases was certainly far larger because testing was still limited. Washington State and New York City were already experiencing surges. Only 31 deaths were directly attributed to COVID-19 at the time, mostly in Washington. But as Dr. Anthony Fauci, director of the National Institute of Allergy and Infectious Diseases, testified to a congressional committee that day, "Bottom line, it's going to get worse."[3]

Suddenly, the virus changed everything, from entertainment, to work, to school. Following the World Health Organization announcement, the S&P 500, a broad stock market index, fell 5 percent and another 10 percent the next day. By March 23, it had fallen by more than a third from its peak on February 19.[4] Many businesses started to close, some for good, putting millions out of work. After canceling a game on March 11, the NBA announced it was suspending the rest of the season. Interviewed following the suspension, Dallas Mavericks owner Mark Cuban said, "Do we send our kids to school tomorrow? Is it that big? It's like out of a movie. It doesn't seem real."[5]

Schools across the country closed that week. The Washington, D.C., public school system, where my four-year-old attended prekindergarten, announced it would be closed the following Monday to reassess safety protocols. Gathering with other parents at the playground after school that Friday—unmasked at the time, of course—we wondered when D.C. public schools would reopen. The consensus was that it might be as much as two weeks, and we agreed that surviving with our kids at home that long would be tough. My son did not return to school in person for more than a year.

That week, like many other Americans, my wife and I both learned that our workplaces would switch to mandatory telework for an unspecified number of weeks. We assumed the pause was going to be brief, so like most people in our situation, we left our workspaces as if we expected to return soon. As the *Washington Post* described it, a year later, many American offices felt like they were frozen in time.[6] Calendars were still on March 2020; desks were littered with notes on projects completed from home months ago; any plants brought in to brighten the space were now dead.

We were lucky we could work from home. Many Americans were required to continue working in person, taking on the risk of exposure to COVID. More than 20 million Americans quickly had no work at all.

Starting at the beginning of March, but accelerating through March and April, the U.S. economy paused as schools shut down and businesses either closed or moved to telework to prevent the virus's spread. Although the pause would not last long, the impact of the economic changes in March and April 2020 were felt for years. This chapter paints the big picture of the massive economic contraction that came from pausing so much economic activity. We'll return to how the pause affected individuals and groups throughout the book.

We would only learn the true depth of the pause slowly. Reliable economic statistics take time to collect, clean, and report, so economists and journalists were often grasping at more quickly available but less reliable data. Throughout this chapter, I highlight the differences between what we knew at the time and what we learned later, and how poor reporting created additional confusion. Those differences matter because decisions at the time were made with the information available—information that was often murky and quickly changing.

But even with the murky information available, the economic situation was scary.

The Eve of the Pandemic

To understand how deep the economic changes in March and April were, it is helpful to understand what the economy looked like on the eve of the pandemic. Up through February 2020, the U.S. economy had expanded nearly continuously since the end of 2009, when the Great Recession—the recession caused by the financial crisis that peaked in the fall of 2008—began to recede. The most straightforward and human-centered way to measure this expansion is to look at the share of the population with a job. The Bureau of Labor Statistics (BLS) releases a monthly report based on surveys it conducts of households and businesses. The household survey asks people whether they are employed or looking for a job and gathers some basic information about them such as age, sex, and race or ethnicity.

After bottoming out in December 2009 at 58.9 percent, the percentage of Americans with a job increased nearly continuously for the next ten years. Often called the employment-to-population ratio, the percentage of Americans with a job peaked in February 2020 at 61.1 percent (Figure 2.1).[7] The continuous expansion was the longest in U.S. history.[8] But even at its peak in February 2020, a much smaller share was working than in 2007, which was itself lower than in 2000. Many factors contributed to this fall—from an aging population, to increased competition with China and the decline of manufacturing, to falling real wages.[9] But the long-term decline suggests that the U.S. economy was leaving many people behind even during the longest expansion in U.S. history.

And even for people who were employed, wage growth had continued to be slow. Real wages (average wages adjusted for inflation) did not increase between 2009 and 2014, and then increased only slowly after that. So even though more people were finding jobs, they were not getting paid much more, on average, for them.[10]

But the expansion meant that many people who had traditionally had difficulty finding a job were included. The Black employment rate has been lower than white employment since the standard statistics were first measured in the 1970s. Black employment typically falls more quickly during a recession and recovers more slowly, a phenomenon

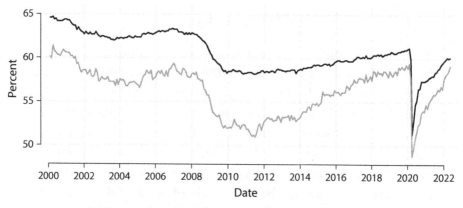

FIGURE 2.1. The share of the U.S. population employed fell dramatically at the start of the pandemic, just as the Black employment rate was starting to catch up. (*Source*: Bureau of Labor Statistics.)

referred to as "first fired, last hired."[11] The Black employment rate started out lower and fell by more during the dot-com crash of 2001 and during the Great Recession in 2008 (see Figure 2.1). The differences are large. During the Great Recession, for example, the Black employment rate fell by 7.4 percentage points while the overall employment rate fell by just 5 percentage points. Because the Black employment rate started out lower, a Black employee was about 50 percent more likely to lose her job.[12] But the long expansion from 2009 to 2020 had brought more and more Black employees into the labor force, and the employment gap in February 2020 was the lowest since at least the 1970s.

This discussion has focused on employment, not unemployment. The unemployment rate tends to get the most focus from journalists and commentators, but unemployment is a weird, nonintuitive, and often misleading measure of whether people have jobs. The "unemployment rate" is the percentage of people who did no paid work in the previous week and are actively looking for a job, based on the BLS monthly survey. The BLS counts someone as "looking" if they made "specific active efforts to find employment sometime during the 4-week period ending with the reference week."[13] Being active might mean attending a job fair or applying for a job posting.

What makes the unemployment rate misleading—and why many economists prefer other measures—is that it can change based on whether people are looking for a job. People who want a job but are discouraged and not actively looking do not count as unemployed. People who might start working, but only if they find a job that pays enough, do not count unless they are actively looking. Those may seem like minor distinctions, but they matter a great deal in practice, especially during the early stages of the pandemic when shutdowns made job search difficult or impossible. For example, many more American women might want to work if they were paid enough to afford child care, but those women do not count as unemployed unless they are actively looking. A great economy paying high wages might bring them into the "labor force," which is the number of people who are employed or looking for a job; a weak economy offering only low-paying work will discourage them from seeking jobs.

By most overall measures, the U.S. economy looked very healthy in February 2020. Employment was high. Gross domestic product (GDP), the dollar value of all economic activity, had been steadily increasing since 2009. By July 2019, the U.S. had experienced its longest period of steady growth ever. Real GDP, which adjusts the dollar value for inflation, had grown at a nearly continuous 2.3 percent annual rate. Wages had not kept pace with growth and, as the next chapter will show, many people still found it hard to make ends meet. But the expansion was finally starting to reach Black Americans, and there were signs that the tight labor market might be finally pulling wages higher.

The Bottom Falls Out

In the week ending on Saturday, March 14, 2020, about 250,000 people filed an initial unemployment insurance claim, slightly more than a week earlier, and about the same as a year earlier.

In the week ending March 21, 2.9 million filed an initial unemployment insurance claim. The next week, another 6 million people filed. The week after that, another 6.2 million filed. Those devastating numbers actually understate the scale of job losses, since people who were not

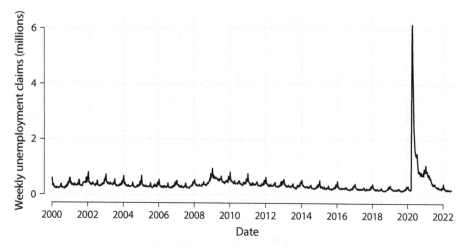

FIGURE 2.2. Initial unemployment insurance claims increased by more than 20 times. (Not seasonally adjusted. *Source*: Employment and Training Administration.)

formally employed, such as Uber drivers or those who were self-employed, were not initially eligible to file for unemployment insurance. The number of unemployment claims was so large that it is hard to even see the Great Recession in 2008 and 2009 or the 2001 dot-com recession when they are plotted together as in Figure 2.2.[14] Although claims fell off after April 2020, that was mostly because there were so few people left to lay off or furlough.

The U.S. had never experienced so many job losses so quickly. Headlines included the terms "unthinkable" and "terrifying" as the job losses shattered records.[15] During the peak of the Great Recession, the number of claims never topped one million, meaning that the peak pandemic unemployment claims were more than six times larger than the worst of the Great Recession. The peak before that was just over a million claims in 1982.

Although these numbers were terrifying, the way they were reported made them seem even worse. The increase in claims was so large that it broke the standard seasonal adjustments that the BLS uses to smooth out regular changes each year. During normal times, many economic data series change in predictable patterns from month to month. For example, every year there are large predictable swings in unemployment claims within the year. One reason for the swings is that some industries, such as construction, farming, and tourism, primarily work only when the weather is good. These swings are evident in the yearly spikes in Figure 2.2. The BLS makes seasonal adjustments to take the predictable swings out so that the trend is clear.

For the week ending March 28, 2020, for example, the BLS adjustment added close to a million claims for seasonal reasons—nearly 14 percent of the total—to the numbers actually reported by state unemployment systems.[16] The BLS reported the actual numbers several pages after the adjusted ones, but the most dramatic numbers were what the news media reported. Whether any seasonal adjustment made sense during the pandemic is questionable because nothing was normal about the pandemic. The BLS's approach, by not taking into account that the pandemic was not just normal seasonal variation, significantly overstated the number of claims (the BLS fixed its approach by September).[17]

Seasonal adjustments can also hide real ups and downs that families must deal with, which are often seasonal. For example, in normal years, about twice as many unemployment insurance claims are filed in January, when the holiday retail surges end, as in September, when agriculture and construction are usually still bustling along. While many people losing jobs at the same time every year is predictable, it does not make it easy for the people involved. Managing income variation within the year is a challenge for many families.[18] Removing the large seasonal variation erases this important economic problem from the standard statistics, making it easy to ignore.

While unemployment claims were the first statistics to come in, the underlying system for collecting them was not built to be a real-time data source, or to deal with an unprecedented shock like a pandemic. The fundamental problem with using unemployment claims to evaluate the state of the U.S. economy is that the underlying data collection was primarily set up to administer federal funds to state employment agencies, rather than to produce an economic statistic. Unemployment claims are collected from state systems, many of which could not handle the influx in claims early on. After the initial surge, much of the variation from week to week was from states processing backlogs or removing duplicate claims, making it difficult to track how many Americans were actually losing jobs in a given week.[19] The pandemic also revealed just how out-of-date and inefficient many state unemployment systems were. As we will see, many states were unable to process claims in a timely manner, leaving people without the funds they were entitled to just when they needed them most.

When the BLS's regular unemployment statistics finally came out in early May, they showed just how devastating March and April had been. The monthly "employment situation report" from the BLS is the basis for the employment numbers in the previous section and in Figure 2.1. The report is usually released the first Friday of the month and is based on a survey that takes place in the middle of the previous month. Unlike unemployment insurance claims, this report is designed to provide an accurate understanding of the labor market. But collecting and processing more accurate information takes time, so the report captures unemployment from several weeks earlier. When the BLS released its April report in early May, the number of employed Americans dropped by 22 million from the middle of March to the middle of April.[20] To give a sense of scale, more people lost their jobs in a month than were employed in all of California. Figure 2.1 shows this employment drop: from February to April 2020, the percentage of people employed dropped nearly 10 percentage points. In just two months, 16 percent of the people with a job lost it.

Even these more accurate numbers did not fully capture the devastating job market. The peculiar nature of pandemic layoffs made it harder to collect information. Many people had not been explicitly laid off, but the place they worked was shut and they were not getting paid. They should have been classified as unemployed but were instead reported as "absent for other reasons." Correcting for the misclassification, the actual unemployment rate was likely a devastating 17.7 percent, 3 percentage points higher than the 14.7 percent the BLS reported for April.[21] Moreover, the household survey the BLS uses to collect the unemployment statistics had a response rate about 15 percentage points lower than in months before the pandemic. This lower response rate is potentially concerning because the people who were not responding may be exactly the ones having the most problems. Normally, surveys correct for this kind of nonresponse by reweighting results to make them representative again. But with such a massive change in employment and response rates, the appropriate way to reweight the results may not have been clear. With so much changing so rapidly, it was very hard to collect accurate statistics during the early months of the pandemic. But understanding what was happening mattered for making good policy, for government budgets that would have to adjust, and for everyone trying to figure out just how bad things were.

Overwhelmed Unemployment Systems Failed

The newly unemployed turned to their state unemployment offices to file unemployment insurance claims. Most states were unprepared to deal with the massive increase in unemployment insurance claims, which meant that many people waited weeks or even months for the money that was rightfully theirs, just when they needed it most. Chapter 4 will discuss the impacts these delays had on household finance in greater detail.

According to U.S. Department of Labor standards, states with "acceptable levels of performance" processed and paid benefits promptly so that at least 87 percent of people claiming unemployment insurance received their first payment within three weeks.[22] Even the "acceptable" level could leave 13 percent waiting more than three weeks. Furthermore, not meeting the "acceptable" level does not carry any penalties for states, although they are required to have a plan for addressing the problem. Before the pandemic, almost every state was "acceptable." Forty-four states paid more than 90 percent of claims within three weeks and many were above 95 percent. Not all states did as well; North Carolina paid less than 80 percent of its claims within three weeks.[23]

During the pandemic, claims were rarely paid promptly. In June 2020, when the backlog was at its largest, the first payment for only 52 percent of claims occurred within three weeks; 22 percent took more than eight weeks.[24] In many states, the share of claims paid within three weeks dropped to less than a quarter by October 2020.[25] Unacceptable.

There were several reasons why states were unable to process claims quickly. First, state computer systems were often outdated and simply unable to deal with the deluge. New Jersey, for example, put out a call to computer programmers who knew the old programming language its systems were based on because it did not have the expertise to maintain its systems.[26] Second, the archaic computer systems and poorly designed forms made errors more likely, and any error would slow down processing because it might require a human to step in and make a change. With so many applications, even as states attempted to hire more people to deal with the influx, anything that required a human intervention was likely to be slow. Finally, states faced many fraudulent claims. One of the reasons why payments were not automatic was to prevent and reduce fraud. Programs put in place to catch fraud also slowed down processing. Fraud prevention might not have produced much delay during normal times, but it was a large drag during the surge.[27]

Some of these problems were long-standing and could have been fixed before the crisis. States that had acted to develop better systems before the crisis did far better than others. Despite the pandemic flood of claims, Virginia, Colorado, and Montana still had "acceptable" first payment percentages. Meanwhile, Florida made the first payment for 22 percent of claims in three weeks as of June 2020. Maryland made it for 14 percent. But states that paid claims quickly were also targets of fraudulent claims, which appear to have escalated during the pandemic as criminal organizations got into the unemployment-insurance claims business.[28] Not only did fraud cost the government money, but it slowed payments and made it harder to claim insurance for the truly unemployed. To deal with fraud, for example, Colorado instituted new rules requiring phone verification in July, which caused claims, whether fraudulent or not, to fall by 40 percent.[29]

Even six months into the crisis, many states still had not reached "acceptable" levels of timely payment. In September 2020, the first payment for nearly half of claims took longer than eight weeks in D.C., Indiana, Maryland, Michigan, and Ohio; and a horrific two-thirds of South Dakota's and Kentucky's claims took more than eight weeks.

For comparison, only 5 percent of North Dakota's claims took that long. In Montana, despite early problems with fraud, only 3 percent took more than eight weeks. Some states served their citizens well; others did not.

Stay-at-Home Orders and Voluntary Stoppages

While there are other ways to describe what occurred in March and April, the term "Great Pause" seems the most apt.[30] Unlike in a normal recession, we intentionally stopped doing many things. The NBA season: paused (other sports soon followed). Going to the office: paused. Employment in industries requiring contact with others: paused. Going to school, having meals in restaurants, traveling: all paused. We could still physically do those things, but they posed a risk of spreading infection, so we collectively made a decision to suspend many activities.

This rapid and simultaneous economic pause distinguishes the initial stages of the pandemic from other recessions. For example, in the Great Recession, the sudden stop in financial markets after the collapse of Lehman Brothers in September 2008 took time to spread to other parts of the economy. Lower stock market wealth and less consumer credit meant fewer purchases. Bank credit became less available, which meant successful businesses could not expand and hire more employees, and troubled businesses could not reorganize and had to liquidate. These effects took time to spread and cause employment and production to decline outside the finance industry, so the depth of the recession was not until a year after the worst of the financial crisis.

As the virus spread, state and local governments implemented stay-at-home orders. The particular restrictions varied widely, but they typically involved requiring everyone who could work from home to do so and allowing only certain "essential" workers to continue in person. By April 1, 89 percent of the population was under some sort of stay-at-home order.[31] As employers told employees to stay home and businesses shuttered, trips outside the home fell precipitously. According to the Bureau of Transportation Statistics, the number of trips fell by about a third from the beginning to the end of March.[32] Nearly real-time data from cell phones told the same story: average travel distance declined by 48 percent from the beginning to the end of March.[33]

The available evidence suggests that government policy ordering shutdowns had only a minor effect compared with individual and employer decisions. In a working paper examining the effects of the pandemic on the labor market, Alexander Bartik, Marianne Bertrand, Feng Lin, Jesse Rothstein, and Matt Unrath found that "shut-down and re-open orders account for only a modest portion of the changes in labor markets and economic activity during the crisis; the overall patterns have more to do with broader health and economic concerns affecting product demand and labor supply rather than with shutdown or reopen orders themselves."[34] The evidence is persuasive: the fall in employment took place as the public ceased going out because of the risk of the virus as cases increased. State stay-at-home orders responded to the same concerns but occurred after the major employment declines. Stay-at-home orders may still have been an important signal to the public about what behaviors were and were not acceptable, but they were not the main cause of the economic decline.

The early employment losses were largely in jobs that require human contact: those associated with restaurants, travel, and indoor gatherings of all sorts. Employers closed their doors for several reasons: because demand had disappeared as consumers stayed home; because of concerns for spreading the virus; and as a result of various stay-at-home orders as states and local governments sought to slow the virus's spread. A large share of the job losses in small businesses reflected firms that closed entirely, though many subsequently reopened. Businesses that were already struggling were more likely to close. Lower-income workers were more likely to be laid off and less likely to return to work through July.[35]

Spending Drops

With much of the country staying at home and with little knowledge of what was safe, many people decided to delay or not make purchases because of safety concerns. Others were newly unemployed or concerned they might be. With the future looking more uncertain, many people decided to reduce spending. Economists call a change in spending because of an increase in uncertainty "precautionary" behavior. During the pandemic, several research groups developed new ways to measure these consumer decisions much more rapidly than before.

My colleagues Éva Nagypál, Christa Gibbs, and I gathered some of the first evidence of this consumer decline. When a consumer applies for new credit to purchase a car or a home or for a new credit card account, most lenders will seek information about the consumer from one of the three large nationwide credit bureaus. These credit inquiries typically appear almost immediately in credit records when a consumer's credit report is pulled. Other credit and consumer spending data often take longer to get reported.

When we compared the first week of March 2020 with the last week of March, auto loan inquiries dropped by 52 percent, new mortgage inquiries dropped by 27 percent, and revolving credit card inquiries declined by 40 percent.[36] The drops were significantly more pronounced for consumers with higher credit scores, suggesting that a drop in income from unemployment was only part of the story. Even consumers who, at least by their credit score, were doing pretty well were avoiding new inquiries. States with more unemployment insurance claims and more COVID-19 cases had much larger declines in auto loan inquiries. In short, consumers were staying home and avoiding large purchases and were doing so more in places where cases were the largest.

State laws also hampered some purchases. Auto inquiries in Pennsylvania fell to nearly zero in March, a precipitous decline larger than any other state. Before the pandemic, Pennsylvania required a notary public signature for car sales, making online-only sales impossible. The Pennsylvania legislature eventually loosened these restrictions, but its residents were effectively unable to buy cars for a month.[37] As we will discuss in Chapter 5, this was one of many instances of governments and citizens muddling through as we figured out how to operate in the pandemic economy.

Other information soon came in that confirmed the decline in spending. One team used partnerships with private payment-processing firms to develop close-to-real-time consumer spending measures. Over the month of March, consumer spending dropped by 28 percent. Almost all of the decline occurred in the second half of the month.[38]

Government statistics eventually caught up and confirmed the precipitous fall in spending. Retail sales declined by 8.7 percent over March 2020. Retail sales, which make up 42 percent of personal consumption expenditures, fell even more in April, declining by 22 percent from February (seasonally adjusted).[39] Restaurants were the worst hit: sales at restaurants fell by 55 percent from February to April 2020.

In a sign of changing consumption habits, spending at grocery stores was 28 percent higher in March and 11 percent higher in April than in February 2020. More people were eating at home and many households sought to stock up their pantries. We'll dig deeper into the enormous changes these consumption shifts caused, from shortages and hoarding in Chapter 5 to supply chain backups in Chapter 10.

Gross Domestic Product Falls

Because GDP is calculated quarterly, we had to wait until the end of April for GDP in the first quarter (January through March), and until the end of July to see the full impact of the Great Pause. Around 70 percent of GDP is consumer spending, so economists knew the fall in spending meant that GDP would fall. The question was, by how much?

Although GDP numbers are often treated as the most important indicator of an economy's health, they are actually estimates based on many underlying data sources and surveys, some of which are not updated frequently. GDP estimates are calculated by the Bureau of Economic Analysis (BEA), and the first or "advance estimate" of GDP is based on limited data and a lot of extrapolation. Typically, the BEA will revise its estimates several times as new information comes in. Revisions can sometimes be extensive, and measurement is particularly difficult during a turbulent time such as the pandemic.

In the second quarter of 2020, U.S. GDP declined by 9 percent (seasonally adjusted). For the previous five years, GDP had grown by an average of 0.57 percent a quarter, so any decline was a big departure. A 9 percent decline in a single quarter was a depression-level decline.

The second-quarter fall was particularly large and scary, although poor reporting made it seem much worse than it actually was. Rather than reporting the growth rate of GDP in a quarter, the BEA reports the "annualized" growth rate, which is how much GDP would grow if it grew at the same rate for four quarters. If that sounds complicated and a bit odd, it is. A rough approximation is that the annualized growth rate is four times the quarterly growth rate. The practice makes some sense during normal times when changes in GDP growth rates are relatively small and it is useful to be able to compare quarterly growth to annual growth.

Reporting on an annualized basis was misleading during the pandemic. GDP would not fall for four quarters at the second-quarter rate, so the annualized number was not useful in understanding the pandemic's impact. When the BEA reported that GDP had declined in the second quarter, the number it reported was that GDP had declined by 33 percent on an *annualized* basis. The key additional nuance was missed by most journalists and news organizations in their headlines and often in the text itself, producing falsely apocalyptic news coverage. For example, NBC had the incorrect headline, "Economy in Reverse: Initial Jobless Claims Rise for Second Week, GDP Falls by Record 33 Percent," although the article later included the key modifier "annualized."[40] To their credit, some reporters understood the difference, and some news organizations managed to report the still-scary quarterly GDP numbers correctly while warning about using the annualized numbers.[41]

This GDP decline was the largest since reporting began. It was also likely larger than the first two quarters of the Great Depression, although the Great Depression extended for much longer.[42]

Stocks Tumble but a Potential Financial Crisis Is Averted

Faced with a rapid reduction in demand, businesses shutting down, and an uncertain future, the stock market fell rapidly. From its peak on February 19, 2020, to the trough on March 23, the S&P 500 fell by 34 percent.

The S&P 500 covers about 80 percent of all U.S. equities and all of the largest companies by market capitalization.[43] The fall in the value of these equities alone wiped out around $10 trillion of wealth.

Worrying signs of a potential financial crisis accompanied the stock market fall. During March, the markets where several important financial securities are traded developed substantial problems. Two of the most important markets—for Treasury securities and mortgage-backed securities—became "dysfunctional."[44] Problems in markets for corporate debt also emerged. The price of corporate bonds plummeted as it became more difficult for sellers to find buyers.[45] It appears that many sellers across financial markets were seeking liquidity—the ability to sell an asset immediately for cash.[46] But the markets were seizing up, perhaps because of disruptions as many traders worked from home, so ironically, the rush to sell left normally very liquid markets (markets with many buyers and sellers and where trades can happen quickly) less liquid, which encouraged more people and institutions to sell because they were worried about lack of liquidity. These kinds of cycles can spiral out of control and lead to a financial crisis.

To deal with a potential crisis, the Federal Reserve reduced interest rates to nearly zero and reintroduced many programs from the 2008 financial crisis to keep markets liquid and support bank lending. Reducing interest rates is the standard way the Federal Reserve, known colloquially as the Fed, approaches a recession. While the Fed can only directly control the federal funds rate—the rate it lends to banks overnight—other interest rates typically follow this rate. So when the Fed cut the federal funds rate from about 1.5 percent to nearly zero on March 15, 2020, and said it would keep rates close to zero for an extended period, that helped lower other interest rates.[47] With lower interest rates, businesses find it less costly to borrow and expand, which helps increase investment, and consumers pay less for new mortgages, auto loans, and credit cards, which helps consumer spending.

To help keep markets liquid and interest rates from rising, the Fed began making substantial purchases of Treasury securities and mortgage-backed securities, a program called Quantitative Easing. Between March 11 and April 29, the Fed bought approximately $300 billion in mortgage-backed securities and $1.68 trillion in Treasury securities. It maintained and increased these purchases over the next nine months, so the Fed's balance sheet nearly doubled between March and December 2020.[48]

The Fed also began offering direct support to securities firms and money market mutual funds and even opened up lending to foreign central banks. Through its Primary Dealer Credit Facility, which it brought back from the 2008 financial crisis with backing from the U.S. Treasury, the Fed offered loans to financial institutions called primary dealers at low interest rates in exchange for a wide range of securities.[49] Primary dealers help securities markets function, so providing these firms with the financial backing may have helped keep the dysfunction in securities markets from spiraling out of control. The Fed also used another program from the 2008 financial crisis, lending to banks to keep the market for money market mutual funds liquid.[50] Money market mutual funds invest in very liquid securities such as Treasury securities and are used by businesses and individuals as a place to keep funds that may be needed soon or unexpectedly. Within the financial system, they operate a bit like checking accounts but pay interest. Large withdrawals in early March and the disruptions in securities markets had left these mutual funds in disarray, so the Fed program may have helped keep problems from spreading. And the Fed started lending dollars to foreign central banks, including the European Central Bank and the Bank of Japan, in exchange for foreign currencies. These loans are called "swap lines" because the central banks swap currencies. Much of international commerce and finance depends on dollars, and these international dollar markets were also seizing up. The swaps allowed foreign central banks to help stabilize foreign dollars markets whose problems might have spilled back to the U.S.[51]

Finally, the Fed introduced new programs in which it lent directly to major employers and bought existing corporate bonds. According to the Fed, the goal was to provide "companies access to credit so that they were better able to maintain business operations and capacity during the period of dislocations related to the pandemic."[52]

These "emergency lending facilities" show just how serious the Fed considered the economic conditions. The Fed normally does not directly purchase corporate bonds, and even lending to firms with these kinds of securities as collateral had not happened since the previous financial crisis. As Fed chair Jerome Powell said on April 29, 2020, when describing the actions the Fed had taken, "Many of these programs rely on emergency lending powers that are available only in very unusual circumstances, such as those we find ourselves in today. We are deploying these lending powers to an unprecedented extent, enabled in large part by the financial backing and support from Congress and the Treasury. We will continue to use these powers forcefully, proactively, and aggressively until we're confident that we are solidly on the road to recovery."[53] In one of the few good things to come out of the 2008 financial crisis, the Fed was able to move rapidly because it had already developed these programs and still had the expertise to deploy them effectively.

Following the Fed's interventions, financial markets quickly began operating more normally.[54] By August the stock market had reached its prepandemic peak and would keep on climbing. It is difficult to tell whether a financial crisis was imminent and was headed off by timely policy, or whether financial markets would have been fine on their own. But a financial crisis on top of the economic crisis created by the pandemic would have been terrifying. A financial crisis would have meant that, just when they needed it most, households and businesses would have been unable to access their own funds or borrow to continue operating during the pandemic. During the Great Pause, much economic activity halted. A financial crisis might have meant many closures were permanent. If we were going to restart smoothly, financial markets and corporations had to be able to access funds they had saved and access credit markets to smooth things over. In a rare bit of good news during this period, what looked briefly like a looming financial crisis quickly dissipated as financial markets began to operate normally again.

Facing Ruin?

We may have avoided a financial crisis, but the bottom had still fallen out for much of the economy. As more than 20 million people lost their jobs, as the stock market dried up, and as consumer purchasing fell, at the end of March it looked like we were entering a financial apocalypse for many families. As we'll see in the next chapter, many families were already financially precarious. So as people lost their jobs, it seemed likely that many families were going to have to make severe cuts soon. Would they skip food and medical care? Would they miss mortgage payments and default on debt, bringing down banks and starting another financial crisis, just as the initial market disruptions were calming down? To answer these questions, we need to understand how families coped before the pandemic.

Marcus

The pandemic economic collapse hit Marcus particularly hard. When he took the survey in June 2019, he was feeling fairly confident about his finances. Marcus, a Black man in his late thirties, lived by himself in a metro area in the South. He had a steady job with a predictable income earning about $30,000 in 2018, which he described as normal.[55]

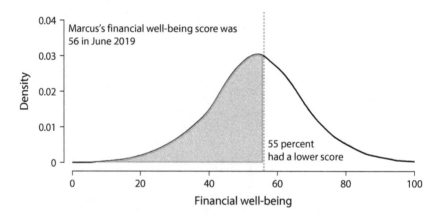

Marcus felt that he was saving for the future, although his choices did not always suggest saving was a priority. He had less than $100 in the bank but felt that if he had a $1,000 emergency fund, he would be well protected. He had a retirement account. His rent was around $750 a month, which was pretty manageable, although he was hoping to move in the next six months. He had a car and an auto loan, but the payments were not too bad.

Marcus often felt that he had money left over at the end of the month and had very little concern that the money he had or would save wouldn't last. Together, these responses left him with a financial well-being score of 56, slightly above the middle nationally. The figure shows how Marcus compares with people from a national survey in 2016.[56]

But while Marcus felt financially secure, his actual finances were more precarious. He had had some difficulties paying some debts several years ago, leaving him with a low credit score. He also had no credit card, so without any money in the bank, Marcus did not have any ready ability to spend more should a problem arise. As a result, a combination of events led to Marcus having trouble paying bills three or four times in the previous year. The most recent time, about four months earlier, a combination of funeral fees and taxes resulted in an unexpected $4,000 expense. He sold something he owned to cover the bills, but the event does not seem to have caused him broader financial issues.

Marcus was beginning to realize that he needed to be more careful. The survey, by asking a series of questions about his finances, may have gotten him to focus for the first time. Marcus wrote in a comment at the end of the survey, "Thank you for helping me realize some of the decisions I have been making."

Early in the Pandemic

In June 2020, Marcus's financial status had deteriorated. He had been laid off because of the pandemic, so his income had gone down. Meanwhile, his expenses had gone up. He never felt as if he had money left over at the end of the month, was very concerned that the money he had or would save wouldn't last, and felt that because of his money situation, he would never have the things he wanted. His financial well-being score had plummeted.

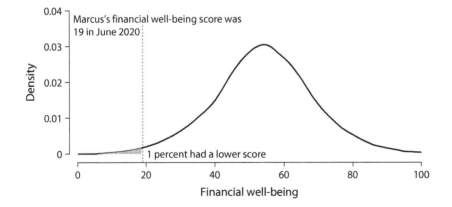

The lost income when his work closed down caused a series of cascading financial effects. He negotiated some lower payments and a lender offered some flexibility on his car loan. He sold something. He paid some utility bills late. He used up all of his savings and reduced his expenses in other ways. But he still had difficulty paying some medical bills and did not pay all of his cell phone bill one month.

One reason for his financial distress is that Marcus does not seem to have benefited from government assistance. He did not receive any unemployment benefits and did not receive an Economic Impact Payment ($600 sent to most Americans as part of the CARES Act). We do not know why Marcus did not receive any assistance. Perhaps his job was informal so he was not eligible for unemployment benefits and did not file taxes, which the IRS used to decide eligibility for Economic Impact Payments. While the U.S. Treasury automatically deposited most Economic Impact Payments, many people slipped through and never received their money. But he did receive some flexibility on rent. He also received some flexibility on his auto loan after he reached out to his auto lender.

Late in the Pandemic

By February 2021, things had turned around somewhat. Marcus had been recalled to his job. He was no longer as optimistic financially as he had been before the pandemic, but his financial situation was not as dire as

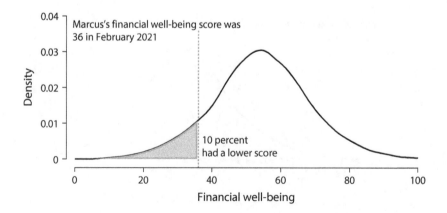

when the pandemic first hit. He had drawn down all of his savings and the one retirement account he had. He still felt as if his money situation kept him from having the things he wanted in life.

And other things come up, even during a pandemic. Marcus had some car repair expenses, and more legal fees and funeral expenses. Because all of his savings had been depleted, these expenses caused him to have trouble paying all his bills about once a month. To deal with these problems, Marcus sold more of his things and cut back on nonessential spending. And he borrowed from his family to help tide things over. While it is possible Marcus's family had substantial resources, it is likely that his troubles also put a strain on his family.

Because of the pandemic, Marcus did not get a medical issue treated. He was concerned about virus exposure and his provider had limited available service, so he delayed treatment.

3

Making Ends Meet before the Pandemic

EVERYONE FACES financial ups and downs through their lives: the unexpected car expense or cell phone replacement; promotions, unemployment, and retirement; a big medical bill. Everyone, including the well off, has to manage through these ups and downs. As the ups and downs of life accumulate, we all have to balance income, expenses, and saving for the future. But for many Americans basic expenses are high compared with their income. The combination of low income and high expenses leaves little margin, so when financial bumps hit, they can add up and lead to bigger financial problems. And the pandemic was a huge financial bump for many people.

Many households were financially fragile before the pandemic. One way to think about this fragility is how well households could respond to shocks such as pandemic unemployment. The Making Ends Meet survey asked all respondents in 2019, "If your household lost its main source of income, about how long could you cover expenses by, for example, borrowing, using savings, selling assets, or seeking help from family or friends?" The question asks respondents to think broadly about their financial situation rather than to consider only a narrow source of funds such as in a checking account. The question thus captures how long a household, using all resources available to it, could cover its expenses after losing its main source of income without significantly altering its lifestyle. Figure 3.1 shows how households responded.[1]

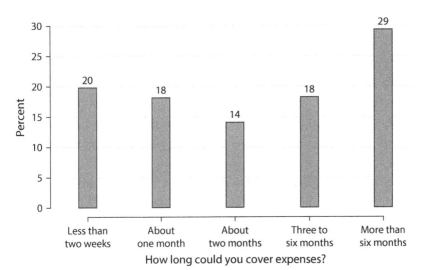

FIGURE 3.1. Before the pandemic, half of American households could not cover expenses for more than two months if they lost their main income source. (*Source*: 2019 Making Ends Meet survey.)

Even putting together all sources of funds, many households were not prepared to weather even a brief income drop. One-fifth of households would not be able to cover expenses for more than two weeks without their main source of income. Thirty-eight percent who lost their main source of income could cover their expenses for less than one month, and 52 percent could cover expenses for two months or less.

So leading into the pandemic, many households lacked a financial cushion. Figure 3.1 illustrates why the financial situation in March 2020 was so concerning. As unemployment spread, we were only weeks from many households having to cut their expenses.

These cuts would hurt. Families would reduce food spending and medical spending. The pain would also spread. A family spending less at the grocery store means the store earns less and maybe employs fewer people. Economists call these feedback effects "multipliers" because cuts in one place multiply, affecting more and more people. So as the pandemic hit and the economy shut down, widespread financial fragility was not just a concern for the newly unemployed. It mattered for everyone.

Why were so many families financially fragile? Each family has its own story, but there are some common themes. Income that has not kept up with expenses; large, often unexpected, expenses; variable incomes; and not enough of a financial cushion to always make ends meet in the middle.

This chapter draws heavily from the Making Ends Meet survey because we will return to many of these same themes and measures again and again as we examine the pandemic's progress. While some of the approaches are unique to the survey, others benefit from substantial prior research on household finance.[2] But because the Making Ends Meet survey occurred before and during the pandemic, it offers unique insights into what changed.

Regular Income and Expenses

The average American household spent one-third of its entire budget on housing in 2019. The next biggest expenses were: 17 percent on transportation, 13 percent on food (nearly half on food outside the home), 11 percent on insurance and pensions, and 8 percent on healthcare.[3] These categories are usually considered necessities. Although there is typically some wiggle room, cutting these expenses means a change in lifestyle and may be impossible in the short run. Everything else—the wants—fits into the remaining 18 percent. These wants include all of the education, clothing, entertainment, and personal care that make life more fun or help us invest for the future. Of course, the division between wants and necessities is somewhat arbitrary. For example, food away from home is often a want and is one of the first things people cut when they need to reduce expenses, but it is sometimes a need if you travel for work. And while we all need to keep ourselves clothed, for most people clothing costs are primarily about wanting to look good rather than the minimum necessary to avoid the elements.

Because necessities spending is such a large portion of its budget, the average American household has relatively little ability to reduce its spending in the short term and can only do so in the long term by changing the way it lives. For example, a family could reduce the amount

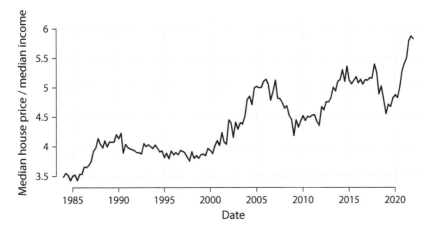

FIGURE 3.2. The median house price has increased faster than median income. (*Source*: Author's calculations from Census Bureau and Department of Housing and Urban Development.)

it spends on housing by moving to a cheaper part of the country. But the adults would need new jobs, likely at lower pay; the kids would need to move schools; and their friend, family, and social networks would be broken. Moving also costs money, making it out of reach for many families without much savings.

Over the last 40 years, housing costs have gone up faster than average incomes. Figure 3.2 shows how the median house sales price compares with the median household income.[4] In 1985 the median house cost 3.5 times the median income. During the early 2000s housing bubble—which, when it popped, culminated in the 2008 financial crisis—the median house sold for more than five times the median income. After a brief fall, house prices increased again and have been high compared with incomes since then. After a brief decline in early 2020, house prices increased rapidly in the second half of 2020 and through 2021, an issue we will come back to. Some of the increase is because houses have gotten bigger; we are paying more because we are getting more. But the increased house size is a problem all by itself; there are fewer small "starter homes" that are affordable for young or low-income people, which has kept many from homeownership.[5]

Many households are paying far more of their income for housing than the average. Affordable housing advocates usually define households as housing-cost burdened if they spend more than 30 percent of their income on housing and severely cost burdened if they spend more than 50 percent. By this definition, more than 30 percent of households (nearly 40 million) were cost burdened in 2019, and of these, nearly half were severely cost burdened.[6] Renters, often the youngest and poorest, were twice as likely to be cost burdened. Black and Hispanic households are more likely to rent, and more than 50 percent of renting Black and Hispanic households are cost burdened.

Meanwhile, average wages adjusted for how much they can buy have barely changed since the 1980s (we will return to this point when discussing how the pandemic altered the labor market in Chapter 10). Because housing is the biggest cost for most households, the increased housing costs are a big reason the median wage does not go any further than it did 40 years ago. Other costs have increased as well. American households spent 3.5 percent of their budget on healthcare in 1984.[7] The share had more than doubled to 8 percent by 2019. This amount only captures households' out-of-pocket expenses. Employers and the U.S. government pay even more healthcare expenses; total U.S. healthcare spending increased from 10 percent to 18 percent of GDP in 2016.[8] Rising healthcare spending is another major reason that wages have not increased. For employers, total compensation includes both wages and benefits, and the cost of providing health insurance rose with healthcare costs. As employers spent more and more on healthcare benefits, these increases ate up regular wage increases or were passed on to employees.[9]

Financial Shocks

Against these increasing costs, stagnant wages, and little adjustment margin, Americans must also deal with frequent financial shocks. Unexpected bills, expenses, and income variability were a fact of life for most families before the pandemic. Marcus and Sofia had large unexpected expenses from deaths in the family. Marcus had some legal bills.

TABLE 3.1. Households are often exposed to unexpected expenses.

Household experienced a significant unexpected expense in the last year (percent)	
A major medical or dental expense	29.2
A major vehicle repair or replacement	26.8
A major house or appliance repair	20.9
Taxes or fees	19.6
A TV, computer, or mobile phone repair or replacement	19.6
Giving a gift or loan to a family member or friend outside your household	11.7
Some other major unexpected expense	11.0
Increase in child care or dependent care expenses	8.3
Legal expenses or fines	7.9
Theft or robbery	2.6
Experienced any of the above significant unexpected expenses	**68.8**

Source: 2019 Making Ends Meet survey.

And then both of them lost income as their jobs shut down during the pandemic. How common were these sorts of experiences before the pandemic?

The Making Ends Meet survey asked families whether they had experienced a "significant unexpected expense." In June 2019, nearly 70 percent of Americans lived in households that had at least one significant unexpected expense in the previous year. Table 3.1 reports the most important events. Medical bills were the most common; nearly 30 percent of respondents live in households that experienced a large unexpected medical bill or expense.

All of the things that make modern life work can break down, so repairs or replacements for cars, houses and appliances, and mobile phones are also important sources of unexpected expenses. For example, I had to replace my phone early in the pandemic when it unexpectedly stopped working; 20 percent of Americans face a similar frustration each year. For some it can be more than a frustration. Visiting one of the many repair shops that now cover urban areas illustrates how important phones are to many people. They are the way many people connect to their family and their jobs. When your phone is broken, you might miss the shift change or the babysitter canceling. As a recent *Wired* headline put it, because being connected is now often part of being employed, "smartphones are a new tax on the poor."[10]

A car breaking down can cause even larger problems. 27 percent of households had a major expense because of a car breaking down. When you depend on your car to get to your job, a breakdown is not just an inconvenience, it can be your livelihood. Residential segregation and high housing costs have pushed many poor families farther from jobs.[11] The only way to get to jobs is to commute, and a broken-down car can make that impossible.

Not having money to repair a car or phone may mean lower income, such as a missed shift or getting fired, which leaves less money to make the repair. This negative cycle is an example of what economists call a "poverty trap," where not having money makes it harder to make money or costs more money, keeping people poor. Residential segregation often means that poor people live in areas with few jobs. Because public transportation often does a poor job connecting areas where poor people live to areas with jobs—often by structurally or explicitly racist design[12]—the only way to get to a job is often with a car. So if your car breaks down, you cannot get to your job and cannot earn the money to fix it, and you get trapped in poverty. Recent evidence suggests that longer commutes and being stuck at the bottom of the income ladder are strongly related.[13]

Meanwhile, nearly half of Americans lived in households that had a significant drop in income in the previous year (Table 3.2). Not all drops in income are unexpected or even unwelcome. For example, 9 percent report that a household member retired in the previous year. Yet for many people a reduction in work hours (19 percent) or a period of unemployment (17 percent) is unexpected and unwelcome. Frequently, higher expenses and reduced income come from the same source, such as a car breaking down. Even more common is for illness or injury to cause a decrease in income and an increase in expenses.

Even as median real wages have not increased, household incomes have become less stable. Household incomes have become substantially more volatile from year to year since the 1970s.[14] The likelihood that a household would experience a 25 percent or greater decline in income

TABLE 3.2. Households often face income drops.

Household experienced a significant drop in income in the last year (percent)	
Reduction in work hours	18.7
Period of unemployment	17.1
Worked less because of illness or injury	10.7
Changed to a lower-paying job	9.4
Other significant drop in income	8.7
Retired	8.6
Loss of government benefits	5.5
Could not work because someone in your household was in jail	1.7
Experienced any of the above significant drops in income	**45.7**

Source: 2019 Making Ends Meet survey.

over a two-year period increased from 7 percent in the early 1970s to 10 percent or more by the 2000s.

This year-to-year increase in volatility hides even more volatility from month to month, and even week to week. A quarter of American households reported in the 2019 Making Ends Meet survey that their income varies somewhat or a lot each month. Variable self-employment income and overtime were important reasons for this variability. But the most important reason income varied was because of irregular or variable work hours, which affected about 60 percent of households with variable incomes. Being on an irregular or on-call work shift means that a worker may not know from day to day or week to week whether she is going to work or how much she is going to earn. One reason for irregular work hours is a practice called "just-in-time" scheduling, in which managers only call in workers when they need them. For businesses, just-in-time scheduling tends to keep direct wage costs low. For example, a restaurant might require its servers to work past their scheduled shift if there are more diners, or a hotel might cancel shifts if there are fewer bookings than expected. But rather than businesses absorbing the uncertainty, they are passing this volatility onto the workforce. The income uncertainty is one bad consequence, but perhaps even worse is the uncertainty about when you will work and the problems it creates for the rest of workers' lives, especially child care.[15] It is difficult to get child care at the last minute and difficult to cancel it.

When a Shock Becomes a Problem

Most negative financial shocks do not cause financial problems. They are still unpleasant: spending time and paying money getting a car fixed means that we don't have that time and money available for other things. But many families have readily available funds in a bank account or the ability to borrow on a credit card to deal with unexpected emergencies. When these funds are not sufficient, a shock can become a financial problem. For some households, an unexpected income drop or a big expenditure shock such as a car repair may cause significant hardship. Other households may be better equipped to weather such shocks. Whether these shocks cause hardship or can be smoothed over is a key measure of financial hardship and health.

Overall, 40 percent of Americans reported that they or their household "had difficulty paying for a bill or expense" at least once in the previous year (Figure 3.3).[16] If they could point to a specific event, 77 percent reported that the event was unexpected. The most common reasons for having difficulty were also the most likely to be unexpected. For example, the event was unexpected for 85 percent of respondents who reported that medical expenses or fees caused them difficulty. And as Table 3.1 shows, having a large medical expense in the previous year is very common.

Having enough income makes it much easier to pay all the bills. Figure 3.3 shows how frequently different groups reported having difficulty paying a bill or expense. Respondents with lower incomes were more likely to have difficulties, but 18 percent of respondents in households with annual income of more than $100,000 reported having difficulty paying a bill or expense in the previous year. Even high-income people have trouble sometimes.

People in rural, suburban, and urban areas all have problems at about the same rate. Although it is often easy to focus only on the plight of the urban poor or rural poor, difficulty paying bills is common everywhere. People in rural areas often earn less, but they have lower expenses. Con-

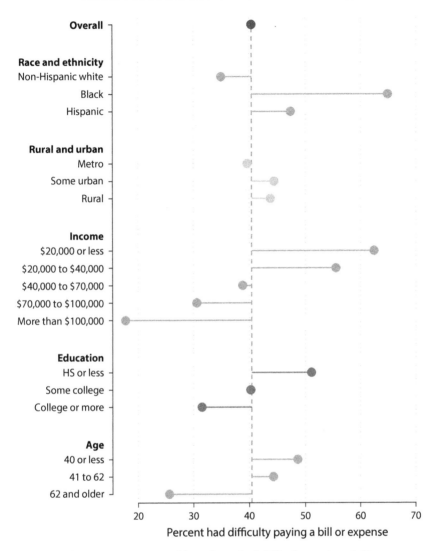

Figure 3.3. In 2019, 40 percent of Americans had difficulty paying a bill or expense in the previous year. (Percent in the Making Ends Meet survey who reported having difficulty paying a bill or expense in the last 12 months.)

versely, high housing costs absorb higher incomes in urban areas. Everyone is struggling to make ends meet.

On average, Black households were more than twice as likely as non-Hispanic white households to have difficulty paying a bill or expense. Hispanic households were somewhat more likely than non-Hispanic white households to have trouble. One reason for these difficulties is that the median Black household has approximately 10 percent of the wealth of the median non-Hispanic white household.[17] The median Hispanic household has about 12 percent of the wealth of the median non-Hispanic white household. Chapter 7 discusses some of the reasons for these disparities.

More frequent difficulty paying bills is one way the wealth gap between Black and white households produces real differences in the kind of lives people can live. For example, facing an income drop of the same size, Black households cut their spending by 50 percent more than white households.[18] Hispanic households cut their spending by 20 percent more. While all households may need to reconsider their spending when income changes, Black households make much bigger changes. One reason for this higher sensitivity is lower wealth. It is easy to smooth over temporarily reduced income with enough money, but because Black households have lower wealth, they have to adjust more to try to match spending to income. Often that means eating less or eating lower-quality food, not paying some utility bill, or making some other sacrifice.

Dealing with Difficulty

Having difficulty paying a bill or expense generally means households have to choose among painful sacrifices. There are five broad ways to deal with a financial problem in making ends meet: using savings, borrowing, cutting back on other expenses, not paying all of the immediate bill or expense, and seeking additional income. Often households choose more than one approach, spreading the pain around. Figure 3.4 shows how frequently households choose different options when faced with difficulty paying a bill or expense. While each of these strategies may help with the problem now, they often do so by delaying the problem for later.

When faced with a financial shock, for many families, savings are enough to cover the problem. After all, 70 percent of families faced a significant unexpected expense, but far fewer had difficulty paying a bill

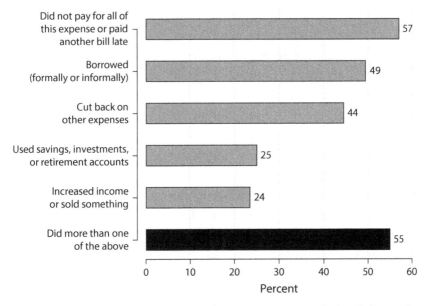

FIGURE 3.4. Households use many overlapping strategies to deal with financial difficulties. (What households in the 2019 Making Ends Meet survey did when they had difficulty paying a bill or expense. Options are not exclusive.)

or expense. Indeed, dealing with the things that come up is an important reason to have savings. Compared with other options, using savings or investments to deal with a difficulty is not as prominent a strategy in Figure 3.4, at 25 percent, because it is generally only when savings are not sufficient that families report having difficulty paying a bill or expense and turn to other strategies. Still, when families need to tap into retirement accounts or investment accounts to deal with an immediate problem, they are often trading off financial security later for a solution today. It may be a good trade, but it is a costly one.

Nearly 60 percent of families delayed paying the bill or expense that caused the difficulty or a different one. Not paying a bill or expense may cause difficulty in the future by, for example, having a utility cut off, causing eviction, having a delinquency on a credit record that increases the costs of borrowing, or having the debt referred to a collection agency. But sometimes there is no way to pay a bill or another bill can be delayed with lower costs. About half of the families that delayed paying a bill negotiated a lower or delayed payment. While negotiating generally will not make the expense go away, it may give a family time to adjust and keep the problem from getting bigger.

When people have trouble paying a bill or expense, they borrow about half the time. Borrowing can take many forms. About 25 percent borrowed informally from friends and family, 28 percent borrowed using a credit card, and 12 percent borrowed from a bank or some other financial institution. (Some families borrowed in more than one way, which is why the percentages sum to more than 50.) A borrower agrees to pay back the loan, generally with interest, which reduces the resources available in the future. So while borrowing allows you to deal with the problem today, it does so by moving the problem into the future and magnifying it. If borrowing allows you to spread the costs over time or delay them until your income is higher, and so avoid making painful cuts, then it has made you better off. But sometimes it leaves you with fewer ways to respond to future problems and higher expenses.

People also borrow to buy things they want or need without a financial problem. Consumer credit can take many forms, but the most common are not backed by collateral, meaning there is nothing for creditors to repossess if someone does not pay back their loan. Instead, creditors may seek to collect the debt in other ways and typically report delinquent debt to credit bureaus, which may make it harder for the borrower to get credit in the future. The following are the most widespread forms of consumer credit:

- Credit cards are widely used for payments, and around 80 percent of adults have one. The amount someone can borrow on a credit card depends on the credit limit. Many introductory limits or limits for people with poor credit scores are $300, while credit limits for high-income people with good credit can be $20,000 or more.
- Personal loans are offered by a variety of financial institutions, including banks and online lenders. They often have lower interest rates than credit cards and typically do not require

collateral. Personal loans typically vary from about $500 to $50,000. Sometimes these loans are marketed as a way of consolidating other debt, especially credit card debt, at a lower rate.

- Home equity loans or lines of credit are loans that use the equity in a house as collateral. Because of the collateral, these loans often have much lower interest rates than credit cards or personal loans.
- Payday loans are short-term loans, based on proof of employment. Borrowers give payday lenders the right to pull the money from a bank account on the borrower's payday if the borrower does not roll over the loan. These loans are often for about two weeks and typically carry a $45 fee for an average loan size of around $300. That $45 fee may not seem like much, but since most payday loans are rolled over many times,[19] it is common to pay more in fees than was originally borrowed.
- Auto title loans allow people to borrow using the amount they own of their car's value as collateral. These loans are typically for less than $1,000. The typical interest rate on these loans is around 25 percent per month. Like payday loans, auto title loans are frequently rolled over. If someone does not pay their auto title loan, the auto title lender may take the car.
- Pawn loans allow people to borrow a portion of the value of something, such as jewelry or a laptop, that they give to a pawn shop to hold. Pawn loans can often continue indefinitely as long as the borrower keeps making interest payments. But if the borrower misses a payment, the pawn shop can sell the item.

Nearly half of families cut back on other expenses to deal with difficulty. As we saw at the beginning of the chapter, about three-quarters of the average household's budget goes to necessities that are often difficult to adjust. Frequently, the only adjustable expenses are food or the medicine to treat a chronic medical condition. Sometimes cutting back also spreads costs into the future. For example, a delay in a needed expense for a medical treatment or car maintenance reduces expenses now but may lead to bigger troubles later. Cutting back is very common, but it can also be very painful.

A different strategy is to increase income today. Sometimes that might mean working an extra shift or taking a part-time job. Or it might mean selling something. When Marcus was faced with difficulty during the pandemic, he sold some of his things. Sometimes selling things is a big sacrifice, such as selling the necklace your grandmother left you; other times it may be part of the way you planned for the future by acquiring salable goods. Yet the term "fire sale" is often used for a forced sale to raise funds, usually at low prices. Selling things because you need to usually means selling them for less than their value. Selling the coffee pot, for example, may raise a bit of cash now, but it also may make life more expensive in the future. Maybe you go without coffee, but snap at your boss and get fired. Maybe you go to a coffee shop and, over time, pay much more than you got for the coffee pot. Maybe that cup of coffee in the morning was one of the few things in life you looked forward to, so life is just harder for a while.[20]

The emphasis on future costs shows how today's financial problems tend to cause future financial problems. This negative cycle is another example of a poverty trap. It is easy to see how it happens: A bad financial shock causes you to borrow on your credit card. But now you also have interest payments, making it harder to pay other debts. When the next shock hits, things are even tighter, so you miss some credit card payments, wrecking your credit and causing your card to be canceled. So when your car breaks down, you no longer have a credit card, which forces you to sell something or take out an even more expensive payday loan. A downward spiral.

Of course, not all shocks, even shocks that cause financial difficulty, cause a downward spiral into poverty, but financial problems tend to be grouped. Figure 3.5 shows how frequently people reported having difficulty paying bills or expenses in 2019 if they had at least one difficulty. Among families that had at least one difficulty, only 17 percent had only one, while 34 percent had three or four, and 27 percent had five or more difficulties. Each time, a costly sacrifice may have made the next difficulty more likely.

People facing difficulties often deal with them in overlapping ways. When people had difficulty, 55 percent used more than one way to deal

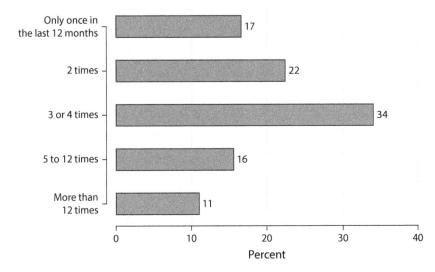

FIGURE 3.5. When people have difficulty paying one bill or expense, they often have difficulty repeatedly. (Response to "How often did you have trouble paying a bill or expense in the last 12 months?" in the 2019 Making Ends Meet survey.)

with it in Figure 3.4. The complexity of these financial arrangements by people facing financial difficulty led Daryl Collins, Jonathan Morduch, Stuart Rutherford, and Orlanda Ruthven to call them the "portfolios of the poor."[21] For rich people, a financial portfolio contains different kinds of assets to diversify risks and plan for different goals: a retirement account, a house, mutual funds for investments, and a checking account or a line of credit to deal with immediate needs. For people with less money, the portfolio is often less formal but more complicated, with many sources of income, expenses, and small debts. Sometimes there is money in the bank. Family and friend networks can help out in bad times but may also call on you. Some bills can be ignored for a while. For example, perhaps the electric utility company may not shut off the power until three notices. Or perhaps the landlord will give you some time to get the rent in. But push these too far and the consequences may be dire. Many people carry multiple credit cards. Or have payday loans. Managing this portfolio is difficult; keeping track of what needs to be paid now, and what can be delayed, and making sure there is enough for the big expense like rent that cannot be delayed is hard. And any mis-judgment can lead to problems, from overdraft fees to eviction. So often it makes sense to use more than one strategy. All may be painful, but using more than one strategy may spread the pain around.

Thinking about different strategies to make ends meet as a kind of investment portfolio is helpful to explain the complexity and harsh realities many families face. Many high-income Americans with retire-ment or investment accounts will recognize this portfolio approach. Focusing on the most commonly available credit, about 80 percent of the population has a credit card (the rest either do not want one or can-not get one). About half of people with a credit card use it to pay for things, but pay the full bill every month. The other half revolve debt from month to month at an average annual interest rate of around 14 percent. The rates for people with poor credit scores can often be 25 percent or higher. Average revolving credit card debt before the pan-demic was around $5,000. In portfolio terms, for someone with credit card debt, paying down that debt—a form of savings—has a riskless return of around 14 percent. That is an amazing return on investment! If you have an investment that offers 14 percent without risk, you should put as much money into it as you can. In fact, it is so good that if some-one offered returns that good, you should be suspicious. Infamously, Bernie Madoff's fund gave 11 to 12 percent every year, stock market up years and down years alike, but only by running a Ponzi scheme that eventually imploded.[22] That something like half of the population is voluntarily giving up such a high return, and is even willing to dissave at this rate by adding to the debt, suggests that they frequently face hard choices where now wins out over tomorrow.

Financial Well-Being and Financial Health

Throughout the book, I discuss how financial health, measured in dif-ferent ways, changed over the pandemic. There are many ways to think about financial health. This chapter started with one way: how prepared households were for an income disruption. Another might be whether the household could pay all of its bills. The Financial Health Network, for example, combines measures like these into a single measure of financial health.[23]

A different approach is to ask how someone feels about his or her finances. This approach is distinct from the other measures of financial health, which could, at least in principle, be measured exactly and comparably across people and households. How people feel about their finances is more subjective. That does not mean it is not important. People should feel financially secure based on their own standards, not someone else's.

To help capture how people feel about their own finances, I return repeatedly to the financial well-being measure that I introduced with Marcus. Financial well-being means different things to different people. The Making Ends Meet survey includes five questions that capture some of these dimensions. The questions can be combined to create a score summarizing an individual's financial well-being. The Consumer Financial Protection Bureau developed these questions to capture the multiple dimensions of financial well-being.[24] Table 3.3 shows these questions the way that respondents to the survey would see them.[25]

In June 2019, the mean financial well-being score among the survey respondents to all three Making Ends Meet survey waves was 51.1.[26] This number does not mean much on its own, but it is a good way to track how Americans are doing during the pandemic. The key advantage of the Making Ends Meet survey is that, because it returned to the same people over the pandemic, we can understand how their financial well-being changed in response to their circumstances. While I have emphasized that financial well-being is distinct from other measures of financial health, in practice they tend to be very closely related. People who are having difficulty paying bills or expenses tend to have low financial well-being.

There are big differences in how Americans perceive their financial well-being. Just as with objective measures such as having difficulty paying bills, Black Americans have much lower financial well-being than non-Hispanic white Americans. In addition, financial well-being tends to increase with income and with age. We will see some of these differences as we meet different people throughout the book.

TABLE 3.3. Five questions that capture financial well-being. (Five-question Consumer Financial Protection Bureau Financial Well-Being scale.)

How well do these statements describe you or your situation?

	This statement describes my situation . . .				
	Completely	Very well	Somewhat	Very little	Not at all
I am just getting by financially.	❏	❏	❏	❏	❏
I am concerned that the money I have or will save won't last.	❏	❏	❏	❏	❏
Because of my money situation, I feel like I will never have the things I want in life.	❏	❏	❏	❏	❏

How often do these statements apply to you?

	This statement applies to me . . .				
	Always	Often	Sometimes	Rarely	Never
I have money left over at the end of the month.	❏	❏	❏	❏	❏
My finances control my life.	❏	❏	❏	❏	❏

Making Ends Meet before the Pandemic

Americans face frequent unexpected expenses. Their incomes go up and down. And somehow they need to have the funds available at the right time to pay the regular expenses and deal with the unexpected ones. Savings are the way many families smooth over these shocks. But keeping savings against the unexpected requires not spending today, which can be hard. Most low-income families are able to plan for less than a year in advance.[27] Many others turn to credit—half of households with a credit card are borrowing repeatedly on it. But credit is expensive. It is often more expensive to be poor, which makes it harder to save, leading to more expensive problems.[28] A vicious cycle.

Frequently not everything lines up and families face difficult choices to cut back, to use even more expensive credit, to borrow from their family, to default, or to go delinquent. This cycle of costly shocks requiring costly sacrifices was widespread before the pandemic. It is certainly not the only reason families feel financial hardship, but it is typically the unexpected shock that pushes families over the edge. More fundamental are high expenses for things like housing and child care and low pay compared with those expenses. Combined high expenses and low pay mean many families are always on the edge. Before the pandemic, most low-income families were not saving. Spending and income were about equal for nearly half of low-income families, and spending was greater than income for more than 20 percent.[29]

As unemployment increased through March and April 2020, many families were already on the financial edge, one shock away from painful choices and sacrifices. It appeared the financial apocalypse had come and widespread suffering was imminent.

Instead, as we'll see in the next chapter, the CARES Act transformed household finance during the pandemic.

John

John was one of the people who had trouble making all of the expenses line up before the pandemic. A white man in his midforties, he lived in a small town in the Midwest with his wife. They had three children, one of whom had just started college. John and his wife both worked full time, and their combined income the previous year was around $80,000.

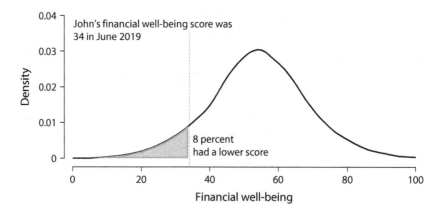

Many families in middle age face multiple financial pressures from different directions. Income growth, which is typically high in the twenties and thirties, often slows down after age forty—and sometimes starts going backward. Meanwhile the expenses keep increasing: mortgage, car, children, perhaps helping elderly parents. Many people face their first real medical expenses in their forties. And retirement, which at thirty seemed too far off to even think about, is starting to get closer. Many people have not built any retirement savings by their forties, sometimes because they tried to save but needed to spend the savings in an emergency, other times because it just did not seem pressing. But saving for retirement cannot be put off forever. These competing pressures are sometimes called the "midlife squeeze." Alternatively, people in midlife are referred to as the sandwich generation, caught between caring for young children and elderly parents. As financial and familial responsibilities tend to peak in midlife, it can be stressful and financially challenging to make everything balance.

In June 2019, John was facing many of these pressures. He and his wife shared their finances, but John was responsible for making the decisions, and the stress of trying to make ends meet—and not always succeeding—was getting to him. They had a mortgage and an auto loan, which they were paying steadily. John had a modest credit card debt he was paying a balance on. They had retirement accounts and some investments outside of the accounts. Yet they found it hard to save; John said they usually spent as much as their income.

One of their big new expenses was a student loan John and his wife took out to help their eldest daughter, who started college in 2019. John felt strongly about his daughter's education, writing in a comment, "People really try but it just seems to take a lot of money to live comfortably. That's why I tell my daughter to get her education so hopefully she can live a better life than me." John himself had attended college for a couple of years but had not finished. Perhaps he felt held back by his lack of degree, seeing jobs he knew he could do just as well go to people with college degrees.

The previous year seems to have been the culmination of many expenses and shocks that left John feeling as though his financial situation was out of control. His financial well-being score was 34, below 90 percent of the population. He felt that his finances always controlled his life.

Their family had difficulty paying a bill or expense about once every other month last year. The most recent time it was a combination of medical expenses, an auto repair, and helping a family member. We do not know exactly how John helped a family member. Perhaps it was the new education loan. But John also said that a family member got married. While it was likely exciting, John may have felt obligated to help with the expenses, putting another strain on their budget.

Like many people, John used a variety of strategies to deal with the problems, including not paying all the bills at once, cutting back on other expenses, increasing his income, taking money from savings, taking out a bank loan, and using a credit card. Even with all of these options, they still cut back on food and regular household expenses to make ends meet.

John also reported a drop in income because either his or his wife's work hours were cut, which may have contributed to the financial pressure.

John and his family still managed to have some financial cushion, perhaps because they had spread the cost of the expenses among so many options. They had about $2,000 in a checking account, and John felt they could cover their expenses for about two months if they lost their main income source.

Early in the Pandemic

John's overall financial well-being improved slightly between June 2019 and June 2020. He had a brief period of unemployment and reduced work hours because of the pandemic but by June 2020 was working full time again. Otherwise the pandemic did not seem to have affected his family much. As with many families, his children's school was closed for a time, and they could not buy enough of a necessity because it was not available in stores. Perhaps they started to ration toilet paper.

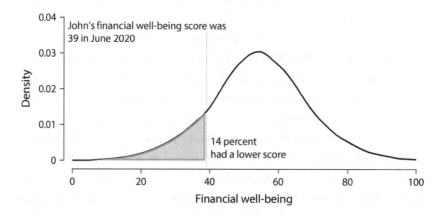

It was a difficult year for John in other ways. It appears he and his wife divorced and she moved out. Although we do not know the details of their arrangement, divorce can be financially costly, in addition to its personal difficulties.

John's family had difficulty paying bills about three times in the previous year. Medical expenses were a problem, as was an auto repair and helping a family member who may have had problems because of the pandemic. As often happens, overdrafts compounded the problems. John or someone in his family had overdrafted about six times in the year before June 2019 and they had more overdrafts in June 2020. At a standard $35 fee per overdraft, that could add up to $350 or more. But unlike most people who overdraft, John said he expected to overdraft the last time it happened, so overdrafting may be part of his strategy to make ends meet.

Late in the Pandemic

John's financial situation seems to have improved again by February 2021. He was working full time. By February 2021, he and his family (not counting his ex-wife) likely received Economic Impact Payments worth around $4,000.

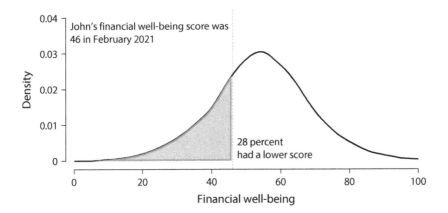

Perhaps coincidentally, John reported that they had about $4,000 put aside for emergencies. Despite a major medical expense, a car repair, and some legal expenses (perhaps from the divorce), John did not have any difficulties paying bills or expenses in the year before February 2021, a big change from the previous year. But he had withdrawn some money permanently from a retirement account, in a sign of how difficult it can be to balance saving and expenses in middle age. Their household expenses had increased while income was about the same, which likely made it even more difficult to save.

4

The CARES Act

THROUGH THE SUMMER of 2020, the economic and policy community held its breath. We had watched the increase in unemployment. Seen the shuttered businesses. Stuck at home, we wondered when the widespread financial suffering would start.

All of the available data indicated that Americans were not prepared for this financial apocalypse. As we discussed in the previous chapter, many households were already on the edge before the pandemic. Half of households did not have the savings or ability to borrow to weather a two-month drop in income without reducing their spending. When the pandemic hit and millions lost their jobs, it appeared that severe financial suffering was just around the corner.

But to our surprise, by August it was clear that the widespread financial suffering we feared was not happening. When I got the data from the June 2020 Making Ends Meet survey, I had to double-check that I had not accidentally opened the survey from the previous year. Could financial well-being actually have improved during the pandemic? Was it possible that fewer Americans were having difficulty paying bills? Had savings really increased during a devastating recession? Yes! By almost every measure, Americans were financially better off on average by June 2020 than they had been in June 2019.

Two factors explain the seeming paradox. First, unable to go out to bars or restaurants or to travel, Americans rapidly reduced their spending in March and April. Second, the Coronavirus Aid, Relief, and Economic Security Act, or CARES Act, helped maintain the income of unemployed consumers, provided cash to many businesses that had lost revenue, and sent direct payments to most Americans. As a result, average incomes increased during the pandemic even as spending fell. Later pandemic relief bills built on this success.

Reduced spending and higher income meant that many Americans went from a situation where they were almost always on the financial edge to a situation where they had substantial financial space. As Charles Dickens's Mr. Micawber explained to David Copperfield, misery is when your income is below your expenses, and happiness is when your income is above your expenses.[1]

This chapter tells the story of how America went from what looked like coming financial misery in March 2020 to financial happiness in June 2020. But not every program was effective, and some made a difference only because they shoveled money at a problem. Individual programs sometimes had issues reaching the neediest Americans, and the money often took its time going out. And as we will see in Chapter 7, not everyone benefited; there were a substantial minority of households who got left behind during the pandemic.

CARES Act Provisions

The $2.2 trillion CARES Act was written, passed, and signed rapidly in response to the pandemic. It contained hundreds of billions of dollars in unemployment assistance, direct payments to individuals, grants to small businesses, and many other provisions to help specific industries or aid in the pandemic response. After its signing on March 27, the U.S. Treasury, the Small Business Administration, and states rushed to implement it.

The CARES Act touched many areas. Table 4.1 summarizes the act's major provisions and their budgetary impact.[2] The amount authorized and the bill's cost estimates are based on Congressional Budget Office estimates over a ten-year budget horizon, the standard time frame for evaluating congressional bills.[3] The $2.2 trillion price tag is somewhat misleading, since all of that money was not spent right away. Many of the largest provisions involved immediate spending in 2020, while others,

TABLE 4.1. Major CARES Act provisions.

Major CARES Act provisions

Provision	Cost ($ billions)
Federal Reserve facility to lend to businesses, states, and municipalities	454
Paycheck Protection Program and other small business aid: Grants and loans to small businesses to help maintain payroll	377
Economic Impact Payments to households: Payments of $1,200 per adult and $500 per child	293
Expanded unemployment insurance: Added $600 per week and covered self-employed and other workers not normally eligible	268
Reduced business taxes: Reductions in caps on interest deductibility and operating losses; delays in employer payroll tax payments	186
Health-related spending: Hospital and public health funding, Medicare, veterans, CDC, FDA, and NIH	153
Aid to state and local governments	150
Transportation support: Grants to public transit providers and airports, other support	71
Other spending: FEMA disaster fund, other spending	60
Other loans to specific industries: Airlines, national security firms, U.S. Postal Service	56
Employee Retention Credit: A tax credit for businesses affected by the pandemic that maintain employees on payroll	55
Expansion of SNAP and other benefits	42
Education support: Support to schools and universities, deferred student aid payments, other programs	40
Reduced individual taxes	20
Mortgage forbearance: All borrowers with a federally backed mortgage could request a delay of payments for up to six months	—
Eviction moratorium: Prohibited evicting renters in federally owned or insured housing	—
Total CARES Act spending authorization ($ billions)	**2,225**

Source: Committee for a Responsible Federal Budget.

primarily tax breaks, were spread more evenly over the ten-year horizon. Some of the most important provisions, including mortgage forbearance and a limited federal eviction moratorium, had no direct impact on the federal budget. Those costs were being shouldered by banks, mortgage servicers, and landlords, not directly by the government.[4]

By the size of the authorization, the biggest provision was to support new Federal Reserve lending facilities with $454 billion. This amount is both misleadingly large and misleading small, however, as it was to support several lending programs, so it authorized the Federal Reserve to make up to $1.95 trillion in loans. With this backing, the Federal Reserve set up nine facilities to support lending to a range of borrowers. We discussed some of these programs in Chapter 2 during our examination of the Federal Reserve's attempts to keep another financial crisis from occurring. The CARES Act money provided additional funding for these facilities, especially programs to support lending to large corporations and other businesses. Because these were lending programs, the government would only lose money if the loans were not repaid, and the CARES Act authorization provided the Fed the necessary backstop to make potentially risky loans that might lose money.

Ultimately, however, these programs had almost no effect beyond their impact calming the market. Only about 1 percent of the amount authorized was lent by December 2020.[5] Because these were emergency programs designed as backstops, once markets were operating normally again, many corporations found they could get better terms from regular capital markets. Small businesses, on the other hand, were wary of debt and had better terms from other CARES Act provisions, so overall these facilities were little used.

The CARES Act provided $377 billion in grants and loans to help support small businesses, of which most—$349 billion—was for the Paycheck Protection Program run by the Small Business Administration. This program provided loans to small businesses that could become grants if they were used to support payroll. The program later received an additional $321 billion in funding under the Paycheck Protection Program and Health Care Enhancement Act signed into law on

April 24, 2020,[6] and an additional $284 billion in the December 2020 relief bill, making it the largest pandemic relief spending.

Two provisions in the CARES Act were particularly important for households: $293 billion for Economic Impact Payments made directly to every adult earning below $75,000 in 2018 and $500 to every child; and $268 billion to expand unemployment insurance benefits. The expanded unemployment benefits included an additional $600 per week to all unemployed workers. The provision also expanded who could receive benefits to include the self-employed and independent contractors such as Uber drivers. This money, as we will see later in the chapter, proved transformational for many families.

The CARES Act allocated $186 billion to reduce business taxes primarily by allowing people who own businesses to reduce their taxes on their nonbusiness income if they had losses in the business ($135 billion).[7] This provision expanded an accounting loophole allowing mostly very wealthy people to reduce their taxes.[8] The CARES Act also allowed greater flexibility for corporations to offset taxes with losses ($26 billion) and greater deductions for interest payments on debt ($13 billion). Many of these provisions were structured to have the greatest reduction in taxes in 2020 and 2021, and then to have smaller positive effects over the next nine years, effectively allowing many corporations and business owners to delay taxes.

The CARES Act also authorized spending on several other programs:

- $153 billion in health-related spending, $100 billion of which was for hospitals and public health. The rest went to increased funding for federal health agencies—including the Centers for Disease Control and Prevention, the Food and Drug Administration, and the National Institutes of Health—and additional funding for Medicare, military healthcare, and veterans' healthcare.
- An Employee Retention Credit ($55 billion), allowing payroll tax credits to businesses who employed workers at a loss during the pandemic.[9]

- Spending provisions to aid industries directly affected by the pandemic, including airlines, airports, and public transportation in general. The CARES Act also provided funds to help school districts operate safely and for higher education.

Several provisions had little direct budget impact for the federal government, but had large impacts for households, lenders, and landlords. The CARES Act required mortgage lenders with federally backed or owned mortgages, about 60 percent of all mortgages, to offer borrowers a delay in payments if they were affected by the pandemic. Many private lenders also offered some sort of assistance, although not all were as generous. The CARES Act also paused interest accumulation and payments for federal student loans, which are more than 80 percent of all student loans. In addition, the CARES Act halted evictions of renters in properties with federally backed mortgages, covering about 25 percent of renters.

Economic Impact Payments

The face of the CARES Act for most people was the Economic Impact Payments (EIPs), or "stimulus checks," as they were often called. Adults whose adjusted gross income on their 2018 taxes was $75,000 or less were entitled to receive $1,200; married couples filing jointly and earning $150,000 or less got $2,400. The amounts began to decrease above $75,000 annual income, dropping to zero at $99,000 for individuals.[10] The EIPs also included an additional $500 per dependent, phased out at the same income thresholds.

There were some important restrictions on who was eligible for EIPs. The most notable was that all filers had to have a social security number valid for employment. Moreover, EIPs were only made to married couples filing joint returns if both were eligible, unless at least one spouse was a member of the military.[11] Noncitizens who used Individual Taxpayer Identification Numbers to file their taxes were not eligible. These provisions excluded unauthorized immigrants, but also the many legal immigrants, U.S. citizen spouses of immigrants, and children in mixed-status households. The Migration Policy Institute estimated that 5.1 million U.S. citizens and legal immigrants were excluded, as well as 9.3 million unauthorized immigrants.[12] Later relief bills made mixed-status families eligible retroactively, allowing them to claim the CARES Act payments.[13]

The IRS and Treasury worked quickly to get the money out. Nearly 80 million EIPs were deposited directly in bank accounts in the week following April 10, about 45 percent of all eligible payments. For tax filers who had paid or received a refund using direct deposit to a bank account recently, the IRS still had the bank account information and used it to deposit the money.

Many tax filers who did not have current bank information had to wait several weeks for a paper check. By the end of May, the IRS had mailed or deposited 89 percent of all eligible payments.[14] The last 11 percent was the most difficult. Nonfilers—who are often low income—typically had to wait much longer, and many never received their EIP.[15] The IRS was still trying to reach around nine million people in September 2020 who had not claimed their EIP.[16] Other nonfilers may have received less than they should because the IRS did not automatically include the additional $500 per dependent for people who do not normally file a tax return.

The program faced several challenges.[17] One bottleneck was the speed with which the Bureau of Fiscal Services could print and mail checks for the IRS. In an attempt to get around this problem, starting in the middle of May, the Treasury began mailing prepaid cards instead of checks for some recipients. But many people threw out the plain envelope containing the EIP cards. On the other hand, mailing checks created a burden for some recipients because many households—around seven million[18]—do not have or use bank accounts. The check-cashing industry generated approximately $67 million in revenue from consumers who used check-cashing services to access their payment.[19]

Despite these problems, the evidence suggests that the EIPs were broadly successful at reaching and helping households maintain spending during the pandemic. When the Making Ends Meet survey asked about EIPs, more than 80 percent of respondents whose 2018 incomes

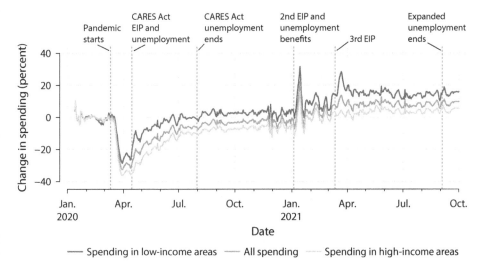

FIGURE 4.1. Spending dropped as the pandemic started, but it rebounded sharply as Economic Impact Payments were deposited, particularly in low-income areas. (*Source*: Affinity Solutions and Opportunity Insights.)

would have made them eligible remembered receiving the check, and more likely received one but did not remember it.[20]

Spending increased by about 8 percentage points in the week immediately following the first EIP deposit (Figure 4.1).[21] For people living in the lowest-income zip codes, spending increased by nearly 17 percentage points over that week. That is a huge increase, especially considering that spending had dropped around 35 percent in those zip codes in the last several weeks of March. From the figure, it looks as if the EIPs by themselves were responsible for about half of the return to normal spending. Jumps in spending from later EIPs are also clear in the figure. But the relationship between overall spending and the EIPs might be explained by other factors. For example, unemployment benefits, which were delayed in many states, may have been deposited in big lump sums around the time the EIPs were deposited. So how do we determine whether the EIPs themselves were effective at boosting spending?

When researchers looked at what happened when individuals got the EIPs, the evidence that they made a big difference for spending, particularly for low-income people, was compelling. One research group used ano-nymized data from a nonprofit that helps individuals track their spend-ing and savings by putting all of their accounts in one place.[22] They compared how these individuals' spending changed on the days just before and after they received the EIP. Compared with the day before receiving the EIP, spending increased by about 6 percent on the day after and was higher for more than a week. Moreover, the spending in-creased primarily among people without a lot of extra cash. People with less than $100 in their accounts spent over 40 percent of the EIP within the first month. People with more than $4,000 did not change their spending by a statistically meaningful amount.

What did people spend their EIPs on? Nearly half used some of the money to pay for food and other essential purchases, 40 percent used it for rent or mortgage payments, 40 percent used it for utilities, and 44 percent used it to pay a credit card bill or other debt. Of course, many people used the payment for multiple things, allocating some to food and some to bills. These spending categories spiked sharply in the days fol-lowing receipt of the EIP.[23] Many people were clearly on the edge.

Yet despite this rise in spending from the depths in March, less than 40 percent of the EIPs were spent within a month on average, and some estimates suggest an even lower percentage.[24] The rest of the money went into savings. The EIPs thus contributed to a remarkable rise in household savings during the pandemic.

Giving consumers money to spend is a common economic policy response to a recession. In both the 2001 and 2008 recessions, direct payments or tax rebates were used to help stimulate the economy. The idea is that part of the reason for the recession is that people are not buying enough. By giving people some money or reducing their taxes, they will spend a bit more and help pull the economy out of a recession. The EIPs worked differently because large parts of the economy were intentionally shut down. As Paul Krugman argued persuasively, the EIPs and other components of the CARES Act were "disaster relief with a dash of stimulus."[25] Indeed, a prime argument *against* later EIPs in March 2021 was that they might be stimulative, rather than purely disas-ter relief, and so might cause inflation.[26]

Because their primary purpose was to reduce economic suffering, not necessarily to jump-start the economy, their stimulus impact is a bit beside the point.[27] In fact, the payments were spent differently from previous recessions. More of the money went to debt payments and food than in previous recessions.[28] And rather than spend all of it, many households used the money to reduce debts and provide themselves a greater financial cushion. As the pandemic wore on, consumers did start making big purchases eventually on physical goods they could still buy: big durable things like exercise bikes and televisions, largely imported. We will explore the widespread consequences of this shift in Chapter 10.

Expanded Unemployment Benefits

The CARES Act expanded unemployment benefits in several ways. The Pandemic Emergency Unemployment Compensation program extended unemployment insurance by an additional 13 weeks. Normally, most states cut off unemployment insurance after 26 weeks. The Pandemic Unemployment Assistance program also expanded the eligibility for unemployment insurance benefits to the self-employed and to people whose work history was too short to qualify prepandemic. Importantly, people working in the "gig" economy, such as Uber or Lyft drivers, were also included. Most gig workers were self-employed contractors and therefore not eligible for unemployment insurance except under the new program.

The CARES Act also established a new $600 weekly supplement for all unemployed, including those newly eligible, called the Federal Pandemic Unemployment Compensation supplement. This supplement was a big deal. The average unemployment benefit in February 2020 was $387.[29] In most states, unemployment benefits replace half of wages up to some maximum. The median weekly earnings in the U.S. were $934 in the fourth quarter of 2019.[30] Under the new program, the average unemployment benefit would be $987, slightly more than the median earnings before the pandemic.

The majority of the pandemic's unemployed came from industries where the average earnings were less than the national median, so the

$600 supplement was a big boost to income. Research that compared the amounts that unemployed workers would have been earning without the pandemic relief program and what they should have received under the new federal supplement in May 2020 found that 69 percent of the unemployed would have received benefits that exceeded their lost earnings. For the median unemployed worker, the expanded benefits replaced 134 percent of their prepandemic earnings.[31]

Most unemployed received more unemployment income than they had earned while employed before the pandemic. Sometimes a lot more, not counting the EIPs. This situation created some complex unfairnesses that we will explore more in Chapter 7. Many workers deemed essential, such as grocery clerks, kept their jobs but now found themselves earning less than many people who were now unemployed, and meanwhile they faced the extra risks of working during a pandemic.

However, the situation for unemployed Americans was often more stressful than the numbers might suggest. As we saw in Chapter 2, many states were slow to pay unemployment benefits during the pandemic. Those problems were particularly acute for the new federal benefits and for people who were newly covered by the provisions of the CARES Act. State systems, which were already overwhelmed, also had to make changes to provide additional money and allow new people to apply. Just 29 states were paying the $600 supplement by April 16.[32]

The delays in paying unemployment benefits led to financial hardship for many people. Among families that received unemployment insurance by the February 2021 Making Ends Meet survey, 37 percent report waiting four or more weeks to receive their benefits.[33] Figure 4.2 shows that those families were much more likely to have difficulty paying their bills.[34] Families who waited four or more weeks were 20 percentage points more likely to report having difficulty paying a bill or expense. Meanwhile, some households whose members experienced a period of unemployment did not report receiving any unemployment insurance. These households were even more likely to have difficulty paying a bill or expense. Other surveys suggest that similar problems arose when households had to wait, including an increase in unmet medical care and difficulty paying for food.[35]

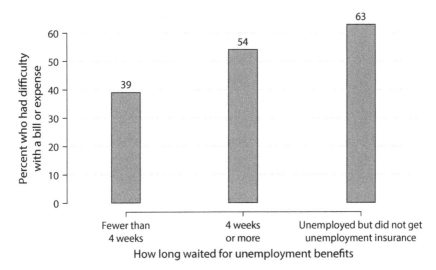

FIGURE 4.2. People who had to wait longer to get unemployment benefits were more likely to have difficulty paying their bills. (*Source*: 2021 Making Ends Meet survey.)

When households did receive their expanded unemployment checks, they spent and saved more. Using anonymized bank account data, a research team at the JPMorgan Chase Institute showed that the spending of the unemployed increased by 22 percent when they started receiving unemployment benefits.[36] Moreover, the unemployed roughly doubled their liquid savings between March and July 2020.

The additional $600 unemployment benefits ended on July 31, although the unemployed would have still qualified for regular unemployment benefits. The Pandemic Unemployment Assistance expansion of unemployment insurance to independent contractors continued until the end of the year (it was subsequently renewed, but only at the last minute). In perhaps the best evidence that the unemployment benefits were helping, with the expiration of the $600 supplement, spending by the unemployed declined in August almost to the prepandemic baseline. The unemployed spent two-thirds of the accumulated savings they had built up since March in August alone.[37]

One smaller program did provide some additional unemployment relief after July. A presidential memorandum authorized the Federal

Emergency Management Agency (FEMA) to use disaster funds to administer a new Lost Wage Assistance program.[38] Because FEMA was using already appropriated disaster funds, the amount of funding was limited. No more than $44 billion could be spent from the Disaster Relief Fund, a special fund the federal government keeps to respond to natural disasters. FEMA initially only committed to providing three weeks of benefits to each state that applied.[39] It eventually clarified that all states that applied by September 10, not just the first states that applied, would be eligible for up to six weeks of funding.[40]

The Lost Wage Assistance program provided that $300 of additional unemployment assistance could be paid to people eligible for the Pandemic Unemployment Assistance as long as they were eligible for at least $100 in unemployment insurance per week,[41] which meant that roughly a million people were not eligible.[42] The odd exclusion was because the law authorizing these disaster funds had a required 25 percent cost share with states.[43] It initially appeared that states would have to put in an additional $100 per recipient, which might have meant that some states either could not or would not participate. Later guidelines fudged the source of the funds to consider existing payments part of the cost share. Funds ran out in September for the states that applied in early August, while states that applied later continued the additional payments into October.

Despite continuing high unemployment, it was not until December that a new relief bill with more money for unemployment insurance was passed. We will return to these programs in Chapter 7.

The Paycheck Protection Program

Small businesses are often financially fragile. Using accounts that small businesses maintained at Chase Bank, the JPMorgan Chase Institute found that about half of small businesses could cover expenses for fewer than 15 days in 2018. Almost 90 percent of small businesses in majority Black or Hispanic areas could cover expenses for fewer than 15 days.[44] At the end of March 2020, things looked bleak. Many small businesses had lost most or all revenues but still had expenses. Nearly 43 percent of small businesses that responded to one survey had temporarily closed.[45] A majority of businesses in the survey planned to seek a loan for pandemic relief if they were eligible.

The Paycheck Protection Program (PPP) authorized by the CARES Act helped provide forgivable loans to small businesses to maintain their payroll. The economic reasoning behind the program was to keep small businesses from closing permanently and keep workers attached to small businesses. Small businesses rarely have access to extensive capital markets, partly because they often lack substantial collateral. So when the pandemic caused demand for many services to plummet, small businesses without a large cash buffer had to immediately reduce costs by furloughing workers. Even with lower employment costs, keeping a business from shutting entirely generally requires some income to pay rent and utility bills, maintain inventory, and perform maintenance on any equipment.

The U.S. was thus at risk of "a cascade of small business bankruptcies."[46] Such a cascade would have produced long-term economic damage, because once a business closes it takes time and money to start a new one. Existing businesses have trained employees, supply relationships, and specific investments that cannot be sold if a business shuts down entirely. These assets are often intangible but may be the most valuable part of a business. To take a personal example, I was concerned that the little French bistro that had recently opened in my neighborhood would go under. Not only would the owners lose the business they had just built, but our neighborhood would lose a nice place to eat. (They converted to selling takeout fried chicken buckets, an example of innovative "muddling through" I discuss in the next chapter. It was good fried chicken.) It is likely another restaurant would eventually take its place, but the new owners would have had to remodel, hire new staff, and establish new supply relationships, all of which take time and money.

Ideally, once it was safe to reopen, existing firms would be able to start back up again quickly. Allowing a wave of failures to ripple through the economy, harming other businesses and their employees, would have deepened the recession. Small businesses, often defined as firms with fewer than 500 employees (although most small businesses are much smaller), account for 47 percent of private-sector employment, so a wave of failures would have had big employment consequences.[47]

Keeping workers attached to businesses, even if they were furloughed, would also help the recovery in several ways. First, it would make restarting straightforward: rather than hiring, small businesses could just recall workers. Second, many workers have what economists call "firm-specific capital," which is just a technical way of saying that all businesses and industries have different ways of doing things. Workers with experience at a business know how to make the specific accounting software work, or which vendor to call, or a big customer's specific needs. Someone else could learn these things, but not at once, so a new employee is likely to be less productive than her predecessor. Third, even without firm-specific capital, businesses and employers often take a while to find a good match between the employee's skills and the business's needs. Employees who are not a good match will often quit or get fired, so established businesses have often found employees who are particularly good for the business. If a business shuts down and fires all of its employees, it will not be able to start up again with the same firm-specific capital and employee match quality, so it will be less productive.

In the face of this potential wave of failures, the PPP was designed to help small businesses survive, maintain payroll, and keep workers attached. Businesses could apply for loans up to 2.5 times their prepandemic payroll. These loans could be converted to grants under some conditions, although as the program evolved, these conditions changed slightly. To be forgivable, most of the loan had to be spent on payroll costs and other covered eligible expenses such as rent or utility payments. In addition, the firm could not reduce employment below its prepandemic level or reduce employee compensation for specific periods.[48]

The program went through several revisions as the Small Business Administration (SBA)—the government agency tasked with administering the program—and policy makers heard from small businesses. As it became clear that the pandemic was not going to end within two months, Congress passed the Paycheck Protection Flexibility Act in early June 2020. The act extended the covered period when funds needed to be spent from 8 to 24 weeks to be eligible for loan forgiveness, reduced the amount that had to be spent on payroll from 75 percent to 60 percent, and made these changes retroactive to loans already made.[49] The act also loosened how long borrowers whose loans were not forgiven had to repay the loan. "Second Draw" PPP loans authorized under the December 2020 relief bill expanded forgiveness-eligible expenses to include worker health protections, insurance costs, some supplier costs, and some other categories.[50] The American Rescue Plan Act in March 2021 made some additional small modifications, including expanding eligibility for nonprofits.

To distribute the funds, the SBA turned to banks, which typically have existing relationships with small businesses and generally already offer SBA-guaranteed loans. There were good reasons to turn to these existing relationships to get money out fast, but it also created problems. While banks were not making or backing the loans, they did need to verify the business existed, check its payroll, and administer the funds. Doing so carries both some administrative cost and some potential risk for the bank. The SBA's rule implementing the PPP allowed banks to rely on borrowers' statements, rather than independently verify information, so the bar seemed low for participation.[51] To encourage banks to participate, the PPP had a generous fee structure considering that banks were acting only as intermediaries: 5 percent of the loan up to $350,000.[52]

Demand for the PPP far exceeded available funds initially. Within three weeks, the SBA had already approved all of the money allocated in the CARES Act. On April 16, the SBA said the PPP would not be accepting new applications.[53] The rush left many small businesses out. Congress quickly passed another $321 billion in funding at the end of April and the funds started flowing again.

The high demand and the limited capacity of smaller community banks and credit unions meant that the initial funds went to larger, better-connected businesses in richer and whiter areas. The smallest businesses, where the proprietor would have to stay up late filling out forms and which might only qualify for a $20,000 loan, were largely left out. Because banks got percentages of the loans, they benefited from facilitating the largest loans to the largest employers. When the SBA was

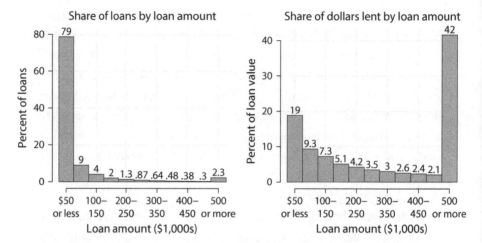

FIGURE 4.3. Most PPP loans went to the smallest businesses, but most money went to the largest businesses. (The distribution of loans and the dollar value of PPP loans by loan amount. *Source*: Author's calculations from the Small Business Administration.)

forced to release data by court order in December 2020, it became clear that 1 percent of PPP borrowers received approximately one-quarter of all PPP funds in 2020.[54]

The largest employers have the largest payrolls, so the design of the program meant that the largest businesses that qualified were going to get most of the funds. Most employees at small businesses work for the largest "small" businesses, while most small businesses have few employees. Figure 4.3 shows how the loans were distributed over the entire program.[55] Over the entire program, 79 percent of loans were for $50,000 or less, but only 19 percent of the funds were for these smaller loans. Only 2.3 percent of the loans were for $500,000 or more, but these loans accounted for 42 percent of the total lending.

The PPP, built as it was on existing banking systems, served bigger and white-owned businesses better than businesses owned by other groups. PPP loans in majority-nonwhite areas were approved later than in majority-white areas, according to one analysis of SBA data.[56] Part of the problem was the initial reliance on the existing small business lending network of banks and credit unions. Nonwhite-owned businesses are much less likely to be well banked. Consolidation and branch clo-sures since the 2008 financial crisis have also left many communities with fewer banks and credit unions. Black-owned small businesses were half as likely to have bank funding compared with white-owned busi-nesses in 2019.[57] Lack of existing access meant that it was harder for nonwhite-owned businesses to apply and made them less likely to be in the first round of funds. For example, while online lenders are a main source of credit to Black-owned businesses, they were not allowed to take part until April 14, 2020, and the first round of funding ran out on April 16. Beyond the inequities in access, some analysis suggests that Black applicants for PPP loans were less likely to be approved compared with white applicants with similar profiles.[58]

The program's limited initial success in reaching truly small busi-nesses is clear in the PPP loan data. For the loans given through April 16, less than half were for $50,000 or less, compared with 80 percent overall in Figure 4.3 for the entire program. Nearly 60 percent of the funds given out in the first wave were for $500,000 or more, compared with 42 percent over the entire program.

Stepping into some of the gaps left by banks, online lenders and on-line intermediaries—sometimes called "FinTechs" because they use technology in finance—helped connect many of the smallest small businesses to servicing banks. Nontraditional lenders, mostly using online-only platforms, were disproportionately used by small busi-nesses to access the PPP in areas with fewer bank branches, lower incomes, and more minority residents.[59] In the first round of PPP fund-ing, banks lent disproportionately to areas with the least economic impact from the pandemic. These nontraditional lenders provided more loans than traditional banks to the areas that were hit worse by the pan-demic. Overall, these nontraditional lenders made 54 percent of the PPP loans to Black-owned businesses even though they only accounted for 17 percent of all PPP loans.[60]

Partly to address some of the access issues, the December 2020 relief bill made the fees for small loans even more generous.[61] Sensing an op-portunity, two online startups, Womply and Blueacorn, helped connect borrowers and lenders for about 10 percent of the total PPP funds disbursed in 2021.[62] In the process, the two startups collected around $3 billion in fees.

The PPP was massive. Over the entire program, 94 percent of small businesses received at least one loan.[63] Including the original March 2020 CARES Act authorization, the PPP and Health Care Enhancement Act at the end of April, and the December 2020 relief bill, the PPP dispersed $800 billion to 11 million businesses and paid around $50 billion in fees to banks.[64] By February 2022, the SBA had forgiven 99 percent of the money for which it had received an application for forgiveness (it had still not received an application for about $100 billion in loans). The program stopped taking new applications on May 31, 2021.

Was this money well spent? The answer is not straightforward since it depends on what we consider success and on what type of businesses we consider. In understanding the effectiveness of the program, it is worth keeping in mind that the U.S. has an established system for supporting laid-off workers directly—the unemployment insurance system. For the PPP to be effective at paycheck protection, it needed to keep workers attached to businesses long enough for the businesses to reopen, allowing these businesses to reopen more quickly. Under these circumstances, the valuable firm-specific capital and firm-worker matches would be preserved. If we judge the program only on how well it provided "paycheck protection," then it needed to be not much more costly than unemployment insurance, which sent money directly to unemployed workers. Instead, if we view it as a small business preservation program, rather than an employment program, then we might measure success by whether it prevented failures.

The evidence that it was effective at keeping workers attached to businesses is mixed and not supportive of the program. The PPP did keep some workers on payroll during the loan period, but that period was not long enough to keep workers attached during the pandemic and the employment effect seems rather small. Following the end of the covered period of a loan, small businesses reduced the number of people on their payrolls.[65] Around 900,000 jobs were lost as small businesses met their requirements for PPP forgiveness in the first wave of funding.

Several research teams examined the PPP and reached similar conclusions: that the program protected relatively few jobs at a high cost per job. Using different data sources, the research teams compared the employment changes of firms below 500 employees with firms just above 500 that were ineligible for PPP loans.[66] While the estimates vary a bit, the research suggests that the PPP increased employment for eligible firms by between 1 percent and 3 percent as of June 2020. The estimates are quite similar to the estimates when the program ended, suggesting that the program saved few jobs and did not protect the jobs it did save when it ended. The estimated cost per job preserved during this relatively short period was between $200,000 and $377,000. That is a lot more than the wages of the jobs preserved.

Using these estimates, it would appear the PPP was a huge bust: we could have paid far less to these workers in unemployment benefits, protecting them from financial harm. And it seems unlikely that the firm-specific capital was worth that much (especially because many of the workers protected were laid off eventually anyway). One estimate is that around three-quarters of the funds did not go to paying workers, which was why the program was so expensive for each job preserved.[67] Instead the funds went to business owners, who are mostly high income. Three-quarters of the PPP benefits went to households in the top 20 percent of the income distribution. The PPP was thus a highly regressive program.

One reason for the limited impacts may be that there was no relationship between where funds went and the economic dislocation. Almost every small business received funds, not just small businesses in the areas with the largest pandemic economic impact. In fact, the least pandemic-affected areas got more funds initially.[68] The funds frequently went to firms that were not planning to reduce payroll, creating a relatively small impact on employment. One reason for the lack of relationship between funds and pandemic economic dislocation is that the funding went through banks. Banks in the hardest-hit areas—and in areas with more Black and Hispanic residents—were less good at processing PPP loans, so businesses in these areas were less likely to get a loan in the first round of funding.[69] Partly because of these location issues, the PPP did not have a substantial impact on local economic conditions or business shutdowns.

It is also possible that the employment effects were larger for the smallest firms. The approach of comparing firms with somewhat fewer than 500 employees and firms with somewhat more than 500 gives a clean comparison. But it is a comparison of the effects of the program for the largest firms. As Figure 4.3 shows, most loans were fairly small and went to firms with fewer employees. But most of the money went to the largest firms, and the largest firms have most of the employees. So even if the effects of the program are larger for the smallest firms, that would not increase the employment effect of the program much.

To illustrate why the program may not have had a large employment effect, dozens of restaurant chains received the maximum $10 million PPP loan, including TGI Fridays, P. F. Chang's, Black Angus Steakhouse, and Legal Sea Foods.[70] As Figure 4.3 illustrates, these large loans were the bulk of the PPP funds. These firms employed many people, some of whom could no longer work because of the pandemic. But it seems that the PPP largely just replaced private funding for these largest "small" businesses; rather than receiving a grant from the government, they would have borrowed from banks or used other sources of funds.[71] It is certainly possible that many of these firms would have laid off most or all of their employees without the funds, but many of the layoffs occurred eventually anyway. Moreover, the firm-specific capital and employee-firm matching value for chain food service is likely to be relatively low given the large turnover rate in the industry, so the economic value of keeping workers attached to these firms is not likely to be high. The PPP's high cost and low employment benefit for these larger firms suggests the program could have been much less costly and still have provided the same employment effect and protected the smallest businesses.[72]

Most European countries took a different approach. Furloughed workers still received 60 percent to 80 percent of their wages directly from their employer, who sought reimbursement from the government.[73] This approach keeps workers attached to the business and is about as costly as paying unemployment benefits. It also avoided the financial suffering caused by delays paying unemployment insurance. Because workers were still on payroll with their employer, it was the business applying for the money, not the worker. As a result, European unemployment increased much less than in the U.S. initially, although many workers were actually furloughed.[74] It appears there were far less expensive ways to achieve similar ends.

Despite its name, perhaps judging the Paycheck Protection Program on its impact on job retention misses its more valuable impact in keeping small businesses from failing. The evidence here is also mixed but somewhat more promising. One research team found that the PPP provided significant benefits to business financial health and prevented closures.[75] These effects through June 2020 were large and appear to have grown over time. Similarly, another team found that many firms used the loans for rent and to build up savings, strengthening their balance sheets.[76]

By preventing business failures and allowing firms to keep paying bills and build up savings, perhaps the PPP had larger employment and economic effects in the long term. Avoiding a wave of failures and having stronger firms that could hire again when demand came back helps economic growth and employment in the longer term. It is harder to study these impacts because they require more time and also rely on less reliable comparisons. While the PPP was disappointing in the short term, given the massive amount of money spent on it, perhaps it had an impact in the longer term.

Student Loan Freeze and Mortgage Forbearance

The CARES Act introduced new flexibilities for federal student loans and for federally backed mortgages. The federal government is central to both the student loan and mortgage markets. About 82 percent of student loans are held directly by the federal government.[77] And the federal government, directly or through Fannie Mae and Freddie Mac, backed 62 percent of mortgages in December 2019. So the CARES Act offered flexibility to most borrowers in these markets. Figure 4.4 shows the percentage of people with a loan who received assistance with it.[78] Nearly everyone with a student loan received assistance. Between the student loans freeze, mortgage forbearance, and assistance offered by private companies on credit cards and auto loans, 20 percent of people received some sort of loan assistance by June 2020.

All federal student loans were automatically set with zero payment due and no interest accumulation. Effectively, loans were frozen at the start of the pandemic. Moreover, not making payments would not affect your credit record, and collections for defaulted loans mostly stopped (the Department of Education continued to garnish the wages of around 400,000 borrowers in violation of the CARES Act for a time).[79] The freeze meant that student loan borrowers could forget about their loans until the flexibilities ended. The flexibilities only paused payments and interest, though; they did not forgive the loans. While the CARES Act provided these flexibilities only through September 30, 2020, they were extended multiple times—often at the last minute and for the "final" time—through at least December 2022, nearly three years after the pandemic's start. The last extension in August 2022 also included substantial debt forgiveness.[80] As Figure 4.4 shows, even as other forms of loan assistance declined to nearly zero or their prepandemic levels, the share who were benefiting from some sort of assistance remained close to 20 percent through June 2022 because of the nearly universal student loan freeze.

For borrowers who were struggling, forgetting about student loans allowed them greater flexibility to deal with other problems. And even for borrowers who were not struggling, paying student loans that were not accumulating interest was not necessarily the best financial move. Paying down more expensive debt—and all debt is more expensive than zero interest—was likely a better use for funds. Even just putting the money that would have gone to payments in the bank preserves more flexibility if a shock happens.[81] All told, the interest and payment freeze allowed student loan borrowers to not pay $80 billion in interest from March 2020 to March 2022.[82]

Mortgage forbearance allowed people to delay payments on their mortgage for a while. It did not forgive the loan or the interest but granted additional flexibility. Mortgage forbearance was not automatic,

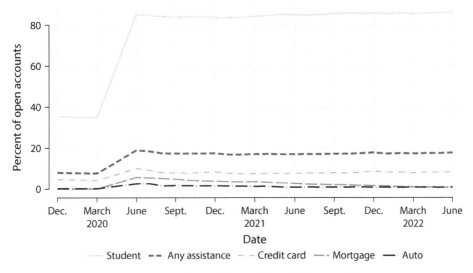

FIGURE 4.4. Loan assistance during the pandemic. (Percent of open accounts with no payment due but a positive balance. *Source*: Author's calculations from the Consumer Financial Protection Bureau Consumer Credit Panel.)

but mortgage servicers were generally required to reach out to borrowers who were having difficulty to discuss options. As a result, most people who were having trouble paying their mortgage were able to enter a forbearance program. For example, 75 percent of people who reported having difficulty paying their mortgage in the Making Ends Meet survey received some mortgage forbearance.[83]

These programs varied somewhat by lender and type of loan, but generally someone could halt mortgage payments for six months and renew forbearance for another six months. Fannie Mae and Freddie Mac, two of the largest mortgage holders, allowed extensions for up to 18 months' total forbearance. At the end of this period, there were several options depending on the loan type. Borrowers could choose to repay the missed payments all at once or over several payments once forbearance ended. More common, however, was to add the missed payments to the end of the loan. This option kept the monthly payments the same—important for any families already on the edge. From March to May 2021, one estimate suggests that mortgage payments worth $31 billion were delayed.[84]

Many mortgage forbearance recipients were facing significant financial difficulties. In the Making Ends Meet survey, 79 percent who received mortgage flexibility had a significant income drop from unemployment or reduced work hours during the pandemic.[85] Using anonymized Chase bank account data, the JPMorgan Chase Institute found something similar: families who missed mortgage payments because of forbearance were much more likely to have experienced large income drops.[86]

A third of mortgage forbearance recipients made all their payments even though they could have skipped some.[87] These homeowners may have been worried about their financial future and applied for the flexibility as a precaution. Perhaps the other policies in the CARES Act left them with more cash than they were expecting, so they were able to keep up their payments. Forbearance under the CARES Act was not supposed to hurt credit scores, but everyone may not have understood that. Some people may have been concerned that missed payments would still cause them problems, such as harming their credit score or causing them to lose their homes, so they preferred to make all payments unless it was absolutely necessary to miss one.

Forbearance seems to have helped counteract what would have been an increase in inequality as happened in the Great Recession. Before the pandemic, mortgage difficulties were uncommon for all racial and ethnic groups. But during the pandemic, low-income, Black, and Hispanic households were more likely to have difficulty paying their mortgage.[88] These groups were also more likely to receive forbearance, so they avoided having problems that would lead to foreclosure.[89] Mortgage forbearance thus helped avoid repeating one of the Great Recession's worst consequences.[90] Wealth losses because of foreclosure during the Great Recession were concentrated among Black and Hispanic families following the decline in housing prices and increase in foreclosure rates. These families had often bought more recently as housing prices increased and so were more exposed when prices decreased.

The CARES Act did not require forbearance for credit cards or auto loans. Nonetheless, many lenders did voluntarily offer some programs.

Relatively few consumers took advantage of these programs, perhaps because they were unaware of them. The gap between need and use is wide for these discretionary programs, an issue we will return to in Chapter 7.

Business Tax Reductions

Between the Employee Retention Credit ($55 billion), corporate and individual owner loss provisions ($135 billion), and other tax breaks such as on retirement account withdrawals, the CARES Act provided around $240 billion in tax reductions to businesses. The total allocated for tax reductions was similar to the amount spent on expanding unemployment insurance or Economic Impact Payments. These tax reductions were controversial. Many businesses that were not affected by the pandemic received substantial tax reductions.[91] They were also highly regressive, mostly reducing taxes for people with high incomes.[92]

The available research on the impacts of these provisions suggests they provided little pandemic relief, although they certainly reduced taxes at the expense of government revenue. One study examined how public corporations discussed the impact.[93] Public corporations must file with the Securities and Exchange Commission quarterly statements discussing events that have a "material impact" on their business. Few corporations felt the CARES Act tax provisions were important enough to discuss for their business. Firms in states or industries most affected by the pandemic were not more likely to discuss these provisions, suggesting that the provisions were not effective at providing pandemic relief to affected industries. Moreover, less than 15 percent of firms discussed the Employee Retention Credit, which was directly aimed at reducing job losses during the pandemic.

In fact, the Employee Retention Credit seems to have been largely unused, although the evidence is not entirely clear why. One problem may be that the rules for eligibility were opaque and the program was not well known, so uptake appears to be low. For example, despite extending the program into 2021, it seems that only $1 billion in credits had been claimed as of May 10, 2021.[94]

The largest tax provision allowed owners of some businesses to use the businesses' accounting losses to reduce their personal income taxes. One estimate suggests that 82 percent of the benefits, about $115 billion, would go to about 43,000 taxpayers with more than $1 million in annual income.[95] It is difficult to see how this tax provision made any difference to financial suffering or economic activity during the pandemic other than reducing taxes for people with high incomes.

Americans Were Better Off Financially Because of the Pandemic

Many Americans were not prepared for even a small financial shock, let alone the pandemic financial apocalypse that descended in March 2020, so it looked in March as if a wave of financial misery was about to crash. Instead, the average American was doing *better* financially in June 2020 than a year earlier by just about any measure. When we asked people how they were doing in the June 2020 Making Ends Meet survey, fewer said they were concerned their money would not last and more said they had money left over at the end of the month.[96] The share of consumers who said "my finances control my life" declined by 8.0 percentage points, from 42.7 percent to 34.7 percent. Combining these questions into the financial well-being score I introduced in Chapter 3, average financial well-being increased by a full point, from 51.1 to 52.1. This increase is substantial. For comparison, before the pandemic, a one-point increase is associated with an increase of household income by approximately $15,000, a five-year age increase, or a 20-point increase in credit score. The share of consumers who had difficulty paying a bill or expense fell by 4 percentage points, from 40 percent in June 2019 to 36 percent in June 2020.

Other research found similar broad improvements in how Americans perceived their finances. The Financial Health Network developed a FinHealth Score based on survey questions that ask how well people are doing in their spending, savings, borrowing, and financial planning habits. Based on its measure, the share of Americans who were financially healthy (doing well along all financial dimensions) increased from 29 percent in April 2019 to 33 percent in July 2020.[97] The share of Americans who reported paying all their bills on time increased from 66 percent to 69 percent.

Americans did not just feel better off financially; by virtually every measure, they were better off financially on average. A research team used anonymous bank account data to examine household spending and liquid account balances during the pandemic.[98] They found that households across the income distribution cut spending from March to early April. Between April and June, spending rebounded for lower-income households. Further, low-income households also drove an across-the-board increase in liquid assets.

Credit card debt fell across the country, falling by around 10 percent between March 2020 and June 2020.[99] This decrease was widespread. The average credit card debt fell in areas with low average incomes as well as in areas with high average incomes. Credit card debt fell in majority-white census tracts, majority-Black census tracts, and majority-Hispanic census tracts. Credit card debt fell even for the most financially vulnerable consumers.[100] As we saw in the last chapter, half of people said their household could cover expenses for two or fewer months if they lost their main source of income. It was these households that worried me the most as pandemic unemployment spread in March and April 2020. Yet as Figure 4.5 shows, credit card debt fell sharply for these people as well.[101] Credit card debt stayed lower through 2021, indicating these impacts were long lived.

This fall in credit card debt during the pandemic is remarkable because credit cards are often the first option that households turn to when they have trouble. Between 75 percent and 85 percent of households have a credit card, making it the most widespread form of consumer credit. Many households hold little liquid savings. For the majority of households with a credit card, the amount the household could spend with a credit card—the difference between its credit limit and its debt—is larger than the amount it has saved.[102] Consumers who have difficulty with a bill or expense most often cut back on other expenses or do not pay a bill. But they are more likely to use a credit card

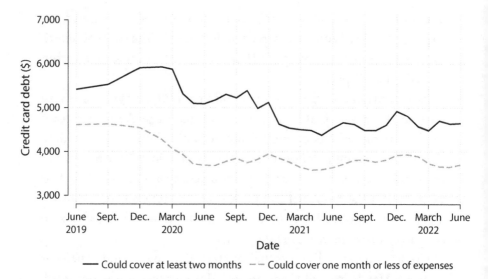

FIGURE 4.5. Credit card debt fell for consumers who were financially vulnerable before the pandemic and stayed lower for two years. (*Sources*: Making Ends Meet survey and Consumer Financial Protection Bureau Consumer Credit Panel, adjusted for inflation.)

than any other source of funds, including using savings, dipping into retirement savings, or selling something. (Although borrowing from friends and family is nearly as important.)[103]

In the aftermath of the 2008 financial crisis, credit card debt fell because credit card limits were cut.[104] People were forced to cut their spending substantially because they could no longer borrow, spreading the troubles banks were having to the rest of us. With the incipient financial crisis in March 2020, it seemed possible that something similar might happen during the pandemic. Instead, credit card–issuing banks did not cut limits.[105] Credit card limit growth slowed a bit at first but then picked up again. Unlike during the Great Recession, people reduced their credit card debt during the pandemic not because their limits were cut but because they reduced spending and saved more.

Credit card issuers did not cut limits because consumers were far more likely to pay their bills. Delinquencies declined substantially during the first months of the pandemic.[106] New delinquencies declined for auto loans, mortgages, and credit cards from March to June 2020. Moreover, accounts that were already delinquent were less likely to become more delinquent, suggesting that even when people were struggling, things got better, or at least less difficult. Student loan delinquencies fell to nearly zero, because all federal student loans were automatically put into a zero-payment-due plan. The CARES Act required new mortgage forbearance options and prevented people who were using these options from being reported delinquent to credit bureaus. Private companies also offered additional loan flexibilities. So some of the decline in delinquencies occurred because people had additional options when they were having problems. But the decline also occurred because fewer people were having problems in the first place.

More expensive forms of debt like payday loans, pawn loans, and overdrafts declined as well. These debts are not generally reported to the big credit bureaus so are more difficult to track. Yet people redeemed pawn loans at unprecedented rates.[107] Veritec Solutions supports state regulatory systems that regulate payday loans. It showed that payday loans declined by nearly 60 percent from the beginning of March to May 2020 in the states that use its systems.[108] While payday loans increased a bit after the CARES Act additional unemployment benefits expired in July 2020, they declined again following later relief bills and were still down 60 percent through June 2021. Overdrafts also fell. Partly, people had more money in the bank and so were less likely to overdraft unintentionally. Many banks also waived overdraft fees.[109]

Not everyone's finances improved, but more people's finances improved than declined. In any normal year, there is substantial flux in household finances. Averaged across households, things usually look pretty constant, but the average hides that some households are doing better and some are doing worse. Every year, some people get promoted and others lose their jobs. We will look at who got left behind in Chapter 7. But first, the next chapter considers the many ways we muddled through the pandemic as it forced us to find new ways to do things.

Joan

Joan's family benefited from the pandemic aid. Joan, a white woman in her late forties, and her husband lived in the Southwest with their daughter. Joan was a teacher and her husband was self-employed. Joan had a college degree and a master's degree, likely in education. She and her husband earned about $60,000 in 2018.

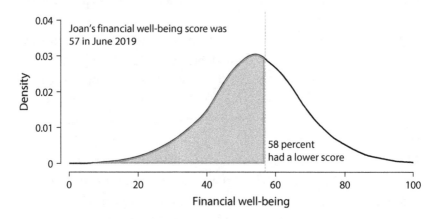

Joan never expected that they would be having difficulty. She considered herself quite frugal. She told us in a comment, "I don't think my financial behavior is that 'unusual.' Most of my friends and family carry a lot more debt than I do. I hate to 'owe.'" She disliked financial risk as well, saying she would turn down the chance to win a substantial prize for a smaller amount without any risk. This worry about risk and dislike of debt carried into how she saved: she wanted at least $5,000 in an emergency fund and reported they could cover more than six months of expenses if they lost their main source of income. She had a credit card and paid off the balance every month. Her family had money in checking and savings accounts, as well as retirement accounts and other investment accounts.

Because of all of this saving, Joan's family was financially well cushioned before the pandemic. They had not had difficulty paying bills or expenses recently. They still had a small amount left on an education loan for Joan's master's degree, but they owned their house outright, so had no rent or mortgage payments to make, which helped keep their expenses manageable.

Early in the Pandemic

When Joan returned the June 2020 survey, her husband was now unemployed because of the pandemic. He applied for unemployment insurance, but it took more than a month to arrive. When it did arrive, it included the additional $600 per week as part of the CARES Act. Although we do not know what Joan's husband did before the pandemic, many people who were self-employed were only eligible for unemployment insurance through the expanded federal benefits authorized by the CARES Act. Part of the reason his benefits may have taken as long to arrive as they did was that many states were not able to easily extend benefits to the newly covered applicants. Although we do not know his exact income, it is likely that these federal extended unemployment benefits more than covered his lost wages.

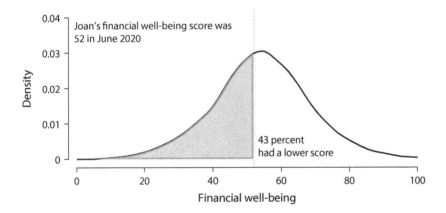

Combined, Joan and her family likely received Economic Impact Payments worth $2,900 in April, a good portion of their prepandemic income. Joan felt herself lucky, writing, "If I had lost my job, our whole financial situation would be dire—but thankfully, being a teacher has given me dependable income & benefits. And it is still considered 'essential' during the pandemic! Not to mention that I love teaching!"

All of this government aid and her stable job meant that Joan felt that her family's financial situation was pretty stable, despite her husband's unemployment. In fact, Joan reported in June 2020 that their income had not changed much from the previous year even though her husband was unemployed. As was true for many families, the amount they had in savings actually went up from June 2019 to June 2020.

The pandemic affected them in other ways. Joan's child's school was closed to limit the spread of the virus. Joan was unable to buy some necessities because they were unavailable in stores.

Late in the Pandemic

By February 2021, Joan's financial situation had further improved. Her husband had resumed working. Perhaps as their state's stay-at-home order lifted, he was able to restart his self-employment business. Joan reported that both their income and the amount they had in savings had increased over the previous year.

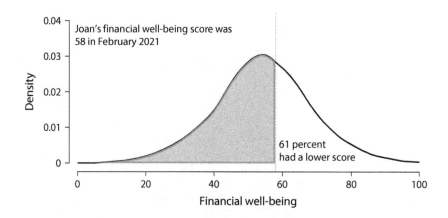

But in a reminder that a family's financial situation is just part of its story, especially during the pandemic, Joan reported a death in the family. Perhaps one of her parents passed from COVID-19. Joan also delayed some medical treatment because she was concerned about coronavirus exposure and her medical provider was closed.

PART II

The Pandemic Settles In

5

Muddling Through

SUDDENLY IN MARCH 2020, other humans were suspect. To illustrate how profound a change it was, a year later, many people felt uncomfortable seeing crowds gathering maskless in prepandemic movies.[1] As one commenter put it, "Like all of a sudden, the most terrifying thing about 'Jurassic Park' is the social proximity of crowds, not the fact that dinosaurs are trying to take over the island."[2] Movies or television shows that came out as late as 2019 were suddenly part of the old world, where people gathered in large groups, touched each other, and went maskless.

It took some time to figure out what was safe and what was not. Partly, the Centers for Disease Control and Prevention were curiously silent and slow to give guidance.[3] We were still learning about the "novel coronavirus" and how it was transmitted and what was safe. It was initially suspected that some spread came from contact with doors, tables, cash, and mail. It eventually became clear that the main transmission channel was through respiratory droplets from an infected person.[4]

While information on respiratory transmission was slowly coming out, however, many companies instituted new cleaning regimes.[5] As Derek Thompson of the *Atlantic* pointed out, this "hygiene theater" became a great and costly distraction with real opportunity costs. Economists use the term "opportunity cost" to describe what you must give up in order to get something. The value of cleaning is that it is a visible and reportable step. Companies could talk about their deep-cleaning protocols. They advertised how they were cleaning in an effort to encourage customers to return. It is much harder to report how good your ventilation is. But someone had to do the new cleaning procedures—in person and therefore at risk of infection themselves. All the money and attention that companies and governments were spending cleaning, they were not spending on other procedures to make people safer or pay their employees.

Beyond hygiene theater, we still had to figure out how to navigate a new economic world in which being close to other people was dangerous. Perhaps paradoxically, it became antisocial to be social.

The pandemic made clear all the ways that human contact is necessary for so many things. The sudden decrease in expenditures for travel and restaurants is the most obvious. It quickly became apparent that loud bars, with people packed tightly together and forced to speak at loud volumes, were some of the riskiest places for transmission.[6]

But if you were house hunting, how safe was it to go to an open house? Go to the grocery store? Work at a grocery store? To give a sense of how difficult the new world was to navigate, Wirecutter, the *New York Times'* product review site, posted an article on April 23, 2020, on how to use laundromats safely.[7] For many people, clean clothes were not possible without some degree of contact, which carried some risk. But if you do not have a washer and dryer in your apartment or house, you would eventually have to venture outside and deal with the risks. We had to learn how to navigate that risk, in laundromats and everywhere else.

In many ways, the most consequential muddling through we did was in figuring out how to perform many jobs while working from home. And there was a great deal of muddling: a video call with someone who could not figure out how to use the mute button, unexpected outages, no sound. A Supreme Court justice forgot to mute and was infamously heard flushing the toilet during remote arguments.[8] Yet the consequences of this massive work-from-home experiment are likely to be felt for years, altering how many people work in profound ways, so I will discuss working from home's larger implications in Chapter 8.

Between stay-at-home orders and individual decisions, Americans rapidly changed many aspects of their lives starting in March 2020. This chapter describes some of the ways we adapted to the new realities and their impacts on the economy. The rapid evolution in how we worked, what we did for "fun," what we chose to buy, and who we were with caused ripple effects through our lives. Some of the effects were weird, others tragic, but most of all they show us adapting to the new reality as best we could.

Delayed or Forgone Medical Care

Perhaps surprisingly, healthcare spending plummeted during the pandemic. Compared with spending at the end of 2019, spending on healthcare was down 20 percent from April through June 2020 as people delayed or ignored nonessential medical care of all kinds.[9] In one poll in the four largest U.S. cities during July 2020, about one in five respondents reported they or someone in their family was unable to get needed medical care during the pandemic. These kinds of delays can be costly for health. Three-fifths of these families reported negative health outcomes as a result.[10]

I had a dentist appointment scheduled on March 21, during the first week of shutdowns in Washington, D.C. I tried calling to cancel but could not get through. My dentist, like many other nonessential health providers, had likely told the staff to stay home. Eventually, the practice would post instructions on its website, but that first week everyone was still figuring out what was safe and allowed under emergency orders. (I did not go to the dentist for two years—it was not a priority, seemed risky, and is not very pleasant to begin with—and then I was scared to go because I might have new cavities. But I did floss more during the pandemic!)

My experience with delayed medical care is common. When we asked Making Ends Meet respondents in February 2021 about their experiences, 34 percent reported that they or someone in their household delayed or skipped medical treatment during the pandemic. Of respondents who skipped, 65 percent did so at least partly because they were concerned about COVID-19 exposure, 40 percent because their local government limited nonessential medical treatments, and 45 percent because their medical provider closed or had limited service (the options for responses to the survey were not exclusive). Even during the pandemic, medical costs were an important factor: 36 percent of those who reported they had delayed or skipped treatment did so because they "were concerned about the cost or couldn't afford it."

The lack of readily available care meant that COVID-19 killed many people indirectly. One estimate calculated that COVID-19 was directly responsible for only about two-thirds of excess deaths (deaths more than one would expect) during the first several months of the pandemic.[11] There was a surge in deaths from diabetes, dementia, hypertension, heart disease, and stroke.[12] The lack of prompt care for these chronic conditions can be especially deadly. Forgone preventive care also has negative consequences. As the authors of one journal article calculating how many fewer cancer diagnoses there had been put it, "While residents have taken to social distancing, cancer does not pause."[13]

Two friends of mine had heart attacks and died during the pandemic. One had an appointment with a cardiologist scheduled but had delayed it during the spring of 2020. Perhaps you have a similar story. Would our friends and family members be alive if, rather than second-guessing whether it was safe to visit a physician for that seemingly minor chest pain, they had just made an appointment? Perhaps. While we cannot know for sure whom the virus killed indirectly because of disruptions like these, it is clear that the virus killed hundreds of thousands indirectly, in addition to the people it killed directly.

Routine childhood vaccination rates dropped by 80 percent early in the first month of the pandemic.[14] By June 2020, vaccination rates were close to normal, but then declined again. The catch-up vaccinations were not sufficient to make up for the decline, however, leaving many children months behind on routine vaccinations. Some may never receive all of these life-protecting treatments. The decreased vaccination rate provided an additional threat to in-person learning for the 2021–22 school year.

On the other side, delayed and forgone care placed many hospitals in a difficult financial situation. With people canceling nonemergency procedures and postponing care, a major revenue stream for many hospitals suddenly disappeared. At the same time, hospitals faced new costs to prepare for and treat COVID-19.[15] Hospitals put in place new safety protocols and prepared for a surge in patients.

One additional cost was an increased price for face masks and other personal protective equipment, if they were available. Shortages of N95 face masks—the masks with the best filtration—continued for more than a year into the pandemic despite multiple manufacturers starting to produce them.[16] One reason for the shortage is that the U.S. imported more than half of its masks before the pandemic and had to switch to new suppliers.[17] These new suppliers did not have preexisting relationships with hospitals or brand recognition among consumers. The market was also flooded with cheaper masks that did not have the N95 certification but claimed they did, which sowed mistrust in potential buyers, particularly distrust of unfamiliar suppliers. This situation left the newly certified manufacturers with millions of masks they could not sell, despite continuing high demand.

Supply not meeting demand because of a breakdown in trust is what economists call a market failure. The economist George Akerlof first wrote about this failure in the used-car market, so it is typically called the "lemons problem." When buyers cannot tell the difference between good and bad products, the price buyers are willing to pay for goods of uncertain quality may not be what good-quality sellers are willing to sell for, so the good sellers leave. But that just leaves the average quality worse, so consumers are willing to pay even less, driving even medium-quality sellers from the market. The market unravels until only bad-quality sellers offering "lemons" are left.

The more sophisticated hospital buyers eventually figured out whom to buy from, although massive fraud continued.[18] For consumers, the market appears to have unraveled almost entirely. Counterfeit masks became ubiquitous. Most of the top fifty best-selling masks on Amazon in November 2021 were counterfeit or made fraudulent claims, for example.[19] With mask mandates continuing or reappearing through 2020 and 2021, consumers were left to fend for themselves throughout the pandemic. Awash in false claims we were not qualified to sort through, we still had to muddle through. So we bought masks that did not offer their promised protection, often unaware that we were being swindled.

We would have been much better off if quality surgical masks had been widely available.[20]

There were some positive healthcare developments. Many of the barriers to widespread adoption of remote medical appointments were knocked down during the pandemic. For example, Medicare allowed far greater flexibility in who could receive telehealth services and what was reimbursable.[21] The investments made to understand how to provide quality care remotely may have big payoffs for hard-to-reach patients in rural areas. Some kinds of care will always have to take place in person, but the pandemic innovations may lead to better care in the long term and expand the kinds of care that can be delivered remotely.[22]

Buying a New Home

Early in the pandemic, home sales plummeted. Existing home sales were down slightly in March but were down 23 percent in April and 30 percent in May compared with February 2020. These numbers were similar to what we saw in mortgage applications in Chapter 2. But by June, buyers and sellers had figured out how to sell and close, so in June, and especially July and August, home sales rebounded and soon hit peaks not seen since the flipping boom in the mid-2000s.[23]

One reason for the drop in sales is that it took time to figure out how to buy and sell during the pandemic. One difficulty was that open houses—unscheduled visits where many people could come at the same time in an enclosed space—no longer worked during the pandemic. Realtors and sellers quickly adapted to provide individual self-guided tours or virtual tours.[24]

The time it took from an accepted offer to closing—when the title transfers and the seller gets the money—increased substantially early in the pandemic. Closing times increased from 43 days in February to 60 days at the end of March. Part of the slowdown was that, with historically low interest rates, there was a refinance boom. Lenders did not have as much capacity—they were navigating working from home as well—so getting a mortgage took longer. In addition, other steps required some work-arounds. For example, final walkthroughs were sometimes done virtually or not at all.

More pressingly, many loans required an inspection and appraisal, which typically needed to occur in person with the appraiser on-site. The Department of Housing and Urban Development issued guidance that allowed desktop-only appraisals (an appraisal only based on information available without actually entering the home) and exterior-only appraisals for properties being purchased with a Federal Housing Administration–backed loan.[25]

Buying a home requires a lot of paperwork. The closing process in particular requires signatures from several parties: the buyer, the seller, the lender, and a title company that facilitates the transaction. Several innovations allowed many of these paperwork steps to occur with less human contact. "Curbside closings" involved the title officer completing the paperwork with one party, then bringing it out to the car, rather than completing the paperwork with everyone present in the same room. And in many instances, "no-touch" closings could take place entirely online using an online notary.[26] The new industry buzzwords "curbside closings" and "no-touch closings" by themselves indicate an industry that was rapidly innovating.

Some lenders had already been working to streamline the mortgage process. These lenders were well positioned to take advantage of the changes and increased their market share because they were more quickly able to adapt. Rocket Companies, the largest U.S. mortgage lender and the company behind the online lender Rocket Mortgages, increased net income by more than 900 percent from 2019 to 2020.[27] Many of the innovations that Rocket Mortgages had pioneered, including virtual showings and better online options, will likely last.

But not all lenders were as adept at managing the new world. Intermediation markups—the difference between how much it costs lenders to acquire capital and the rate they lend at—increased substantially. Even though interest rates were near zero, so lenders faced a very low cost of capital, the decline in interest rates was not passed on to consumers as much as one would normally expect. Research suggests that it was difficult for traditional lenders to expand during the pandemic. They could acquire the funds at historically low rates, but did not have the staff to make as many loans. And they could not expand rapidly because hiring and bringing new staff in was more difficult.[28] In addition, the massive increase in unemployment and forbearance introduced new risks to the marketplace. Lending became tighter for the riskiest segments of the market, and interest rates rose sharply in April 2020.[29]

House prices had not declined in the initial stages of the pandemic and in June they started to rise dramatically. The average price of houses sold increased by nearly 30 percent from June 2020 to June 2021. As the pandemic dragged on, many people began to rethink where they wanted to live. But with a fixed housing supply in the short run, an increase in demand meant that prices increased dramatically. Once the industry had figured out how to get through the pandemic capacity constraints, buyers started making offers for this limited supply and prices started increasing. These increases contributed to housing affordability issues and inequality, both of which we will discuss in the next chapter.

Shortages Early in the Pandemic

Did you have a hard time getting toilet paper in the spring of 2020? Bread? Cleaning supplies? My family did. And 44 percent of respondents to the February 2021 Making Ends Meet survey said they could "not buy enough of a necessity because it was not available in stores" over the previous year.

Three trends combined to produce these shortages. First and most directly, the pandemic itself affected the supply of many goods. Many meatpacking plants were shut down in April and May as workers there were exposed to and caught COVID-19.[30] The daily capacity at cattle and hog meatpacking and processing plants declined by as much as 45 percent in May 2020.[31] Prices surged and some products became unavailable. Tyson Foods, one of the largest meat processors, took out full-page ads in the *Washington Post,* the *New York Times,* and the *Arkansas Democrat-Gazette* to defend its safety record—and advocate for financial assistance—after massive outbreaks caused it to close several plants.[32]

Second, demand suddenly surged for many consumer goods and supply chains were not set up to meet this new demand. The Great Pause produced a sudden change in consumption patterns. With restaurants mostly shut down, Americans started cooking more at home, so demand for food purchased at grocery stores surged. With offices shut down, workers no longer bought a sandwich from the shop downtown or a burrito from a food truck, but instead made their own sandwich at home. And they no longer visited the restroom at work, instead doing their business at home. The amount of toilet paper we needed did not change, but where we needed it did.

These changes in consumption led to shortages because the household and business supply chains are different.[33] Demand for household consumption of toilet paper and food went up, and the regular consumer suppliers of these products were not able to meet this demand quickly during the pandemic. Suppliers of commercial toilet paper could not easily respond to the consumer market because the supply chains and even the products are different. For example, many offices use huge industrial rolls of toilet paper with special dispensers. To take just one problem, the bar codes for commercial rolls are different from consumer rolls, which made it difficult for shippers and stores stocking these rolls. Muddling through, suppliers started putting little code stickers on commercial rolls repurposed for consumer use, similar to the stickers on pieces of fruit in grocery stores.[34] Similar problems occurred for many consumer staples such as flour, eggs, and beans. Not many consumers want 50-pound bags of flour or 20-pound bags of dried beans. In response, some restaurants became mini grocery stores to meet demand and make up for lost sales.[35] They were using their commercial supply chains to meet consumer demand.

Third, the most discussed reasons for shortages early in the pandemic were hoarding and panic buying—acquiring much more of something than one needs, perhaps out of fear that it will not be available in the future. Hoarding likely contributed to some extent, adding to the surge in home demand. But shortages continued even after many retailers placed limits on amounts, suggesting that the broad increase in home demand was largely responsible.

The underlying economic problem was that retailers either could not or would not raise prices. Higher prices would have limited hoarding. Higher prices would have induced more restaurants or business supply vendors to alter their supply chains or products to serve the home market. As many states declared health emergencies in March 2020, they also implemented antigouging laws that limited the ability of retailers to increase prices (these are often accompanied by antihoarding laws that appear to be rarely enforced). Research using Google Shopping Trends suggests that these laws made it more difficult to find hand sanitizer and toilet paper.[36] Even without limitations from price-gouging laws, retailers may have also decided that the extra profit from raising prices was not worth the cost of bad press. Rather than share the pain of more costly items in short supply, the shortages created by not raising prices just created winners who got toilet paper at an artificially low price and losers who could not buy any. Compounding the problem, 33 state attorneys general called on eBay, Amazon, and Craigslist to police individuals selling toilet paper online at a high price.[37] These sellers might have been making a windfall profit. But they were responding to a real need from people desperate for toilet paper.

While tight toilet paper supplies did not last long, they did create some great pandemic muddling through. Bidet sales skyrocketed. And some people started getting creative, including with reusable toilet paper alternatives.[38]

The Great Pause produced some shortages in surprising areas such as coins. Coins stopped circulating as frequently because people were not using them in person.[39] Signs started popping up in stores asking customers to pay with a credit or debit card. One convenience store offered a free beverage to anyone who would exchange $5 in coins for bills.[40] Coin shortages may not seem like a big deal (or like "small change"), but they can have a big impact, as retailers' actions suggest. Shortages of small denominations are problematic because the inability to make correct change may prevent purchases from happening. For example, if you only have a $20 bill and want to buy a candy bar, but the merchant cannot give you change, maybe you do not make the purchase. Both you and the merchant lose. A shortage of the right denominations can therefore be a drag on economic activity.[41]

Retailers and restaurants adjusted to coin shortages and customer demand for little contact with new innovations. No-touch menus became more common, for example. Customers would scan a QR code (a block of black and white squares in a unique pattern) with their phones, which would lead them to a special website for ordering and paying for the meal. Such digital interactions have some advantages for restaurants. They can update their menu and prices quickly and automatically and learn more about their customers.[42] But it took widespread adoption by restaurants, and customers learning how to use the new tools, to make the new ordering method common.

As supply chains adjusted, shortages became less common. By September 2020, meat prices had fallen to prepandemic levels, for example.[43] And by the fall, toilet paper was no longer hard to come by in general, although local shortages still occurred from time to time. But some specialty items were still in high demand and difficult to find. With gyms closed, home workout equipment was often unavailable and prices surged. Video game consoles were sold out everywhere. Home office furniture was difficult to find as people settled in for what was looking by then like an extended period of working from home. And as people spent more time entertaining outside, pools, tents, and trampolines became difficult to find.[44] Patio heaters became a hot commodity as the weather turned cold.

In 2021, many of these supply difficulties occurred in reverse, creating new supply problems in unexpected places. For example, as restaurants opened up in the spring of 2021, meat prices surged again as demand increased.[45] In Chapter 9, we will discuss the late-pandemic supply chain problems that emerged as the world economy struggled to adapt to changing buying patterns.

Comparative Advantage Unravels

During the Great Pause, many services, such as haircuts, and goods, such as bread, suddenly became unavailable. Sometimes state stay-at-home orders meant nonessential services had to shut down. Yet even when these orders were relaxed, many people decided to stay home rather than take additional risks or expose others. The decision to cut spending on high-contact services was particularly prevalent among people with high income and in high-income areas.[46] As a result, small business revenue in high-income areas fell by more and job losses among low-wage workers who worked in high-income areas were especially large. Yet consumers still wanted many of these goods and services, so they started performing for themselves services they used to pay others to perform for them. (We should not forget the other side of this story, the millions of people who used to do these jobs and were now unemployed.)

I cut my own hair for more than a year during the pandemic. It reached a point in June 2020 where I felt so unkempt that I got out the clippers I had bought years before. Because I was working from home, the only people outside my family who saw me were on a webcam from the front, so my inconsistent cutting was not too evident. The barber I used to go to was definitely better at cutting my hair than I am. Many others decided that the pandemic was a good time to see what their hair looked like long (not bad, after the intermediate awkward phase) or what their beard looked like (perhaps not a keeper). As Lauren Kent put it on CNN, "This hasn't just been a bad hair day, it has been a bad hair year."[47]

With more time available and many products unavailable, people also started making products they used to buy. For example, many people took up baking, so much so that sourdough starters became a pandemic joke.[48] Demand for specialty flour surged, partly because standard baking flour was unavailable.[49]

What baking, home haircuts, and the many other services Americans started performing during the pandemic have in common is that they showed we were shifting to doing for ourselves what we used to pay someone else to do for us. During normal times, people make tradeoffs between "home production" and "market production" based on their available time and skills. For example, it sometimes makes sense to pay a skilled chef to prepare dinner, rather than doing it at home. Or an industrial baker to bake bread, rather than doing it ourselves.

Whenever we pay someone else to do something that we could (in principle) do ourselves, we are finding a gain from trade due to "comparative advantage" and "economies of scale." Both concepts go back to the fundamental economics insights from Adam Smith and David Ricardo, some of the first economists, writing around 1800. Comparative advantage occurs when we pay whoever is comparatively better at something—the skilled chef—because our own relative skills are better used on something else. Economies of scale occur when doing a bunch of the same thing is more productive. Professional bakers are more efficient than home bakers partly because they make bread in larger batches, so the time it takes per loaf is much lower. They also have bigger ovens, an investment that makes them more productive. During the Great Pause, many services and goods were suddenly unavailable and these gains from trade based on comparative advantage and economies of scale disappeared. Meals were still getting made, but not in the most efficient way.

To get a sense of the costs, consider a concrete example of home-made bread. When we could not find any sandwich bread for a month but still wanted to make sandwiches for our two young children, my wife learned how to make sandwich bread. It was delicious! But the cost of the bread was large. The direct costs of a single loaf of bread (flour, yeast, gas for the oven) were likely as large as the loaf of bread we used to buy at a grocery store. But the opportunity cost—the full cost of something, including the time it takes to do it—was much larger. We did not have any child care at the time, so we were trying to keep our two children entertained while doing full-time jobs. My wife was making two loaves at a time, so there were no economies of scale. And while she became more experienced, a skilled baker could make much more bread more quickly. Taking into account the cost of her time, this bread was likely more than ten times more expensive than any bread we had ever had. We started buying bread again when it became available, even though her bread tasted better.

The Great Pause caused comparative advantage to unravel in many ways. Very expensive bread or bad haircuts are just two examples of how, rather than using the services of someone who is comparatively better at doing something, we instead made do.

One way this unraveling affected many Americans surfaced around Thanksgiving in November 2020. Because of social distancing and travel guidelines, Thanksgiving gatherings during the pandemic were much smaller than normal. One consequence was a glut of large turkeys. But a hidden consequence is that many people were cooking their first turkey or other Thanksgiving favorites rather than joining their extended families and friends.[50] Thanksgiving gatherings benefit from economies of scale. Turkeys are a very efficient way to feed many people but are not so great for two people. Thanksgiving gatherings also benefit from comparative advantage: some people make better mashed potatoes than others. So these smaller Thanksgivings lacked scale, gains from trade, and experienced chefs, which meant a lot of dry or undercooked turkey and less variety.[51] To say nothing of missed family and friends.

One hidden way that the unraveling of comparative advantage worked is it made the decline in GDP we discussed in Chapter 2 seem larger than the actual decline in economic activity. Actual economic activity declined less because of the way that GDP is measured. When we eat at a restaurant, the "value added" of the meal preparation (the value of the meal minus the cost of the inputs required to make it) is counted in GDP. But when we cook at home, or care for our own children, or clean our own houses, rather than pay someone else to perform these services, these services are nonmarket production, so they do not count in GDP. During the Great Pause, there was a massive increase in home production. Some of the increase was driven by unemployed workers with more time on their hands, some by forced substitution as schools and restaurants closed. Americans kept consuming many services but ceased spending for them, so they no longer showed up as readily in GDP.[52]

The fact that nonmarket production does not count in GDP has a pernicious effect: it tends to undervalue work in the home, such as child care or cooking, that is still more often done by women. For example, if two stay-at-home moms care for their own children, their work does not count in GDP. But if they agree to pay each other to take care of each other's children, suddenly the child care they each provide is market production and counts in GDP. The ostensible reason is that it is difficult to value work that does not carry a market wage. But GDP is already an approximation from many imperfect sources, and long-standing surveys measure the amount of time people spend on unpaid home production. For example, one estimate suggests that if American women were paid the minimum wage for their unpaid home labor, it would be worth $1.5 trillion in 2019, about 7 percent of GDP.[53] Millions of families found themselves in a similar situation in the spring and summer 2020: doing a lot more unpaid and uncounted labor at home that we used to pay others to do for us.

Dating, Marriage, Divorce, and Friends

The pandemic reshaped dating. Tinder, a dating app, reported that 2020 was the busiest year in its history.[54] Of course, as a growing dating app, some of that growth would have occurred absent the pandemic. Match Group dominates the online dating business, owning Tinder, OkCupid, Match, Hinge, and almost every other dating site you might have heard of, except Bumble.[55] Match Group's revenue increased 23 percent over 2020 and its average subscribers increased 12 percent.[56] Tinder users were more engaged, sending 19 percent more messages per day in February 2021 than in February 2020. Despite all this activity, in a survey during the pandemic, 60 percent of Tinder members felt lonely.

Dating quickly became virtual. Before the pandemic, virtual dates were uncommon. Typical app users might connect or match (for example, if both "swipe right" in Tinder), start chatting through the app, then set up a date in real life (or "IRL"). But this process was disrupted during the pandemic as meeting in person declined and many typical places to meet were shut down. From March to June 2020, video calls between users increased by 84 percent on Bumble, the second-largest dating app.[57] Tinder quickly launched video calls and reported in March 2021 that nearly half of its members had a video chat with a match during the pandemic.[58]

Because meeting in person was no longer the ultimate goal, the geography of dating changed. Tinder added "Global Mode," which lets people match anywhere.[59] Bumble expanded how far it would match people.[60]

Dating, just like most social interactions during the pandemic, came with new restrictions that needed to be negotiated. The dating apps, for example, added new ways of identifying whether you were ready to meet in person or only virtually.[61] According to Tinder's analysis of its users' messages, the term "wear a mask" became far more common as users negotiated how to see each other in ways they were comfortable with.[62] As vaccines rolled out, disclosing your vaccine status became important. As testing became widespread, asking whether a date was worth dipping into a limited stash of rapid tests became a new measure of how serious things were likely to get.[63] And just as with many other areas of our lives that we had to muddle through, sex came with a whole new range of issues around transmission and consent. While these concerns may seem a bit funny now, for New Yorkers in the spring of 2020 who could hear the sirens and see the overflowing hospitals on the news, they were anything but. The New York City Health Department put out an advisory on safe sex during COVID-19 to help people navigate the new normal, including advice on virtual sex and wearing a face mask during sex.[64]

Some of these changes will persist.[65] Video dates are an intermediate step that lets people get to know each other somewhat before committing to a first in-person date. Why commit to dinner and a movie, only to be sure half an hour in that there will be no second date? And perhaps the need to set up boundaries and discuss what safety protocols make everyone feel safe beforehand will improve communication around all forms of consent. Tinder thinks so. In a report analyzing user messages, it wrote, "The pandemic brought up more discussions of personal boundaries" around masks and safety, which will "make conversations about consent more commonplace and comfortable in the future."[66]

For those on the other end of the dating obstacle course, the pandemic was a tough time to be getting married. It was also a tough time to be in the marriage business. For example, my cousin canceled her wedding in June 2020. She and her fiancé did get married in a backyard ceremony with only their parents attending. Her sister video-called onto a tablet set up on a stool to watch. It was not the lovely wedding with all of their family and friends that they had planned (we celebrated with them in summer 2022).

My cousin's experience was sadly common. Looking at marriage filings in five states and metropolitan areas through October 2020, one study found marriages in 2020 were down between 15 and 30 percent compared with 2019.[67] Other research came to similar conclusions.[68] Some of the decline is directly because of shut-down orders in March and April 2020 as county clerk offices closed. But the declines continued during 2020 even after it was generally possible to obtain a marriage license, suggesting that many couples were delaying marriage.

The decline in marriage certificates also understates the decline in marriage ceremonies and receptions. Many small businesses provide event planning, catering, floral arrangements, baking, and dresses (plus many other things) for wedding ceremonies and receptions. With couples canceling or scaling back their weddings, these vendors suffered a massive decline in business.

Wedding planners interviewed by *Brides* magazine think many of these trends will continue.[69] Smaller weddings, outdoor ceremonies, and more civil marriages seem likely to persist. A small boom in weddings occurred in 2021 as couples who canceled their weddings finally had them. But the Delta and Omicron variant surges in the summer and fall of 2021 also led to cancellations and downsizing.

Many postponed weddings had to change significantly from what the bride and groom had originally planned. Among the most awkward problems, a smaller wedding meant disinviting some people.[70] But with many weddings postponed two years, friendships and priorities change. The people you "podded" with might not have been close at the beginning of the pandemic (and you may be tired of them), but it might be hard not to invite them to your wedding. Meanwhile, friends you might not have seen for years might no longer seem priorities.

The idea that an expensive wedding is necessary is relatively new. Rebecca Mead, in her book on the wedding industry's growth, describes the spread of the idea of the large, lavish, and expensive wedding.[71] After all, throwing a fancy party for yourself, your fiancé, and your closest friends and family is great, but it is a tough way to start out your adult life when you often have the fewest resources. The average cost of a wedding may have declined in 2020. (Although these costs are always suspect, since they are usually collected by bridal magazines or wedding registry websites—which have an interest in encouraging more wedding spending—from couples who spent a lot on their weddings.)[72] Just as many people saved more because they could not spend, perhaps the pandemic will halt wedding inflation and convince couples that expensive parties and marriage ceremonies do not have to go together.

Surprising many, divorces also declined by 12 percent in 2020.[73] The divorce drop appears to have occurred internationally as well, suggesting it is part of a broader pandemic phenomenon.[74] One reason divorces declined is that many civil courts and county clerk offices were closed during the first months of the pandemic, making it impossible or much harder to file. Divorce may have been one of the things we could not figure out how to muddle through. Another reason may be that the pandemic increased financial concerns and uncertainty.[75] Divorce can be expensive. Most obviously, it splits up the household, so any savings from living together disappear. But the drop may only delay an eventual surge in divorces, and limited evidence suggests divorces picked up again in 2021.

People had to figure out dating, marriage, and divorce during the pandemic. But more broadly, we had to figure out all of our social connections. In his book *Bowling Alone*, Robert Putnam documents a long-term decline in social connections.[76] People are less connected to family, friends, and social networks than they used to be. Rather than join a bowling league, we now watch online videos, or play video games, perhaps at the same time as friends, but not in the same room. The pandemic may have reinforced these trends. With everyone now suspect of carrying a deadly disease, it became more difficult to maintain social connections. For single-person households—about 25 percent of all households—the pandemic was often isolating.[77] Work often absorbed more time. What else was there to do? Pandemic hobbies spread, but these were often poor substitutes for the social interactions we gave up.

Measuring the social costs of more isolation is hard. But they exist. We may have muddled through some things, but the lost connections, the year or more of our lives when we saw fewer people, traveled less, did not hug our parents or grandparents, have real costs. With other people suspect, we often did not make new social connections or deepen the ones we had. Those scars may be with us long after the virus's economic effects fade.

Lisa

All of the shops are on the main road that runs through Lisa's small town in the intermountain West. There's the grocery store, the coffee shop, the hardware store, and the elementary school. The town runs along this main road in the narrow, flat area along the valley floor. Behind town, a hiking trail leads up the steep hills. After raising three kids there, Lisa and her husband likely loved the area.

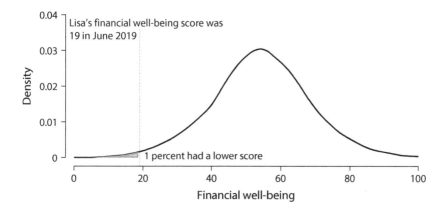

But those three kids had been a financial strain. "I have three children and my husband and I have put them all through college," Lisa wrote in the June 2019 survey. "We have had a child in college for the past 11 years and therefore have not had any money for ourselves. Our life has been a struggle for the past 11 years and we have one year left with our youngest in college. There is simply never enough money."

Lisa, a white woman in her late fifties, was feeling particularly financially strained in 2019. Between trying to pay off loans they had taken for the previous children and the new loan for her youngest daughter, who started college in 2017, they were stretched beyond their means. She and her husband together earned about $80,000 each year; she was working part time while he worked full time. But with several student loans, a mortgage payment of several thousand dollars, the payments for the auto loan, and several unexpected expenses, all of their income was always spoken for. They had less than $100 in their checking account and had maxed out their credit card. Because they had so little in their accounts, they kept overdrafting, adding to their expenses.

As a result, Lisa and her husband had difficulty paying bills or expenses more than 12 times in the previous year. Because the underlying problem was too little cash, there was not a specific reason for most times they had difficulty. A bill would come due, but there was not any money to pay it immediately. So they would shift money from somewhere else, or not pay another bill, pushing the problem down the road. The last time they had difficulty, they did not pay all of the expense, paid another bill late, and sold something, and Lisa took on some additional hours at her job.

Early in the Pandemic

Lisa's family was already barely getting by before the pandemic. Things got complicated as the pandemic hit and her family had to muddle through. She and her husband kept their jobs, so the primary problem was not lower income but changing expenses. "Since the pandemic began," Lisa told us, "two of my adult children have moved into my house along with their pets, so I now have four people, three cats, and a dog living in my house." Perhaps Lisa and her husband and their children were all trying to work remotely, bumping up against each other, interrupting each other's work calls, the dog demanding attention, the cats demanding obeisance. Perhaps the kids were unemployed and always borrowing the car to go for a hike or go snowboarding. In some ways it must have been nice having the kids at home again. But with more people and pets, their expenses went up. Lisa wrote, "My household expenses have increased and I have owed taxes on our personal return for 2019 and 2020 which I never used to. It is very stressful."

Those taxes loomed large for Lisa. On top of their already tight finances, these big new expenses were responsible for her having difficulty paying several bills in the previous year. She had started working full time to help bring in additional income. Things got so tight that she pawned something—maybe some jewelry—because it was the fastest way to raise the money.

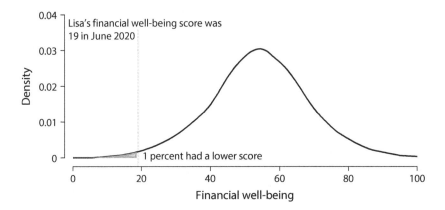

Even though they all had medical insurance, one of the things they had difficulty paying for was a medical expense.

Lisa's family benefited from the student loan payment pause. For nearly three years they did not have to make payments on their parental student loans. The loans did not go away, but not making payments freed a lot of money each month.

They also applied for and received forbearance on their mortgage and stopped making payments for six months starting in June 2020. Unlike for student loans, interest continued to accumulate on the mortgage, but it is likely that when they left forbearance in December 2020, they worked with their mortgage servicer to add the missed payments to the end of the loan without increasing the monthly payment. In the meantime, their expenses went down by around $3,000 a month.

The Economic Impact Payments also helped. All of the adults (not counting the cats and dog) received $1,200 from the CARES Act in April 2020, and they would have each received another $600 in January 2021 and $1,400 in April 2021. These payments would have more than covered the unexpected medical expense and helped Lisa's family get out of the financial swamp they had been slowly, but surely, sinking into before the pandemic. And while Lisa's direct expenses had increased—food for four adults, three cats, and a dog is expensive—the family's total expenses, including the children's, had likely declined substantially. Rather than their two adult children renting somewhere else, they were avoiding this expense. Like millions of other families, the pandemic showed them unexpected ways to adapt.

Late in the Pandemic

The pandemic financial assistance helped Lisa to not feel so pessimistic about her financial situation and her financial well-being improved slightly. She was still not feeling financially secure in February 2021. Partly, she had continued to have difficulty paying all the bills. But they had found ways to cut back on expenses and Lisa had continued working additional hours to bring in more income. They had left mortgage forbearance in December 2020 even though they could likely have extended it for another six months. By January 2022, they had paid off the auto loan, which freed up some more money. Lisa's credit score had improved and her credit card limit had increased. But in a sign that things continued to be tight, Lisa had maxed out her card again after several months.

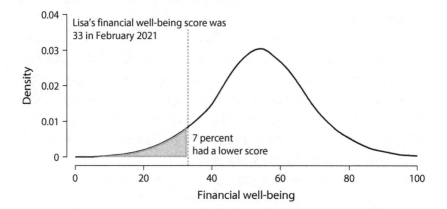

6

Pandemic Relief after the CARES Act

THE REMARKABLE speed and impact of the CARES Act surprised many people, myself included. By July 2020, the act's policies, taken all together, had remarkably transformed household finance. Savings were up, credit card debt was down, households had fewer difficulties paying their bills and expenses, and their financial well-being was up in June and July 2020.

Yet these positive trends had started to reverse as the CARES Act policies expired. After all, few expected in March that the pandemic would go on for so long. The extra $600 unemployment benefit expired at the end of July 2020, for example, and the expansion of unemployment benefits to contract workers and long-term unemployed was set to end in December.

As it became clear that the pandemic would extend well beyond 2020, policy makers began to work on new bills to extend or expand on the provisions of the CARES Act. What shape would policy take as the pandemic continued? Two new pandemic relief bills—one passed in December 2020 and one passed in March 2021—were the last major pandemic economic policy interventions. These bills largely continued policies introduced in the CARES Act. They increased unemployment benefits by $300 per week, extended unemployment benefits to contract workers, provided more money to the Paycheck Protection Program, and provided new rounds of Economic Impact Payments.

By continuing and extending these policies, the new bills continued the transformation. The average household was financially better off in February 2021 than before the pandemic and remained so through summer 2021. We already looked at the surprising improvement following the CARES Act. This chapter rounds out pandemic policies and looks at how well pandemic policies, taken together, protected households from financial calamity.

The December 2020 Relief Bill

The 5,593-page Coronavirus Response and Relief Supplemental Appropriations Act was unveiled on Monday, December 21, 2020, and passed both houses of Congress by wide margins within hours.[1] It was hotly debated for months before passage and the subject of a great deal of last-minute behind-the-scenes back-and-forth. The act combined about $900 billion in pandemic relief with a $1.4 trillion omnibus spending bill to fund the federal government in 2021. The federal government's fiscal 2021 year actually started on October 1, 2020, but it had been working under temporary budget appropriations.

I refer to the pandemic portion of the act as the December 2020 pandemic relief bill for lack of a better name. Because many of the most important elements were only worked out at the last minute, it never received a catchy name like the CARES Act or the later American Rescue Plan Act. The president did not sign the bill until Sunday, December 27, after last-minute "waffling."[2] During the delay, several benefits expired. The negotiations and chaos surrounding the December 2020 relief bill made it hard to tell whether it would actually go into effect until the last moment. It was a messy time.

Because it combined 12 separate appropriations bills to fund the federal government and a pandemic relief package, the Coronavirus Response and Relief Supplemental Appropriations Act was the longest bill ever passed. Although it contained a lot, much of the pandemic relief was a continuation or reinstatement of policies from the CARES Act. The most important provisions restarted unemployment benefits from the CARES Act that had lapsed.

- The bill provided an additional $300 weekly unemployment benefit on top of state unemployment benefits. The CARES Act $600 additional benefit ended on July 31, 2020, although the Lost Wage Assistance program provided a smaller benefit for several weeks in August and September.
- The bill also reinstated the Pandemic Unemployment Assistance from the CARES Act, which made freelancers and independent contractors eligible for unemployment benefits. Their CARES Act eligibility for benefits ended on December 26.
- And the bill extended how long the unemployed could claim benefits by another 11 weeks. The CARES Act had added an extra 13 weeks of benefits for unemployed who had used up their benefits. Unemployment benefits generally last for 26 weeks depending on the state. This provision was very important because unemployment benefits were expiring for workers who lost their jobs at the beginning of the pandemic.

The new benefits under the relief bill were mostly set to expire in March 2021. (The American Rescue Plan Act, which I discuss next, extended most of them through September 2021.)

Because it took several weeks for archaic state unemployment systems to change benefits, the last-minute passage of the bill created benefits gaps.[3] The delay signing the bill until after the benefits expired added to the difficulties. One study found that only 28 states were able to start benefits in about two weeks; 12 states had a three-to-five-week delay.[4] By January 30, 2021, a month into the new program, there was no indication that 11 states were paying Pandemic Unemployment Assistance, nor that 13 states were paying Pandemic Emergency Unemployment Compensation, which likely means these states had not yet implemented the programs. The delayed benefits were eventually paid. But with many households only barely making ends meet, a delay in benefits can have real consequences; $300 the week after the rent is due is not the same as $300 the week before. Given the difficulty many states had with unemployment insurance programs, allowing these programs to expire made them less effective at helping the unemployed.

The December 2020 relief bill also provided a new $600 Economic Impact Payment to adults and children under 17. Adults and children were eligible for the full amount if parental income was less than $75,000 for single parents and $150,000 for married parents.[5] Above $75,000, the payments fell as income decreased, dropping to zero for adults earning $87,000 or more. This decline was much more rapid than in the CARES Act.

The December 2020 relief bill also contained other money for programs. These included the following:

- $285 billion for small businesses under the Paycheck Protection Program. Chapter 4 discusses the impacts of this spending in the context of the full program.
- $54 billion to K–12 schools and $23 billion for colleges and universities.[6]
- $25 billion in rental assistance.[7] It also extended an eviction ban originally implemented by the Centers for Disease Control and Prevention in September 2020 for one month. This ban would later be extended several times. I will discuss renters, this money, additional money in the American Rescue Plan, and the eviction moratoria in Chapter 7.
- To help combat an increase in food insecurity, the bill increased Supplemental Nutrition Assistance Program (SNAP) benefits by 15 percent for six months.[8] SNAP replaced what used to be called food stamps. The program provides funds that can be used at approved grocery stores to about 10 percent of American households.
- The bill funded several other programs, including a range of public health measures, funds to expand access to high-speed internet, and funds for the child care industry.[9]

The bill also banned surprise medical bills starting in 2022.[10] As we saw in Chapter 3, medical bills are one of the primary causes of financial difficulty. Nearly 60 percent of households with a major medical or dental expense had difficulty paying a bill or expense, according to the Making Ends Meet survey.[11] Among other things, the relief bill banned "balance bills" when patients are treated by an out-of-insurance-network care provider at an in-network hospital.

Many of the provisions in the December relief bill were temporary. The extended unemployment benefits were set to expire in March 2021 after just 11 weeks, for example. Their expiration set the stage for the final large pandemic relief bill.

The American Rescue Plan Act

Congress started debate on the American Rescue Plan Act in February 2021 and passed it in early March. Symbolically, the president signed it into law on March 11, 2021, one year after the World Health Organization declared the start of the pandemic. The act committed $1.9 trillion in relief,[12] about as much as the CARES Act and twice as much as the December 2020 relief bill.

The American Rescue Plan continued the $300 expanded unemployment benefits to September 2021. These benefits were going to expire on March 14. The combination of a last-minute passage and creaky state unemployment systems meant that some unemployed had delays in receiving benefits, again.[13] However, because the American Rescue Plan was largely a continuation of unemployment policies from the December 2020 relief bill, states had fewer delays implementing it.[14] Many states ended these benefits earlier than September 2021. I will discuss the impact these early cutoffs had and the other benefits' expiration in September in Chapter 9.

Meanwhile, about a quarter of the unemployed in March 2021 had been out of work for at least a year.[15] The end of the unemployment "benefit year" typically means a big drop in benefits.[16] The December 2020 relief bill and the American Rescue Plan allowed the unemployed to continue to receive Pandemic Extended Unemployment Compensation through September 2021, even if their benefit year ended, so it largely prevented big benefit drops in March.

Many families had received significant unemployment benefits in 2020 and were facing a big tax bill. Unemployment benefits are taxable, which catches many people by surprise, as they reasonably figure, "Why should the government tax money it's giving me!?" According to one online survey in October 2020, 39 percent of people did not realize unemployment benefits were taxable.[17] The problem with not knowing unemployment benefits are taxable is that, unlike for wages, taxes are not typically withheld automatically from unemployment benefits. In some ways not withholding makes sense; during normal times, unemployment is typically short term, so it is not clear how much to withhold. But with the increase in long-term unemployment during the pandemic, not withholding automatically meant that for many people used to withholding or not aware that unemployment benefits are taxable, a big tax bill was accumulating that they were not ready for, leading to a scary tax-time surprise. We saw in Chapter 3 that unexpected taxes and legal fees are one of the more common financial shocks households face, and financial shocks like these can cause substantial suffering. Adding to the confusion, unemployed workers can opt to have some withholding from unemployment benefits. But many states, including California, did not apply the withholding to the $600 added unemployment benefit from the CARES Act.[18] So even many people who had tried to prepare for taxes and were doing the right thing were caught by surprise when they prepared their 2020 taxes.

To deal with this looming problem, the American Rescue Plan Act exempted the first $10,200 of 2020 unemployment benefits from income taxation, significantly alleviating the brewing taxable unemployment benefit mess. Households that had already filed received refunds automatically.

The act also sent a new round of Economic Impact Payments. Individuals with incomes below $75,000 received $1,400, which declined rapidly to zero for individuals earning $80,000 or more.[19]

The American Rescue Plan Act provided $350 billion to state and local governments. While, early in the pandemic, it appeared likely that state and local tax receipts would crater, most states weathered the pandemic better than expected. Total state tax revenues from April to December 2020 were down just 1.8 percent compared with the same period in 2019.[20] The small decline is starkly different from the 2008 financial crisis, which caused a large long-term decline in most state's revenues.

During the pandemic, some states that rely on tourism (Hawaii and Florida) or energy (Alaska, Texas, Louisiana, and Florida) had much bigger tax revenue declines.

State tax revenues barely fell for several reasons. Partly because of the extensive federal aid, including extended unemployment benefits, individual income did not fall in most states, which in turn kept state income and sales taxes from falling. Also, after a brief fall at the start of the pandemic, the stock market did well, keeping capital gains taxes high. And states with progressive income tax systems did better than expected because the pandemic primarily affected low-income workers who provide a smaller share of revenue.[21] Because high-income workers largely kept their jobs and their incomes, tax receipts did not fall much.

At the same time, city and local budgets were still facing shortfalls. Many cities' tax receipts declined substantially because of the decline in the value of commercial real estate.[22] Cities are typically heavily reliant on real estate taxes. As companies reduced the amount of office space they used because so much of their workforce was remote, one projection suggested commercial real estate values would decline by 7.2 percent nationally compared with before the pandemic. This decline directly reduces city tax receipts. States and local governments also needed to spend more on unemployment benefits and direct expenses to deal with the pandemic.[23] Even flat tax receipts would still leave many states and local governments with big budgetary holes.

These funds were only slowly put to use. At the end of 2021 most cities had not yet used much of their allocated funds. The American Rescue Plan provided $130 billion in flexible funding to cities, counties, and tribes, a large share of these local governments' budgets. But by July 31, 2021, when these cities had to declare the amounts they had spent and on what, nearly half of the largest cities had yet to use any funds.[24] Only half the funds were available initially; the rest became available in 2022. Many local governments waited to see what their full budget shortfalls would be before committing to funds.

The American Rescue Plan provided an additional $21.6 billion in rental assistance in addition to the $25 billion in the December 2020 bill. We'll discuss these funds in Chapter 7. Housing vouchers and homelessness assistance also received $10 billion.

As with prior pandemic relief, the American Rescue Plan provided funding for many public health measures. It funded the vaccine rollout ($9 billion), including some funds dedicated to reaching underserved communities.[25] Also included were funds for vaccine development and manufacturing ($20 billion), and testing and hospital reimbursement ($25 billion). And the American Rescue Plan significantly expands eligibility for insurance subsidies under the Affordable Care Act.

Finally, the American Rescue Plan expanded two programs with significant consequences for low-income households' finances. First, it extended the 15 percent increase in SNAP benefits in the December 2020 relief bill through September 2021. The increase would have expired in June.

Second, the act raised the child tax credit from $2,000 to $3,000 for children six and older and to $3,600 for children under six. It also raised eligibility to 17. More consequentially for low-income households, the credit was fully refundable, so low-income households received money if they paid less than the child tax credit in taxes. Previously, households that did not pay enough in taxes to get a full credit also did not get any benefit over the amount of their taxes. Since the households that pay the lowest taxes are also the poorest, the child tax credit was somewhat regressive (although it phased out for households with incomes over $200,000, making it progressive at the top end of the income distribution). In addition, the American Rescue Plan Act authorized monthly payments that made the child tax credit act much more like a universal child allowance. Eligible parents started getting a monthly deposit in July 2021.

The combination of unemployment benefits, progressive Economic Impact Payments, the child tax credits, expanded insurance subsidies, and SNAP benefits means the American Rescue Plan Act significantly expands direct financial assistance to low-income families. As Dylan Matthews in Vox put it, the American Rescue Plan Act launched "the second war on poverty."[26]

When most people use the term "poverty," they mean households facing financial deprivation, with all of the problems associated with it that we saw in Chapter 3. But "poverty" has a technical definition as well. The poverty rate is the proportion of households that fall below a particular income threshold.[27] The threshold is adjusted for the composition of the household so that, for example, a four-person family needs to earn more than a two-person family to be out of poverty. The poverty threshold was originally developed by Mollie Orshansky, an economist working for the Social Security Administration, in 1965.[28] It was based on the amount of income a family of four would need to afford three times a basic food budget—which at the time included a lot of meat. Since then the poverty line has been updated for inflation and food budgets have changed substantially, so this original connection has been lost. Now the poverty line is just a convenient way of measuring how many poor there are using a widely agreed-on threshold for what "poor" means.

Poverty is a poor way to measure policy effectiveness, but it is widely used nonetheless. Why is poverty a bad way to measure policy? First, we do not stop caring about people just because they pass some arbitrary threshold. A family earning just a bit more than the threshold is not doing well financially, yet it does not count. A policy that improves this family's situation would be considered a failure if we measure the policy's impact on poverty. Second, and more perniciously, some policies may reduce poverty but are clearly harmful. Suppose I told you about a great program to give money to people close to the poverty line so we could bring them above the poverty line. But if we pay for the program by cutting funding for homeless shelters, we have reduced poverty, but made the lives of the desperately poor worse. Few think that is a good trade-off. A final problem is that the official poverty measure excludes important government benefits such as public housing, Medicaid, and SNAP benefits from the calculation.[29] By excluding such benefits, the official poverty measure does not calculate deprivation correctly, making it worse than useless because it encourages reaching incorrect conclusions about a policy's impacts.[30] Better poverty measures include these benefits.

Measuring poverty including these benefits, poverty fell by a historic amount from 11.8 percent in 2019 to 9.1 percent in 2020.[31] But poverty increased after the CARES Act's expanded unemployment benefits expired. An Urban Institute analysis projected that the American Rescue Plan Act would reduce the poverty rate by more than one-third, from 13.7 percent without the act to 8.7 percent with it.[32] Black poverty would fall by 42 percent from what it would be without the act. Because of the unemployment benefits, poverty would fall by half for unemployed workers compared with what it would be without them. While the expanded Child Tax Credits were active from July to December 2021, child poverty fell by about 30 percent.[33] Families who received the expanded Child Tax Credits were much more likely to have enough to eat.[34] Truly, a war on poverty.

Pandemic Relief Policy Overall

Most American households received some sort of government aid between March 2020 and September 2021. Coming up with an average number of dollars households received is challenging, because pandemic relief varied by state, income, number of children, and unemployment status. So instead of trying to estimate a "standard" amount of aid, it is more useful to calculate the aid different kinds of families would have received, and compare that dollar amount with how much aid they would have received if prepandemic policies had continued unchanged. Even that number can be hard to calculate; unemployment benefits vary by employment and income history, and Economic Impact Payments and child tax credits depend on children's ages and custody status. In most states, regular state unemployment benefits replace about half of an unemployed person's income for at most 26 weeks, although states vary significantly in their replacement rate, with some replacing less than a third of wages.[35] Many states also have a maximum weekly benefit so that high-wage workers receive a smaller share of their wages.[36]

Consider four hypothetical families:

- The Adams family: Mr. Adams, a single father, earned $50,000 per year before the pandemic. He remained employed during the pandemic and has one child under six.

- The Burns family: Ms. Burns, also a single parent, earned $50,000 per year as a self-employed contractor before the pandemic. She was unemployed for the entire pandemic and has one child under six.
- The Cook family: A four-person family with two children under six and two adults earning $80,000 per year before the pandemic. Mr. Cook kept his job during the pandemic, but Mrs. Cook lost her job in March 2020 and did not return to work before July 2021.
- The Davis family: A four-person family with two children under six and two adults earning $80,000 per year before the pandemic. Mr. Davis left his job in September 2020 to take care of their children and could not find work when their children's school reopened.

These families do not represent all families, but they do capture some of the important variations that would have affected benefits. Table 6.1 summarizes these families' situations and the aid they would have received.[37]

These families' experiences differed substantially during the pandemic. Some had periods of unemployment, others did not. But because of pandemic policies and particularly the expanded unemployment benefits, their incomes barely changed in 2020. Table 6.1 shows how much these different families received and how their incomes in 2020 compared with 2019. Even though both the Burns, Cook, and Davis families experienced unemployment, their income in 2020 was only slightly lower than in 2019.

The Adams family did not have an unemployment period. The largest impact on its finances was $1,700 in Economic Impact Payments in 2020. The Adamses' income increased slightly because of these payments.

The pandemic aid had a larger impact on Ms. Burns. As a self-employed contractor, she would not have been eligible for any unemployment benefits before the pandemic. Without pandemic-related assistance, the Burnses' income would have dropped to zero after the pandemic started, so her only income in 2020 would have been what

TABLE 6.1. Pandemic cash assistance to families in 2020.

Family	Adams	Burns	Cook	Davis
Adults	1	1	2	2
Children	1	1	2	2
Unemployed?	No	Yes	Yes	Yes
Annual income before pandemic	$50,000	$50,000	$80,000	$80,000
2020 income without any assistance	$50,000	$14,423	$51,538	$67,692
2020 nonpandemic state unemployment benefits	0	0	$10,000	0
2020 pandemic assistance	$1,700	$32,450	$20,400	$7,123
2020 income with assistance	$51,700	$46,873	$81,938	$74,815
2020 income compared to before pandemic (percent)	103	94	102	94

she made in the first several months of the year—a quarter of her normal income. Instead, the extended and expanded unemployment benefits, along with Economic Impact Payments, meant that the Burnses received 94 percent of their prepandemic income.

The Cook family also had one adult who was unemployed. Two incomes help provide an additional buffer against income falls, but losing one income for most of the year would likely still have been painful. Because of the CARES Act, however, the Cooks' income would have been 2 percent higher in 2020 with pandemic aid than without it.

Mr. Davis quit his job in September 2020 to take care of their children, whose school was shut down. Normally, leaving your job for family reasons makes you ineligible for unemployment insurance in most states. But the Department of Labor issued guidelines in August 2020 saying that parents who could not work because they needed to care for children whose schools or daycares were closed would be eligible for benefits.[38] The Davises received unemployment benefits and Economic Impact Payments, which meant that their income only fell 6 percent in 2020.

Regular unemployment benefits would have done little or nothing to protect the Cooks, Davises, and Burnses from a major income loss. The Burns and Davis families were not eligible for regular unemployment benefits and would not have received any aid. And the Cooks received twice as much pandemic unemployment aid as they did regular unemployment benefits. It was pandemic policy, not the regular safety net, that prevented families like these from serious financial suffering. At its heart, the pandemic paradox turns out not to be so complicated. Because of pandemic unemployment benefits, incomes for the unemployed largely did not decline, so we avoided widespread financial suffering.

Furthermore, although Economic Impact Payments contributed to these households, they were relatively unimportant for the unemployed. Economic Impact Payments received a great deal of attention and substantial funding, but because they were not targeted at households in need and were relatively small, their contribution to these families' bottom lines was far less significant than the changes to unemployment benefits. Of course, the families I chose are not the poorest. For a family with much less income, the Economic Impact Payments would have been more important.

How did these families fare in 2021? Table 6.2 shows how much each family would have received assuming the unemployed parent was unemployed for the entire year. The December 2020 relief bill and the American Rescue Plan Act extended unemployment benefits and added $300 weekly through September 2021. The additional weekly benefit was less generous than the CARES Act's $600 additional benefit, but it lasted substantially longer.

Mr. Adams was not unemployed but received $5,600 in Economic Impact Payments and $1,600 in child tax credits, so the family's income increased by 11 percent. The Burnses were facing more difficulties. Pandemic unemployment benefits now provided just two-thirds of their prepandemic income. But without pandemic assistance and changes to unemployment rules, the Burns family would have received no aid at all. Meanwhile, the two-income Cook and Davis households maintained 94 percent of their income and now look identical. The major

TABLE 6.2. Pandemic cash assistance to families in 2021.

Family	Adams	Burns	Cook	Davis
Adults	1	1	2	2
Children	1	1	2	2
Unemployed?	No	Yes	Yes	Yes
Annual income before pandemic	$50,000	$50,000	$80,000	$80,000
2021 income without any assistance	$50,000	0	$40,000	$40,000
2021 nonpandemic state unemployment benefits	0	0	0	0
2021 pandemic assistance	$5,600	$32,927	$35,162	$35,162
2021 income with assistance	$55,600	$32,927	$75,162	$75,162
2021 income compared to before pandemic (percent)	111	66	94	94

difference between these two families and the Burnses is that with two adults and two children, they received twice as much in Economic Impact Payments and child tax credits.

Again, without the pandemic aid, the situations of the families with an unemployed parent would have been dire; the Burnes's income would have fallen to zero and the Cooks' and Davises' incomes would have fallen by half. It was pandemic policies, not the regular social safety net, that protected these families.

Household Finance through the Pandemic

Together, the three large pandemic relief bills transformed Americans' finances through the pandemic. Much of this section draws directly from research I did with Cortnie Shupe using the Making Ends Meet survey.[39] Other research provides a similar view. Despite the pandemic, the average American was better off financially during the pandemic. Even financially vulnerable groups were better off. First, the overall numbers.

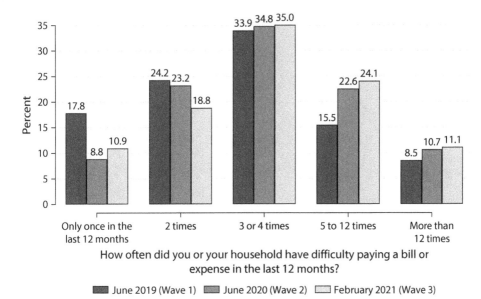

FIGURE 6.1. Consumers with difficulty paying a bill or expense had difficulty somewhat more frequently. (How often Making Ends Meet respondents reported having difficulty in the last 12 months in each survey wave, if they reported having difficulty.)

Fewer Americans had difficulty paying bills during the pandemic. The share reporting difficulties declined by 5 percentage points, from 39 percent before the pandemic to 34 percent in February 2021. Difficulty paying bills or expenses declined for almost all demographic groups. For example, African Americans and low-income households were less likely to have difficulty during the 12 months preceding February 2021 than during the prepandemic period.[40]

While fewer people had any difficulty overall, Figure 6.1 shows that for people who did have difficulty, difficulties were somewhat more frequent.[41] More people had difficulty five to twelve times and more than twelve times. Perhaps reduced spending and financial assistance helped people who might otherwise have had occasional difficulty avoid it. But people who did not receive assistance still faced a difficult economy with high unemployment, making difficulties more frequent and harder to avoid.

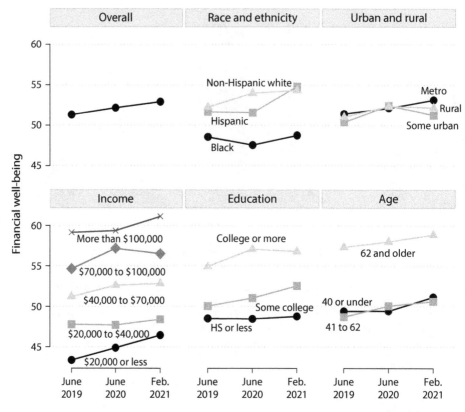

FIGURE 6.2. Financial well-being improved for almost all groups, although the improvements were larger for some groups. (*Sources*: 2019, 2020, and 2021 Making Ends Meet surveys.)

Households felt better about their finances too. The individual stories of Marcus, Joan, John, and other Americans show the ups and downs of financial well-being. Against the ups and downs, it can be hard to spot a trend, but average financial well-being increased by 1.62 points, a huge increase. Figure 6.2 shows this overall increase and the increase by groups.[42] Before the pandemic, there were big gaps between groups. Financial well-being tended to increase with income, for example. For comparison, the overall financial well-being increase is so large that it is similar to the average difference in financial well-being between a household earning $30,000 and a household earning $50,000 before the pandemic.

Financial well-being increased across race and ethnicity groups, income groups, and education groups. High-income people felt better about their finances, perhaps because they were saving more. And low-income people felt better about their finances, perhaps because they were saving more or had been helped by unemployment insurance or Economic Impact Payments. The increases for some groups are larger than others, but we cannot be confident these differences are meaningful. All surveys have some uncertainty in their estimates, and as we look at smaller groups that uncertainty gets larger. What is meaningful is that almost everyone seemed to be doing better during the pandemic, but the differences between groups remain large.

Other research also concluded that financial status generally improved for most groups. The Financial Health Network's aptly named financial health score—an index based on eight survey questions that is conceptually distinct but closely related to the Consumer Financial Protection Bureau's financial well-being scale—improved from April 2019 to April 2020 and again in April 2021.[43] Financial health seems to have improved almost everywhere: the share that was financially healthy (doing well on almost every question) improved, even as the share that was financially vulnerable declined. Financial health improved for low-income people, as well as for all major racial and ethnic groups. Financial health improved more for Black Americans than for non-Hispanic white people.

Measures that do not depend on surveys showed strong improvements as well. Using anonymized Chase Bank accounts, the JPMorgan Chase Institute reported that median checking and savings account balances, which had increased sharply at the beginning of the pandemic, were still higher than before the pandemic through 2021.[44] By September 2021, high-income families' balances were 40 percent higher than before the pandemic. Low-income families' savings were 50 percent higher (although low-income families had lower bank balances before the pandemic, so this change is a smaller dollar amount). As we saw in the last chapter, wealth increased across the spectrum of wealth distribution. Using the same data, incomes grew across the country over 2020 and 2021.[45] The growth was particularly large for the lowest-income workers.

Looking in the opposite direction, financial distress measures fell. My colleague Ryan Sandler showed early in the pandemic that delinquencies on most types of credit accounts fell by about half early in the pandemic and continued to be low, perhaps even falling a bit more through 2020.[46] In April 2021, new delinquencies on auto loans, mortgages, and credit cards were about half what they had been in January 2020. And even accounts that were already delinquent were less likely to become more delinquent, suggesting that even struggling borrowers were doing better. Delinquencies stayed substantially lower through at least June 2022.

Bankruptcy filings also fell sharply. Consumers can generally file for two kinds of bankruptcies, named for the chapter of the bankruptcy code they come from. Filings for chapter 7 bankruptcies, which generally involve selling all nonexempt assets but wipe away most debts (but generally not student debt), fell by 22 percent from 2019 to 2020.[47] Chapter 13 bankruptcies, which generally include a repayment plan, were down 46 percent. Part of the decline early in the pandemic was likely due to the fact that it became harder to file with courts shut down, but as courts learned to work remotely, filings could have rebounded.

Looking at a different approach to financial stress, credit card debt fell substantially at the beginning of the pandemic and, remarkably, fell again in early 2021 and remained low through summer 2022. Credit card debt fell even for the most financially vulnerable (see Figure 4.5).

Pandemic Relief's Role in the Improvement

Pandemic relief policies were central in these household financial improvements. We have seen hints of this role over and over again in this book. For example, as Economic Impact Payments were deposited, spending went up. Credit card debt declined as policies channeled money to households. As Tables 6.1 and 6.2 showed, pandemic unemployment benefits appear to have been the largest contributor to maintaining incomes.

To understand just how important unemployment insurance was, let's look at its role in improving financial well-being. Overall, about 15 percent of people in the February 2021 Making Ends Meet survey

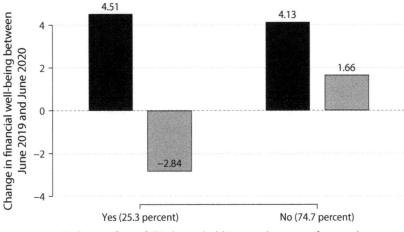

FIGURE 6.3. Unemployment insurance helped improve financial well-being during the pandemic. (Change in financial well-being from June 2019 to June 2020 among Making Ends Meet respondents who did or did not have a significant fall in income because of unemployment and did or did not receive unemployment insurance.)

reported receiving unemployment benefits since March 2020. Conditional on receiving some unemployment benefits, 84 percent also received the additional $600 weekly supplement at some point during the pandemic. Figure 6.3 breaks the respondents into four groups by whether they received unemployment insurance and whether they reported a drop in income because of unemployment.[48] The bars show the change in financial well-being for each group between June 2019 and June 2020.

The biggest group, 72 percent, was people who did not have an income drop because of unemployment and did not receive unemployment insurance. Their financial well-being increased by 1.66 (the bar at the right). This change is almost the same as for everyone in Figure 6.2, which makes sense because this group contains most people. Economic Impact Payments likely helped with this increase, but much of it was from decreased spending and increased savings. As the Adams family in Tables 6.1

and 6.2 illustrated, most families that received only Economic Impact Payments would not have had large changes in income.

Where policy clearly made a huge difference is for the unemployed. The financial well-being of people with income drops but who received unemployment benefits increased by 4.51 points (the first bar), substantially more than people who did not have an income fall and did not receive unemployment benefits. This group is about 11 percent of the population. To repeat: the financial well-being of Americans who lost their jobs but received unemployment insurance increased by more than the financial well-being of Americans who did not lose their jobs!

The two middle groups in Figure 6.3 are a bit more complicated. Just like Marcus after Chapter 2, about 14 percent of respondents report their household experienced a large drop in income from unemployment but they themselves did not receive unemployment insurance. The average financial well-being of this group fell by 2.84 points. The way the questions were worded, it is possible that a family member was unemployed but the respondent him- or herself was not. About 3 percent reported receiving unemployment insurance but did not report having a fall in income from unemployment. I suspect they are answering that way because the unemployment benefits kept their income from falling. This small group appears similar to the larger group who had an income fall and received unemployment insurance.

Put a different way, the reason that overall financial well-being increased is that financial well-being increased for all but one group: people with a significant income drop because of unemployment who did not receive unemployment insurance. Other evidence using administrative tax data shows that big income falls became much less likely in 2020 compared with 2019 or during the Great Recession because of unemployment insurance.[49] An important reason there was a lot less financial suffering than we saw in Chapter 3 is that far fewer Americans were exposed to big income falls. When Americans did suffer unemployment, the pandemic social safety net was often (but not always) there to protect them financially. Importantly, as was clear in Tables 6.1 and 6.2, it was *pandemic* policies, not the regular unemployment system, that were central.

Economic Impact Payments' importance is less easily measured. Most people were eligible for these payments, and almost everyone who was eligible got one. These payments increased spending in the short term (see Chapter 4). But in the long term, because most people got one, there is no good comparison group. What the financial picture would have looked like if nobody had gotten them or if they had been targeted differently is a difficult question. Based on the timing or the changes in credit card debt or spending, it seems clear that the Economic Impact Payment deposits pushed up spending. They also appear to have increased savings. While not everyone who got one needed it, the Economic Impact Payments seem to have been broadly successful at helping people pay for what they needed immediately, reduce debt, and save more for the future.

Yet because they were not targeted at specific groups, the Economic Impact Payments were fairly expensive for the disaster relief they provided and their stimulus effect was somewhat beside the point. Yet broad-based relief that fills in gaps that might be missed by other programs has advantages. Unemployment benefits often took a long time to get distributed, whereas the Economic Impact Payments were typically distributed fast. Broad relief makes it less likely someone will be missed. Broad relief is also popular, which might help other, more targeted programs politically. It is this delicate political question of who got help and who needed help that we turn to next.

Who Got Help and Who Needed Help

Programs targeted at specific kinds of trouble, such as mortgage forbearance or rental relief, also helped. But to understand these more targeted programs' importance, we need to answer two questions: Did the people who got help need it? And did the people who needed help get it?

Before looking at the evidence, it is worth acknowledging that there were substantial gaps in some programs, allowing money to flow in problematic ways. There appears to have been substantial organized unemployment insurance fraud. This problem is distinct from whether the unemployed Americans who did get help deserved it. We should certainly prefer not to shovel money toward international criminal organizations! We examined the scale of this problem in Chapter 4. Whether we could have reduced this fraud while at the same time getting aid to those who needed it in a timely manner is a hard question. Delays getting many people the unemployment benefits they were legally due caused substantial hardship. Modernized state unemployment systems were better at getting money to the unemployed and preventing fraud. Similarly, Paycheck Protection Program funds often did not go to the businesses most affected by the pandemic and some funds went to fraud. Designing better systems that get money to the right people and businesses is important. Rather than focus on the money that went to fraud, this discussion focuses on whether the people who did get it legitimately were suffering financially.

When human beings, not criminal organizations or businesses, received targeted aid, were they in financial need? Yes. When Cortnie Shupe and I looked at the February 2021 Making Ends Meet survey, it was clear that people who received assistance or flexibility typically faced financial hardship.[50] About three-quarters of people who received auto loan, credit card, rent, or mortgage flexibilities also experienced a significant income drop. Over 95 percent of people who reported receiving eviction protection also report having experienced a significant income drop. Moreover, a large share of those benefiting from eviction protection measures also missed or delayed payment, not only on rent but also on medical bills, utilities, and other regular household expenses.

Federal student loans are the clear exception. All federal student loans were automatically put into a zero-payment-due plan. So people receiving federal student loan flexibilities were less likely to be experiencing problems than others receiving accommodation, and only 54.5 percent of those receiving a suspension of student loan payments had also suffered a significant loss of income, a far lower percentage than for those receiving other forms of assistance.

Other analyses reached similar conclusions. When the JPMorgan Chase Institute looked at mortgage forbearance in its Chase bank account data, it found that "families in forbearance were more likely to have lost labor income and received unemployment benefits than families not in forbearance."[51]

The second question is whether people in need got assistance. This question might initially seem identical to the first question. But it is possible for a program to reach only people in need but not reach many people in need. Here the evidence is harder to obtain and less conclusive. In the February 2021 Making Ends Meet survey, most people who had a significant income drop did not receive assistance on any loans or rent. Only 12 percent of people with a significant income drop and a mortgage received mortgage assistance; only 16 percent of renters with a significant income drop received rental assistance or accommodation. Perhaps the reason relatively few people with income drops received any flexibility is that the general aid from unemployment insurance and Economic Impact Payments was sufficient for most people, so an income drop did not automatically mean problems with the rent or mortgage. But whatever the reason, most families having financial difficulty did not receive more assistance for their loans or rents.

The targeting was somewhat better for specific assistance aimed at specific problems. 75 percent of people who reported having difficulty with mortgage payments received mortgage flexibility. Among renters who deferred or missed a rental payment, 38 percent reported receiving payment flexibility assistance. This flexibility would have come almost entirely from landlords, as almost no federal rent assistance had been dispersed by February 2021. And while state and federal eviction moratoria covered most renters, only one-quarter of renters who were having difficulty reported directly benefiting from eviction protections. It is likely, however, that many renters indirectly benefited from eviction protections but did not realize they benefited unless they were acutely at risk of being evicted.

Again, the exception that proves the rule is student loans. Among people with student loans, nearly everyone with a problem paying the rent or mortgage, a credit card bill, or utility or who had a significant income drop reported benefiting from student loan deferment. The remainder may have had private student loans or may not have been aware that their student loans were in a zero-payment plan or may have already been in a plan.

The relative success of student loans and mortgage forbearance at reaching people with financial problems suggests something important about policy: the most common kinds of assistance were automatic or were widely available, and consumers were informed about them. Federal student loans were automatically put into a zero-payment-due plan, so nearly all consumers with a problem who also had a federal student loan received assistance. (The remainder are likely private student loans, which we cannot directly distinguish.) Mortgage servicers for federally backed mortgages were required under the CARES Act to grant forbearance if a consumer requested it and attested to a financial hardship caused by the pandemic.[52] Federal agencies and government-sponsored enterprises backing these mortgages and some private servicers conducted outreach to mortgagors who were delinquent to inform them of forbearance options.[53] And Consumer Financial Protection Bureau regulations generally require mortgage servicers to inform struggling borrowers of forbearance options or the availability or other options to reduce loss.[54] On the other hand, forbearance programs for credit cards or auto loans depended on the choices of specific creditors. Eligibility standards differed both within and across industries, and consumers may have been unaware of how to participate in them.

The difference between mortgage forbearance during the pandemic and help for struggling homeowners following the 2008 financial crisis is stark. During the pandemic, Black and Hispanic homeowners were more likely to miss payments, but they were also more likely to make use of forbearance. Because forbearance was easily available with little documentation, it was widespread. Unlike in the aftermath of the 2008 financial crisis, when programs to help struggling homeowners required extensive documentation and servicers could not keep up, pandemic forbearance was almost automatic. As a result, minority borrowers benefited more and the pandemic reduced one racial and ethnic gap.[55] We will return to differences between pandemic policies and policies following the financial crisis in Chapter 11.

Taken together, pandemic relief policies succeeded tremendously in their primary mission, although they did so partly by spending huge amounts of money. Unemployment insurance kept financial misery from spreading. Economic Impact Payments were a lifeline for many families. Some more targeted programs, such as mortgage forbearance, were widely used by struggling homeowners. Others appear to have missed the mark. And where people, for whatever reason, slipped through the cracks of unemployment insurance or other programs, the costs were large. The next chapter takes a closer look at who got left behind and why.

Samuel

Samuel's family experienced the benefits of these pandemic policies. Samuel lived in the Los Angeles metro area in one of the most highly income-segregated areas in the U.S. Samuel and his family could see this segregation directly. On one side of their neighborhood were some light industrial businesses and restaurants. Samuel likely rents an apartment in one of several two-story apartment buildings in the center. On the other side were ranch-style homes with pools in the back. Although Samuel's apartment is mere blocks from these homes, there is no way to access them directly. A wall surrounds the ranch homes, blocking them off from the rest of the neighborhood.

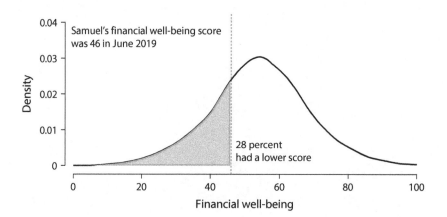

Samuel's approach to his financial life suggests that helping his family get over this wall was important to him. Samuel, a Hispanic man in his late fifties, was likely born in another country and moved to the U.S. when he was much younger. Whether he is an immigrant or not, his preferred language is English and he took the survey online in English despite there being an option to take it in Spanish.

Samuel had built a good financial life in his adopted country and a strong financial foundation for his kids. He had a high school degree, but his two daughters were attending college; the most recent had just started and still lived with him. He likely wanted his teenage son to go to college as well. Samuel and his wife took money from their savings to help pay for their daughters' tuition but did not take out an education loan. Because one daughter still lived with them, it is likely she went to one of the community colleges in California's excellent network, where tuition is generally more affordable than state or private universities.

To build this stable life, Samuel and his wife both worked full time, earning about $55,000 a year. They had very little debt: some credit cards they paid off every month and a car loan. Their biggest expense was for housing—they live in California, after all—and they spent about a third of their income on rent. Keeping their expenses less than their income meant that they were typically saving at least a bit. Because they had a savings cushion, when his wife's hours were cut for several months in 2019, the family did not suffer broader financial consequences or have trouble paying bills. Samuel was very careful with credit; he had actively worked to improve his credit score, which was excellent, and checked it frequently. Samuel was also very cautious, saying that you need to be very careful dealing with people. At the same time, he wanted to help us understand his experience, writing, "I did my best to fill out this survey," in a comment.

Early in the Pandemic

All of this financial stability and upward mobility could have been in jeopardy during the pandemic. Samuel was still working full time in June 2020, but his wife had been furloughed like millions of others. She applied for and received unemployment insurance, including the $600 weekly CARES Act supplement. But it took more than four weeks for the first payment to start. During this time things seem to have come close to the financial edge. They had difficulty paying the rent but managed to make it through each month. Perhaps the $2,400 in Economic Impact Payments they received in April 2020, while they were waiting for the unemployment benefits, made all the difference just as it did for many lower-income families. They also cut back on nonessential spending. As a result of these ups and downs, Samuel's financial well-being declined slightly in June 2020 from the year before.

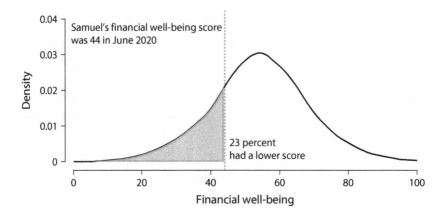

Late in the Pandemic

When the unemployment benefits kicked in, Samuel's wife would have been earning more than she did when fully employed. By February 2021, they were both working full time again. They had each just received $600 from the December 2020 relief bill (and would each receive another $1,400 in March 2021). All told, their incomes in 2020 had been slightly higher than in 2019, although between unemployment and unemployment benefits starting and stopping, it had been a bumpy year. Still, Samuel was optimistic. His financial well-being was higher than it had ever been. They were spending a lot less and continued to spend less through 2021, judging by their credit cards. If they both remained employed, their income would

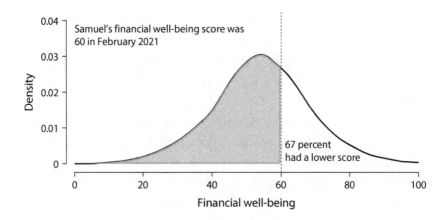

have likely been up as well, so they would have been saving more. They bought a car in May 2021, just before prices for used cars shot up. Although their financial situation appeared dangerous for a while, the financial security that Samuel had worked so hard to achieve was still intact, thanks in part to unemployment insurance.

7

Left Behind, Again

SCIENCE FICTION author John Scalzi once tried to explain privilege in a way that might make it more tangible for those who have it but often do not realize it. He wrote, "In the role playing game known as The Real World, 'Straight White Male' is the lowest difficulty setting there is."[1] The point is not that straight white males never falter. Instead, privilege means that you can take more hits and when you do fail (as everyone does sometimes), the consequences are not as bad. Although Scalzi was primarily focused on gender and race, these characteristics intersect with income and wealth. As we saw in Chapter 3, for example, African Americans were almost twice as likely to have difficulty paying a bill or expense as non-Hispanic white Americans. Part of the reason is that they are somewhat more likely to have large unexpected expenses. Lower income and wealth mean that African Americans often live in older housing and drive older cars, which are more likely to have problems. And they have a lower wealth buffer to deal with those problems when they arise.

This chapter examines the many ways individuals and groups were left behind during the pandemic. The first several chapters showed a remarkable improvement in overall financial health. These improvements are real. But averages hide diversity. Even as most people's finances improved, some people's finances did not improve. Of course, people are moving up and down the financial ladder all the time, even without a pandemic. We should expect some people's finances to deteriorate as their incomes go down or expenses mount for reasons that have nothing to do with a pandemic.

Pandemic policies such as unemployment insurance, Economic Impact Payments, and mortgage forbearance were very important in keeping financial suffering from spreading for everyone, particularly people already likely to have trouble. Including this support, income and wealth increased for the poorest households. Pandemic policies' effectiveness at protecting households' finances broadly was even more important for groups who were already at risk. So while this chapter will focus on groups who got left behind, it could have been far worse. The Great Recession, for example, devastated Black and Hispanic households' wealth, and they were far more likely to lose their homes.[2]

Yet the groups that benefited the least or were the most likely to slip through the cracks were often the groups that were already having trouble. Most prominently, the pandemic's health impact fell disproportionately on Black, Hispanic, and Native American households, and it exacerbated the negative trends for whites without a college degree. A "shadow pandemic" of domestic partner violence seems to have raged largely unseen (as is often the case). There are some important nuances, however. Renters, already frequently at risk of eviction, found significant protections and formal evictions dropped sharply, but they were largely left out of direct support for nearly 18 months. In other words, once you peer behind the averages, things are messy. They nearly always are.

Job Losses and Who Was Already at Risk

The prepandemic differences in all forms of financial health were stark. In Chapter 3, we saw that in 2019, 65 percent of Black Americans had difficulty paying at least one bill or expense, compared with 47 percent of Hispanic Americans and 35 percent of non-Hispanic white Americans. Most, but not all, of these differences are explained by income: 18 percent of households earning more than $100,000 had difficulty, compared with 62 percent of households earning $20,000 or less.

As pandemic shutdowns spread in March and April 2020, it was often the most financially disadvantaged Americans who were the first fired. Early analysis of initial job losses found that Hispanics were much more likely to lose a job relative to non-Hispanic whites, while African Americans were only slightly more likely to be unemployed relative to non-Hispanic whites.[3] Of course, since non-Hispanic whites also suffered big job losses in March and April, no group was doing well.

The differences are largely explained by industry and occupation. Hispanics were more likely to work in industries, such as restaurants and hotels, with the highest layoffs. African Americans, on the other hand, were slightly more protected, relative to both Hispanics and non-Hispanic whites, by the industries they were employed in.

As the pandemic wore on, white workers were more likely to be called back or get new jobs. Males were also more likely to be employed. So as of March 2021, while there were 5 percent fewer white men employed than before the pandemic, there were nearly 10 percent fewer Black women and 8 percent fewer Hispanic women.[4] (Meanwhile, the percentage of Black men employed fell only slightly more than that of white men, and the percentage of Asian men and women employed fell by less.) Again, the industry mix was crucial. While other industries were able to come back, industries that women worked in, and especially Black and Hispanic women, such as hospitality and child care, were much more likely to remain closed.

Employment declines were concentrated among low-wage jobs. Four in five jobs lost during the pandemic were earning in the bottom 25 percent. Meanwhile, the number of high-wage jobs actually increased by nearly a million compared with 2019.[5]

Pandemic aid policies were largely successful at keeping this increase in unemployment, particularly for the lowest-income earners, from becoming financial hardship. But they did not protect everyone, and just because we avoided financial hardship even for most low-income households does not mean everyone benefited equally.

Health and Wealth

The pandemic exacerbated existing inequality. Inequality is a tricky concept: after all, it just means "not equal" and so is all around us. Why should we care about inequality? As economist, philosopher, and Nobel

Prize winner Amartya Sen puts it, we care about the freedom to make more choices.[6] Higher incomes help people achieve freedom from hunger and disease and have more scope to choose their own path in life. Although they approach it from a very different direction, Milton Friedman (another Nobel Prize winner) and Rose Friedman similarly argue in *Freedom to Choose* that "equality of opportunity . . . is an essential component of liberty."[7] We want everyone to have the opportunity to make their own way in life. Of course, the Friedmans' conception of inequality differs from Sen's in radical and important ways. But the common thread is that we should care about whether everyone has the opportunity to pursue and achieve the life they value.

Not everyone has such opportunities. And the pandemic restricted these opportunities even more for some. Of course, measuring freedom of choice is hard, so instead we'll focus on two approximations. Most of us would choose to live longer (provided we were healthy), so health inequality is one useful measure. And the ability to make choices about how and where to live, to be free from financial worries, and to choose a job or other activities we find most fulfilling rests squarely on wealth. Both health and wealth became markedly more unequal during the pandemic, although with important nuances. We'll explore both.

Wealth Inequality

With more wealth, I could choose not to work, just as retirees do. Or I could choose how and where to work. I could choose to make my voice heard in politics or public affairs. Or I would be free—there's that word again—to live as I do now. Wealth is a good approximation of the choices I face and how limited they are. And as we saw in Chapter 2, lack of wealth is about being forced to make difficult choices about what to give up to make ends meet.[8]

Wealth inequality is large and has been growing. Figure 7.1 shows estimates of the total net wealth and how much of it is owned by different groups.[9] The bottom 50 percent—the half of the population with the least wealth—had just over $2 trillion at the end of 2019. The bottom 50 percent thus had 1.8 percent of the $111 trillion total wealth. It is a bit

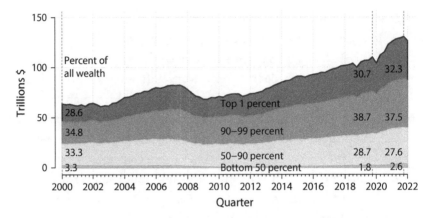

FIGURE 7.1. The wealth owned by the top 1 percent increased sharply during the pandemic, but so did the bottom 50 percent's wealth (if you squint). (Wealth owned by each wealth percentile group, adjusted for inflation. The numbers show the percentage of wealth owned by each group in 2000 quarter 1, 2019 quarter 4, and 2021 quarter 4. *Source*: Federal Reserve Board Distributional Financial Accounts.)

hard to see the bottom 50 percent in Figure 7.1 (hint: they are at the bottom) because, relative to the other groups, they hold so little wealth. The housing crash and unemployment following the 2008 financial crisis sharply diminished their net wealth to an inflation-adjusted low of just $280 billion in 2011. The bottom 50 percent only returned to the inflation-adjusted wealth they held in 2006 in 2019. In wealth terms, for most people the Great Recession had only just ended when the pandemic began.

These estimates come from the Distributional Financial Accounts, a program by the Federal Reserve Board to combine survey estimates on the distribution of assets and liabilities with financial accounts that measure the aggregate value of these assets and liabilities.[10] There are many approximations to get these numbers, but they are a serious attempt to measure something hard.

Meanwhile, the top 1 percent of people held $34 trillion, 31 percent of all wealth, despite being a much smaller group. And even in the top 1 percent there is a lot of inequality. The top ten richest people (all white men) owned $692 billion in 2019,[11] about 0.6 percent of all wealth in the

United States. The top ten richest men's wealth was about one-third of the wealth held by the poorest half, 150 million people.

There is also plenty of inequality among the bottom 50 percent, just as in the top 1 percent. A significant portion of the bottom 50 percent have negative net worth. Many families have little, if any, money in their checking and savings accounts and carry substantial credit card debt. Having negative net wealth is not necessarily a bad thing. For example, someone with student debt incurred from obtaining an MBA that will substantially boost her earnings may have negative net worth but high earnings potential. The most valuable asset owned by most working people is their own labor, which will earn money now and in the future. But future labor income is not a financial asset, so it is not included in these calculations.

Between 2000 and 2019, wealth had become more and more concentrated at the top end. The share owned by the bottom 50 percent almost halved, from 3.4 percent to 1.8 percent. Much of this reduction comes from increasing liabilities such as credit card debt and mortgage debt. Even those at 50–90 percent, the wealth distribution's "middle class," lost share. Instead, proportionally it was those at 90–99 percent and particularly the top 1 percent who held a larger share. These top wealth groups thus captured almost all of the total wealth increase over these 20 years. The bottom 90 percent were only slightly wealthier in 2019 than they had been in 2000.

The wealth owned by the top 1 percent of the wealth distribution increased sharply during the pandemic. The top 1 percent keeps much of its wealth in the stock market and similar assets, so when the market fell at the beginning of the pandemic, its wealth—and the wealth of those at 90–99 percent—dipped sharply. But then the stock market came roaring back, and with it the wealth at the top end. Over the next two years, the top 1 percent's wealth increased by $10 trillion, or nearly a third. The share of all wealth held by the top 1 percent increased from 31 percent at the end of 2019 to 32 percent by the end of 2021, although some of these gains diminished as financial markets declined in 2022. And those ten richest men? Their wealth more than doubled to $1.3 trillion by the end of 2021.[12]

As unemployment increased in March and April 2020, earnings suddenly dried up for many families. Yet the bottom 50 percent's net wealth increased 25 percent from about $2 trillion to $2.5 trillion. What happened? The March 2020 CARES Act, the December 2020 relief bill, and the March 2021 American Rescue Plan Act provided significant unemployment insurance and cash to many families in the bottom 50 percent. These families increased their savings and paid off debt.[13] Many families reduced their spending, increasing savings even more. Moreover, the student loan payment suspension and mortgage forbearance reduced the payments of many families who might have been struggling. While this assistance did not directly decrease debt—the forbearance programs delayed payments but did not forgive debt—the assistance did mean that less money was flowing out from households and fewer households were not able to pay their bills and thus avoided entering negative spirals.

The already large racial wealth gap did not expand during the pandemic, but it did not shrink either. The overlap between wealth inequality overall and racial and ethnic wealth inequality is large. At the end of 2019, African Americans held 4.1 percent of wealth, despite making up 13.4 percent of the population; Hispanics held 2.3 percent of wealth, despite making up 18.5 percent of the population; and non-Hispanic whites held 84.3 percent of wealth, while making up only 60.1 percent of the population.[14] These shares did not change during the pandemic. But a substantial Black and Hispanic middle class holds much of the wealth of these groups, so unchanging shares do not mean financial suffering was equally distributed. Wealth inequality is so large that very minor changes at the bottom are nearly invisible as a percentage share of the total, even though these minor changes can have a huge impact on millions of people's lives.

So did wealth inequality increase? It depends on what you think is the most important. The wealthy got wealthier and increased their share of total wealth. But the poor got wealthier also and increased their share. Wealth's increasing concentration at the top end is a growing political and economic concern. Growing wealth inequality is a problem because it distorts the market and government in favor of rent seeking, entrenched wealth, and reduced growth, and so reduces freedom of opportunity.[15]

But the increase at the bottom end is one sign that there was a massive reduction in financial suffering that may have long-term benefits for American society. As we saw in Chapter 3, poor, Black, and Hispanic households were more likely to have difficulty paying all their bills and expenses. Because they hold lower wealth, their spending is also much more sensitive to income falls, requiring them to make spending cuts on food and medical care and pay bills late.[16] Pandemic policies largely protected families from these cuts and gave them some financial buffer. This financial reset had widespread consequences in the pandemic's second year and beyond, as we'll see in Chapter 9.

More fundamentally, you have to be alive to have the freedom to choose how to live your best life. While the pandemic had a complicated effect on the wealth distribution, its effect on the health distribution was disturbingly clear.

Health Inequality

Life expectancy fell 1.8 years in 2020. Figure 7.2 shows this devastating fall.[17] The 385,000 deaths from COVID-19 in 2020 explain three-quarters of the decline.[18] Life expectancy dropped to the same level it had been at in 2000, erasing 20 years of progress. This decline is likely the largest single-year decline since the 1918 flu pandemic,[19] which killed around 675,000 people in the U.S. out of a population around 100 million.[20] The rest of the decline was largely from an increase of deaths of despair, which we will discuss next, as more people overdosed and, as we saw in the last chapter, the pandemic reduced regular medical care, indirectly causing many additional deaths.

Life expectancy at birth is a bit of an odd measure. Although life expectancy sounds like it measures how long people live, it is actually a kind of average age of death from a given year. Technically, it is how long a group of newborns would live if they were to die at each age at the same rate as the people of that age died in a given year. But it is exceedingly

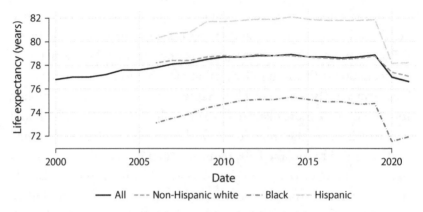

FIGURE 7.2. Life expectancy fell by 1.8 years in 2020. The already large life expectancy gap between Black and white Americans increased sharply. (*Source*: See notes.)

unlikely that newborns today will die at the same rate as 70-year-olds today in 70 years. Hopefully, nutrition, public health, and medical advances will have reduced mortality by then. Health researchers interested in specific populations often focus on death rates specific to those populations, such as the infant mortality rate or the maternal mortality rate, but life expectancy is a useful way of capturing how healthy the overall population is.

Death came for Black and Hispanic Americans far more frequently during the pandemic. Life expectancy in 2020 fell by 1.4 years for non-Hispanic white Americans, by 3.7 years for Hispanic Americans, and by 3.2 years for non-Hispanic Black Americans. Figure 7.2 shows these declines. Black Americans already had substantially lower life expectancy than whites, so the decline opened the gap even more to 5.9 years. Before the pandemic, Hispanic life expectancy was 3.1 years higher than the non-Hispanic white life expectancy. This gap is not a mistake and even has its own name, the "Hispanic epidemiological paradox," and extensive research on why it occurs.[21] But the gap fell to only 0.8 years as Hispanic life expectancy plummeted during the pandemic.

The Black-white life expectancy gap had been closing since 2006. Black life expectancy increased substantially until 2014, although it started declining in 2015. Meanwhile, white life expectancy had stalled as opioid overdoses and other deaths of despair spread. The pandemic erased all of the gains made in closing the gap since 2006.

Based on COVID-19 death rates, it is likely that life expectancy for Native Americans fell by even more. The National Center for Health Statistics does not calculate official life tables for Native Americans, Asian Americans, and Pacific Islanders, so there are no standard life expectancy numbers for these groups.[22] But the available mortality data suggests that Native Americans died of COVID-19 at much higher rates and younger ages than whites.[23] The differences are stunning. Compared with non-Hispanic whites of the same age, Native Americans were 2.4 times more likely to die of COVID-19, Hispanics 2.3 times more likely, and Blacks 2.0 times more likely. Meanwhile, Asian American death rates appear comparable to those of white Americans.[24]

Why was the pandemic so much more devastating to Black, Hispanic, and Native Americans? For many of the same reasons that Black and Native Americans often have worse health outcomes in the first place, as well as some issues that are specific to COVID-19: lack of health insurance, lack of money to pay for medical care, lack of healthcare access, and work in high-exposure jobs. Which of these reasons is the most important is hard to disentangle and there may be other, even more important, reasons we don't yet understand. More research is sure to come.

While the Affordable Care Act increased health insurance coverage, 21.7 percent of Native Americans lacked health insurance in 2019, along with 20.0 percent of Hispanics, 11.4 percent of Blacks, 7.8 percent of whites, and 7.2 percent of Asians.[25] Healthcare costs matter even with health insurance. As we discussed in the last chapter, in February 2021, 34 percent of Making Ends Meet respondents had delayed or skipped medical care during the pandemic. 36 percent did so because of cost. Around 49 percent of Hispanic respondents and 60 percent of Native Americans skipped care because of cost (although our sample of Native Americans is small, so this number could be much bigger or much smaller), compared with 39 percent of whites and 41 percent of Black Americans.

Black, Hispanic, and Native Americans also faced lower access to testing, hospitals, and vaccines. For example, during the summer of

2020, when testing for COVID-19 was still scarce and potentially life saving, the unmet demand for testing in Black and Hispanic neighborhoods was much larger.[26] So Black and Hispanic Americans faced longer wait times or could not get tests, adding to the burden of missing work. Similar gaps opened up when vaccines became available, and a racial vaccination gap developed.[27] And throughout the pandemic, most low-income communities had no intensive healthcare services available.[28] Of course, rural Americans and poor Americans of any race faced many of the same issues. But race and wealth are tightly connected.

Preliminary estimates shown in Figure 7.2 suggest life expectancy for Black and Hispanic Americans stopped falling in 2021, but life expectancy fell by another 0.3 years for white Americans in 2021. New variants swept through the unvaccinated in 2021, killing many more. From June 2021, when vaccines were widely available, to March 2022, around 234,000 preventable deaths occurred.[29] Nearly one-quarter of COVID-19 deaths were easily avoidable.

So many of us did not need to die. The increased deaths and decreased life expectancy in the United States were much worse than in other high-income countries.[30] Life expectancy declined in the average high-income country by 0.22 years in 2020, one-seventh as much as in the United States. These calculations, using preliminary life expectancy estimates, suggest that the gap in life expectancy between the United States and the rest of the rich world increased from an already bad 3.3 years in 2019 to a devastating 4.6 years in 2020 and a terrifying 5.26 years in 2021. While the U.S. began vaccination earlier than most countries, our vaccination rates stalled, so that by summer 2021, when the Delta and then Omicron variant waves hit, most U.S. deaths were preventable.

Our health was already worse than that of other high-income countries, and the pandemic increased the gap. One reason for the gap is the deaths of despair discussed next. But the other reason is the lower life expectancy of Black Americans, which fell even more during the pandemic.

Our healthcare system was already the most expensive in the world. We spend at least a third more per person on "healthcare" (much of it not directly on health) than the next most expensive rich country and nearly twice as much as the average yet have significantly worse health outcomes.[31] Spending more and getting less is a broken system. The tradeoff might be worth it if our healthcare system were prepared for disasters such as the pandemic. It was not.[32]

Deaths of Despair

In their book *Deaths of Despair and the Future of Capitalism*, economists Anne Case and Angus Deaton describe how deaths from suicide, drug overdose, and alcoholism rose dramatically in the last two decades.[33] These deaths rose particularly quickly for white Americans without college degrees. The increase has caused something that was once unthinkable: a decline in life expectancy for white Americans. These deaths affect both men and women.[34] Case and Deaton link these deaths of despair to the social and economic stagnation of the white working class. For many people, particularly in rural areas, good, well-paying jobs are scarce. As a result, family structures have broken and social connections have declined. Hope for a better future is in short supply. Prescription opioids pushed by a broken healthcare system hooked many people, while other people turned to alcohol. Many Black families had suffered their own version of this collapse two decades earlier, as manufacturing jobs left cities and crack cocaine spread.

The pandemic exacerbated all of the trends leading to these deaths. Unemployment spiked, reducing economic opportunity. Social distancing reduced contact with friends, family, and neighbors. Social distancing was more pronounced in some areas than others, but group meetings for drug addiction were generally shut down almost everywhere, at least initially. With the closure of these meetings and other forms of support, many addicts lost one key to keeping them from relapsing. And traumatic events, such as terrorist attacks or natural disasters, make relapses more likely.[35]

Deaths of despair were up dramatically in 2020, and this increase continued into 2021. Preliminary estimates from the Centers for Disease Control and Prevention (CDC) suggest that drug overdose deaths were up 30 percent, to 93,000, in 2020 and kept on increasing.[36] The increase was driven by the spread of fentanyl, a synthetic opioid, but deaths from overdoses of methamphetamine and cocaine also rose.[37]

Americans also drank a lot more during the pandemic.[38] Alcohol purchases spiked in the first weeks of the pandemic.[39] How we purchased alcohol also changed. Online sales, which had been a small portion of sales before the pandemic, more than doubled, even as retail sales also increased by more than 20 percent through May 2020.[40] Of course, some of this increased home consumption was because bars and restaurants were closed, so the total alcohol consumption did not increase by as much. Home drinking likely involves less drunk driving, so it may be less immediately deadly, but it may well be more detrimental in other ways. Drinking alone is considered one of the primary signs of burgeoning alcoholism, for example.[41] In one small study, nearly 50 percent of respondents reported drinking more because of stress, 34 percent because of increased availability, and 30 percent because of boredom.[42] It seems many people, isolated and with nothing to do, turned to alcohol to numb the pain.

Women, in particular, appear to have been drinking more during the pandemic.[43] Alcohol consumption increased faster for women than for men in the last several decades, so there was almost no gender gap before the pandemic.[44] The increase during the pandemic may have more than closed the gap. More women also seemed to be drinking to cope with stress.[45] Drinking to cope can be especially dangerous because people who do so are more likely to be unable to stop drinking, even when it is harming other parts of their lives such as work or social interactions.[46] As the boundary between home and work blurred, the wine bottle was always in easy reach.

We may not know for years whether the spike in alcohol consumption or drug overdoses during the pandemic will fall away or continue to create long-term problems. Perhaps as the isolation and stress, both economic and emotional, of the pandemic recede, so will some of the coping mechanisms we sought. Yet the pandemic may have only accelerated the preexisting trends. We may find that some of the bad habits we picked up during the pandemic are hard to break. And as Case and Deaton showed, these trends were already having a devastating impact on the white working class. The immediate deaths from drug overdoses were already up. It takes longer to drink yourself to death than to fatally overdose on drugs, so these deaths may just be the start.

In one rare sign of good news, about 3 percent fewer people committed suicide during 2020 compared with 2019.[47] Other countries seem to have had similar falls,[48] suggesting that there was something common going on rather than U.S. specific. One explanation is that, with people stuck working or sheltering at home, it was harder to escape family members who had greater opportunities to intervene.

Mental health more generally was hard during the pandemic. The causes differed: my family, stuck together, often saw too much of each other and would have liked more space. Others, sheltering alone, felt isolated. As a *Washington Post* article put it in April 2020, "If you're scared, anxious, depressed, struggling to sleep through the night, or just on edge, you're not alone."[49] Polls and surveys regularly found that mental health had deteriorated broadly. In June 2020, 31 percent of U.S. adults reported anxiety or depressive disorder symptoms, 26 percent reported symptoms of a "trauma- and stressor-related disorder" related to the pandemic, and 13 percent reported starting or increasing alcohol or drug use to cope with stress from the pandemic. Mental health challenges were particularly prevalent among racial and ethnic minorities.[50]

The mental health impact of past disasters, such as Hurricane Katrina, the Chernobyl nuclear meltdown, or the SARS pandemic, was large and long lasting.[51] We do not yet know what the long-term consequences of the pandemic will be, and we may never be able to cleanly distinguish effects. The summer of 2020 was tumultuous for other reasons, as was the U.S. presidential election and its aftermath. But it does seem safe to say that the impacts on mental health will be large and ongoing, whether or not they result in spreading deaths of despair.

The Shadow Pandemic: Intimate Partner Violence

More immediately, intimate partner violence appears to have increased sharply during the pandemic. During the initial weeks of the pandemic, calls to police departments to report domestic violence increased by

10 percent to 20 percent across many cities as lockdowns started.[52] One survey, conducted over ten weeks starting in April 2020, found that financial stress from lost income due to the pandemic was closely related to increased intimate partner violence.[53] Previous research suggests that alcohol tends to exacerbate intimate partner violence,[54] and people were drinking more at home.

Social isolation, financial and emotional stress, and alcohol created a toxic combination for increased intimate partner violence. Moreover, those suffering from violence had fewer places to turn to get away from abusive partners as shelters and hotels closed and social networks were disrupted. The United Nations called the increase in intimate partner violence, particularly against women, the shadow pandemic, while *Time* called it the pandemic within the pandemic.[55]

Intimate partner violence seems to have been up around the world.[56] Studying such violence is always fraught because it is often not reported. During the pandemic, with different services shut down in different places, reporting was likely uneven. The number of intimate partner physical assaults reported by hospitals diminished in some places and increased in others.[57] With many nonessential healthcare services shut and fewer ways to escape abuse, fewer victims may have gone to the hospital; abuse may not have fallen, just gone unreported.

When victims did seek medical help, the abuse seems to have been more severe. Characterizing the severity of abuse is difficult, but examining injuries at Boston hospitals, a team of radiologists found both a higher incidence of intimate partner violence and greater severity during the first two months of the pandemic.[58] Comparing the injuries with previous years, the radiologists suggest that many victims may have delayed reaching out to healthcare or other support services until the abuse had progressed in severity.

As the pandemic subsided and exit options reopened, intimate partner violence seems to have declined. But the trauma from sheltering in place with an abuser may last much longer.

Essential Workers

Because quitting generally makes you ineligible for unemployment insurance, many "essential" workers were suddenly in a bind starting in March 2020. Their jobs were deemed essential for the public, so they did not lose them because of shut-down orders. But they were often low paid to begin with, and their jobs often came with much more risk than before. Because the $600 expanded unemployment benefits were so large, from March through July 2020, many would have earned more if they had been fired and would not have faced so much risk.

Some private firms, including Amazon, Target, and Starbucks, gave small hazard pay bumps of $1 or $2 an hour in the first few months.[59] Others, including CVS and Walgreens, made one or two bonus payments. But most of these hazard pay bumps expired in May 2020 and were typically quite small.

The unfairness was striking to many. With unemployment so high, many essential workers had few options to reduce their risk or earn more. The power imbalance was bad enough that economist Suresh Naidu asked whether the pandemic had "turned the workers we call heroes into something closer to forced labor."[60] Not only were essential workers often earning less than the unemployed because of the expanded benefits, but their jobs, often not great to begin with, were suddenly much more risky. As Katherine Thomas, who worked at a grocery store, told NPR, "I felt very angry. I have to go to work. And I make less money, being essential. Six hundred dollars a week—that's almost the whole paycheck for me. Even with hazard pay, I still don't make that much money."[61]

While there were policy proposals for pandemic premium pay or "patriot pay" to help equalize the situation, they were never passed into law.[62] The American Rescue Plan Act provided $350 billion for state, local, and tribal governments to use for pandemic recovery, some of which could be used for essential worker premium pay.[63] Yet it seems that few governments allocated much, if any, funding to essential workers.[64]

By the time the labor market tightened in the summer of 2021, many essential workers had had enough. It is telling that many of the same firms that had given no hazard pay or only a small bump suddenly had to offer much bigger pay increases to keep and attract employees. We will return to this shift in worker power in Chapter 10.

While the lack of hazard pay applied to all essential workers, many healthcare workers faced additional issues that took time to resolve. Most acutely, our hugely expensive healthcare system was somehow not prepared to provide basic personal protective equipment even to healthcare workers dealing directly with potential COVID-19 patients. This failing not only exposed the healthcare workers themselves but harmed our ability as a society to deal with the pandemic. By increasing the risk that healthcare workers would get sick, the lack of protective equipment both increased demands on the healthcare system and reduced the supply of healthcare, thus contributing to the overall decline in life expectancy.[65]

The lack of protective equipment was also a personal issue placing many healthcare workers, already working at increased risk during the pandemic, at even more risk. Nurses resorted to reusing face masks and wearing trash bags as disposable coverings.[66] While some of the shortages eventually became less severe, many persisted through 2020.[67] Part of the problem, as we discussed in the previous chapter, was a market breakdown from poor quality or fraudulent suppliers. To illustrate the absurdity of the situation, one serious study examined the effectiveness and risk of putting a clear plastic bag, sealed at the neck, over the head to avoid breathing potentially contaminated air. "Although this might offer better protection from infection than current Centers for Disease Control and Prevention recommendations for homemade cloth masks in situations of last resort, it also introduces risks of hypoxia and hypercarbia due to rebreathing," write the authors, recommending that this method only be used as a last resort.[68] Indeed.

Many healthcare workers felt let down by the system. While they were overworked, scared, and stressed by the death and suffering around them, the system was not providing them basic protective equipment. And as the pandemic wore on, many people were not taking basic protections to prevent transmission. The unfairness became particularly acute once vaccines became widely available. Having worked so hard to get us through the pandemic, healthcare workers found it frustrating to treat new pandemic waves among those who had not tried to protect themselves, and many felt as if society had let them down again.[69]

Renters, Evictions, and Affordable Housing

The pandemic intersected with a massive housing affordability problem and a preexisting eviction crisis. During the pandemic, much attention and many resources went to helping homeowners. Meanwhile, renters and landlords suffered through a patchwork of often unsuccessful policies. General pandemic policies briefly alleviated the financial consequences for many renters but left the larger structural problems unchanged. The pandemic may even have exacerbated them as housing prices and rents soared, making housing even less affordable. Still, it showed us a path forward for the long-simmering eviction crisis that had hurt so many families.

Before the pandemic, roughly a million households were formally evicted each year.[70] For comparison, there were about 400,000 mortgage foreclosures in 2016. A foreclosure occurs when a lender repossesses a home, generally evicting the former owners. Foreclosures peaked at 1.2 million in 2010 following the aftermath of the 2008 financial crisis.[71] This surge was considered a national emergency at the time and prompted large policy shifts, much research, and substantial funding to prevent foreclosures (much of it unsuccessful in dealing with the immediate crisis). Yet renters experienced as many evictions each year as during the worst of the Great Recession, without a corresponding sense of panic. Moreover, because there are fewer renter households, renters are more than two times more likely to be evicted than homeowners are to be foreclosed. One estimate is that 2.34 percent of renter households were evicted in 2016, compared with around 1 percent of mortgages in foreclosure, which can take months to complete.[72]

An eviction is a formal legal process in which a court orders a tenant to leave. Most data on evictions capture only these formal evictions. But being forced to leave is much more common; recent estimates suggest that there are as many as 5.5 informal evictions for every formal eviction.[73] A formal eviction often makes it very hard for a tenant to rent in the future, so often just the threat of an eviction, legal or not, is sufficient to get a tenant to leave. For example, a landlord may threaten eviction and perhaps pay the tenant a bit to leave. Or the landlord may illegally lock the tenant out without a formal eviction. These informal evictions are likely common, but they are difficult to track. Among the problems, surveys that rely on mailing to an address likely undercount people who are moving around a lot. And people with eviction experience may not have the most positive views of government agencies, so they may not be willing to respond to surveys.

Renters are younger, poorer, and more likely to be Black or Hispanic.[74] As Chapter 3 showed, all of these characteristics are associated with being more likely to have difficulty paying bills. More than 60 percent of renters had difficulty paying bills in the 2019 Making Ends Meet survey, compared with 36 percent of households with a mortgage and 20 percent of households that owned their home outright.

Why are renters so financially vulnerable? Because they are often caught in a difficult bind. The places with good, high-paying jobs are generally the most expensive to live. And the cheapest places to live often have the fewest jobs. So you can choose to try to live in an expensive area, and devote much of your (hopefully higher) income to paying for housing, or live in a less expensive area but have fewer options for jobs and income. Either way, much of your income will go to housing. And in many places, the worst housing is only a bit less expensive than the best housing, so there are few ways to reduce your housing budget much, even by commuting.[75]

Lack of affordable housing affects lower-income homeowners just as much as renters. Buying and renting are just different ways to pay for housing, although rent and home prices are not as tightly linked as one might expect. But renters are typically poorer and more exposed to shocks, so housing affordability is often a bigger problem for renters. In 2019, nearly 50 percent of renter households paid more than 30 percent of their income to housing, and about 25 percent paid more than 50 percent of their income.[76] For low-income renters, the situation is even more dire: 62 percent of renter households with incomes under $25,000 (approximately the poverty line for a family of four) paid more than 50 percent of their income for their housing.

Affordable housing, whether renting or owning, is at the heart of many financial issues. The problem often comes down to not building densely enough in the places people want to work and live. And despite some small but important steps to address the issue, such as California allowing duplexes,[77] there has been little recent movement toward addressing the deeper issue.

So when the pandemic started, America was already suffering a chronic eviction and affordable housing crisis, even if it was often hidden. Renters were already more vulnerable and were more likely to lose their jobs during the pandemic.[78]

Yet renters overall were financially better off during the pandemic, just as most other people were. All of the pandemic financial aid, including expanded unemployment insurance and Economic Impact Payments, helped the average renter avoid financial calamity. Although these policies were not targeted specifically at renters, they were most helpful to low-income households. Overall, renters' credit card debt decreased substantially (although not by as much as homeowners') and their financial well-being went up.[79] Government aid seems to have been key. For example, following the expiration of the CARES Act's expanded unemployment benefits in July 2020, renter credit card utilization increased sharply, then declined sharply following the Economic Impact Payments and renewed expanded unemployment benefits in the December 2020 relief bill. These shifts indicate that renters were particularly sensitive to changes in these general relief policies and to the end of these policies.

Evictions started falling precipitously after the first week in March 2020. Figure 7.3 shows an estimate of formal evictions during the pandemic.[80] To smooth out noise, the figure is a rolling four-week average. It is tempting to look to pandemic policies to explain the fall, but the fall comes before these policies would have had much effect. Instead, like many other things in the economy, it simply was not possible to file an eviction in the first months of the pandemic because most courts were shut down for civil filings and hearings, so evictions could

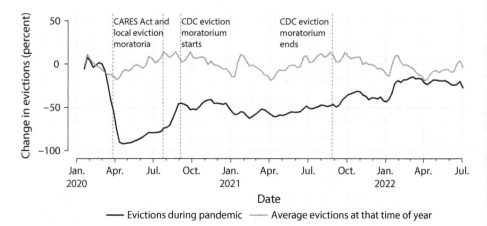

FIGURE 7.3. Eviction filings fell abruptly at the start of the pandemic, stayed low through 2021, but then rebounded in 2022. (Four-week moving average. *Source*: Author's calculations from Eviction Lab.)

not proceed. By April 2020 evictions had fallen more than 90 percent from their prepandemic average.

Short-term eviction moratoria also contributed to the fall, but they mostly expired after several months. The CARES Act provided a 120-day moratorium on evictions from housing with federal financial backing, which were about one in four rental units.[81] The CARES Act moratorium ended on June 24, 2020, although it required a 30-day notice period. At the start of the pandemic, 42 states had introduced some sort of eviction moratorium.[82] But most local moratoria were limited to several months, so many ended over the summer. Following the CARES Act eviction moratorium's expiration, evictions increased, although the four-week average in Figure 7.3 was still 50 percent below normal at the beginning of September.

On September 4, 2020, the CDC issued an order prohibiting evictions for unpaid rent.[83] To be eligible, renters had to attest that they were at risk of homelessness or moving into overcrowded conditions. The CDC's stated reason for the order was that people evicted would not be able to isolate themselves and were at risk of experiencing homelessness and moving into group housing, which would help the virus spread. The eviction moratorium was extended several times. The original order expired December 31, 2020, but was extended in the December 2020 pandemic relief bill for another month. The CDC then extended the moratorium three separate times through July 31, 2021.

The CDC's use of its public health authority for such an order had no precedent.[84] Evictions and rental laws are normally state and local decisions, not federal ones. Courts eventually found that the CDC had exceeded its statutory authority but allowed the moratorium to expire as planned on July 31, 2021. The CDC issued a new order on August 3, 2021. The new moratorium was a bit more narrowly focused on counties with high COVID-19 rates. But courts quickly halted enforcement of this order, effectively killing federal eviction moratorium efforts.[85] State and local eviction limitations or outright moratoria continued for several months, most importantly in New York, California, and New Jersey, but had almost all ended by early 2022.

How effective were these moratoria at protecting renters? It is hard to sort out the effects of pandemic policies like expanded unemployment insurance and Economic Impact Payments from those of eviction moratoria. Direct cash assistance that improved renters' overall financial status also made it easier for them to pay the rent. But the timing of the fall in evictions in Figure 7.3 suggests the CDC moratorium had an effect. Evictions had been increasing over the month before it went into effect, and then they stopped increasing. Some states or cities imposed stronger restrictions or restrictions that were in place before the CDC moratorium. Areas with active local eviction moratoria in August 2020 before the CDC moratorium had many fewer evictions than those without. The August 2020 evictions increase in Figure 7.3 occurred mainly in these areas without moratoria. The increase stopped after the CDC moratorium, suggesting the CDC and local moratoria did prevent many evictions.[86] Regional court decisions also ended the moratorium earlier in some areas in 2021, and evictions increased in the areas covered by these decisions.[87] While the exact contribution of the CDC moratorium is difficult to discern, these comparisons suggest it was significant.

All told, there were around one million fewer formal eviction filings from March 2020 through March 2022 than there would have been absent the pandemic.[88] This number is an approximation. Matthew Desmond, the author of *Evicted*, started the Eviction Lab at Princeton University with Peter Hepburn and Renee Louis. One of the primary goals of the Eviction Lab was to track evictions. Tellingly, while a great deal of effort goes into tracking mortgage delinquencies and foreclosures, there are no standard or national sources for evictions. The Eviction Lab fills some of that gap by collecting data from the handful of cities and states that make it possible to collect eviction filings. These states and cities may not be representative of the nation as whole, although they are spread out geographically, so they make a national estimate possible. While the Eviction Tracking System is not a complete tracking of all evictions, it is the best information available and a huge step beyond the data void that existed before it. Figure 7.3 is based on the Eviction Tracking System. Other data collections that cover areas that only partially overlap with the Eviction Tracking System show a similar eviction decline, so we can be confident evictions fell by around half, even if the exact magnitude is harder to pin down.[89]

Landlords may have been more likely to encourage tenants to leave without a formal eviction, so the fall in formal evictions in Figure 7.3 may overstate the fall in involuntary moves.[90] Yet a main way landlords force tenants out is through the threat of eviction, so this change may have reduced involuntary moves more broadly, even if landlords were still trying to push tenants out.

Eviction moratoria protected tenants at the expense of landlords who could no longer evict tenants who did not pay rent, although they could generally evict for other reasons. But landlords overall do not appear to have suffered financially. Partly, general pandemic aid was very effective at helping renters, especially renters who would have struggled without the pandemic, so there does not appear to have been a widespread increase in missed rent.[91]

Unlike mortgage delinquencies, which get reported to credit bureaus, there are no standard sources for rent delinquencies, but the available data suggests only a minor increase in rent delinquency, not closely tied to eviction moratoria.[92] The National Multifamily Housing Council, which represents the rental housing industry, collects rent payment data from about 11 million apartments that are professionally managed.

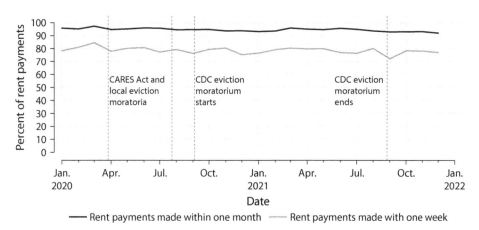

FIGURE 7.4. Most renters still paid rent during the pandemic and non-payment does not seem to have increased during the eviction moratorium. (*Source*: Author's calculations from National Multifamily Housing Council.)

It is likely that people who live in professionally managed apartments face less eviction risk than renters overall, but these data are still useful for understanding the overall trends. The National Multifamily Housing Council asks its members to report two numbers: the share of rent payments due from the previous month that are made within the first week, which is a close approximation of "on-time" payments, and the share made within one month. Both measures suggest that the pandemic did not bring immediate increases in rent delinquency (Figure 7.4).[93] The percentage of rent payments made within a month was 95.1 percent in February 2020, 94.5 percent in August 2020, and 93.5 percent in February 2021. Through 2021, there was a slow decline in the percentage of rent payments made on time. Notably, decreases in on-time rent payment are not closely related to eviction moratoria. Instead, on-time rent payments increased slightly following the Economic Impact Payments and expanded unemployment benefits but were fairly stable.[94] The wave of missed payments that many feared at the beginning of the pandemic never materialized.

Smaller landlords were perhaps more likely to have problems, but even the average small landlord was not financially hurt during the pandemic, although some did suffer. Using anonymous Chase bank account data, the JPMorgan Chase Institute examined the rental revenue and balances of landlords with a mortgage on a multifamily or investment property or whose small business bank accounts show they rent out a residential property.[95] The owners in their sample typically had fewer than three rental properties. Small landlords do appear to have lost money in the first several months of the pandemic. Median rental revenue was down 20 percent in April and May 2020, but it was up 10 percent in June 2020 over 2019. Over the rest of 2020 and through May 2021, rental revenues were nearly the same as in 2019. Meanwhile, landlord expenses fell in April and May 2020 by more than revenues fell, so the median small landlord ended the year with a 30 percent larger cash balance. Landlords with federally backed mortgages, for example, were generally eligible for mortgage forbearance if they needed it.[96] Other landlords delayed repairs.[97]

Small landlords in some cities did lose rental revenue, but it seems to have been mostly because rents fell as people moved out of expensive areas. The JPMorgan Chase Institute study found that small landlords in New York, San Francisco, and Miami—some of the most expensive rental housing markets—lost rental revenues. But landlords in the areas surrounding these cities lost far less, if any, revenue, as people moved to the suburbs, increasing rents there.

Putting landlords and renters together, because of the unprecedented general pandemic aid, most renters were still able to make their rent payments, so most landlords still got the rent. Meanwhile, the average small landlord, who also generally benefited from this aid individually, did not suffer financially. Formal evictions were halved for nearly two years, preventing around one million evictions.

Yet the averages hide the acute difficulties faced by some renters and landlords. Despite the fall in evictions, around a million families were still evicted during the pandemic. These families' experiences were still painful, even if there were fewer of them. Landlord spending fell because many were spending less on upkeep, leaving many families with worse housing. The drop in revenues at the start of the pandemic or tenants' difficulty paying during it harmed other landlords. Any income fall can be a hardship, even if it is later made up. In a May 2021 survey that Avail—a resource for independent landlords—developed with the Urban Institute, 60 percent of independent landlords said they were not suffering any financial loss due to partial or missed payments in the previous three months.[98] But of the 40 percent of independent landlords with recent financial losses, about 60 percent reported experiencing six or more partially or fully missed rent payments since April 2020. At least early in the pandemic, Black and Hispanic landlords were facing greater financial struggles, but they were also more willing to work with tenants.[99] These landlords' experiences were also painful, even if they are not common. And while pandemic aid and eviction moratoria may have kept the pandemic from exacerbating the affordable housing crisis, those problems did not go away.

Notably absent from the story so far is the nearly $50 billion in rental aid that the December 2020 relief bill and the American Rescue Plan Act allocated. This money was sadly irrelevant through August 2021 because almost none of it made it to landlords to cover rent. While the money did go out more quickly after that, and some areas were more effective at getting it out than others, that this money did not go out in a timely manner is one of the most notable policy failures during the pandemic.

By the end of October 2021, ten months after the first money was allocated in the December 2020 relief bill, only $12 billion had been distributed to renters, less than a quarter of the amount available. Figure 7.5 shows the cumulative rental assistance funds dispersed.[100] To put that in perspective, the Paycheck Protection Program managed to run through $350 billion in just three weeks and most Economic Impact Payments were mailed or deposited within three weeks after authorization. Still, by October 2021, more than two million families had received some assistance.

Because the federal government had never provided significant rent relief before and many states had no rent assistance programs, disbursing the money was not easy. But to point out the obvious: the reason this discussion is in this chapter is because the federal government had never provided significant rent relief before and many states had no rent assistance programs. Rental relief was difficult because it was not a policy priority during the pandemic and had not been one before the

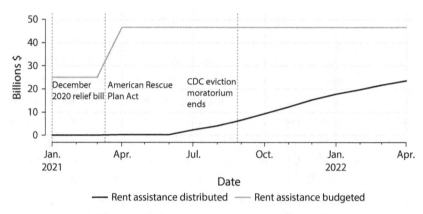

FIGURE 7.5. Rental assistance funds went out very, very slowly. (Rental assistance budgeted and distributed. *Source*: Author's calculations from U.S. Treasury.)

pandemic. Renters, particularly low-income renters, were an after-thought. They, and their landlords, were left behind, again.

Why was it so hard to distribute the money? A fundamental problem, from which many others spring, was that the program distributed funds to state and local governments. Each of these governments had to figure out how to apply for the funds and set up a process to distribute them. Some relied on third-party vendors, but that required a new government procurement. Rules around government contracts mean it is often difficult to do them quickly, especially for a new program. Other local governments tried to distribute the money themselves, with varying degrees of success. The most successful governments already had established rental assistance programs that could be readily adapted. In other words, rather than setting up one program, more than 400 state, local, and tribal governments, often understaffed to begin with, had to figure out how to set up 400 programs.[101] It is hard to build these programs, and state and local governments rarely have the capacity to do it quickly and well, unless they have already worked to set up similar programs.

And so, unsurprisingly, many of these programs were really bad to start with. They were bad in different ways, however, so there was no easy national fix. For example, the New York program could not accept paper applications initially, a major hurdle for many applicants.[102] Even

New York's online application was extremely difficult to use for months.[103] Other programs made the process extremely complicated or required excessive documentation.[104] Still others could not process applications in a timely manner.[105] Part of the problem is that, at least initially, renters were required to document that their income had been harmed due to COVID-19, which is often hard to do. The U.S. Treasury eventually clarified in August 2021 that "self-attestation" of an income drop was sufficient.[106] But this clarification came eight months in, when most programs had already been set up.

In contrast, mortgage forbearance and the Paycheck Protection Program required only a self-attestation of COVID-19 harm from the very beginning and were part of the CARES Act in March 2020. To be fair, mortgages are typically well documented, while rental contracts are not, so there was perhaps a greater possibility of fraud. But the Paycheck Protection Program only required self-attestation of harm from small business owners, whose COVID-19 harm and expenses are not necessarily any better documented than rental contracts.

The delay setting up these programs is clear in Figure 7.5. It took about six months before funds started going out beyond a trickle. This is not meant to diminish the hard work of state and local government staff who set up these programs; six months is actually quite fast to set up a new program with some sort of need verification to distribute funds, even in the absence of a pandemic. But it does illustrate how largely irrelevant these funds were for so long.

A separate problem was that receiving the money often required tenants and landlords to work together. Many landlords and tenants had been working together throughout the pandemic. For example, 38 percent of tenants who had problems paying the rent say they had received rent flexibility in the February 2021 Making Ends Meet survey, before any federal funds had been distributed.[107] But many tenants and landlords had not worked together and were not interested in doing so. Many landlords refused to take the rental relief money because it required them not to evict for another year or because it required a cut in rent.[108] Some of the initial problems came from requirements of the December 2020 relief bill, which, for example, required offering assistance to landlords before reaching out to tenants. The funding in the American Rescue Plan was more flexible.[109]

The most successful programs managed to overcome these obstacles, often because they could build on preexisting programs. For example, Philadelphia's Eviction Diversion Program required landlords to participate in mediation and apply for rental assistance before filing an eviction.[110] The program helped Philadelphia distribute all of the federal funds available and apply for more.

As funds started to flow in the second half of 2021, evictions did not increase sharply even after the CDC's eviction moratorium ended. Formal evictions were still down about 30 percent from average in December 2021 and about 25 percent through spring 2022. Yet as the rental assistance ran out in 2022, evictions started to rise. Evictions typically rise in January. In the midst of the pandemic, they had not risen in January 2021, but rose in January 2022, nearly returning to prepandemic levels (see Figure 7.3). Rent, meanwhile, had increased sharply through 2021, making housing even more unaffordable. While the pandemic had briefly turned down the heat on the simmering eviction crisis, it had done little for the underlying problems.

Who Else Did We Miss?

Miles-long lines of cars outside food banks became common during the pandemic.[111] Food bank directors reported surges in demand in the first few weeks of the pandemic and demand continued to be higher than normal for some time. An Associated Press analysis of nearly 200 food banks found that the amount of food distributed was about 50 percent higher in the second, third, and fourth quarters of 2020 than it had been a year earlier.[112] Food banks reported that the need was worse than during the Great Recession, and the lines evoke images of Great Depression soup lines. Yet other parts of this book have shown that average financial status improved during the pandemic and fewer people had difficulty paying bills. Unprecedented unemployment insurance and Economic Impact Payments increased average savings.

Both can be true. It is possible for most people to be doing financially better while some are financially struggling. The surge in demand from food banks and other food insecurity measures suggests that the people whom pandemic policies missed were facing real hardships.

So whom did we miss? The short and humbling answer is that we do not know for certain, but the food lines suggest a sizable population was not successfully reached by pandemic policies. Surveys—including the Making Ends Meet survey—have a difficult time reaching people who move around a lot or have no fixed address. We often know very little about populations that are difficult to reach. For example, our best estimates of people experiencing homelessness and bird populations are done using the same method: a point-in-time count. Volunteers spend a night in January enumerating people experiencing homelessness, looking in places they might be sleeping or staying. The Audubon Society organizes a similar event to count bird species each February.[113] The reason both take this approach is the same: with a population that moves around a lot and is often hiding in plain sight, an accurate count requires an intensive effort all at once. Spreading the effort over time risks missing some people and double-counting others. It got even harder to learn about difficult-to-reach populations during the pandemic; many large cities called off their count of people experiencing homelessness in January 2021 because of safety concerns.[114]

Not all, or even most, of the people who were suffering financially despite pandemic aid were experiencing homelessness. Instead, the difficulty reaching them illustrates the limits of our knowledge. It also illustrates that many programs have holes. People experiencing homelessness may not have qualified for unemployment insurance, but many would be eligible for Economic Impact Payments. Unless you filed a 2018 or 2019 tax return, you needed to apply to receive the payments. And the IRS needed a bank account or an address to mail checks to. These are large hurdles for someone experiencing homelessness. The IRS, aware of the difficulties, reached out to community groups to let them know that people experiencing homelessness were likely eligible for Economic Impact Payments.[115] My guess is that only a small share ended up receiving money, but given the limited information, it is only a guess.

People experiencing homelessness are perhaps the most difficult to reach and most likely to be overlooked, but many other Americans are difficult to reach and may be overlooked for other reasons. Some people might have been working off the books, so might not be eligible for unemployment insurance, perhaps because they were undocumented immigrants. Others may have had some irregularity in their unemployment insurance application, causing it to be delayed or rejected. For people who were unemployed and did not get unemployment insurance, such as Marcus after Chapter 2, the costs were large.

While we cannot be sure who was missed and how much their financial situation deteriorated, the scale of the problem is potentially large. One-sixth of the U.S. population might have been mostly or entirely left out from aid.[116] Even as Chapter 6 shows pandemic policy's broad success at preventing financial suffering, this chapter points to specific groups that were left behind. Surely there were others, even if they are more difficult to measure. Additional research may give us a better idea of the scale and perhaps how to better reach people in the future. Cold comfort to those who needed more help during the pandemic.

———

Part III turns to the pandemic's aftermath and the long road to a post-pandemic world. The pandemic fundamentally altered where Americans work, and those changes suggest new possibilities for both businesses and employees. But the pandemic also put many lives on hold and forced short-term compromises that will have long-term consequences. It kept school children from progressing, pushed parents out of the work force, and caused many people to retire early. As the pandemic fitfully receded, supply-chain snarls and rising inflation caused problems, but a surprising increase in new businesses and a stronger labor movement produced new opportunities. The road back to normal was bumpy; hold on for blind curves and potholes ahead.

Tamira

Tamira had long struggled to make ends meet. In June 2019, she said that she was just getting by financially and felt that her finances controlled her life. It seems that her many financial problems had left her uncomfortable with her ability to manage her finances. When asked how confident she was in her ability to make complex financial decisions, she responded, "Not at all."

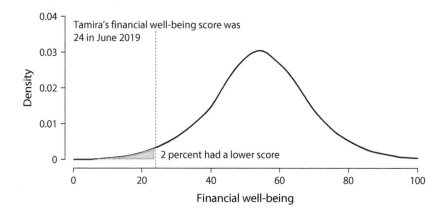

Tamira, a Black woman in her late thirties, lived in a large metro area in Texas. She and her partner rented an apartment, paying around $1,500 a month in rent. In 2019, she had a car and an auto loan, which she was slowly repaying. It seems likely, given that she lived in Texas, that she needed the car to get to work. She and her partner earned around $50,000 between them in the previous year. Her household income was about the same from month to month. Tamira did not say how she was employed, but she was looking for a new job.

Tamira's family's high housing expenses and car payments meant there was little left over every month. They had no money in checking or savings accounts and could cover expenses for less than two weeks if they lost their main source of income.

Partly because she had so little financial buffer, Tamira had difficulty paying bills and expenses about once a month in 2019. The most recent time she had difficulty, her income was unexpectedly $300 less than she thought it would be because her partner got sick. Because they had less income, they were late paying the rent. Tamira had health insurance, but her partner did not. They had to pay a major medical expense because of the illness. She expected more medical expenses to come.

Tamira had to deal with several other unexpected expenses in the past year. Her car broke down and had to be repaired. She faced some legal expenses as well as unexpected taxes. To help tide her over, she turned to a pawn shop for a loan sometime around December 2018. Like many people with pawn loans, she had yet to fully pay it back six months later. She had had a credit card several years ago but failed to make some payments, so she no longer had one. The unpaid credit card debt was still on her credit record and kept her credit score very low.

Yet Tamira was also working toward a better future. Her son had started college in 2019. To help pay for it, she took out a parental education loan, which added to her expenses. The loan was for more than $20,000, a large amount given her income. She checked her credit score regularly using the free website AnnualCreditReport.com, which was set up by the major credit bureaus. She knew her score had gone down recently but was trying to improve it. She also reported that she expected to move in the next six months. Perhaps she wanted to move, or perhaps her landlord was pushing her out because of the missed rent.

Like many people her age, Tamira felt comfortable with the internet. She had a cell phone, which was the primary way she accessed the internet, although she also used a computer at work and home. She took the survey at home on her laptop, which she also used to pay bills online.

Tamira was also part of a larger community. If faced with a large expense, she said she would turn to friends and family. She felt that most people can be trusted. She turned to family and friends for financial advice. And she had large expenses because she loaned money to a family member.

Early in the Pandemic

When Tamira took the survey in June 2020, the previous year and pandemic had been difficult. She was laid off because of the pandemic and her partner was also unemployed, although not because of the pandemic. She was actively looking for a job, but the prospects were bleak. Their income was down from the previous year.

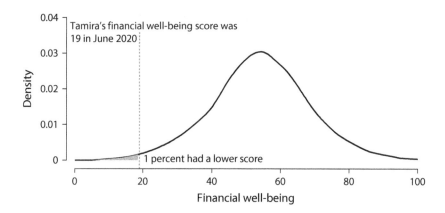

Before the pandemic started, the education loan she took out for her son had proved difficult to pay. They were still having difficulty paying bills and expenses about once a month, but the education loan was the most recent problem. She was unable to pay the full amount when it came due. And trying to pay left them financially extended in other ways. Tamira reported having difficulty paying for medical expenses, rent, utilities, other regular household expenses, and even food because of the bill. To help deal with some of these problems, she took out a payday loan, which she still owed money on as of June 2020, as well as a new pawn loan.

The CARES Act student loan payment pause seems to have been particularly helpful for Tamira. From March 2020 through at least January 2022, the balance did not change, indicating she was not making payments and no interest was accumulating. For Tamira, who had already had trouble making some payments and was laid off during the pandemic, not having this extra expense was important. She delayed making some other payments, perhaps on the car, because a lender offered flexibility.

Their family continued to face unexpected expenses, such as a mobile phone that broke and had to be replaced, and continuing legal and medical expenses. But everyone was finally covered by health insurance.

Late in the Pandemic

Tamira did not return the third wave of the survey. She moved between June 2020 and February 2021, so perhaps the survey never reached her. It is possible she was evicted, whether formally or informally, because of the missed rent payments. Tamira may be one of the people we missed.

However, the credit bureau data linked to her survey suggested that by February 2021, things were looking brighter. In January, she got a new credit card. The credit limit was a standard low starter limit of several hundred dollars, but it made some payments a lot easier. The amount she owed on her auto loan had diminished, so perhaps she started receiving unemployment insurance and was able to pay down some of her debts. And she continued to benefit from the student loan payment pause.

PART III

The Pandemic's Aftermath

8

Work from Home

THE PAST AND FUTURE OF WORK

THE SENSE that there is a proper division between "work" and "home" is new. Until the development of rapid mass transportation at the end of the nineteenth century, almost no one could live far from where they worked because transportation was expensive and slow. Remains from early hunter-gatherer societies suggest that any crafting was done close to where they lived.[1] Shopkeepers or skilled artisans, such as shoemakers, would typically live above their shop, housing their families and apprentices. Farmers lived near the fields and often with the livestock. Even as industrial development introduced large factories, many "cottage industries," such as weaving, continued to exist through the Industrial Revolution. As upstairs-downstairs dramas such as *Downton Abbey* illustrate, many service workers continued to live on the premises. The invention of mass transportation, cars, and the ability to construct large apartment buildings and remove sewage allowed greater density and greater separation between work and home. Yet caring for children and the household is still performed in home, even if it is often forgotten and not counted in GDP.

So when about half the workforce suddenly started working from home in March 2020, it was in many ways a return to an earlier life. One large difference: work does not necessarily stop when the sun goes down. In early societies, light was expensive and low quality, so most work needed to be completed during the day.[2] Many of remote work's benefits and costs to workers and their employers are a result of this modern ability to work anywhere and anytime.

Even measuring remote work is new. As a result, the evidence about remote work during the pandemic can appear inconsistent. Different surveys defined remote work differently: some measured only remote work that occurred because of the pandemic, others measured work-days rather than workers who can work remotely, and still others considered all workers.

All measures agree that the transformation to remote work occurred rapidly starting in March 2020, peaking around May 2020, and then slowly declining. One study calculated that the percentage of paid full days worked remotely increased from about 5 percent prepandemic to over 60 percent in May 2020. The percentage declined to about 45 percent in November 2020, before increasing again during the winter 2021 surge.[3] Other studies found a similar increase.[4] In May 2020, the Bureau of Labor Statistics added a question on remote work to the Current Population Survey (the source for unemployment statistics). Figure 8.1 shows the percentage of employed workers who said they had worked remotely at any point in the past four weeks because of the pandemic and said they had not been working remotely full time before the pandemic.[5] Close to 40 percent of workers in May 2020 were pandemic remote workers; by June 2021, only 16 percent were. Throughout the pandemic, non-Hispanic whites were more likely to work remotely, while Hispanics were the least.

By fall 2021, it was clear remote work was here to stay. While the Bureau of Labor Statistics asked about remote work because of the pandemic, Gallup asked about any remote work. According to Gallup surveys, about 69 percent of the workforce was working remotely some or all of the time in April 2020.[6] While the percentage fell to 53 percent in January 2020, it was still 45 percent in September 2021.[7] Even as the pandemic faded and the share reporting remote work because of the pandemic fell, as seen in Figure 8.1, the share in Gallup's poll who were working remotely was nearly constant. By spring 2022, most people who could work remotely were still doing so because they preferred to work remotely, not because their office was closed.[8]

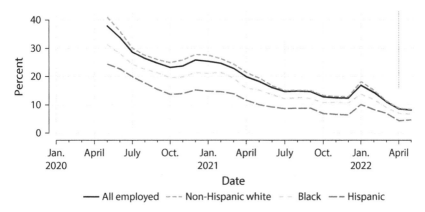

FIGURE 8.1. In May 2020, 40 percent of employed were working remotely because of the pandemic. (Percent of employed who worked remotely in the last four weeks because of the coronavirus pandemic. *Source*: Author's calculations from Bureau of Labor Statistics Current Population Survey.)

Remote work had become the preferred option during the pandemic, not just a necessity.

Office occupancy rates tell a similar story; people were not going back to offices, even two years later. Office occupancy rates in the biggest metro areas plummeted from close to 100 percent to below 20 percent at the beginning of the pandemic. By March 2022, office occupancy rates were still at only 40 percent of their prepandemic levels.[9] Meanwhile, restaurants were at close to their prepandemic levels. People were going out again, just not to the office.

The pandemic massively increased the remote work share, but it also transformed the remote work experience. Before the pandemic, remote work for a full workday was rare for most people. Estimates from the American Time Use Survey conducted by the Bureau of Labor Statistics suggest that in 2018, 25 percent of workers sometimes worked from home.[10] But "sometimes" hides that, for most people who did work from home, it was occasional and not for a full workday—for example, the teacher who took home papers to grade or the office worker who answered emails on the weekend. Only 15 percent of workers had days they worked exclusively from home, and of those, only a quarter worked from home three or more days per week.

Even before the pandemic, the ability to work remotely was highly concentrated among white, high-income professionals. While 30 percent of white workers could work remotely in any capacity in 2018, only 20 percent of Black workers could and 16 percent of Hispanic workers could. Remote work for a full day at a time, which indicates that, at least occasionally, all work could be completed remotely, was even more rare: 15 percent of white workers had days they worked exclusively remotely, compared with 11.2 percent of Black workers and 5.7 percent of Hispanic workers. The main difference in who could and did work remotely was education; 29 percent of workers with at least a bachelor's degree had days they worked remotely exclusively, compared with 7 percent of workers with less education.

As the pandemic started, the people in some professions found the transition easy. A Pew survey in October 2020 found that, among adults who said that "for the most part, the responsibilities of my job can be done from home," 71 percent were working remotely full time, compared with 20 percent before the pandemic.[11] Nearly 90 percent said it had been easy for them to have the technology and equipment they needed to do their jobs, and nearly 80 percent said they had adequate workspace. And these professions largely stayed home: Gallup found that in "white-collar" professions that are performed in an office with a computer, about 67 percent were working remotely through September 2021.[12]

People invested significant time and money in improving their new home workspaces. According to one survey, the average person working from home devoted 15 hours and $561 dollars in new equipment to make working from home possible.[13] These investments added up to around 0.7 percent of GDP. Late-night television hosts recorded from home with new lighting and cameras, radio and podcast hosts recorded from their closets, and webcams shot up in price, when they were even available.[14] Many companies also helped pay for necessary work-from-home equipment and invested in new technologies to allow online collaboration and communication.

Because of this investment, the remote work experience improved substantially. Before the pandemic, for example, it was much harder to participate using a phone to call into a meeting when everyone else was physically there. You could not read the facial expressions that everyone else could. The slight delay made it harder to take part in the regular flow of conversation. When the pandemic sent everyone home and video teleconference software became widespread, suddenly we could have meetings where not being physically present was not a problem.

Of course, for the people who did not have adequate workspace or child care, the mix of work and life was difficult. "Desks are the new toilet paper" became an expression late in summer 2020 as students and remote workers realized they were likely to be home for extended periods and needed a better setup.[15] People got creative. One woman, tired of sharing her workspace with her kids and husband, turned a spare bathroom into an office by putting a desk above the toilet (it worked surprisingly well).[16] Others moved into the kitchen, used ironing boards, or borrowed some space from a child's bedroom.[17]

Juggling child care, online school, roommates, and spouses was difficult and stressful for many people. The privilege of a home office, a desk, and a good chair that did not cause agony after several hours became a new fault line among those who could work remotely, adding to the existing fault lines between workers who could not work remotely and the unemployed.

Surprising many, despite the challenges of remote work, people working remotely produced just as much. Partly, they just spent more time working. For example, one study of a large Asian IT firm that suddenly switched to work from home during the pandemic found that average weekly hours increased by about four hours.[18] Hourly productivity declined somewhat, especially for parents, but because hours increased, weekly output hardly changed. Other research that tracked meetings and email metadata across metropolitan areas in North America, Europe, and the Middle East found that the average workday increased by nearly 50 minutes.[19] People spent less time in meetings, but they met more frequently and sent more emails.

New work patterns emerged as the boundary between home and work disappeared. Measuring when Microsoft employees were using their keyboards, a Microsoft research team found that 30 percent had a new work spike from 6 to 8 p.m.[20] Many workers found they could now work outside regular business hours and without being physically at the office. For some, this allowed them greater flexibility during the day. For others, it was just more time to work. Other teams appear to have used the time to meet with team members in different time zones, embracing the possibilities of remote work, as well as its potential downsides.

Employers, employees, and experts mostly agree that productivity increased or held steady. In several surveys of employees, most felt their productivity had improved.[21] Mercer, a human resources consulting firm, surveyed 800 employers, and 94 percent said productivity was as high as or higher than before the pandemic.[22] When the *San Diego Union Tribune* interviewed a range of experts in November 2020, all 13 felt that people were as productive or more so.[23]

The primary reason for increased productivity is fewer wasted hours commuting. We spent 60 million fewer hours per day commuting from March to September 2020, by one estimate.[24] One of the most hated parts of the day for many people is their commute. People find their morning commute the most unpleasant time spent during their day, much worse than child care, housework, shopping, and working.[25] Yes, most people would rather work than commute. Importantly, commuting is time spent for work, but it is not time spent working. It is time we do not spend doing something we want, and we are not compensated for it by our employers. Dead time. So it is perhaps not a surprise that without a commute, one of the things people did with their time was work a bit more. On average, Americans spent about 35 percent of the time they saved by not commuting working more and the rest on a range of activities, including chores and child care.[26]

Productivity also increased because, it turns out, a lot of "work" is not really productive. Part of the change was that many were able to focus more on the parts of their jobs that create the most value. For example, in one pandemic survey that asked people to go through a typical day from the previous week, people described being in big meetings 10 percent less and spending 9 percent more time on externally focused work such as talking to customers.[27] People reported doing more work that they considered important and far fewer tasks they considered tiresome. As Julian Birkinshaw, Jordan Cohen, and Pawel Stach, who conducted the research, describe it, "Working from home gives us a bit of breathing space: We don't have colleagues or bosses badgering us, and we don't get drawn into meetings by force of habit, just because we happen to be around. The result is a reassuring increase in us making time for work that matters most to us." One way that remote work may enhance productivity is by focusing on work's outcomes rather than just appearing busy. Many managers and workers measure work by attendance—time in the office—while remote work encouraged us to focus on outcomes.[28] It is easy for a lazy manager to see people at their desks and so consider them "at work," without thinking about what they are doing. But good management focuses on achieving good outcomes, not on the appearance of work.

Many managers responded to the new environment poorly, attempting to micromanage or use technology to perform constant monitoring. Alison Green, writing in *Slate*, described some horror stories, from requiring several check-ins every hour that reduced productivity to asking employees to install spy software on personal laptops.[29] For companies that did not convert well, Green points out that they tended to think monitoring is management.

And some workers responded to this monitoring creatively or used the lack of physical surveillance as an excuse to slack. Sales of "mouse jigglers"—a product that makes it seem as if a worker is at her computer by simulating mouse movements—boomed.[30]

Of course, some things are lost by not being physically present with others. While existing teams may have found it easy to transition, perhaps we will find that building new teams to handle new problems is harder when everyone is remote. For example, a study of Microsoft employees' communication patterns found that they were less likely to communicate across groups during the pandemic.[31] Business groups across Microsoft became less interconnected. It is possible that over the long term, less sharing across groups may lead to less agility or innovation. Or maybe it just leads to less time spent in unproductive meetings.

Remote work may also reduce innovation. There is some evidence that proximity to others helps foster innovation and creativity.[32] Laboratory and field experiments suggest that meetings in person are better at generating creative ideas than virtual meetings.[33] But virtual meetings were just as effective at deciding which ideas to pursue and building team trust. Some executives fear that not being physically together will depress innovation, which is necessary for long-term productivity and income growth. Apple chief executive Tim Cook has publicly expressed skepticism that teams working remotely can be as creative.[34] Jamie Dimon, chief executive of banking giant JPMorgan Chase, was another skeptic, suggesting as he started to bring people back to the office in 2021 that being remote "does not work for young people. It doesn't work for those who want to hustle."[35]

As Dimon suggested, it may be harder to learn from experience virtually, so younger remote workers may not have the same career development, be able to find mentors, or be able to network in the same way. As Amanda Mull argued in the *Atlantic*, "Young people who work remotely risk remaining unknown quantities. And unknown quantities don't become beloved colleagues, or get promoted."[36]

It is hard to pinpoint exactly what is lost for young workers and how important it is. It may take years before we see how the pandemic remote work experience changed early-career development, and as of spring 2022 the scholarly literature did not have much to say. Maybe missing peer relationships make it harder for people to figure out how to do their jobs. Maybe lost networking opportunities make it harder to get the next job. Maybe reduced mentorship hampers on-the-job learning. Yet hard to measure is not the same as unimportant. I direct, help train, and mentor junior colleagues just starting their careers. I can't help but feel that my junior colleagues did not get the same on-the-job experience while we were working remotely, although what they are missing is harder to pin down. If I could identify it, maybe I could do it better.

Yet the in-person office was not always promoting Black or Hispanic workers or women or making them feel like valued team members. In a fall 2020 Gallup survey, Black women were less likely to feel they were valued members of their team or that their coworkers treated everyone fairly.[37] Alarmingly, while Black women were the least likely to agree that they were valued, at 33 percent, only 42 percent of white men felt valued, suggesting there is a broad lack of respect in the workplace. Only 13 percent of Black women and 19 percent of white women felt that there were plenty of opportunities to get good jobs in their communities, compared with an also alarming 22 percent of white men.

So it is unsurprising that only 16 percent of Black knowledge workers were eager to return to the office full time, compared with 30 percent of white knowledge workers.[38] One reason: half of Black men said their sense of belonging at work had improved when working remotely, compared with a fifth who said it had declined. In interviews, many Black women preferred working from home, away from microaggressions and constant code-switching.[39]

By spring 2022, workers who had shown they could productively work remotely refused to accept that they needed to return to the office full time. Against the tight labor market at the end of the pandemic (see Chapter 10), employers more or less capitulated. As a *Wall Street Journal* headline pithily expressed it, "Remote Work Is the New Signing Bonus."[40] While the mix of full-time remote, full-time in person, and hybrid—sometimes remote—differed, by spring 2022 even remote work's staunchest opponents had accepted that they could not return to the old days. In his April 2022 letter to shareholders, JPMorgan Chase chief Jamie Dimon had accepted that hybrid and fully remote work were there to stay.[41] Pushback from his (largely white and well-paid) office workers forced him to change his plans for returning to office.[42] But some jobs could not be done remotely, and these employees would still be in the office full time. The janitors, security guards, and retail bank employees, who were more likely to be nonwhite before the pandemic, had to work in person through the pandemic, and would continue to work in person after it.

A switch to remote work has the tantalizing possibility that it might create a more equal workplace. It is true that young workers may find it more difficult to become "beloved colleagues," but someone will still end up getting promoted. Perhaps by removing some of the irrelevant social aspects, remote work will make more evident the contributions of people who might have been overlooked before. Maybe we should care less about being "beloved colleagues" and more about who does good work, no matter what they look like or whether they play golf to ingratiate themselves with the boss. Management may have to adapt, focusing less on visible face time and more on measurable results, but that seems like a good thing too.

Over the long term, "working from home will stick," write economists Jose Maria Barrero, Nicholas Bloom, and Steven Davis, although it will not be as pervasive as during the height of the pandemic.[43] It will stick for several reasons. For one, with all of the investments and innovations we have made in remote work, we are better at it than we were before, so we should do more of it. In addition, many companies, managers, and workers have experienced productive remote work, so they now know that remote workers can be productive and how to incorporate them into teams. Because the pandemic created a massive forced experiment in remote work, it broke the previous reluctance to try new approaches.

Depending on how important remote work becomes, it has the possibility to more broadly transform economic geography—where we work and live and play. At the city level, there will likely be fewer people downtown, changing the demand for office space and downtown services such as sandwich shops and bars. As a sign of the times, the pharmacy that used to rent the bottom floor of the building where I worked in downtown Washington, D.C., cleared out during the pandemic. It served people working in the surrounding buildings and so likely had no business with people working from home. At the same time, my local residential pharmacy has been increasingly busy.

These kinds of retail shifts from downtown to suburb were very common during the pandemic. Economists Gianni De Fraja, Jesse Matheson, and James Rockey call it "Zoomshock."[44] Because people were spending more of their time during the pandemic working from home in residential areas, they had much greater demand for services in these areas and correspondingly less demand for services in city centers. But the retail and service space was still predominantly in the city center, so supply still needed to catch up with the shift in demand. The larger the shift to remote work is after the pandemic, the larger this shift in services will be.

There are real costs to this kind of relocation, even if there are benefits. Barrero, Bloom, and Davis predict that the shift to remote work will lower expenditures on services such as meals and shopping in major cities by 5 percent to 10 percent in the long term.[45] Other research suggests the benefits of remote work will flow mainly to highly educated workers who can relocate.[46] The service workers who used to support these office workers will find fewer jobs and may be forced to relocate to suburbs to match the new demand. When those prosperous people spread out in suburbs, service workers will have to follow, often encountering greater commutes and less concentrated public transportation.

Beyond metro areas, remote work may begin to reshape where people live and work across the U.S. During the pandemic, some firms took the opportunity to rethink where they were located. Many technology companies announced that their workers could work anywhere, permanently. Even the companies themselves started moving. Oracle announced it was moving its headquarters from Silicon Valley to Austin, Texas.[47] It joined several other firms, including Hewlett Packard, in moving out of California. REI, an outdoor equipment retailer, had just finished a brand-new 400,000-square-foot building outside Seattle, but decided to sell it in August 2020.[48] The experience during the pandemic convinced REI's leadership that they could operate effectively remotely, but they planned several satellite locations. As one executive explained, "We've seen and we've heard from our employees that they see a lot of benefits of working remotely." Rather than being concentrated in one very expensive city, REI, Oracle, and Hewlett Packard were becoming more distributed. Many other businesses followed suit.

During the pandemic, many workers found they could work from anywhere they had a good enough internet connection. For some, that meant relocation to a suburban area within the same metro area. Others made longer moves to rural areas or other states where the cost of living was lower.[49] Others gave up a fixed address altogether: RV sales and rentals grew substantially.[50] Interest in retrofitted custom vans with sleeping and storage platforms, some costing hundreds of thousands of dollars, also exploded under the Twitter hashtag #vanlife.[51]

Remote work became a way for some places and countries, such as Barbados, Bermuda, and Costa Rica, whose tourism revenue had dried up during the pandemic, to attract visitors.[52] Able to do their job anywhere, many people flocked to these and other tourist locations.[53] The tax implications of working in a foreign country for a U.S. employer are complicated. They are even complicated working remotely outside your "home" state, since employers owe unemployment insurance and other taxes based on the location of work. These issues partly illustrate a complicated, almost metaphysical, question (except to state tax collectors): Where is work "done" if the employee is working in one place for an employer with no single location? While tax collectors will surely answer this question, it illustrates how far we have come. Home and work used to occur together. Then they separated, but only as far as workers could commute. Now that much work no longer needs a physical location and can be performed anywhere, there is no physical bond tying work to home.

All of these trends meant that big cities lost residents. Of course, people move into and out of big metro areas constantly. Retirees tend to move out of the expensive big city, while young new workers move in to get the higher-paying jobs. In recent decades, the pull of cities has been greater, so city populations, and particularly inner-city populations, have been growing. These trends reversed during the pandemic. The pandemic accelerated the move-outs as people nearing retirement decided to make the move now, perhaps while continuing to work remotely. On the other side, young people no longer had to move to get a remote job. And families looking for more space and home offices were more likely to move farther out to the suburbs.[54] The net effect was a reduction in city population, particularly in the Northeast, and an increase in suburban and southern and western state populations. For example, Texas had the largest inflows.

Relative to the overall population, these changes in population flows are modest. Yet even modest changes in population can have big effects. One of the most immediate is the rapid increase in prices for larger houses in metro areas and any housing in smaller towns and cities. The incomers, often still earning big-city remote work incomes, bid up the prices of the limited houses available in smaller cities and towns, often pricing out locals. One of the hottest housing markets during the pandemic was Boise, Idaho, for example, where housing prices increased 32 percent from May 2020 to May 2021.[55] Other smaller cities saw similar price increases.

This relocation may bring both businesses and employees to new places, moving away from dense metro areas. These moves may upend where we work and how important the biggest cities are for our economy and so may be the pandemic's most enduring change.

A fundamental economic question is why we have large and expensive cities in the first place. In the nineteenth century, most major U.S. cities were located on ports and served as trade hubs. The finance industry—necessary because it was slow and costly to move goods from place to place—grew alongside them.[56] But railroads soon reduced the importance of being on a river or a port, so why do people and businesses continue to congregate in the most expensive cities when housing and office costs are so much less expensive in other parts of the country? Amazon, for example, chose to put its HQ2 in two of the most expensive areas in the country, the D.C. metro area and New York. Why not go someplace cheaper?

It turns out that the value of density is often larger than the costs, so big cities are even more valuable to be in than they are costly. The term economists use for this phenomenon is "agglomeration effects," which is just a fancy way of saying "what happens when everyone is heaped together" (the Latin word *agglomerare* means "to heap up or mass together"). While there are several kinds of agglomeration effects, one of the most important comes from labor market size. When a business wants to hire more engineers, it helps to be where the engineers are. And when engineers want to be hired, they need to move to where the businesses are. This dynamic creates a feedback loop, reinforcing the advantages of some areas over others and leading to geographic winners and losers.[57] Partly because of this dynamic, income has become more unequally distributed geographically over the last 40 years. The big metropolises have been thriving. Meanwhile, smaller cities and rural areas have largely been left behind.

The firms and employees moving out of expensive areas because of pandemic remote work may be the first signs that remote work has broken this reinforcing labor-market agglomeration effect by allowing a national labor force. If so, it may unlock huge productivity gains because productive employers and employees no longer have to live and locate in expensive cities with limited housing supply.[58]

A national labor market may also improve the match between employers and employees. Incomes tend to increase with age. One reason might be experience, but another is that workers may find the right match for their skills. When an employer and employee who are well matched find each other, they can be more productive together. A national market increases the size of the possible match pool so employers can find the best match, not just the local one.

Remote work also makes the cost of switching employers much smaller. Rather than move your entire family, maybe you just use a different laptop when you switch employers. Over time, more switches may mean better matches as workers and employers are more willing to give each other a try and find the best fit. Lower switching costs may also increase bargaining power for some workers who can hop to new employers. As we'll see in Chapter 10, in late 2021 and 2022, job switching became more common, although it is difficult to tell what role remote work had.

To understand how remote work might improve matching, consider what is sometimes called the "two-body problem" of spouses trying to find good jobs in the same city. The relationship of three heavenly bodies such as the earth, the moon, and the sun is chaotic—small changes to initial conditions can cause large changes in outcomes eventually. There is no exact mathematical solution to the three-body problem, only better and better approximations. Borrowing from this classic physics problem, the two-body problem is when a married couple with specialized skills, such as two PhDs, try to find jobs in the same place. Although PhDs with jobs are generally well compensated, there are not many jobs for people with highly specialized skills, and they are not necessarily in the same place. Finding two highly specialized jobs in the same place is hard and often requires compromise or a trailing spouse whose career suffers.

A national market would break the curse of geography for this highly specialized labor market. Spouses could live together no matter where they "worked." Match quality would improve as highly specialized skills were available for their best uses, perhaps unlocking innovations.

The benefits of remote work may not flow to workers.[59] The national labor market and better matching may unlock new productivity. And workers may benefit from less time commuting, from moving to less expensive areas, or from being able to choose where they want to live based on something other than where they are employed. But some of the time saved commuting may just go to longer working hours. Employers may pay remote workers less, whether or not the worker is less productive, and will not necessarily pass on productivity increases or longer hours in higher compensation. Still, as offices opened up in 2022, it was the cities with the longest commutes that saw the lowest return to office, suggesting that whatever the trade-off, many employees were happy to pay it.[60]

Perhaps the rapid evolution in remote technologies has broken the link between physical proximity and innovation. Perhaps we have gotten good enough at remote work that it no longer matters where we are located. If so, an unexpected benefit of the pandemic may be that it opened up the possibility of living where we want, not where the historical happenstance of being on a river or ocean port dictates. A national labor market and instant communication with colleagues anywhere may help flatten the growing inequality between flourishing cities and the rest of the country. Or we may find that the social value of physical proximity is necessary for creativity and innovation in ways that are difficult to replicate remotely.

There are significant cost reductions from reduced commuting and big gains from a broader national labor market that lets firms hire the best person, not just the local person. These changes will happen slowly, however, as the new college graduate decides that she does not have to move to the Bay Area to get a great computer programming job but can instead stay in her hometown. As we develop better tools and ways to connect while living far from work—through occasional in-person retreats, for example—perhaps remote work's social and early career costs may diminish. Over the long term, I am optimistic that the pandemic shift in work will produce better lifestyles and productivity. Or maybe I just hated my commute too.

The revolution in the way nearly half of Americans work will have long-term consequences. In the next chapter, we'll see some of the other profound long-term changes from the pandemic.

Amy

Amy's financial journey during the pandemic was largely uneventful. For her, the biggest impacts were the many other social complications of life in a pandemic. Amy, in her late twenties in 2019, identified as white and Asian. She lived in an apartment in the Chicago metro area with her partner.

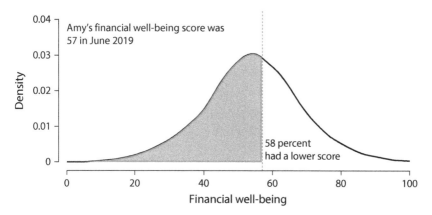

Amy had moved to Chicago a few years ago from another state after graduating college. Amy and her partner both worked full time and between them earned more than $100,000 in 2018. But Chicago is an expensive city. They had recently rented a new apartment and were paying around $3,000 a month. Although housing was expensive, their income was more than suffi-cient to cover it, so they were able to save. Amy said they were saving regularly and could cover their expenses for more than six months if one of them lost their job. Amy took a cautious approach to her finances, perhaps having learned this caution from her parents. For example, Amy felt she needed $25,000 in savings for emergencies, a substantial cushion. And she and her partner had those savings. Amy had the retirement accounts and health insur-ance that typically come with a high-paying professional job in a big city. As a result, she felt confident in her finances and her ability to manage them.

Amy's biggest upcoming expense was a vacation she and her partner were planning.

Early in the Pandemic

Amy and her partner were able to go on their vacation before pandemic shutdowns occurred in March 2020. They stayed employed through the pandemic, and, based on her location and income, it is likely that they both worked from home. They had not been planning to move in June 2019 but ended up moving to a new apartment in February 2020.[61] Hopefully, they had enough space to not interrupt each other's telework calls.

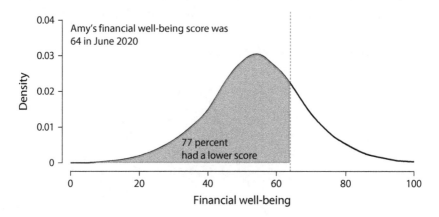

Amy's spending plummeted during the pandemic. Before the pandemic, she regularly spent around $800 on her credit card each month, although she paid it off every month. In April 2020, Amy spent $200. In May, $100. In June, $30. Amy started spending again in the next several months, but her credit card spending was far below where it had been. While we do not know what she stopped spending on, it is likely that she stopped going out to eat and drink, so her social life became much more limited. Drinks or brunch with friends can add up in an expensive city. As a result, she had more savings and her financial well-being score improved. It is unlikely that Amy considered that a good trade.

Late in the Pandemic

Amy had some big news in February 2021: she and her partner had gotten married! Based on what limited information we have from Amy's credit card spending, it is unlikely they had a big wedding. Perhaps it was a purely civil ceremony or an open-air celebration with some friends. Hopefully her parents made the trip from out of state, but perhaps concerns about virus exposure prevented them from coming.

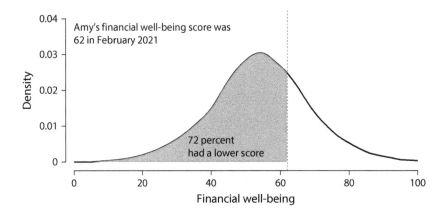

Amy reported that their savings had increased since March 2020. Amy and her spouse did not receive any government aid, so all of the savings increase comes from them spending less. But they did not feel like they were spending less. Amy reported their spending was about the same during the pandemic. But even small changes add up over time. As a result, Amy's financial well-being increased again.

Amy's pandemic experience shows the limits of a financial survey. For Amy, the pandemic's costs were not in unemployment and missed bills. Nor did she directly benefit much from pandemic aid. Instead, the costs were largely in things the survey did not capture. A wedding postponed or performed without her family. Not seeing her friends. Perhaps Amy and her spouse planned another vacation that they had to cancel. Or had to figure out how to exercise with their gym closed. She likely had too many Zoom meetings and worked too hard.

9

The Long Term

HURRICANE KATRINA hit Louisiana on August 29, 2005. After levees intended to hold back the surging water broke, the storm flooded New Orleans. The storm's immediate impacts were devastating: more than 1,000 dead and a mostly unlivable city. But the storm also had long-term consequences. Half of New Orleans's population was displaced for a year and many never returned, preferring their new lives in the cities that had welcomed them over trying to rebuild in neighborhoods that often no longer existed.[1] New Orleans today is a smaller city, and many of its residents came only after the storm. The storm permanently altered the course of a great American city and its residents.

The pandemic's economic effects are much like the hurricane, although with a more successful immediate response. After the devastation in March and April 2020, successful relief policy protected most people buffeted by the pandemic's winds or caught by the rising unemployment waters, even if it missed some people. But as the water subsided, Americans found a changed landscape that they no longer entirely recognized. Many people were faced with difficult choices or had opportunities yanked from them. While they may have done the best they could in the moment and survived the storm, the consequences of those choices and the missed opportunities will be with them for a long time.

The pandemic's long-term effects partly depend on what stage of life people were in when it hit, because where they were determined what choices they faced or opportunities they lost. So this chapter moves in approximately reverse order, starting with early retirements, then moving to women who left the workforce, the long-term unemployed, millennials living through the second economic catastrophe of their working lives, and finally to schoolchildren whose learning was so thoroughly disrupted.

The good news is that these effects are predictions based on past evidence and will be spread over time. By identifying and understanding the pandemic's likely long-term effects, perhaps we can ameliorate them. As G.I. Joe—the original toy action figure to sell dolls to boys— would say at the end of each 1980s cartoon episode, "And knowing is half the battle."[2] Many policies that might have general benefits—better education for low-income children, parental leave, unemployment support and training, more flexibility for parents or to bring the retired back into the labor force—may also have specific benefits for the pandemic cohorts.

The bad news: the social and mental health impacts will also likely be large and long lasting, but they are far more difficult to measure. For example, while we can measure lost learning and quantify its likely impact on earnings, it is harder to predict the consequences of missed social development from remote school or learning with a mask. The mental health trauma of disasters like Hurricane Katrina last for a long time. The pandemic's economic consequences may only be the most visible signs of lasting scars.

Early Retirement

Older workers' employment dropped sharply early in the pandemic, just as that of younger ones did. But while younger workers would largely return to work, many older workers decided to retire. About twice as many people retired in 2020 as in 2019.[3] One estimate is that an additional 1.7 million people retired because of the pandemic who would not have retired otherwise.[4]

Retiring early sounds like a good thing. But many of the people who retired because of the pandemic were not prepared to retire and were not retiring voluntarily. They would have preferred to work longer and build retirement savings. Instead, having lost a job, they accepted that a return to the labor force was going to be hard and made the difficult choice to move on.

Older workers' experience following the Great Recession was bleak, for example. It took them a lot longer to get employed again, and when they found a job, they typically earned a lot less.[5] One reason may be age discrimination. But older workers are also typically paid more. They have general experience and firm-specific experience and, before being laid off, their experience and skills may have been very well matched to their employer. As we discussed in Chapter 4 with the Paycheck Protection Program, layoffs break these business-specific matches. An older worker who is laid off may have been great at her specific job at her specific company. Some of these skills are transferable to a new company, but not all of them. So older laid-off workers can generally expect to spend a long time looking and to earn less than they did before.

Yet in many ways, what we are calling "early retirement" was part of a broader trend of leaving the labor force. As Figure 9.1 shows, the pandemic changes in labor force participation among people age 55 and older were actually quite similar to those for younger workers.[6] Older people were less likely to leave the labor force initially but slowly caught up. By June 2021, the labor force participation rate for people 55 to 74 had declined by 2 percentage points, about the same amount as for younger workers. Because only about half of 55-74 year olds work, about 4 percent of those who had been working had stopped doing so and were no longer looking for work.

While we may call many of the older workers "retired," what many of them really were was "discouraged." Facing a tough job market or dependents to care for, many younger workers also stopped actively looking and left the labor force. Labor economists call these workers discouraged because we generally assume they would like a job but do not think they can get one. As we discussed in Chapter 2, when people stop looking for work, they no longer count as unemployed, which is one reason why unemployment is often a poor way to measure labor market health. Because we tend to assume that people in prime working years (generally defined as age 25-54) should be working, while older people might be considering retirement, we tend to label younger workers out of the

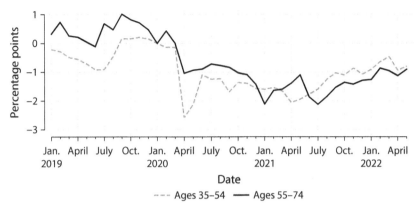

FIGURE 9.1. Facing a tough labor market, many older workers retired. But many younger workers also left the labor market. (Labor force participation rate for 35–54-year-olds and 55–74-year-olds compared with January 2020. *Source*: Author's calculations from Bureau of Labor Statistics Current Population Survey.)

labor force as discouraged and older workers as retired. But by whatever label, millions of older workers stopped working earlier than they had planned.

In addition to the tough labor market, older workers faced substantial new risks. COVID-19 was particularly deadly for older people. While some jobs could be remote, many employers could not or would not allow remote work, so employment carried additional risk that was compounded by age. The combination of lower pay, a tough job search, and COVID-19 risk pushed many to decide that trying to get a job again was not worth it.

These early retirements will have long-term negative consequences for their financial health. The involuntarily retired tended to be less well educated and earned less before they lost their jobs.[7] Because they "retired" earlier than they might have planned, they likely had accumulated less savings than they wanted. Many retired adults are already in poverty or at risk of poverty.[8] Adding millions more who were financially unprepared for retirement will exacerbate the problem. On the other hand, older adults benefited from general pandemic policies, including unemployment insurance and Economic Impact Payments. Moreover, unlike younger adults, they benefit from substantial government aid outside the pandemic, including Social Security and Medicare.

The good news is that many of these older workers might still return to work if they choose to and the labor market is good enough. Involuntary retirement is not necessarily permanent, but it is difficult and often not as rewarding financially to go back to work.

Not all older Americans were suffering. For some the pandemic brought new opportunities at work or eased them into voluntary retirement by showing a better way. College-educated workers were less likely to retire before age 65 during the pandemic than before it, but more likely to retire after age 65.[9] These two trends suggest two opposing currents. In one direction, working from home allowed many older workers the flexibility they had wanted but had not been able to achieve. One of my colleagues, for example, had been planning to retire to live in Montana, close to his daughter and the mountains he loved. Remote work allowed him to move to Montana and keep working, letting us continue to benefit from his experience.

In the other direction, the pandemic gave higher-income workers a chance to rethink what they wanted. There were likely several contributing factors. For some, working from home gave a new sense of what retirement might look like. Not having to go into the office. No commute. More time with your spouse. In addition, the financial status of many wealthier adults improved by late 2020. The stock market, which plunged early in the pandemic, increased substantially, making retirement look feasible. And as working parents were desperate for child care, there was suddenly both an opportunity and a need to spend more time with their grandchildren. As one retiree whose daughter was about to have a new baby put it, "I could have kept working from home, but I had a good run. With everything going on with the kids and the baby coming, and we're financially OK, this was as good a time as any."[10]

Child Care and Women's Labor

Early in the pandemic, I was watching my kids while trying to respond to a simple work email. It took me an hour to compose an email that should have taken five minutes. Just as I would finish reading the question, what I had already written, and prepare to write the next sentence, there would be a new interruption and I would have to start again: "Hey, Daddy! Hey, Daddy? What's nine plus five?" or "Can I watch on my iPad?" or I would realize the one-year-old was climbing or eating or grabbing something inappropriate, maybe all three. My wife and I took turns watching the kids, and I eventually mostly gave up trying to do any work while I was with them; it was too frustrating. I could do good work or be a good dad, but not at the same time.

Millions of other parents faced similar dilemmas through the spring and summer of 2020 and faced new or continuing challenges through 2021. The term that crops up again and again in research and news articles interviewing parents is "juggling."[11] Juggling work or the search for work, child care, and online school, and dropping some of the balls. Child care hours by parents who could work from home—mostly college graduates, as we discussed in the last chapter—doubled during the first months of the pandemic.[12] As economist Misty Heggeness wrote, "Overall, the pandemic appears to have induced a unique immediate juggling act for working parents of school age children."[13]

The early stages of the pandemic were a massive shock to the delicate household gender balance and one that revealed how far from equal we still are. One study through April 2020 found that mothers of young children reduced their work hours by four to five times more than fathers.[14] The early months of the pandemic, with kids at home, meant new disruptions that tended to be hardest on working mothers. As one news article on the research described it, "They go to mommy first."[15]

These gendered adjustments to child care and other household decisions are common. Although it is often useful to think about the household as a single decision-making unit, households are composed of different people with their own desires and ambitions. Yet household members typically also care about other members of the household. This combination of independence and altruism makes studying household "decisions" difficult because what the household does is composed of many individual decisions, but individual decisions depend on what others in the household want. One way to approach how these individual decisions combine to make a household decision is to consider who has power within the household. Social norms around gender and differences in earnings tend to mean household decisions often favor men.[16]

Of course, not all households are alike, but most had difficult adjustments to make. In some, fathers cut back hours more. In single-parent households, the parent—most commonly the mother—had to make difficult decisions about work and child care.[17] For many parents, particularly single parents, grandparents filled the child care gap.[18] In same-sex households, traditional gender norms did not necessarily apply, but there were still hard decisions to make about child care. In some, the parent with a more flexible schedule took on more child care. In others, the lower-earning parent.

While many mothers managed through the summer, despite daycare and camp closures, the breaking point came when many schools did not open in person in fall 2020. Starting in August as schools failed to open in person and continuing through the fall, millions of mothers left the labor force.[19] They either quit their jobs or stopped looking for a job if they were unemployed. Figure 9.2 shows how the labor force participation of parents and nonparents has changed since January 2020.[20] Labor force participation is the share of all people either employed or looking for a job. Until August 2020, there were few differences. Everyone had a big drop in participation in March and April and a big rebound in the subsequent months. But by September, women with children were near April's low in labor force participation again. Their participation stayed lower through June 2021 but started increasing, so that by early 2022 it was about even with other adults, although still below January 2020. On the other hand, the participation of women with children had surged in the second half of 2019, so it was actually slightly higher in January 2022 than in January 2019.[21]

Many mothers decided that the best thing for their family was for them to stop working, at least temporarily.[22] Lack of child care—including in-person school—was a large contributor, although not the only one.[23] Mothers without a college education, whose jobs largely could not be done remotely, were the most likely to face this difficult choice, and the most likely to leave the labor force.[24] The safety of the

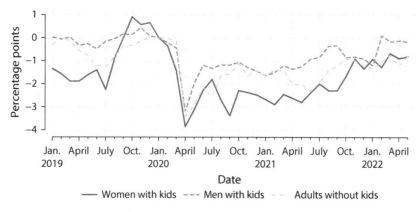

FIGURE 9.2. Some mothers stopped working as schools remained closed in fall 2020, but many had returned by fall 2021. (Labor force participation rate for parents and nonparents among 25–54-year-olds compared with January 2020. *Source*: Author's calculations from Bureau of Labor Statistics Current Population Survey.)

options that were available was a concern for many parents. In a May 2021 survey of parents whose children were not in in-person school, only 10 percent said it was because there was no in-person option.[25] But nearly half of parents surveyed said it was safer for the child or family.

Some parents found they liked having their children home for school, whether for remote learning or homeschool. Around one-fifth of parents whose children were not in person in May 2021 said their child was happier, and one-quarter said the child was doing as well or better academically. Many parents decided to try homeschooling. The share of households homeschooling doubled from 5.4 percent before the pandemic to 11 percent in September 2020 and at least some planned to stick with it.[26]

Leaving the labor force had an immediate impact on family earnings. In the February 2021 Making Ends Meet survey, 9.1 percent of households had experienced a significant drop in income because someone worked less or stopped working to take care of children. And 7.4 percent of households reported a significant income drop because someone worked less to care for others who were sick or injured.

While many mothers who left the workforce or cut back on hours eventually returned to work, the break in employment will have long-term negative consequences. To understand why, it is useful to understand how the gender wage gap—the gap in hourly pay between men and women—arises in the first place. The gender wage gap had been narrowing until recently. But one of the biggest remaining contributors to the wage gap is that many of the highest-paying professions still reward inflexible and high work hours.[27] These professions, which Claire Cain Miller memorably called the "greedy professions," demand complete loyalty and the willingness to work long hours and give up other life goals such as family flexibility.[28]

To understand these greedy professions and how the pandemic is likely to affect the gender pay gap, consider two professions:

- The gender pay gap is large among lawyers and is even larger at the highest-earning law firms.[29] The billable hour, an hour charged to a client that earns the firm money, typically rules in these law firms. For the partners who run the firm, who are still mostly male, even though law school graduates have been more than half female since 2016,[30] more hours mean more money. For them, even the best lawyer who needs to work only 50 hours a week, or needs to stay home occasionally with sick kids, hurts their profits. Gender norms mean women are more likely to seek this flexibility or need to work limited hours. Promotions to partner tend to go to those who bill the most (or who play golf with the partners on the weekend, a different kind of work), so while men and women lawyers may earn similar amounts initially, the pay gap widens as men are promoted. (And, of course, there is explicit and implicit gender discrimination, although that is likely a smaller portion of the gap.)[31] Many female lawyers, even if they start out at the top-earning law firms, move to more flexible but lower-paying jobs in corporations and government. This same pattern holds in many "greedy professions," where there is an overwork premium.[32]
- Pharmacists have one of the smallest gender pay gaps. As research by Claudia Goldin and Lawrence Katz shows, the most important reason is that technology has made it easy for pharmacists to

substitute for one another.[33] Pharmacists who want to work part time, or take a shift schedule that allows them to pick kids up from school, earn almost the same per hour worked as pharmacists who work standard hours. There is no penalty to flexibility.

Pharmacists still get paid less if they work fewer hours, but they do not get paid less per hour. Lawyers do. Because pharmacist-like professions are still not the norm, for most women, especially the most highly paid ones, time away or reduced hours can reduce wages substantially and harm promotion opportunities, leading to a growing wage gap as they age.

The women who left their jobs, reduced their hours, or stopped looking for a new job during the pandemic because of child care will thus tend to face a long-term drop in earnings for two reasons. One reason is that, in the greedy professions, once someone is off track, it is very difficult to get back on and there are large wage penalties for reduced hours or time off. The career-making case went to someone else. The client or customer list is no longer current. Second, skills and experience tend to diminish when they are not being used. These two reasons suggest there will be long-term consequences from these short-term employment disruptions.

Based on estimates of earnings trajectories from previous recessions, one economic model predicts that because women not working lose some experience, the pandemic will increase the gender pay gap by 5 percent.[34] Because the gender wage gap had been narrowing before the pandemic,[35] the predicted pandemic increase will erase a decade or more of progress.

Millions of dreams were delayed as women took a step back from careers. Between two and three million mothers were no longer employed or looking for a job in October 2020 who had been employed before the pandemic.[36] Women with careers they were building as they gained experience. Or whose families needed that second income but had decided they could make do. And while the decision to leave work to take care of children was a heavily female one, some fathers did the same. Faced with difficult choices, these parents made the best choice available for themselves and their families. The best choice available was still costly.

Unemployment Scarring

Leaving the workforce to take care of children can have long-term negative effects on earnings. Economists call such effects "scarring" because the initial "wound" leaves a permanent scar on wages and life circumstances. Employment scarring can also occur for people without children. Anyone who loses his or her job can suffer long-term consequences. These consequences tend to increase the longer someone is unemployed.

A typical definition of long-term unemployment is someone who has been unemployed for more than six months. An important limitation here that has come up before is that unemployment requires actively looking for a job. Women who left the labor force or people who become discouraged and stop looking likely have similar scarring effects but are not counted as long-term unemployed because they are not, technically, unemployed. In February 2020, 19 percent of unemployed had been unemployed for 27 weeks or longer (Figure 9.3).[37] While many of these people likely remained unemployed, the long-term unemployment rate dropped sharply as millions joined the unemployment ranks. Some were soon hired back, but for many, the pandemic wore on and on. By April 2021, 44 percent of the unemployed had been without a job for at least six months; 29 percent had been unemployed for at least a year. As more people were hired through 2021, the unemployment rate came down, but the share of long-term unemployed remained high. As of October 2021, 24 percent of unemployed had been unemployed for a year of more, 1.7 million people. Many had likely been unemployed the entire pandemic.

Any period of unemployment can have long-term consequences for a person's career. Unemployment is not like a line at a coffee shop where the first arrival gets served first; the first people fired are not the first hired, they are often the last to get hired. Past unemployment is one of the best predictors of future unemployment.[38] When people who invol-

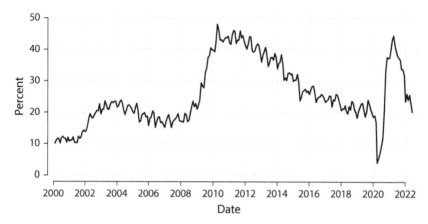

FIGURE 9.3. The share of those unemployed for more than six months increased rapidly but then fell to its prepandemic level. (Percentage of unemployed who are unemployed 27 weeks or over, not seasonally adjusted. *Source:* Bureau of Labor Statistics.)

untarily lost their jobs take new jobs, the new jobs tend to pay less and be less stable. Long-term unemployment tends to be particularly bad for the next job, when it finally comes. Wages on reemployment fall the longer someone is unemployed. Much of the evidence for these problems comes from the Great Recession, which had a similar spike in long-term unemployment that had still not returned to prerecession levels at the pandemic's start. Figure 9.3 shows this slow path down as well as the pandemic's spike in long-term unemployment.

Long-term unemployment may directly negatively affect future earnings. It is also probable that people who are more likely to be long-term unemployed have poorer earnings prospects already, so it is not always easy to clearly distinguish why earnings for the long-term unemployed are lower even after reemployment.[39] One reason long-term unemployment might harm earnings is that skills deteriorate over time. Another may be stigma. Perhaps if you have big holes in your employment history, employers may wonder whether you are reliable. As important, but difficult to study, may be social networks. The vast majority of jobs are filled through networking.[40] For example, a company's internal posting results in an internal hire before the job is even posted externally. Many employed are constantly meeting other people with jobs in their own company and talking to clients and customers, so they are likely to learn about new openings. These contacts and references are still fresh for the recently unemployed, but they diminish the longer someone is out of a job, making it harder to get the next one.

The long-term unemployment scarring may be less bad during the pandemic. Partly, any reasonable employer who looks at unemployment starting in March or April 2020 will understand what happened (although many employers are not reasonable and rely on poorly designed automatic résumé screening). More broadly, long-term unemployment's negative consequences often stem from the income lost because of unemployment. As Chapter 7 shows, while pandemic policies had starts and stops and unemployment insurance often took some time to reach people, the average unemployed person was actually more financially secure during the pandemic than they had been before.

During the Great Recession, long-term unemployment lingered for years; it had only just returned to the prerecession low in 2018. In contrast, while long-term unemployment spiked during the pandemic, it quickly receded and was back to the prepandemic level by June 2022. Some of this decline was because of the tight labor market we will discuss in the next chapter, which meant that many people who wanted a job could find one. But some was because there were fewer people actively looking for a job. They had retired or were home with the kids or were still worried about getting sick. The percentage of the population employed was still 1.3 percentage points lower in February 2022 than in February 2020 (see Figure 2.1). Around four million people were still struggling to find work or had left the labor force because of the pandemic.

Millennials, the Unluckiest Generation

Even before the pandemic, the millennials were already "the unluckiest generation," a term used by Derek Thompson, writing in the *Atlantic* in 2013.[41] At the time, the 2008 financial crisis and the subsequent recession were over, but employment and wages were inching up very slowly.

Millennials, who were just entering the job market or were early in their careers, were having the most difficult time. During the pandemic, they would experience the second economic crisis of their working lives.

Generations are broad groupings of people born about the same time. In research, a group of people born in the same year is called a cohort. A "generational cohort" is the combination of cohorts born over approximately 20 years. Generations and these broad cohort groups are often referred to interchangeably.

Generations are used to broadly describe the common experiences of a group of people of about the same age. Often there is some formative event that most people in a generation experienced. For example, as Tom Brokaw called them, the "greatest generation" served in World War II and rebuilt the world afterward.[42] Pew Research defines more recent generations as the baby boomers, who were born from 1946 to 1964; Generation X, who were born between 1965 and 1980; and the millennial generation, who were born between 1981 and 1996.[43] Of course, there is not much of a difference between the experiences of the cohort born in 1981 and part of the millennial generation and the cohort born in 1980 and part of Gen X. These two cohorts likely have more in common with each other than with the cohort born in 1996. Still, these broad groupings are useful for summarizing the experiences of people of about the same age.

Entering the workforce during a recession can permanently reduce wages and job prospects. There are several reasons why being a member of a "recession cohort"—a group that starts working life during a recession—can cause long-term problems. First, taking longer to find a job leaves recession cohorts with less experience. Second, they may accept a lower wage when they do find a job, which leaves them with lower bargaining power for the next job, and so may hurt earnings for a long time. Third, people in recession cohorts may have fewer job choices and so may not be able to take the job best suited to their talents. They thus have less room for growth. These factors also influence anybody affected by a recession, but the impact tends to be the largest for the people with the least experience who are just entering the workforce, the recession cohort.

The combined impact of these factors is stark; compared with people who started working just before a recession, recession cohorts earn less initially and may never catch up, so their lifetime earnings are lower.[44] They are less likely to marry. They have higher death rates and more deaths of despair from drug overdoses and alcohol (see Chapter 7). These effects seem even more pronounced for high school graduates who start working during a recession than for college graduates.[45] A college education seems to inoculate its recipients against many of society's woes.

Millennials were just starting their working lives during the Great Recession and its aftermath. The oldest millennials were 28 in 2009 while the youngest were 13. Even though the Great Recession ended in June 2009, the unemployment rate did not drop to below 5 percent—a loose measure of a "strong" labor market—until the end of 2015. Nearly every millennial was therefore early in her working career or just graduating high school and college during a high-unemployment era. Economist Lisa Kahn's work on the 1981–82 recession suggests that college students graduating into a recession can expect to earn permanently lower wages. The effects are large: for every 1 percentage point increase in the unemployment rate, initial wages are about 7 percent lower and wages 15 years later are still 2.5 percent lower.[46] Recent work on millennials' experience following the Great Recession has suggested that the scarring effects remain large.[47] The combined effect of earning less for decades and a higher likelihood to be unemployed mean that even if the effects fade eventually, the millennials who entered the workforce with high unemployment will earn hundreds of thousands of dollars less in their lifetimes.

To put some perspective on the differences, on average the total earnings over the first 15 years of their working lives would be $200,000 greater for someone who started working in 2007 than in 2009 using Kahn's estimates.[48] That is the cost of a down payment for a house in an expensive metro area or the cost of a house in a less expensive area. It is the cost of a college education for a child.

On top of this already tough situation arising from the Great Recession, the pandemic hit millennials again, just as they should have been entering the highest earning potential of their lives. Andrew Van Dam, writing in the *Washington Post*, calculated that with the pandemic, millennials have experienced the lowest economic growth of any generation ever.[49] The pandemic helped millennials fall behind the "lost generation" (1883–1900), who experienced the Great Depression. The average growth rate experienced by the greatest generation was more than three times higher.

The pandemic unemployment was also particularly hard on the workforce's youngest members. Millennial employment fell by more than older generations', and the employment of Generation Z (the generation born after 1996) fell by even more.

It is too early to tell whether Gen Z's pandemic scarring will be as bad as millennials' Great Recession scarring. The pandemic was deep, but high unemployment did not last long compared with the Great Recession. The remarkably different policy approaches during the pandemic compared with the Great Recession may prevent the scars from being too severe during the pandemic. But it is likely that some scarring will still occur.

Zoom School

Perhaps you tried to sing happy birthday on a video call during the pandemic. My family did. It does not work. It turns out that the small delay at either end makes synchronizing impossible, so grandma is about two seconds behind everyone else. The technical term for it is "audio latency," and it was a killer for all musicians during the pandemic. The workaround for professionals, according to David Pogue at *Wired*, is no workaround at all: "The musicians film themselves playing their parts individually, at home, on their phones. Then some poor, exhausted editor assembles their videos into a unified grid."[50] Everyone making music together during the pandemic went through some sort of similar process As the pandemic progressed, new innovations appeared, making it easier as we learned to muddle through.[51]

So imagine if you are a new teacher in a prekindergarten classroom, trying to conduct classes online. How do you get kids to sing together with the video lag? To take turns, for each of which they have to mute and unmute themselves? To learn to work together positively with other children? After all, as a Brookings Institution report on prekindergarten found, "developmental science tells us that a key ingredient is the instructional, social, and emotional 'serve-and-return' interactions that occur daily between teachers and children, as well as among classmates."[52] How do you teach when the core reason for prekindergarten is to prepare kids socially, but they are not only socially distanced but interacting only onscreen?

Students and teachers at every grade level and through graduate school faced a similar conundrum: How do we teach well remotely? School's socialization role is most apparent for the youngest grades. But even older students benefit from their classmates. And teachers, professors, and administrators had to figure out how to teach and what to teach remotely. For most educators, remote learning was entirely new.

Millions of children spent the end of the 2019–20 school year and much of the 2020–21 school year taking classes either entirely or mostly online. Many others slipped through in various ways, attending only some classes if any.

The disruptions reduced education significantly. One research team at the consulting firm McKinsey estimated that the pandemic reduced the average student's progress by five months in mathematics and four months in reading.[53] Put a different way, it was as if the school year was about four to five months shorter than normal. They measured the learning gap by comparing test scores across 40 states in the spring of 2021 with the test scores of similar students before the pandemic. Most of the learning gap occurred in the first several months of the pandemic when schools hurriedly shut down. Based on the McKinsey estimates, no progress in math occurred in the final three months of the 2019–20 school year. But in the new school year, the estimates suggest that most schools were more effective despite the challenges. Still, the learning gap increased by another two months over the 2020–21 school year.

Other research points to a similar conclusion: students made about half the progress one would expect over the 2020–21 school year. NWEA is a nonprofit that creates assessments to measure students' achievement and growth. It examined the results of a computer adaptive test (a test given on a computer that gets harder or easier depending on whether students answer questions correctly) given to 5.5 million third through eighth graders in the spring 2021.[54] The reading and math progress across all grades in the 2020–21 school year was about half as large as in previous years. The more time elementary students spent learning remotely, the more they fell behind.[55] Other studies suggest that little to no academic progress occurred at the end of the 2019–20 school year.[56] Many school districts reported that failing grades increased by a third in fall 2020.[57]

This lost education will likely have large negative consequences on students' earnings later in life. Education economists Eric Hanushek and Ludger Woessmann summarized the evidence from prior learning loss episodes.[58] The evidence that lost instruction time reduces education outcomes is based on several natural experiments when external events treated otherwise similar students differently. For example, when teachers strike, students in the striking schools lose instruction time compared with students in nonstriking schools. Based on strikes in Belgium, Argentina, and Canada, the affected students have permanently lower educational attainment and lower salaries once they become adults.[59] In another natural experiment, the German government standardized when school started across states in 1966 and 1967. To make the transition, states whose school year started in the spring had to shorten their school years to transition to a fall start. Compared with students in other states, the students who experience shorter school years had lower earnings when they were adults.[60]

Using episodes such as these, Hanushek and Woessmann calculate that if students lose half a school year, their lifetime earnings will be 4.6 percent lower. The McKinsey and NWEA estimates suggest that students finished the 2021 school year about half a year behind, on average. So the average student affected by pandemic schooling is likely to earn around 4.6 percent less over her lifetime than she would without the pandemic. This number may seem small, but consider that one estimate puts the median lifetime income around $2.2 million in today's dollars,[61] so the lost education cost the average student around

$100,000 in lifetime earnings. There are around 50 million kindergarten through 12 graders, so the total pandemic lost earnings add up to around $5 trillion over their lifetimes.

Lower education harms the student, but it also harms economic growth. The relationship between economic growth and education is not as straightforward as the relationship between individual earnings and education. In one direction, if more education improves skills and innovation, more education increases economic growth. In the other direction, education may just be what economists call "costly signaling." Students can show future employers they are likely to be productive by completing school, but the education does not improve their productivity, it just shows they are good at sitting still and following instructions. Assuming that the productivity and innovation effects are substantial, Hanushek and Woessmann calculate that the half-school-year reduction will reduce future GDP by 2.2 percent. Adding these losses year after year produces stunning numbers: $22 trillion in lost output.[62] While this calculation is sensitive to the underlying assumptions, so the actual amount could be very different, the underlying message is not: over the long term, we are all much poorer because of the lost education.

The average pandemic learning loss is already bad enough, but the learning loss was concentrated in poorer areas and areas with more Black students. As the authors of the McKinsey study put it, "Students in majority-Black schools ended the school year six months behind in both math and reading, while students in majority-white schools ended up just four months behind in math and three months behind in reading."[63] Students in majority-Black schools were already more likely to be behind, so the pandemic worsened existing educational gaps.

The NWEA study found similar gaps. Students of all races and ethnicities had declines relative to the progress they would have made in previous years. Black and Hispanic students in third through eighth grades lost almost twice as much progress as white or Asian students in reading and nearly that much in math.[64] The combined effect is to nearly double the preexisting math and reading score differences between white students compared with Black, Hispanic, and Native American students. Because the education gap was larger, the long-term earnings impact will be larger for these already disadvantaged students, worsening inequality.[65]

Maybe pandemic students will eventually catch up. Many school districts have tried to increase summer school in 2021.[66] The American Rescue Plan Act included $122 billion for school districts to help close some of the learning gaps and pay for pandemic costs. School districts used some of the money to increase summer school, individual instruction for students falling behind, and tutoring.[67]

Yet the evidence from prior lost-education episodes suggests there will be little catch-up. Many disadvantaged students were already behind. And the students who need to catch up the most are the least likely to get additional support, despite the best efforts of educators. For example, early in the pandemic, parents in high-income areas were far more likely to seek out online learning resources as schools closed.[68] This parental involvement likely explains a significant portion of the difference in learning loss between high-income and low-income areas. High-income parents were more likely to continue to work from home and have the time and resources to help their children close the learning gap. In short, the pandemic learning gap may close for white and high-income students but remain or widen for other students. The long-term consequences for these children and for society will be large.

The Long Term

This chapter moves approximately in reverse order, starting from the early retirees, moving through mothers and the labor force, and ending with schoolchildren. The pandemic affected each group differently, but there is a common theme: What happens when we take a year or more out of your life, keeping you from progressing? Retirees who wanted to work for another year to build up retirement savings. Mothers who left the labor force and will find it hard to go back to their careers. Long-term unemployed with a gap on their résumé. Millennials who have had another year or two of savings and income growth cut from their lives. Children who lost half a year of education. All lost some progress toward the next stage of their education, careers, or life goals.

Chapter 2 examined the economy's Great Pause starting in March 2020. The pause extended into our lives in many ways. It often stopped us from progressing to the next stage of our lives, sometimes even pushing us backward. Some of the effects will dissipate. But we are not getting the pandemic years back, and this chapter shows just some of the many ways the pandemic will stay with us. Let's now turn to the pandemic's messy immediate aftermath.

Winona

Things were looking good for Winona in June 2019. She lived in a metro-politan area on the East Coast with her husband and two children. Winona, a millennial in her early thirties, identified as a Native American. She and her husband both worked full time and their income in 2018 was around $60,000.

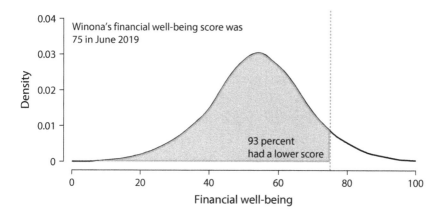

Winona had completed a two-year college degree, likely what is called an associate's degree. Many skilled professions, especially in medical areas, require such a degree. For example, medical sonographers, MRI technicians, and dental hygienists may be required to have an associate's degree in one of these fields. A degree does not guarantee a job but can be a valuable qualification in an expanding field.

With two good incomes, Winona and her husband were building a stable financial foundation. Their household income was stable from month to month, so they did not have to worry much about income variability. They had built up a nice financial cushion, with $5,000 to $10,000 in their checking accounts. They bought a house a year ago. The mortgage payments were well within their income, giving them some financial flexibility. They had retire-ment accounts. Everyone in the household had health insurance.

In 2019, Winona and her husband were saving regularly by putting money aside each month. Because of this saving, they had substantial financial resilience. Winona reported they could cover all of an unexpected $2,000 expense within a week, for example, and could cover expenses for two months even if they lost their main source of income. They had not had difficulty paying any bills or expenses.

Capturing this, Winona's financial well-being score was 75 in June 2019, higher than 93 percent of the population. Echoing this optimism, Winona said that she expected to go on a vacation and buy a car in the next six months.

Early in the Pandemic

Winona was still employed in June 2020, as was her husband, but her financial outlook had darkened considerably. Perhaps her employer had shut down but tried to keep paying the staff. For example, if her employer received a Paycheck Protection Program loan, her employer would have been required to maintain payroll. Even if her employer received such a loan, it may have been clear to the staff that it was unsustainable to keep paying them unless the office reopened.

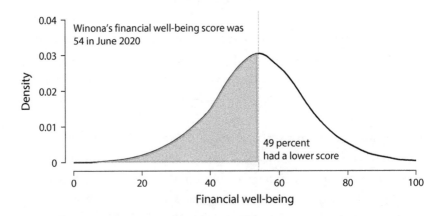

Because of their extensive financial cushion and because they were both still employed, the pandemic had not yet affected them financially. Winona did not report an immediate difficulty paying a bill or expense. But from her responses, it was clear that she was much more worried about their finances. In a big change from the previous year, she felt that her finances controlled her life. Her financial well-being score dropped from 75 in June 2019, among the highest scores, to 54, about the average score.

Late in the Pandemic

By February 2021, Winona's financial situation had deteriorated. She had stopped working because her children's school or daycare had closed and she decided to stay home to take care of the kids. Her husband was still employed. Winona did not report receiving any unemployment insurance. Perhaps she was ineligible because she "voluntarily" left the labor force. Her family likely would have received $5,800 from the CARES Act and the December 2020 relief bill. While their savings had not gone down much, their income had, so Winona felt like her financial situation was no longer nearly as secure. Capturing this change, her financial well-being score declined again. They looked for ways to cut back on food expenses, for example. Judging by her credit card spending, their family was still cutting back through 2021.

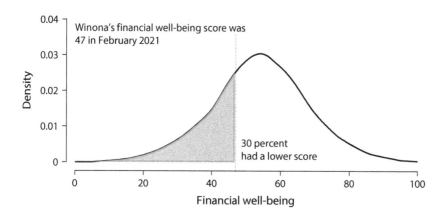

Unlike some of the families described in earlier chapters, Winona's family did not suffer acute financial hardship. Instead, faced with a difficult situation about child care, Winona left the career she had been building to take care of her kids. Going from two incomes to one income was hard on the family, but they had a sufficient financial cushion to weather some problems. The hardest part was the change in trajectory. Winona went from feeling as though she had it all to having to make difficult choices to protect her family.

10

Struggling Back to (a New?) Normal

IN JULY 2021, the group that officially determines the dates of U.S. recessions announced that the pandemic recession had ended in April 2020. The pandemic recession lasted only two months, making it the shortest recession on record.[1] The term "recession" is used popularly to mean "bad economic times," but economists take its meaning literally to be the time from economic peak to trough. In April 2020, the economy stopped "receding," so we were no longer in a recession. Just because things were generally moving in a positive direction after April 2020 does not mean that they were good, just that they were not getting any worse.

While the pandemic recession was short, the lingering economic effects rippled out. Like a giant rock thrown into a pond, the massive economic changes at the pandemic's beginning caused big dislocations. As the pandemic wore on, the waves spread, reached the pond's edge, and reflected back, interacting with each other. Sometimes the pandemic's waves offset, but sometimes they built on each other, producing unexpectedly large effects. Some of the waves will have lasting impacts in surprising ways, as we discussed in the last chapter. Others will die out. One of the most powerful but unexpected waves occurred in the labor market.

In October 2021, workers at Deere & Company went on strike for the first time since 1986. John Deere is a giant farm and construction

equipment manufacturer that makes the iconic green John Deere trac-
tors. The 10,000 union members had twice rejected new contracts
with significant pay increases. Deere workers had continued through
the pandemic, so when the first contract offer was only a 6 percent
raise, one union member described it as a "joke."[2] The final contract
included larger pay increases and bonuses. In a statement following
the union vote that ratified the contract, United Auto Workers president Ray Curry said, "UAW John Deere members did not just unite
themselves, they seemed to unite the nation in a struggle for fairness
in the workplace."[3]

How is it that after years of decline and stagnant wages and the employment devastation at the beginning of the pandemic, labor was in
its strongest position in 40 years? The proximate cause was a tighter
labor market as the pandemic ended. Employers struggled to find
workers across many industries in 2021. The tight labor market had
many repercussions: on pay, on job hopping, on inflation, and on
shortages and supply chain problems as the economy struggled back
to a new normal.

Why the labor market was so tight is more complicated. There are
several partial explanations. One is that child care was still difficult to
find, making it difficult for many parents, particularly mothers, to return
to work. Child care is an example of waves building on each other: in a
tight labor market, it is difficult and more expensive to find child care
providers, which limits the options of parents who need child care and
contributes to a tight labor market. Another reason is that many older
workers had retired, as we discussed in the previous chapter, and did
not seem to want to return. Lingering COVID-19 concerns also likely
contributed to keeping many workers, especially older ones, from wanting to return.

But something deeper also seemed to be happening. The pandemic
gave many people a chance to reset what they wanted from life and
work. The reset occurred in different ways. After being furloughed or
unemployed for months, many people realized that their old jobs were
awful. For years, many employers had pushed risks onto workers while
not increasing pay, leaving many jobs stressful, unpleasant, and with

uncertain earnings. More fundamentally, because of the risks and low pay, many jobs were not serving the primary purpose of working—providing for your family. And even for those who liked their jobs before the pandemic, being furloughed was a reminder that your workplace is not a family. Your family does not fire you when times are hard. Many employers had abused workers' sense of loyalty before the pandemic, pushing workers for more and more hours and sacrifices, but not offering more compensation. Furloughs broke the sense for many employees that they owed any loyalty, beyond the strict contractual kind, to their employers.

Many workers who kept their jobs were also burned out after more than a year of reinventing work. Healthcare workers are the leading example. Their long hours, the additional risks, and the stress of caring for others who were in distress and dying led many to feel overwhelmed. Many quit.[4] But hours increased for people working from home as did child care responsibilities, so people in other industries were feeling burned out as well. As many employers pushed workers to return to the office in person, some employees realized that they preferred working from home and quit or pushed back.[5]

Like Herman Melville's Bartleby, many workers looked at going back or continuing to work at unsatisfying jobs with low pay and said, "I would prefer not to." Stories about quitting in spectacular fashion spread, as many workers finally got to tell their bosses what they really thought of them.[6] Many of the stories are about one too many sudden shift changes or an abusive scheduling system. In Chapter 3, we saw that one of the big problems Americans faced before the pandemic was variable income. Changing shifts and work hours were a big part of the problem. As was low pay.

This chapter presents events as they unfolded through summer 2022, so it can only capture some of the massive pandemic waves that continued to ripple out. As inflation continued to be high, the Federal Reserve started raising interest rates. Russia's invasion of Ukraine in February 2022 produced supply shocks through oil and food markets reminiscent of those in the 1970s even as pandemic supply issues started to ease. The job market continued to be tight but other economic indicators suggested a looming recession. It all added up to a complicated and uncertain economic outlook as pandemic waves crashed and new storms appeared.

The End of Pandemic Policies

The economic changes as the pandemic wound down were closely related to the end of pandemic support policies. Some policies, such as the three Economic Impact Payments, occurred more or less all at once, but others, such as expanded unemployment benefits, wound down slowly. Previous chapters discus the impacts of these programs in greater detail, so here I focus on how and when they ended and the evidence for what happened as they ended.

As economic activity picked up in the summer of 2021, 25 states stopped offering the expanded $300 unemployment insurance benefit from the American Rescue Plan Act early. The entire program ended in September 2021. The stated reason for ending expanded unemployment insurance was that, as we will discuss next, job openings surged and employers were finding it difficult to fill positions in spring and summer 2021. Cutting off expanded unemployment benefits would encourage the unemployed to get back to work.[7]

The staggered end to the program gives a useful comparison group for understanding unemployment insurance in the short term. By comparing the states that cut off expanded unemployment insurance with those that did not, it is possible to estimate how much unemployment insurance was holding back employment in the short term. The answer that several research groups reached was that expanded unemployment insurance was not holding back employment much. Depending on how and whether individual state characteristics are dealt with, the states that ended expanded unemployment insurance early saw only a tiny increase in employment or a slight *decrease* compared with states that waited until September.[8] The unemployed who lost all benefits, not just the extra $300 from the American Rescue Plan, were somewhat more likely to transition to work.[9] By looking at anonymous bank account transactions, one research team isolated the spending impact of the unemployment insurance cutoff.[10] They found a slight increase in employment from the unemployment insurance cutoff. But the unemployed in the early states lost far more income from benefit cuts than the relatively few who became employed earned. As a result, spending for people unemployed in April 2021 in early cutoff states fell by 20 percent compared with late cutoff states. Overall, the research tells a consistent story: The unemployed in early cutoff states were worse off and were only slightly more likely to get a job. They spent less, hurting the early cutoff states' economies.

These differences between states were all in the short term. The additional $300 benefit ended for all states in September 2021. Moreover, because of unemployment insurance, Economic Impact Payments, and individual spending cuts, many unemployed had a substantial financial cushion. The early cutoffs may not have had much effect in the short term because of this cushion. With some savings, people could afford to be choosy and not jump at the first job they came across.

The federal eviction moratorium also ended at the end of August 2021, although its end was a messy and drawn-out affair. A Supreme Court ruling in June ended the first Centers for Disease Control and Prevention moratorium as of the end of July. The Centers for Disease Control and Prevention issued a new moratorium on August 3, which the Supreme Court struck down on August 26.[11] Several states and local governments continued moratoria through the end of the year. As we saw in Chapter 7, after the moratorium ended, evictions started to increase slowly.

Other programs also ended through the fall of 2021, although there is not yet evidence on what happened because they ended. Most federally backed loans had an eighteen-month limit for mortgage forbearance (the exact details differ by who is backing the loan). Most people who applied for forbearance did so early in the pandemic, largely in April 2020 after the CARES Act was passed, so about three-quarters of mortgages that had gone into forbearance exited forbearance by the end of September 2021.[12] For most loans, it was still possible to apply for forbearance while there was a national emergency, which continued through at least 2021. But as the pandemic wore on, fewer mortgages entered forbearance and more exited.

Meanwhile, the student loan payment pause was extended again and again so it was unclear when and whether it would end.[13] When it was extended a final time, through the end of 2022, the Department of Education announced it would cancel up to $10,000 in student loans for most borrowers.[14] Many people, such as Sofia in the introduction who had student debt but had not completed her degree, would have their entire debt canceled. The median borrower saved $133 a month due to the payment freeze, but many had substantially higher savings.[15]

Pay, Hiring, and the "Great Resignation"

Through the summer of 2021, a media narrative took hold: Americans were quitting in great numbers, fed up with poor working conditions and bad pay. There is some truth to the narrative and some exaggeration, but the narrative touched an important underlying trend that was broader than the quit rate. Americans were quitting at slightly higher rates than normal, but they had also been quitting at lower rates since March 2020, so much of it was just catching up. Far more important was the overall tightness of the labor market, which caused pay and other incentives to increase to bring people back into the labor force and allowed many people to switch to a new employer. Together, these trends show the start of a profound change. For the first time in at least forty years, rather than getting weaker, labor was getting stronger.

Since the 1980s, the amount the median American earns has been nearly flat. Meanwhile, U.S. income per person has nearly doubled. Figure 10.1 shows these diverging trends, which together illustrate how the average person has not shared in U.S. economic growth for the last forty years.[16] Gross domestic product per person grew by 93 percent from 1980 through 2019 after adjusting for inflation. Although there are some slight differences based on income earned abroad, GDP per person is a close approximation of how much income we would get if we took the income created by all economic activity and divided it evenly. Meanwhile, the median wage adjusted for inflation increased only 13 percent from 1980 through 2019.[17]

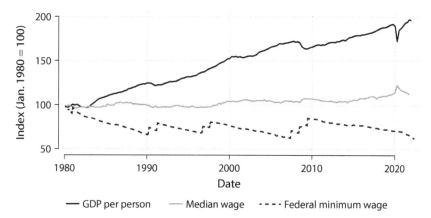

FIGURE 10.1. Real GDP per person has nearly doubled while real median wages have barely changed, and the real minimum wage fell. (GDP per person, median wage, and the federal minimum wage, adjusted for inflation and indexed to 1980. *Source*: Author's calculations from Bureau of Labor Statistics, Bureau of Economic Analysis, and Department of Labor.)

These differences understate the divergence in important ways. The earnings are for wage or salary workers, but we saw in Chapter 2 that the share of the population working had been decreasing, so fewer people are earning any wages at all. Many, but not all, of the people not working would earn below median wage if they were employed—pulling down the average. This change in the composition may seem minor, but who is employed can have a big effect. For example, the sharp increase in median wages at the start of the pandemic is not something to celebrate. It occurred because low-wage workers in retail and hospitality were the most likely to be laid off. The workers who remained earned more than the workers who were laid off, so median wages rose.

One reason median wages have not increased is that the federal minimum wage adjusted for inflation has been declining. Figure 10.1 shows this decline. The federal minimum wage is worth only two-thirds of what it was in the 1980s. Many states have higher state minimum wages, so the federal minimum wage is not necessarily the lowest wage that can be paid. But the federal minimum wage's decline means that rather than feeling pushed to raise wages, employers feel less and less pressure from the wage floor.

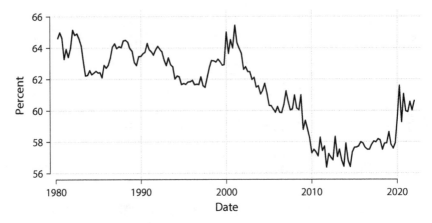

FIGURE 10.2. Labor's share of national income had been declining, but it increased sharply during the pandemic. (*Source*: Author's calculations from Bureau of Labor Statistics.)

The share of national income that goes to paying for labor has been declining since at least the 1980s, with a very sharp decline after 2000. Figure 10.2 shows this decline, although it is surprisingly hard to pin down.[18] Most people's largest income source is from selling their labor. So the declining labor share means that, even as the economic pie has been getting bigger in Figure 10.1, the share that gets divided up among working people has been declining.

In its simplest sense, the labor share is the percentage of total economic outcome that gets paid as compensation for labor rather than to capital. When someone owns a business, they pay their employees, rent space, buy equipment and raw materials, and pay other expenses. The amount paid to employees is the labor share. Everything else is payment for someone who owns "capital." Rent is a payment for land and buildings. The profits to the owner are from her ownership of the business (sometimes offset by the amount she is paying herself).

Of course, there are big differences among wage earners between, for example, the well-paid physician employed by the local hospital and a waiter at a nearby chain restaurant who earns a minimum cash wage of $2.13 plus tips.[19] Both work for wages, so both the physician and the waiter are included in the labor share in Figure 10.2, although the physi-

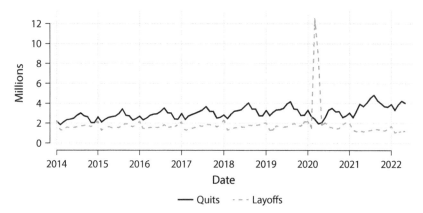

FIGURE 10.3. After being laid off in 2020, more Americans started quitting in 2021. (Total monthly quits and layoffs. Not seasonally adjusted. *Source:* Bureau of Labor Statistics.)

cian earns a lot more. The physician has largely shared in the growth in Figure 10.1, while the waiter has not. Because the trends for these two groups are not the same—the highest earners have been doing better, soaking up a larger income share—Figure 10.2 understates the share that has been going to most people.

Against this backdrop of weakening labor, the pandemic reset our relationships with work. In the spring of 2021, job openings shot up as employers tried to hire, often unsuccessfully. More people started quitting, often to take a new job with better pay or benefits. To attract people and keep their employees, employers started offering better wages and negotiating over benefits like work-from-home that previously would have been nonnegotiable. The U.S. is a big country with a giant economy, so many of these changes are subtle in context. But together they mark an inflection point for labor against the long-term downward trend.

Americans are constantly flowing into and out of jobs. Figure 10.3 shows how many people quit or were laid off each month.[20] A big layoff spike occurred in March and April 2020 when around twenty-two million people were laid off. Outside of that spike, around two million people were laid off every month, with layoffs typically peaking as the holiday retail season winds down. Before the pandemic, between three and four million people voluntarily left their jobs each month. Quits typically swing predictably through the year, peaking around August. As is common during tough economic times, as lots of people were fired, fewer people also quit in 2020 than normal.

In 2021, more and more people started quitting; 3.9 million in April 2021, increasing to 4.9 million in August. Most of these quits were just catching up. People who had stayed in their jobs in 2020 because it was a bad year to look for a job decided that a move made sense in 2021. There were actually more total quits from January 2018 through August 2019 than from January 2020 through August 2021. Still, the number of quits was at an all-time high in August 2021, although it was only 800,000 more quits than in the previous high in August 2019.

Yet news coverage of the "Great Resignation" was suddenly everywhere. That term, coined by management professor Anthony Klotz in an interview with *Bloomberg Businessweek* on how to quit your job,[21] captured a feeling.[22] Part of it was burned-out workers who had stayed in their jobs longer than they wanted—captured by the lower quits early in the pandemic. But part of it was that workers were reassessing what they wanted from jobs. They were pushing back for better conditions with the jobs they had and moving when their employers would not negotiate.

Emblematic of the changes, and of the mood in summer 2021, was the message a large group of employees at a Burger King in Lincoln, Nebraska, left on the big sign out front: "We all quit—Sorry for the inconvenience." The mass quit followed months of hard conditions from the pandemic and from a broken air conditioner that sent at least one employee to the hospital for dehydration.[23] Rachel Flores, the location manager, finally could not take it anymore and put in her two-week notice. When she did, the entire morning crew did the same and put up the huge sign for everyone to see. The employees had finally reached their breaking point. They were chronically understaffed, so Flores was often working back-to-back open-to-close shifts from 5:30 a.m. to 1:00 a.m. And the franchise owners resisted any pay increases to help compensate for the understaffing. "It was just a slap in the face," Flores said.[24] Pictures of the sign went everywhere, capturing a mood. As one of the quitting workers said, "Almost everyone that I know that left has found better jobs making at least the same or more."[25]

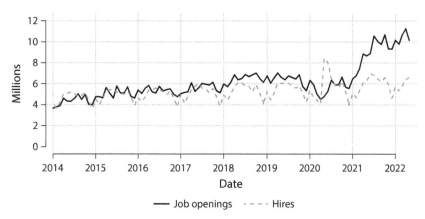

FIGURE 10.4. Hires increased, but not as fast as job openings. (Total monthly hires and job openings. Not seasonally adjusted. *Source*: Bureau of Labor Statistics.)

Workers felt confident quitting because it was suddenly easy to get new, possibly better, jobs. Figure 10.4 shows the number of hires and the number of job openings (on the same scale as Figure 10.3).[26] There was a surge in hires several months into the pandemic as employers restaffed after furloughing or laying off workers. But then, in 2021, the hires increased rapidly. Job openings increased even faster as employers tried to expand.

While hires, quits, and layoffs represent concrete actions by employers and workers that affect both, job openings are more like an expression of employer hiring sentiment. The survey that measures job openings asks whether employers have a position available that they are actively recruiting for.[27] But an employer may or may not have realistic expectations for the pay or qualifications necessary to attract prospective employees. Job openings are just expressions of interest by employers until a hire occurs and employer and employee reach agreement on wages. Still, job openings surged past ten million in August 2021, indicating that employers were seeking to fill a very large number of jobs.

The labor market was extremely tight through 2021 and into 2022, as Figures 10.3 and 10.4 illustrate. Employers wanted to hire. Layoffs were way down. Employees were quitting and taking new jobs at a higher rate. Anecdotal evidence suggests that these trends reinforced each other. As some workers quit, employers put more work on other workers. As their jobs got harder, these workers quit or were lured away by better offers from stressed managers desperate to hire at some other employer.[28] While it is difficult to assess how important this dynamic was, it certainly felt real to many workers. Surveys showed that a large fraction of employees were thinking of quitting or changing careers.[29] Many carried through, as the quits in Figure 10.3 showed.

At the end of 2021, the labor force (the employed plus people looking for jobs) was still at least two million people lower than it had been in January 2020. It was perhaps four million below what it would have been had the steady employment growth from 2010 through 2019 continued. The unemployment rate had fallen—the tight labor market largely meant that those who were looking for a job could generally find one. So an important reason the labor market was so tight was that far fewer people were working or looking for jobs than before the pandemic. The economy could not go back to "normal" because normal meant more people working. The credit agency Standard & Poor's divided the lower labor force participation into two portions.[30] About 40 percent was due to permanent shifts out of the labor force, largely retirement. The other 60 percent was pandemic related and would resolve eventually. But as the pandemic dragged on and new virus variants emerged, that "eventually" took longer and longer to arrive.

Why were fewer people working? First, many had retired, whether by choice or not, for many of the reasons we discussed in Chapter 9. People can decide to unretire. Yet if one has already retired, returning to work at a new job, likely for lower pay and continuing virus risk, would not be attractive for many.

Second, estimates suggest that millions were still dealing with long COVID with symptoms that lasted months or years.[31] Many people found that they had to cut back their hours or stop working altogether.

Third, child care was still a problem. Many parents, particularly mothers, had left the labor force in 2020 to take care of their children. But child care is also an industry with substantial sickness risk and often low pay, so it was difficult to hire. New safety approaches, whether legally required or not, likely also limited child care spots. As an illustration of the reinforcing dynamic, Maggie Koerth, writing at FiveThirtyEight, described how a shortage of school bus drivers made it difficult for parents to return to their jobs, contributing to the labor tightness all around.[32] Driving school buses is difficult, often low paying, and stressful. (I often find ferrying two children hard; the thought of driving 30 makes me shiver.) The cycle fed on itself: because the labor market was tight and not yet normal through 2021, child care was not yet at full capacity, so parents could not fully return to work, contributing to a tight labor market.

Fourth, many people could afford to be more choosy about jobs. Continued retirement is one aspect of this choosiness. Choosiness among younger people likely explains little of the labor force decline because people being choosy are likely still looking for a job, even if they are willing to take their time to find a good one. But choosiness and the high number of quits do suggest a labor market where prospective employees suddenly had bargaining power.

When economists think about labor markets, they are often thinking about a complex matching problem with bargaining power at its center. Employees are constantly leaving jobs and looking for new ones. Employers are trying to find the best match. Employers and people looking for jobs search until they find a good enough match, compared with the costs of searching more. When people looking are desperate, they may accept any job that comes their way, even for low wages and benefits, or one that does not make good use of their skills. When they have a substantial savings cushion or generous unemployment benefits, however, they may be willing to keep looking or bargain harder. This dynamic also affects people with jobs who may demand a raise or the ability to work from home. Their ability to bargain depends on how willing they are to leave the job and look for a new one.

Suddenly, it seemed that workers had greater bargaining power all through the labor market. The willingness to quit, such as the mass exodus at the Lincoln Burger King, is one sign of this change. Successful strikes at John Deere and Kellogg's showed a labor movement with additional power.

An important reason for the greater bargaining power was the improved finances because of the pandemic. The pandemic paradox—that most people's finances improved during the pandemic—is crucial here. People without jobs could take their time looking for a good one and reject bad jobs.[33] People with jobs could afford to quit for new ones. People in retirement could afford to stay there. Women taking care of children were not necessarily financially desperate to return. All of these trends may have been temporary, but they marked a large shift in bargaining power.

In an important variation of being increasingly choosy, a fifth reason for labor market tightness was that many workers had lingering concerns about COVID-19 risk or did not want to return to offices in person. As employers tried to reopen in-person businesses, it was harder to hire for these positions.[34] As vaccinations increased, some of these fears likely diminished, but the spread of virus variants may have rekindled them. It is difficult to tell how important these concerns are, distinct from overall more choosiness. Before and during the pandemic, people without many options often accepted risky working conditions for a paycheck. The desire to work from home and virus fears were new pandemic reasons for workers to be choosy, aided by a financial cushion.

To keep workers and attract new ones, pay started increasing. Figures 10.1 and 10.2 started by showing how the median wage had barely risen for the 40 years before the pandemic and labor's share of national income had declined. Both trends reversed through the pandemic, although inflation—which we will discuss later—meant that wages adjusted for purchasing power did not always increase. Yet Figure 10.1 shows that real wages were still higher than before the pandemic, even as many low-wage workers returned to the labor market and inflation picked up. Wage growth for the lowest-paid workers was particularly strong, more than offsetting inflation, prompting economist Arindrajit Dube to call it a "Great Re-Compression."[35]

Many companies did not adapt well. Some tried to hire as they had before the pandemic, when they had more bargaining power, continuing to offer low pay and benefits.[36] The companies that did the best during the Great Resignation were also the ones that had long invested in their workforce (although not always by choice). A great example is the difference between UPS and FedEx. FedEx's difficulties hiring and retaining drivers, most of whom are "independent contractors," not employees, cost it dearly.[37] UPS, with its unionized workforce, had far fewer quits. Its on-time delivery rate was substantially higher than FedEx's during the 2021 holiday season. Treating your workforce well was suddenly good business.[38] UPS stock was up 31 percent over 2021, compared with 1.5 percent for FedEx. UPS delivered. FedEx did not.

The Supply Chain Backup

The Three Stooges, slapstick comedians from the early days of cinema, had a standard stunt. Having gotten themselves into trouble, they would try to run away through an open door. All three would try to go through a door at the same time, but they would get stuck in the doorway. One would break free and start to go through, only to be pulled back by another. Eventually one might crawl through another's legs and then they would all break through, falling on their faces.

In late fall 2020 and accelerating for the next year, world supply chains resembled the Three Stooges bit, without the humorous payoff. Flush with cash from the decline in spending and from Economic Impact Payments, Americans started buying stuff. Literally boatloads of stuff. All that stuff tried to make its way through America's ports and got gummed up. Of course, the details are a bit more complicated, but the Three Stooges bit captures the basics: too much stuff trying to go through too small an opening, causing backups, and some unexpected workarounds.

It all started with the huge shift to buying stuff in the pandemic. Early in the pandemic, purchases of services that required any contact with a human plummeted. These services fall into two big categories: recreation and entertainment, such as going to the movies or to the gym, fell by more than 50 percent (Figure 10.5).[39] So did accommodation and food services, which include hotels and restaurants. Recreation recovered somewhat as people learned to muddle through and socialize safely. For example, one of my son's classmates had a magician call into a virtual birthday party in late 2020. It was a creative workaround, except we all wished it had been in person. But spending at restaurants and

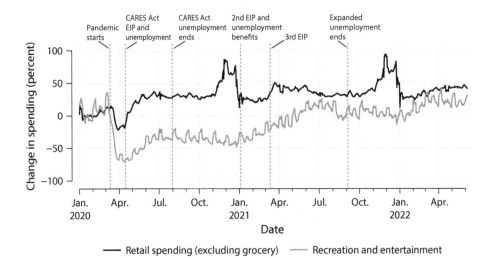

FIGURE 10.5. Americans spent a lot more on physical goods during the pandemic. (Spending by category relative to January 2020. *Source*: Affinity Solutions and Opportunity Insights.)

hotels was low through April 2021 and fell again with the Delta variant surge in July and August 2021.

Meanwhile, stuck at home, Americans were buying more stuff. After a brief and relatively shallow decrease, retail spending surged (see Figure 10.5). By June 2020 it was 25 percent above its prepandemic level. Retail spending normally surges following Thanksgiving for the holiday shopping season, then falls through March. Rather than falling in January 2021, retail spending stayed high, and starting in March 2021, after the third Economic Impact Payment, it was 50 percent higher than prepandemic.

A major reason for high retail spending was that people were suddenly doing at home what they used to do outside the home. They needed to set up home offices, for example. The rise of the home gym illustrates this shift. During the pandemic, gyms were largely shut down (lots of people breathing heavily in close quarters indoors turns out to be a great way to spread the virus).[40] The plummeting gym memberships are part of the fall in recreation spending in Figure 10.5. But many people still wanted to work out. Working from home and finding themselves with more time because they were not commuting, it suddenly made sense for many people to buy equipment to work out from home too. Sales of stationary bikes, regular outdoor bikes, treadmills, weights, and yoga mats boomed, all of which are captured in retail spending. Peloton, which sells pricey stationary bikes and online classes, saw sales nearly double and subscribers increase rapidly.[41] The company had been losing money before the pandemic (and would go through similar problems as the pandemic wound down).[42]

Exercise bikes are largely made in Asia or have many parts made there, even if they are assembled in the U.S.[43] The demand surge meant that more and more bikes needed to come from Asia. And we were ordering more of many other things as well. The global supply chain, however, only had the capacity for one stooge at a time. When three tried to go through, bottlenecks started to appear, and as they kept coming, the bottlenecks spread.

The most obvious bottlenecks were the ports of Los Angeles and Long Beach, which together account for 40 percent of all U.S. imports by sea.[44] These ports handle the massive container ships that transformed global trade.[45] Container ships transport standard shipping containers that are 8 feet wide, 9 feet tall, and 20 feet long (although there is a bit of variation, this is the standard twenty-foot equivalent unit). With the standardization of containers, almost all ships could handle all containers, and ports could specialize in technology like cranes that could rapidly unload the containers into waiting trucks or trains. These trucks and trains were also built to handle the standard container, so the goods could go from factory to final warehouse without ever having to be unpacked, massively reducing the time, labor, and wastage involved. The containers could be stacked securely on the boat or in port waiting to be loaded, allowing everything to be more centralized, including the container ships, which got bigger and bigger.

Standardizing all of these steps brought shipping prices down precipitously starting in the 1950s. Shipping costs fell by around 90 percent following containerization.[46] The largest container ships can handle 24,000 standard containers, equivalent to a train 44 miles long.[47] Container ships got so massive that limitations in size were described by what they could fit through: Panamax was the biggest size that could fit through the Panama Canal (or New Panamax after canal upgrades).[48] Suezmax ships were the largest that could fit through the Suez Canal. The *Ever Given*, which ran aground in the Suez Canal in March 2021 and contributed to the global supply chain backup, was a Suezmax.

Transhipping—moving goods from one form of transport to another—defines our economic lives, even though it is easy to miss. Almost all major U.S. cities grew around their port or role in transhipping. New York's harbor meant that Atlantic traffic would unload there. New York's financial industry grew to support this trade. Other major U.S. cities also formed around these core activities of unloading goods from ships to other ships or trains. The Baltimore port helped the burgeoning tobacco trade, and New Orleans was the key port connecting the vast Mississippi River network. Further upstream, Saint Louis grew because it was at the confluence of the Mississippi and Missouri Rivers. Chicago connected grain from the Midwest to the East Coast and Europe. Even America's legends are built around moving goods. The classic cowboy "cattle drive," central to American mythology, was just the first transhipping step as the cattle went from grazing lands, to the railroad, to the slaughterhouses in Chicago.

Because of containerization and other productivity increases, shipping costs fell so low that transhipping was no longer the defining economic characteristic of our cities. But this specialization also meant that there was no easy way to increase capacity quickly. Only a few ports can handle the bigger containerships, so when these ports were at capacity, there were no easy ways to increase throughput quickly.

As all the exercise bikes we ordered arrived by ship, the Ports of Los Angeles and Long Beach were unloading as quickly as possible. But all those containers had to go someplace and the rest of the supply chain could not keep up. Each container needs a truck and truck driver to move it to the next stop and people to unload it there. There were not enough truck drivers or warehouse workers to unload the containers, so they sat for longer.[49] Containers accumulated, stacked higher and higher, clogging the ports and slowing down the containers getting out.[50] These containers, the three stooges of the supply chain, were all trying to go through a door at the same time and getting stuck.

Many of these problems have the same source: decades of poor pay and tough conditions meant that as more stuff started moving through the supply chain, logistics companies could not retain or hire the people needed to deal with it. Short-haul trucking from port to warehouse—known as drayage trucking in supply chain terminology—is tough work and is often paid by the trip.[51] So as the clogged ports slowed down, drayage truckers' incomes fell, making it harder to keep them employed. Warehouses clogged up as the people needed to unload and process the exercise bikes quit and were difficult to replace.[52]

A narrative that there was a "shortage" of truckers took hold. In an economic sense, there was no shortage of drivers but rather an unwillingness to pay drivers enough to accept tough working conditions. The claim that truck driver shortages existed predated the pandemic but had been thoroughly debunked.[53] The trucking market is a functioning labor market; workers enter and leave based on the wages and working conditions. As Nicolas Rivero pointed out in Quartz, "The real shortage is of good trucking jobs that can attract and retain workers in a tight labor market."[54] As the port congestion caused delays in drayage trucker pickups, their incomes fell. The costs of port congestion and of L.A. traffic were being shifted to the truckers, rather than being absorbed (and possibly passed on) by shippers. So truck drivers quit or were harder to hire without raising wages or improving working conditions.[55] (To point out one unpleasant working condition: port congestion meant longer times waiting to pick up a container, and that in turn meant longer without a bathroom. As one trucker put it, "Sometimes a water bottle is the only bathroom option.")[56]

At its root, the supply chain backup was just part of labor's broader reassessment. Trucking, particularly drayage trucking, had to compete with other options. The supply chain industries—transportation, storage, wholesale trade, and retail trade—were some of the largest contributors to the declining labor share of income I discussed earlier.[57] It is not just that these were hard jobs but that the share of income going to labor in these jobs had been declining. And the industry had long operated by shifting both physical and financial risks onto low-paid labor—for example, by paying by the load rather than by the hour. When there were fewer options, many workers were stuck. With a tighter labor market, the hard conditions, low pay, and risks were a big problem in finding workers. Pay increases helped, but pay was increasing for many jobs, so relatively speaking, trucking and warehouse jobs were not necessarily becoming more attractive.

Meanwhile, the exercise bikes were still arriving at the ports, so ships started to back up at anchorage. Normally, there might be about 17 ships waiting outside Los Angeles to be unloaded. Around 40 ships were at anchor or waiting outside the port in early 2021. By September 2021, there were between 80 and 100. To put that in perspective, these ships are often as large as or larger than the biggest skyscrapers. There are only about 90 skyscrapers higher than 200 meters in New York City.[58] In August and September 2021, it was as if every big building in New York City was floating outside Los Angeles. Around half a million containers with goods worth $24 billion were waiting to be unloaded, each one needing a trip by truck from the port and a warehouse team to unload it.[59]

All these delays meant that, even though we were getting more and more stuff, we were also waiting longer for more of it. As one CNN article memorably described it, "Everything you're waiting for is in these containers."[60] And as supply chain issues gained prominence, many people ordered more stuff to get ahead of holiday shopping. My family contributed. We did more of our holiday shopping earlier, and even then we could not find everything we wanted. Sometimes we settled for something else, sometimes we just bought less. But that demand meant retailers did not have as much income even as we did not get the stuff we wanted. When people trade, each side gets something they want more than what they have given up. I buy a present for my children and give up some money. The retailer gives up a toy but gets money. Both of us prefer what we get to what we give up. These "gains from trade" are real, all around us, and their expansion drives economic growth. When we cannot make these trades because the retailer cannot get the stuff to me, everybody loses like the stooges falling on their faces.

While this discussion has centered on supply chain difficulties that kept goods that had been produced from getting to customers, other challenges—some pandemic related, some not—kept things from being made in the first place. Perhaps the most important was a limited supply of semiconductor chips that go into anything electronic. The demand surge for goods, particularly electronic goods, had soaked up the supply of these chips. The massive and complex chip-manufacturing centers—called fabs in industry jargon—are hugely expensive, have a long lead time to production, and produce a limited output.[61] A fire in some fabs in Japan and the February 2021 Texas power outage had reduced capacity during the pandemic.[62] And Chinese electronics manufacturer Huawei had bought up many chips before international sanctions on it went into effect.[63] So when demand surged, supply was already down, and these chips were suddenly in short supply. The auto industry was particularly hard hit, partly because many companies had reduced their chip orders when demand fell early in the pandemic. As a result, car makers reduced production because they could not find enough chips.[64] Consumer electronics such as video game consoles and tablets were harder to find.

And in spring 2022, a baby formula recall and factory shutdown led to massive shortages. The formula market had already been tight. Sales surged in 2020 as parents stocked up while at home, but sales fell dramatically in 2021 as parents used up their stock. Because formula can expire, manufacturers cut back production in 2021. The pandemic demand fluctuations made it hard to figure out how much to produce. This issue is called the "bullwhip effect" in supply chain parlance because small fluctuations in demand by consumers can lead to larger swings up the supply chain as manufacturers try to catch up with demand or cut too much. It was a problem in many industries during the pandemic.[65]

So inventory was already low when a bacterial infection caused the FDA to recall several formula brands and pause production at the factory that made the recalled formula.[66] Parents were left scrambling and scared. When allergies mean there is only one formula your baby can drink or your picky eater will only accept one brand, not having a steady supply will keep you up at night.

Together, difficulties in shipping, a low chip supply, and firms' trouble hiring explain many of the difficulties Americans experienced buying things. Even if manufacturing took place in the U.S., such as for many cars, production often needed chips that were in short supply or some parts made abroad. Complex multinational supply networks left the ability to finish many products perilous because of shipping delays. Increased wages and firms' troubles hiring made it even harder. The bullwhip effect meant that supply and demand were often chasing each other.

As demand increased and supply could not keep up, prices on many goods started to rise.

Prices and Inflation

Prices for many things fell early in the pandemic as demand collapsed. As demand returned but supply chain issues, limited labor, and other disruptions limited supply, prices surged. The causes behind price rises differed, but they added up to create some of the fastest overall price increases in decades.

Inflation is what economists call an overall increase in prices. It is typically measured using the percentage change in the Consumer Price Index (CPI), which is the cost for consumers to buy a particular basket of goods and services. How much of each good or service is in the basket is determined by the average amount consumers spent on different goods and services as measured by surveys that are typically several years old by the time the CPI is measured. Normally, how people spend their money on average shifts very slowly, so the lag does not matter. During the pandemic, how people spend shifted dramatically, so the CPI was not as accurate a measure of the cost of living. For example, the cost of gasoline is typically a large portion of the CPI basket, but demand for gasoline plummeted in the pandemic's first few months as people stopped traveling and commuting.[67] In fact, because it is expensive to halt oil production, the price of oil briefly turned negative in April 2020 as supply exceeded demand and storage filled up.[68] Very briefly, oil producers were having to pay more to store the oil than they were able to get

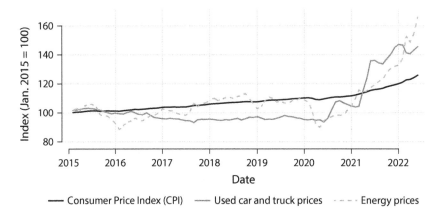

FIGURE 10.6. Prices fell early in the pandemic. Then they increased rapidly in 2021 and 2022, especially for used cars. Just when used car prices were coming down, energy prices shot up. (Consumer Price Index, price index for used cars and trucks, price index for energy. *Source*: Bureau of Labor Statistics.)

for it, so oil was worth less than zero. Because the fall in the price of oil was caused by a fall in demand, the CPI, which still assumed people were commuting, fell by more than the cost of living.

Early in the pandemic, other goods also fell in price, so the CPI, as shown in Figure 10.6, fell significantly.[69] The pandemic's beginning was thus a huge *deflationary* shock—inflation's opposite. The CPI's fall early in the pandemic likely missed the broader sense that the cost of living was going up. Because the CPI basket is fixed, but what people were actually buying during the pandemic changed rapidly, as the oil example illustrated, the CPI was not as good a measure of the cost of living during the pandemic. In 2020, people consumed much more food at home and grocery store prices increased.[70] With summer camps largely shut down in summer 2020, schools not open in person, and daycares shut or restricting the number of children, costs for child care increased by as much as 50 percent during 2020, if child care was even available.[71] Meanwhile, tickets to the local movie theater could not be bought at any price. On net, the effective cost of living increased in April, May, and June 2020, whether the CPI captured it or not; what we wanted to buy was not available, and what we were buying was often more expensive.[72] Although the CPI at the time had not increased much from the year before, 51 percent of Making Ends Meet respondents felt their expenses had increased in February 2021 compared with a year earlier. Only 5 percent thought their expenses had decreased. Consumers certainly felt like life was more expensive, even if the statistics did not yet reflect it.

So when prices started to increase more generally in early 2021, many people were already feeling like life had become more expensive. Most prominently, car prices, after declining early in the pandemic, started shooting up. Between March and June 2021, used car prices increased by 23 percent (see Figure 10.6). In some places, it became very difficult to find a used car at any price. Transportation is the second-largest part of most families' budgets, so these price increases explained perhaps a third of the overall increase in prices measured by the CPI in 2021.

What caused the car price increases? Supply and demand. Early in the pandemic, demand for cars had fallen as we moved around less and worked from home more. Rental car companies had sold off around a third of their fleets, causing the decline in prices. New car production fell. Starting around March 2021, demand picked up again, but the supply was still low. Rental car companies, rather than selling, were trying to buy cars again (rental prices surged as well). New car sales hit a record for the first half of 2021, but car manufacturers were having a difficult time keeping up. The chip shortage and other supply chain woes made it difficult to ramp up production. With limited supply and increasing demand, prices rose.[73]

Increases in demand, the difficulty hiring, and supply chain backups meant that many things, not just used cars, got more expensive. The supply chain difficulties meant the supply of goods manufactured abroad was lower, pushing prices higher. But even for goods made in the U.S., shipping problems meant it was often hard to finish assembling some goods because some components were made abroad or were otherwise difficult to find. New homes could not be finished because key materials were unavailable. Garage doors, gutters, and faucets were hard to find, slowing the supply of new house construction and contributing to the increase in prices we saw in Chapter 5.[74] The chip shortages slowed car production. Difficulty hiring and the demand for all kinds of labor for shipping products meant it was harder and more expensive to get goods to consumers. For example, such factors—inability to get packaging, difficulty hiring, and transportation difficulties—contributed to a severe cream cheese shortage.[75] Plus a cyberattack shut down one cream cheese factory for several days just before cheesecake season.[76] These factors, however, were largely temporary and would be replaced by potentially falling prices once businesses had hired more people and supply chains sorted themselves out, but the transition took longer than many expected.

Less temporary was the increase in consumer spending. If supply had been able to adjust easily, then prices might not have risen. But labor markets and supply chains were not able to adjust easily, so the higher spending pushed prices higher. There was an active debate on how much pandemic policies contributed to this increased demand. As we saw in previous chapters, pandemic policies were remarkably successful at maintaining income. But later policies, particularly the American Rescue Plan Act's Economic Impact Payments, added hundreds of billions to already flush consumer bank accounts. The resulting increase in consumer demand likely increased inflation somewhat. Yet since prices increased in countries across the world where pandemic spending had not been as large, the largest inflation contributor must have been global, not U.S.-specific policies.[77]

Altogether, prices were rising rapidly at the end of 2021 and into 2022. Inflation—the percentage change in prices—was higher than it had been since the 1980s. The increase in used car prices startled anyone trying to buy a car in 2021, but other prices started increasing as well. Many thought the spike in prices was temporary, caused by the supply chain difficulties, and prices would soon stabilize.[78] But price increases proved to be larger and longer lasting than expected. And then, just as used car prices started to come down and some supply chain issues were getting resolved, Russia invaded Ukraine, sending energy and food prices soaring (see Figure 10.6). Rent was also increasing rapidly.

A dirty secret of economics is that the economy-wide costs to inflation below around 10 percent are quite small.[79] To see why, consider what would happen if all prices—including wages, which are the price of labor—went up by 100 percent. In fact, we can easily perform this thought experiment by pricing everything in pennies instead of dollars. There might be some small direct costs from stores having to change their price tags so that $9.99 reads ₵999 (these costs are called "menu costs" in economics because they are similar to the new prices that restaurants update their menus with for the latest catch of the day). But beyond these small costs, everyone would be exactly as well off as they were before, even though the price of everything just increased by 100 times. If this example seems silly, consider that Turkey removed six zeros from its currency starting in 2005 after decades of inflation left a billion lira worth only about 75 cents.[80] The revaluation made it much easier to transact but otherwise left everyone exactly the same. These examples illustrate something important: if all prices change at once, nobody is worse or better off.

But not all prices typically go up at the same rate, so some people end up benefiting from inflation, while others end up losing. Inflation's largest effects are *distributional*—who gets what in a society. If you own a company that makes something that is going up in price faster than inflation, such as cars, you benefit. If you buy from that company, you lose. If you owe debts, such as a mortgage, which you can pay back with inflated dollars, you benefit. If you invest in a financial institution that owns these debts, you lose. If you have savings that earn a return less than inflation, you lose. If you have a low income and spend a lot on food and rent that go up faster than your wages, you lose. If you are a farmer or landlord selling at these higher prices, you benefit. Of course, different people may lose or benefit depending on their particular circumstances and the relative price increases. Increased transportation or fertilizer costs may mean that a farmer is worse off even with increased food prices.

For the most part, these relative price changes balance out across everyone so that the gains equal the losses, which is why the economy-wide inflation costs are pretty small. But that doesn't make the process easy or fair! For example, wages in late 2021 and early 2022 were not generally keeping up with inflation, leaving working people worse off. The owners of the companies employing them, however, were selling goods at these higher prices while paying relatively less for labor, so they tended to benefit. Winners and losers.

Even as inflation increased through 2021, the Federal Reserve kept interest rates low, only starting to raise rates in March 2022. Many felt the rate increases were too little, too late.[81] The supply chain issues and the demand shift to goods appeared temporary or "transitory"—a term the Federal Reserve used so often it became a dirty word[82]—so it seemed that inflation would come down on its own. But as supply chain issues began to resolve and demand shifted from goods to services, new shocks, such as Russia's invasion of Ukraine and new shutdowns in China, kept inflation high.

The Federal Reserve's new policies for inclusive growth meant it did not want to slow a broad recovery too soon. As Federal Reserve chair Jerome Powell told a congressional committee in June 2021, "Those who have historically been left behind stand the best chance of prospering in a strong economy with plentiful job opportunities. And our economy will be stronger and perform better when everyone can contribute to, and share in, the benefits of prosperity."[83] One of the reasons most Americans had not shared in the economic growth over the previous 40 years (see Figure 10.1) is that the Federal Reserve had tended to raise interest rates just as wages started to rise to fight inflation.[84] Moreover, longer economic expansions tend to draw in the people on the margins— those most often left behind.[85] Before the pandemic, employment was still increasing ten years after the Great Recession; Black employment was still increasing particularly rapidly (see Figure 2.1). Even during the longest expansion in U.S. history, we had not yet hit "maximum employ-ment," one half of the Federal Reserve's statutory mandate to achieve maximum employment and stable prices.

But the most substantial price increases in 2022 were for household basics such as food, housing, and fuel that tend to be a large part of low-income families' budgets. Meanwhile, even though wages were increasing, they were not increasing as rapidly as prices. So inflation was raising expenses for many low-income households far faster than their incomes were increasing. As we saw in Chapter 3, such changes can be dangerous for low-income households. While many households still had substantial savings left from pandemic policies, those policies had largely ended.

So the Federal Reserve had a tough balancing act in meeting its dual mandate. Inflation in the first half of 2022 was taking from the have-nots and giving to the haves. A continued strong expansion that increased wages and employment would do the opposite. The Federal Reserve was trying to balance the two with sufficient rate increases to bring down inflation without killing the strong recovery. It started raising rates in March 2022 and raised them rapidly over the next year. As I finished writing this book in July 2022, inflation was still high yet employment was still expanding, so it was too soon to tell whether the Federal Reserve would succeed in both its objectives. The struggle back to the new normal was proving more complicated and longer lasting than it had first appeared.

New Businesses Form

Starting in June 2020, something odd happened: far more new businesses were formed than before the pandemic. Figure 10.7 shows this surge.[86] In the two years before the pandemic, there were about 300,000 applications each month to form new businesses. Those two years were very good years. Over the 12 previous years, the average had been closer to 200,000. In the first two months of the pandemic, applications fell sharply. But by May 2020, there were 300,000 applications again, by June 380,000, and in July 553,000. While the number varied, they remained high through 2020 and 2021.

New business applications are not necessarily all going to become new businesses, but a sizable fraction will. New business applications are collected and processed by the Census Bureau from IRS filings for an Employer Identification Number. An Employer Identification Number (also called a Tax Identification Number) is usually required to obtain a business license or permit, open a business bank account, and pay any employees and business taxes. Many applications are for tax purposes. For example, an Employer Identification Number is necessary to pay taxes for a household employee such as a nanny. The Census Bureau

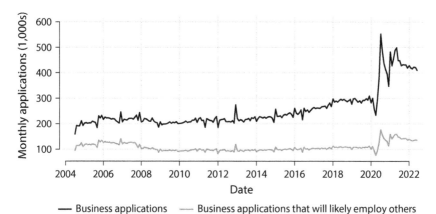

FIGURE 10.7. Applications to start new businesses soared during the pandemic. (Seasonally adjusted. *Source*: Census Bureau.)

excludes these applications and others that are unlikely to represent a new business for other reasons.[87] Many business applications also represent self-employment businesses that will never have other employees. The Census Bureau tries to track what kinds of new business applications have historically turned into businesses with paid employees. It calls these High-Propensity Business Applications, and they do not always move in the same way as all business applications. As Figure 10.7 shows, High-Propensity Business Applications had been nearly flat since 2010 while business applications increased sharply in 2018. The difference between the two lines suggests that the increase in applications in 2018 and 2019 was for reasons other than the founding of new businesses that would expand and hire employees. Perhaps it was due to an increase in self-employment or because of the big tax changes in 2017.

During the pandemic, both Business Applications and High-Propensity Business Applications increased sharply and sustained the increase through 2021, as seen in Figure 10.7. That both moved in the same direction at the same time suggests that new businesses were forming more rapidly by any measure and many of these businesses were likely to eventually have paid employees. Business applications were 83 percent higher from June 2020 through October 2021 than in the ten years before the pandemic. High-Propensity Business

Applications were 45 percent higher. As economist John Haltiwanger—who helped the Census Bureau develop these measures—points out, these increases contrast with the declines that occurred in the Great Recession.[88] Usually, we think that a recession causes people to delay or discard ideas to form new businesses. Instead, the opposite happened during the pandemic.

What is so surprising about this pandemic increase is that entrepreneurial activity had been falling for decades before the pandemic. In 1980, 11.8 percent of firms were less than a year old and they employed 3.1 percent of workers. In 2019, only 8.2 percent of firms were less than a year old and they employed only 1.8 percent of workers.[89] New business starts have fallen in all states and nearly every city.[90]

The decline in new businesses is concerning because it suggests a decline in the kind of economic dynamism that results in economic and job growth. New firms are not the biggest employers, but they are a key source of economic dynamism. New firms grow, create new products, employ more people, and challenge old businesses, and so they help the economy become more productive. Of course, older firms can do these things as well,[91] but it is telling that the biggest companies today did not grow from existing businesses. Apple was not a spinoff from IBM, the computing juggernaut when Apple was founded, nor was Microsoft. More recently, Microsoft did not create Google or Facebook and tried to stifle nascent competitors. Tesla was not founded by GM nor Amazon by Barnes & Noble.

It is important to distinguish small businesses from new businesses. While new businesses generally start small, small businesses are mostly not new businesses and most owners of small businesses are not interested in growing. While much policy focuses on small businesses because there are many of them and they employ a lot of people, small businesses in general are not a source of economic or employment growth. As economists Erik Hurst and Benjamin Pugsley write, "Most small businesses have little desire to grow big or to innovate in any observable way."[92] Instead, it is young businesses, which often start small but may not stay that way, that create most new jobs. Young businesses often fail, so they also destroy the most jobs. But they create far more jobs than they destroy, making new businesses the most important source of employment growth.[93]

Against this decline in new business creation, the sudden increase during the pandemic is thus remarkable and exciting. Like all changes during the pandemic, it may not last, but as Figure 10.7 shows, it has proved relatively durable over nearly two years. About a third of the increase in business applications is in selling things outside traditional retail stores.[94] With in-person retail shut down or customers staying home, it seems many people saw an opportunity to sell something online. Other increases suggest new businesses were rushing into areas not being well served during the pandemic, as remote work and ordering became more common.

Many of these new businesses were started in high-percentage Black areas by Black entrepreneurs.[95] Using business registrations from eight states, a team of economists looked at where and when new businesses registered. These data are different from the Employer Identification Number applications behind the Census data, so they give a different view of business starts. Importantly, the state business registrations also surged starting in May 2020 compared with 2019. The larger the percentage of Black residents, the larger the increase in business registrations. The increase was particularly pronounced in higher-income Black areas.

The increase in state business registrations typically occurred soon after an Economic Impact Payment. Figure 10.7 shows the same pattern, although the series removes seasonal variation, which blunts some of the jumps. While the timing does not necessarily prove that Economic Impact Payments caused the increase in entrepreneurship, it suggests they helped.

The timing and geography of new business starts indicate something important about why business starts were declining before the pandemic. While the evidence is circumstantial, pandemic policies' success in improving wealth and financial security for most people suggests that wealth concentration and the safety net are crucially important. Other possible explanations for the decline in new business formation do not seem to help explain the pandemic increase. Regulations did not change, so while regulation may still be an impediment, it was not sufficient to hold back the wave. Meanwhile, the American entrepreneurial spirit is clearly far from dead. The increased market power of big incumbent businesses that are able to fairly or unfairly outcompete new businesses might have been an important reason for the decline in business start-ups before the pandemic. But the market power of the largest firms increased during the pandemic, although the pandemic disruptions may have altered market power for smaller firms in ways that let new entrants prosper.

Instead, the pandemic experiment suggests that one important element for recapturing business dynamism is to make sure everyone has the financial security to bring their ideas to market. Lack of wealth seems particularly important for Black entrepreneurs. The disparity was important even before the pandemic. Low wealth prevented many Black and Hispanic entrepreneurs from starting businesses.[96] And even when they did start businesses, Black-owned startups were typically smaller and grew less fast because they had lower access to capital.[97]

The pandemic experience echoes the international comparisons. For example, Sweden has had a startup boom in recent years. At least part of the boom likely comes from Sweden's extensive social safety net, which means that a business failure—and most new businesses will fail—does not cause financial suffering.[98]

Some of the increase in business starts surely comes because of the pandemic's devastating effect on employment and small businesses, particularly minority-owned small businesses.[99] Newly unemployed people or owners of shuttered businesses had a lot more time to explore the idea they had been kicking around. But they also had the money to get the idea off the ground because of pandemic policies such as unemployment insurance and Economic Impact Payments and the decline in spending. The pandemic economic changes also meant there were new business opportunities. It is difficult to separate out the impact of pandemic policies from the pandemic. But having the money to start a business nonetheless seems to have been one crucial ingredient.

Some of these new businesses will fail, and many were pandemic dreams that did not develop beyond that. A surge in pandemic self-employment peaked in August 2021. But the tight labor market appears to have attracted many people back in. On average, only 3 percent more people were self-employed in the 12 months ending April 2022 than two years earlier.[100] Two years later, some new businesses owners will still be figuring out whether they could turn their dream into reality.

Ripples Building, Ripples Dying Away

In a sign that some of these changes would be longer lasting, Amazon workers at a warehouse in New York City voted to form a union in March 2022.[101] Amazon is the second-largest employer in the U.S. after Walmart and had massively expanded during the pandemic as shopping turned online. The effort was the first successful unionization attempt for Amazon, which, like Walmart, had aggressively fought and defeated previous union drives.

The successful union drive came from the pandemic. It started when Amazon fired Christian Smalls after a protest about Amazon's pandemic health and safety practices. Smalls went on to start the union effort. And the warehouse employees might not have voted to form a union if they had not been in the stronger bargaining position of a tight labor market. The warehouse had become a "lifeline for the city," delivering all of the physical goods people were buying instead of going out to restaurants or traveling.[102]

Before the pandemic, retail unions had long had difficulty against aggressive antiunion responses. For example, two weeks after the butchers in one store voted to unionize in 2000, Walmart famously announced it would close every in-store butchery.[103] The tight labor market and critical position of their warehouse meant that the Amazon warehouse employees were not as concerned about such retaliation. The pandemic's ripples intersected and built to something bigger.

Yet high inflation, difficulty buying stuff, and, perhaps, exhaustion after two years of economic gyrations left Americans pessimistic in spring 2022. In March, 32 percent of consumers expected their financial position to worsen over the coming year, the highest level since the University of Michigan's consumer sentiment survey started in the 1940s.[104] And in April, preliminary estimates suggested first-quarter GDP declined slightly after growing rapidly since the pandemic plunge two years earlier. The Russian invasion and new lockdowns in China exacerbated supply chain problems again. Inflation reached over 8 percent and the Federal Reserve started raising interest rates. After two years of mostly positive economic news as we recovered from the sudden stop in 2020, things suddenly seemed more uncertain than ever. The stock market fell sharply, reflecting the new economic uncertainty.

Despite this uncertainty, this chapter emphasizes how people started taking more control of their lives. They started new businesses. They quit in search of better opportunities. They held out for better pay. The pandemic ripped control from us all in March 2020. Yet as it faded, more of us had more control of our lives than ever.

The U.S. had weathered and recovered from the pandemic remarkably well. But economies have ups and downs even without a pandemic. As we struggled to return to normal, the massive pandemic economic waves were still intersecting, some dying away, some adding to regular economic ups and downs. Whether higher interest rates would cause a recession; whether labor would maintain its gains; when inflation would fall; whether the overall financial well-being improvements would last all remained unanswered. But we had learned something profound about what was possible.

Marvin

Marvin was proud of the secure financial position he had built when he took the survey in June 2019. He and his wife lived in a rural county in the Pacific Northwest. Marvin, a white man who had recently turned 70, was a veteran. Judging by his age, he likely served in Vietnam. He had a postcollege degree. Perhaps he used the Vietnam-era GI Bill to help pay for some of his education. He worked full time in June 2019, as did his wife. Together their income was about $75,000. They had helped at least one child through college. Marvin wrote in a comment, "From a very early age I was taught to work hard, budget my money, and never spend more than I earn! I have done all three and owe no man."

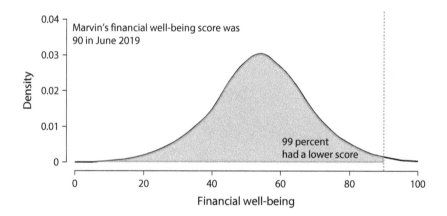

This approach showed: Marvin had no debts reported to the credit bureau. He had a credit card, which he paid off every month. He and his wife owned their house, so their only expenses were taxes and insurance, which added up to less than $500. They saved regularly, putting money aside every month. As a result, they had substantial money in checking and savings accounts and a good retirement account, and they could cover their expenses for more than six months if they lost their main source of income.

Marvin felt this financial security: he had one of the highest possible financial well-being scores.

Late in the Pandemic

Marvin did not return the June 2020 survey, but he did respond to the February 2021 survey. The preceding year and a half had changed his life plans. Marvin and his wife had both retired, but not by choice. They were both laid off and decided to retire rather than look for work. As he wrote in comments at the end of the survey, "Due to COVID both my wife and my jobs ceased and we entered into retirement. We are not in financial 'trouble' but we must be quite careful how we spend. We had intended to both work through July 2021 but began retirement in July 2020. Starting early has squeezed us but we are frugal, we budget and live within our means."

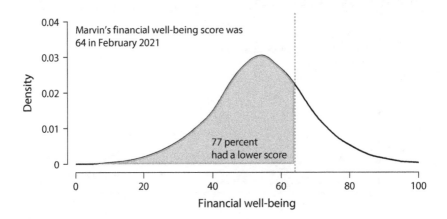

By retiring early, Marvin and his wife had lost a year of earnings and their retirement savings had to last an extra year. Suddenly, what had seemed like a financially straightforward future carried a bit more risk. As Marvin said, they were not in "trouble," but he no longer felt financially bulletproof.

Part of the problem was that, even as they retired and their earnings dropped, their expenses increased. As they retired, Marvin and his wife moved to another state. Perhaps they moved to be closer to grandchildren. In any case, the move was expensive. They did not take out a mortgage and had said they expected to move to a new residence in June 2019. So perhaps they moved to a house they had already bought or perhaps they paid cash. The moving expenses and furnishing the new place show up as Marvin's credit card debt (which he still paid off every month) increased sharply. These moving expenses added up and Marvin had not expected them to be so large. In the year leading up to February 2021, they had an unexpected vehicle replacement, a house repair, unexpected legal expenses, an unexpected computer replacement, and another major unexpected expense. Marvin also reported having a large unexpected gift to a family member.

As a result of the early involuntary retirement and expenses, while Marvin still felt financially secure, his financial well-being was no longer at the very top. Among the changes, he was now somewhat concerned that the money he'd saved wouldn't last.

Beyond the unexpected expenses, the price increases in 2021 must also have been concerning. Having retired, Marvin and his wife were now living on their savings and Social Security. While Social Security increases with inflation, Marvin's savings may not have kept pace. Perhaps he invested in the stock market so had seen his savings boom. But his general aversion to risk and debt suggests he might have preferred less volatile investments, which might not have increased much and did not pay much because interest rates were low.

Like millions of others, Marvin and his wife retired earlier than they wanted, but they were likely not tempted to come back into the labor force even when hiring started up again in 2021. Their old jobs likely paid better than anything they thought they could get easily. And there was the continuing risk of virus exposure. The virus had upset their plans, but they had adapted and were ready to move on.

11

The Pandemic Paradox

THE PANDEMIC allowed us to see what happens when we have a more generous social support system, even if some people were left behind; what happens when we save more; what happens when we have the chance to rethink how and where we work; and what happens when we, at least briefly, return some power back to labor.

What happens is that far fewer of us struggle to pay the bills every month. Far fewer people are evicted. Financial health improves for most people. More of us start businesses. We feel better about our finances.

How could so much good come out of a pandemic that killed more than a million of us? That is the pandemic paradox. We responded individually and collectively in new ways that improved our finances. These responses show us ways our society could be better, fairer, and more productive. Much of what we learned does not need a pandemic, but it took a pandemic to teach us what is possible.

The pandemic showed us that we are still capable of responding to massive threats, making individual and collective sacrifices for the greater good. Other massive societal threats exist, from climate change to inequality. If we can develop a vaccine over a weekend, test and deploy it in less than year, spend $5 trillion for pandemic relief, and alter our lives completely around a common goal, what else can we do?

The overall improvement in our financial lives does not mean we were better off because of the pandemic. $5 trillion is a lot of money even for a country as wealthy as the U.S., and there are costs to this spending, from increased inflation to reduced spending on other priorities or higher taxes. Reduced spending, government transfers, and forbearance policies got money to people and kept problems from ballooning. But many Americans also vastly reduced their spending and limited their social lives to reduce the virus's spread. Financial health improved in part because many people spent less, avoiding going out to restaurants, taking vacations, or visiting family, among other limitations. Improved finances came at the cost of these lost opportunities. To take a personal example, my parents did not come to visit their grandchildren for nearly a year. Sure, they saved money by not traveling, but they would have rather held my wiggling one- and then two-year-old. They will not get those years with my family back. Many families have similar stories.

And it is important to remember the people left behind in the short and long term and those who died. Economic Impact Payments do not make up for increased intimate partner violence during lockdowns, nor will they compensate the children who lost nearly half a year of learning, or bring back our loved ones.

Instead, we should think of our improved finances as mitigating a devastating disaster, a ray of light through the otherwise dark storm of the pandemic. And like a lighthouse in a storm, perhaps we can use that light to find a way forward that leaves us with better financial lives and more security but does not require a pandemic to make it happen.

What have we learned? Often, when we come across a seeming paradox, we discover that previous assumptions were wrong. By finding a paradox, you know that your original premise was false. So let us use this pandemic paradox to reexamine our own thinking. The pandemic forcibly and unpleasantly pushed us to do new things, try new policies, and approach our lives differently. It exposed the flaw in our assumptions that things could not change. We learned a great deal about ourselves, about our society, and about how to conduct policy for the common good.

We Learned We Could Spend Less and Save More

Americans' financial lives improved for two main reasons: (1) they spent less, at least for a while, so had more savings and less debt, and (2) surprisingly effective economic policy got money to most people who

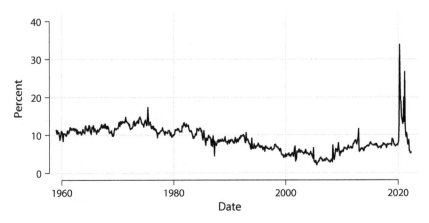

FIGURE 11.1. The personal savings rate had declined since the 1960s. It spiked in the pandemic but then fell. (*Source*: Bureau of Economic Analysis.)

would have suffered otherwise. These two reasons point to different, but not exclusive, ways forward.

Americans' savings were low before the pandemic. We saw in Chapter 3 how few people had the savings or ability to borrow to deal with an income shock. And the important thing: most Americans did not want more savings. When surveys ask households how much they want for "emergencies or other things that may come up," the median household wants only a little over a month of income in such savings and 40 percent of households want less than a month.[1] Moreover, the median household has about what it wants in emergency savings after adding together checking and savings accounts and available credit, although many households also have additional illiquid assets. In other words, before the pandemic, most households, except the poorest,[2] had the emergency savings they wanted. They just did not want very much.

Americans save less than they used to, although measuring how much and why is the subject of continuing debate.[3] Figure 11.1 shows the personal savings rate, which measures the share of total household income that is newly contributed to savings.[4] This amount is then available for new investments in factories or new businesses, so it helps measure how much Americans are contributing to growing the economy. This aggregate savings measure has flaws—among them that it is most closely related to how much those with the highest incomes save—but it can be measured consistently for decades.[5]

The personal savings rate averaged 11 percent in the 1960s. From there, it fell slowly, averaging 4.4 percent from 2001 through 2008. After the Great Recession, the personal savings rate was a bit higher, averaging 7.2 percent from 2010 through 2019. To put the rate into perspective, the European Union also had a low personal savings rate of around 5.5 percent in 2016, although European social insurance programs are more extensive, so Europeans do not need as much savings to self-insure. China had a personal savings rate of more than 30 percent in 2016.[6]

During the pandemic, personal savings spiked, rising to a high of 34 percent in April 2020 and averaging 15 percent from March 2020 through November 2021. Data at the individual level tell the same story. The amount in savings and checking accounts rose sharply for everyone, even for people with low incomes.[7] Credit card debt was way down. Paying down debt is also saving since it reduces the amount you owe. By any measure, Americans put more into savings during the pandemic than they had at any time during the recent past.

Americans saved more because they spent less but their incomes did not go down. Spending declined sharply in March, April, and May 2020. After that, people started slowly spending again, but it was not until the end of the year that spending had returned to prepandemic levels. During this time, people put the difference between their income and their spending into savings, which accumulated substantially. Americans' ability to save more depended on their incomes not declining, and government policies such as unemployment insurance were central here for the unemployed. We will talk about those policies next.

Saving is hard. It requires not spending today for some future need that may not happen. Savings can be stolen or lost. If you have some money, then friends or family may come asking for it. So why deny yourself and your family today?

Because the savings also protect you against financial pain and help prevent you from starting down a negative cycle into one of the poverty traps we saw in Chapter 3. Paying down your credit card debt saves money on interest payments, freeing up more money to save. Having some emergency savings might help fix the car, so you can get to your job when your car breaks down. It is often more expensive to be poor. But the flip side is that having some savings is often much more valuable if you are poor because it helps protect against the extra costs that come from not having money when you need it.

The pandemic showed us that we can drastically reduce our spending. Not everyone can, of course. People whose income largely goes to housing, for example, have limited options. And many expenses are unavoidable—for example, the biggest reason people had difficulty paying bills or expenses was unexpected medical bills, as noted in Chapter 3. But the pandemic's decline in spending shows that many Americans were still spending a lot on wants, not needs. Meals out. Travel. Those wants made life more enjoyable. But spending on them also left many Americans financially exposed. Spending a bit less on wants over time adds up, leaving more savings and more financial security.

The financial advice industry often uses coffee to illustrate how small costs and choices add up.[8] As Suze Orman, who writes financial advice books, puts it, with characteristic directness, when you buy your coffee out, rather than make it at home, you are "peeing" your money away.[9] The typical story goes like this: if you just stopped buying a cup of coffee a day at a coffee shop, you would be able to have some emergency funds. Or, to get even larger numbers, a financial adviser might point out that if you invested that money, in 30 years you would have $100,000. Wouldn't you rather have $100,000 to retire with than that cup of coffee?

Elites have long judged the eating habits of the poor, often with little justification. As the new immigrants with their strange tastes flooded New York starting around 1890, a movement developed to educate these new Americans, particularly the Italians, on proper eating. Schools instructed children in "proper" nutrition, for example. While the movement pretended to have scientific backing, much of its advice was clearly moralistic and nationalistic. Immigrants were taught that pickles, tomatoes, and peppers harmed digestion. Instead, the movement sought to teach these new immigrants to eat a supposedly healthier diet of porridge for breakfast and meat, beans, milk, potatoes, and codfish balls the rest of the day.[10] Supposedly hearty food rather than the vegetable-heavy fare many immigrants were used to. The movement eventually fizzled and we benefited from the Italian American hybrid cuisine that developed, including pizza and pasta and meatballs. Today's lattes and avocado toast are last century's pickles and tomatoes.[11]

During the pandemic, many Americans stopped going out for coffee as much. One estimate suggests that the coffee cups made at home grew from 73 percent to 81 percent during the pandemic.[12] Coffee maker sales boomed.[13] The switch from going to a coffee shop to making coffee at home captures many pandemic trends: the average American was less social; people learned to do it themselves, muddling through where expert baristas used to do the job; many people reduced their outside spending, but they bought a lot of physical goods to meet new at-home needs.

Despite the financial advice industry's moralistic tones and often absurd view that financial security is all about personal responsibility, the pandemic showed that it has a point, although it certainly does not apply to everyone. When many Americans stopped going out for coffee (and lunch, and drinks with friends, and the movies, and traveling, and visiting family, and so many other things), their savings went up. They had fewer financial troubles. They had the capital to start new businesses.

Many of the impediments to saving are outside our control—low incomes, high housing and child care expenses, and frequent unexpected expenses we cannot prepare for—but not all of them are. The pandemic showed that many of Americans can cut back on spending, if they choose to. To continue the coffee example: the thing about coffee is that you can make it at home. It requires a bit more effort, planning, and some upfront costs, which may be too high for some people. It probably does not taste as good (likely because when you make it at home, you typically put in a reasonable amount of cream and sugar, rather than buying a coffee-flavored milkshake). The pandemic forced many of people to make coffee at home or go without. Without the commute, many people had a bit more time to do so. While coffee is not the most important expense Americans reduced, it indicates a broader shift in spending. In at least one survey, most people who made the switch to brewing at home expected to continue.[14]

Perhaps the pandemic showed many Americans that they can make different choices about their spending. Before the pandemic, financial difficulties were not limited to households with the lowest income. Nearly 20 percent of households earning $100,000 or more had difficulty paying a bill or expense in 2019; 30 percent of households earning between $70,000 and $100,000 had difficulty. For the most part, these high-income households had fewer financial difficulties during the pandemic because they were saving more, not because of government aid. Saving more may be harder for low-income households, but having some savings is often even more valuable. The pandemic showed that many Americans could live without some of the things they were buying, even if they did make life more pleasant. And even a little bit more saving adds up—$100,000 in thirty years!—and can help stop the vicious cycles from starting.

There are hints that the pandemic reshaped many people's views on savings. It helped many people realize how little they had saved.[15] More than half of respondents to one survey in 2021 said that having an emergency fund had become a greater priority because of the pandemic.[16] Many people reported wanting to stick with their new savings habits, so some of the pandemic's savings lessons may stick. As one Making Ends Meet respondent put it in a comment in June 2020, "COVID-19 has actually helped us save gas money and childcare costs." By February 2021, this respondent had embraced a new lifestyle, writing, "I've discovered minimalism—it's changed how I view what 'needs' really are. I've gotten rid of 80% of our belongings. I've also decided I'm content with what I have. It's freeing."

We Learned That Better Unemployment Insurance Can Improve People's Lives

Remarkably, paradoxically, financial well-being went up during the pandemic despite all of the economic disruptions and widespread unemployment. A series of policies sent money to almost everyone, channeled funds to the unemployed, and gave money to almost all small businesses. As we saw initially with the CARES Act in Chapter 4 and later pandemic policies in Chapter 6, these policies prevented the pandemic unemployment and business losses from causing widespread financial suffering. In fact, unemployed people's financial well-being increased more than that of people whose families did not face any unemployment. While spending cuts were responsible for the financial improvement of people who kept their jobs or did not face financial disruptions because of the pandemic, it was these pandemic policies that kept people who faced financial disruption from also suffering financial harm. The pandemic exposed the flaw in assuming there is nothing we could do about widespread financial suffering. If we can improve financial well-being during a pandemic, why can't we improve it when unemployment is not widespread?

Most obviously, the pandemic showed us what happens when unemployment insurance becomes more generous: getting fired is no longer a financial disaster. So why did most states limit unemployment insurance benefits to half or less of preunemployment income before the pandemic? The standard reason is that unemployment insurance makes it less painful to be unemployed, so more unemployment insurance may decrease the incentive to look for a new job. The standard reason did not apply during the pandemic because businesses were intentionally shut down. During a pandemic or a big recession, more generous unemployment insurance does not decrease the incentive to look for a job because there are few jobs available. The argument is that if we made unemployment insurance more generous outside recessions, people would just live on the unemployment dole longer.

While it is true that overly generous unemployment insurance might decrease the effort to find a job, most American states offer far too little regular unemployment insurance. Although there is an active debate in economics, the current range of evidence is that unemployment insurance that replaces more than half, but not all, of income provides the right balance, pushing people to find work while still providing substantial financial protection.[17] Such unemployment insurance would be more generous than that available in most states but somewhat less generous than the CARES Act, which replaced more than the lost income for most recipients.

In addition to better benefits, it makes sense to provide them for longer than the typical 26 weeks. Research from the Great Recession and the pandemic suggests that cutting off unemployment insurance has only a very minor effect on pushing people to take jobs faster.[18] Cutting off unemployment does reduce the unemployed's income and consumption, harming the unemployed financially, while only barely changing the incentives.

The pandemic experience also showed that better unemployment insurance can make the labor market as a whole work better. More generous unemployment insurance directly improved people's lives when they received it. But it also helped transform the labor market, shifting power to labor in an important way that has the potential to make most people's lives better even when they are not unemployed. By making everyone, particularly the unemployed, less financially strained, pandemic unemployment insurance and other pandemic policies showed that a financially healthy workforce demands better pay and jobs. No longer desperate for a job and willing to take whatever bad pay, variable shifts, and poor working conditions an employer offers, workers demanded better.

A hidden tragedy during the pandemic was that poorly administered unemployment insurance programs in many states hampered policy, contributed to fraud, and delayed helping people. Many states could not provide benefits with acceptable promptness, harming people whose benefits were delayed just when they needed the money they were due the most. Moreover, antiquated state systems could not handle changes, which made policy worse. The CARES Act provided a flat $600 weekly increase in unemployment benefits to everyone. This situation was profoundly unfair for essential workers who often would have earned more had they been fired. A better policy might have instead replaced a larger share of the unemployed's prepandemic income, such as 75 percent, which would not have created such unfairness. But many state systems could not handle this type of policy change, so we had to settle for a worse policy.[19]

The pandemic also showed the value of automatic and speedy policy. Unemployment insurance is often called an "automatic stabilizer" because it injects more money into the economy during a downturn. No need to have a special session of Congress or worry that elderly senators might come down with COVID-19 (yes, that was a concern during CARES Act negotiations). Because unemployment insurance helps families when they need it, and when they might otherwise cut their spending, it helps keep recessions from getting deeper, automatically.

But normal unemployment insurance replaces too little income in most states and covers too few people. As the pandemic showed, a better system would replace more income and make more people eligible whenever they become unemployed. Such a system would reduce financial fragility outside of recessions and possibly strengthen the labor market. And during recessions, it would automatically help not just the unemployed but everyone.[20]

We Learned Maybe Just Throwing Money around Is Not the Most Effective Policy

While expanded unemployment insurance was the key pandemic policy for households, we spent nearly $4.5 trillion on other stuff as well. Was it worth it? The U.S. economy produced around $21 trillion in 2019. Pandemic federal spending in the two years following March 2022 added up to something like $5.2 trillion, although calculating exactly what was spent within two years is difficult. Spending this large a share of GDP had never happened outside wartime.

But perhaps we were at war against an existential threat, so wartime spending may be the only appropriate comparison. Putting these numbers in context, the U.S. spent around $3.4 trillion on its invasion of Iraq.[21] Exact numbers are difficult since much of the money was spent indirectly on healthcare for wounded veterans, for example, or on additional interest payments. Other estimates that include the broader costs to the U.S. economy—from more expensive oil or from higher interest rates reducing productive investments—come up with even larger numbers after adjusting for inflation.[22] All of these dollar values ignore the invasion's human costs from servicemembers killed and wounded to the 100,000 or more Iraqi civilians who died.

The key difference between wartime spending and pandemic spending is that making war is intentionally destructive. When we build and fire a missile, the value of the missile literally goes up in smoke. Much war spending has no direct economic return, although it is often stimulative in the sense that spending on anything, from building bombs to digging ditches, puts money in the pocket of someone who then spends it, creating income for someone else. In war, we spend money to achieve some policy goal, but most of the money spent is useless beyond that goal.

The federal government spent around $500 billion on pandemic "war" spending. On testing. On developing, buying, and deploying vaccines. On payments to hospitals to provide care, set up temporary wards, and treat elderly. On helping nursing homes develop better protections. This spending would not have been valuable without a pandemic, just like war spending isn't valuable without a war.

The rest of pandemic spending was for economic purposes, mostly through transfers from the federal government. In the giant accounting ledger for the entire economy, the money was moved from one column to another; for every dollar increase in federal debt, there was approximately a dollar increase in small business assets, household income, or state and local balance sheets. Put a different way, most pandemic spending was a transfer from the federal government to someone else in the economy.

So the value of most pandemic spending is the value of redistribution during a pandemic. But not all redistribution is valuable or goes to people who need it. Redistribution during an economic downturn can have big benefits: by giving money to people who would otherwise suffer financially; by helping people spend more than they otherwise would and so increasing growth; and by keeping good businesses that cannot borrow from going under and so harming growth. Redistribution to the wealthy or to businesses that would not have closed has few of these benefits and all the same costs.

In these terms, there are broadly two ways to evaluate pandemic spending on different programs: (1) Did it relieve suffering in the short or long term? For example, unemployment benefits kept many families from suffering financially. And (2) did it increase growth in the short or long term? For example, giving money to the unemployed who might otherwise cut their spending helped keep demand high, so helped keep the recession from being as deep and made the recovery faster. If a policy prevents an economic collapse, that policy likely pays for itself.

Against the benefits—relieving suffering and increasing growth—there is the extra cost of federal debt. In the short term, the costs were nearly zero and perhaps even below zero. The Federal Reserve's massive Treasury buying spree and decision to keep interest rates near zero until March 2022 meant that the federal government paid very low interest rates on the new pandemic debt. And inflation meant that the real value of the debt was diminishing.

In the long term, however, interest rates will rise and future taxpayers will have to pay the debt eventually. When the next crisis hits, perhaps the federal government will have less ability to respond. The debt may crowd out other investments, cause taxes to rise, or reduce future benefits. There are, eventually, real costs to spending, although they are not easy to quantify and may not be as large as the spending itself.

Whether a given pandemic program relieved suffering and increased growth enough depends on how you weigh the costs against the benefits and what you think would have happened without the program. Weighing these factors is hard. While the rest of the book has pointed to the impacts, or lack of impact, of various policies, most pandemic policy dollars were redistributed to someone. The person receiving the dollar benefited, but that dollar has costs.

Taken as a whole, the pandemic paradox still holds: despite a massive recession, household balance sheets improved, financial suffering was largely averted, and the U.S. economy recovered extremely rapidly. Yet we could have achieved those outcomes with far less spending, perhaps causing less inflation as the pandemic wound down.

Figure 11.2 shows what various programs spent, lumped into broad categories.[23] $5.2 trillion is a lot of money! Many of the CARES Act policies were put together rapidly, but later policies had time to consider better approaches, so they have no such excuse. How do the pandemic policies compare?

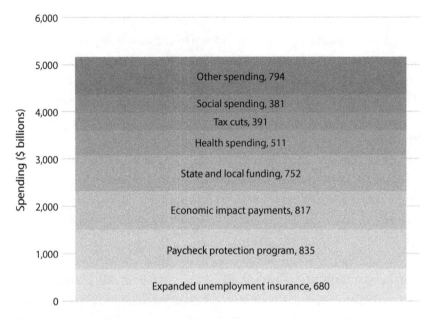

FIGURE 11.2. The U.S. allocated $5.2 trillion to pandemic programs. Not all of it was well spent. (Amount allocated over all bills. *Source*: Author's calculations from the Committee for a Responsible Budget.)

Expanded unemployment insurance ($680 billion). Pandemic policy's star is undoubtedly expanded unemployment insurance. It alleviated suffering and, because it was targeted at someone experiencing difficulty, did so far more effectively, per dollar spent, than largely untargeted programs like the Economic Impact Payments. As Chapter 6 shows, unemployment insurance was the most important income source for families experiencing unemployment. The federal expansion was key; regular unemployment benefits would not have protected people the same way. And so, the unemployed's financial well-being improved. By providing funds to households that would have cut their spending the most, expanded unemployment insurance also likely had a large growth impact.

Paycheck Protection Program (approximate cost: $835 billion). The Paycheck Protection Program protected few paychecks. Instead, it was a transfer to nearly all small business owners, most of whom have high incomes. It was thus a massive and regressive redistribution. Because many very small business owners could not have borrowed on their own, the Paycheck Protection Program likely avoided some small businesses closing down entirely, which would have reduced growth. How many would have shut down absent the program is difficult to estimate. But it could likely have achieved nearly the same effect by targeting much smaller businesses at less than half the cost.[24] And while the initial $540 billion in March and April 2020 was distributed during lockdowns and the severe downturn, during which a "whatever it takes" approach was perhaps reasonable, the additional $285 billion in the December 2020 relief bill was dispersed in a growing economy and after research showing the program's flaws. However, the later money was more likely to go to the smallest businesses and to nonwhite owners, so it made the massive redistribution to small business owners fairer.

Economic Impact Payments ($817 billion total; $141 billion in the CARES Act, $276 billion in the December 2020 relief bill, and $400 billion in the American Rescue Plan Act). It is worth dividing up the Economic Impact Payments from the different bills. As we've seen repeatedly, individual Americans benefited from the CARES Act's Economic Impact Payments. They filled in gaps in other programs and, because they went out quickly, helped tide many families over while dysfunctional state unemployment systems stumbled. But the money also went to many families that were not suffering. Later payments in the December 2020 relief bill and the American Rescue Plan Act filled in fewer gaps and so relieved less suffering. And by 2021, the economy was suffering not from a lack of demand, as in other recessions, but from difficulty supplying goods and services safely. So while all of the payments provided some stimulus, the later payments may have provided too much. By March 2021, household balance sheets were already solid overall and the economy was near capacity. In retrospect, pouring another $400 billion into an economy facing supply constraints contributed some growth, but also some inflation. However, the Economic Impact Payments were also a massive redistribution toward lower-income Americans whose finances improved markedly.

State and local funding ($752 billion total; $244 billion in the American Rescue Plan Act, $191 billion in education assistance, and $150 billion to state and local governments in the CARES Act, plus a series of smaller allocations that add up to $167 billion). State and local governments generally cannot spend more than they take in except for on specific bond issues. After revenues fell precipitously during the Great Recession, state and local governments cut their budgets and employment severely.[25] These cuts slowed the recovery and reduced spending on, among other things, education. So in the initial months of the pandemic, with new costs and falling revenues, there was good reason to be afraid that state and local governments would have had to cut spending and employment. These cuts would have hurt growth and the services that many people rely on. Yet all of the income support to the unemployed, to small businesses, and through the Economic Impact Payments meant that state tax revenues barely fell. As a result, many of the transfers, especially the March 2021 American Rescue Plan Act funds, were supporting new spending, not preventing cuts. They were, effectively, a transfer from future federal taxpayers to current state taxpayers. The programs these funds support may increase growth by funding valuable projects that states would not have done themselves. For example, school funding may help close the pandemic learning loss. Whether these funds relieve suffering or increase growth enough depends on what they are used for—some may be used well, others less effectively.

Health spending ($511 billion, including $158 billion to hospitals and nursing homes, $97 billion for testing, $58 billion for vaccines, and many other provisions). This spending was the closest to "war" spending: money spent to combat a new virus directly rather than for redistribution. While some of it was wasted or not put to very good use,[26] other spending surely saved lives and kept struggling hospitals in business.

Tax cuts ($391 billion total, including $193 billion in business tax cuts in the CARES Act). The largest tax provisions allowed mostly very rich individuals to reduce their taxes. These provisions had little obvious impact on growth or reducing suffering. Other tax cuts perhaps had larger possible impacts by delaying some taxes (at a small cost to the government) but perhaps some benefit to cash-constrained individuals or employers early in the pandemic; or by exempting some unemployment benefits, preventing a tax-time crunch for the unemployed.

Social spending ($381 billion total, including $71 billion for nutrition, $62 billion for child and family services, $39 billion to defer student loans, $106 billion to expand the child tax credit for six months, $62 billion on rental assistance and housing, and $41 billion to farmers). Much of this spending went to struggling families, so it relieved substantial suffering. Individual programs, such as nutrition spending for school meals, the expanded child tax credit, and rental assistance, helped in measurable and profound ways that suggest relieving financial suffering need not be very expensive. Because this spending also went to families likely to spend it, it may have also increased demand and growth.

Other spending ($794 billion total, including $565 billion in loans and direct support for specific industries and $229 billion for many industries including disaster support, transportation, telecommunications, national defense, and higher education). That an additional $794 billion, divided into many different programs, is mostly a spending footnote shows the massive scale of pandemic spending. Much of this money was for loans, so the direct costs of these programs are perhaps only $200 billion. Some of this money was likely unnecessary, while other spending supported necessary pandemic adjustments to existing programs.

Federal Reserve asset purchases ($4.2 trillion, not included in Figure 11.2). By its size, the largest pandemic response was the Federal Reserve's purchase of trillions of dollars of assets across many markets, expanding its balance sheet by something like $4 trillion. Many of these purchases were supported by very small direct lending support from Treasury and the CARES Act to cover any losses, so the direct costs of these programs to the federal budget were small. As of spring 2022, the Federal Reserve had no losses and will send any profits back to Treasury. This spending may have headed off another financial crisis, so its growth effects are potentially large. On the other hand, we do not yet know the impact of having the Federal Reserve suddenly become one of the biggest owners of assets ranging from mortgage-backed securities to municipal bonds, and how it will extract itself from these massive positions.

Unlike previous recessions, the pandemic showed what happens when, rather than doing too little, we maybe do too much. Of course, the pandemic was also different from other recessions. Yet perhaps the biggest lesson, which also makes it difficult to evaluate individual programs by themselves, is that programs supported each other. Because we had sufficient unemployment insurance, income and spending largely held up. So state and local revenues did not decline much, if at all, and businesses that could operate safely had many customers. With the money, fewer people were at risk of eviction, and landlords largely got the rent. And defaults were low, so financial institutions were not at risk, making a financial crisis less likely. With sufficient income support, particularly for the unemployed, other programs become, in hindsight, not as valuable. Yet it is worth remembering the disastrous response to prior recessions to understand the costs of doing too little.

We Learned That We Do Not Have to Repeat Past Policy Mistakes

The defining characteristic of the policy response to the 2008 financial crisis was timidity. Monetary policy that came in only after markets were already spiraling. Too little stimulus. Too little help for regular people. True, some of them had made poor home purchases at the height of the market, but insurer AIG had also made some stupid bets. Yet AIG was "too big to fail," so it was bailed out (and, in turn, the banks it owed money to were bailed out).[27] Individual Americans were not "too big to fail," even collectively, it seems. So many Americans suffered through foreclosures and years of slow employment growth.

During the pandemic, we learned that a large immediate policy response can have a large impact on people's lives. Rather than the slow and timid response to the 2008 financial crisis, a bill almost three times larger than the stimulus bill in February 2009 was passed in the first three weeks of the pandemic. Then another nine months later. Then another three months after that. In total, the fiscal response to the pandemic was more than five times larger than the response to the Great Recession. Rather than the insufficient and ineffective programs that helped relatively few homeowners struggling with their mortgages following the 2008 financial crisis, we had effective and widespread mortgage forbearance and an eviction moratorium.[28]

Stepping back to look at pandemic policies against the broad backdrop of history, pandemic economic policy was extraordinarily effective at preventing financial hardship partly because it learned from past mistakes. It is possible that policies could have been even more effective and more cost effective, of course. And previous recessions were different in many ways, so we should treat comparisons carefully. Among the most important differences, we know what caused the pandemic economic decline, but identifying the cause of recessions generally is hard. It is far harder to treat a patient when you do not know what the disease is. Yet compared with the two closest economic contractions in severity, the Great Depression and the Great Recession, the pandemic economy produced relatively little hardship and the economy bounced back quickly.

The Great Recession starting in 2008 was not nearly as deep as the short pandemic-induced economic coma, but the policy response was smaller and the negative effects lasted for years. The most important work combatting the Great Recession was by the Federal Reserve as it struggled to keep the financial crisis from growing. It is a bit hard to know the appropriate measure of success: Federal Reserve policies broadly defined kept the worst financial crisis since the Great Depression from becoming a depression. But the downturn was so bad that it got its own name—the Great Recession—which is not exactly a mark of success.

In contrast to its slow response to the early problems in 2008, the Federal Reserve quickly deployed tools from the Great Recession starting in March 2020. Stuttering financial markets soon smoothed, perhaps because of Federal Reserve policies, or perhaps they would have smoothed all by themselves. But unlike in the 2008 financial crisis, the Federal Reserve was clearly paying attention from the beginning of the pandemic, which may have been important all by itself. Markets knew the Federal Reserve was ready and willing to "do whatever it takes."[29] Panics tend to be self-fulfilling, so having the Federal Reserve step in can stop them before they even start.

Most estimates suggest that federal spending—what economists call "fiscal policy" to distinguish it from the Federal Reserve's "monetary" policy—helped GDP decline less than it would have otherwise during the Great Recession.[30] But fiscal policy in the Great Recession was distinctly ineffective at preventing widespread financial suffering by people even while it largely bailed out banks and insurers whose investments went bad. Partly, as a percentage of GDP, the one stimulus bill during the Great Recession was several times smaller than pandemic spending.

In addition, Great Recession policy largely failed to help individual families. While peak unemployment was higher during the pandemic, high unemployment did not last long. Unemployment close to 10 percent lasted for years following the Great Recession. Yet the only direct aid to families was a short extension of unemployment eligibility (which normally stops after 26 weeks) and a $400 tax cut.[31] Millions of people lost their homes following the Great Recession partly because policies channeled huge amounts of money to banks but did not require mortgage loan terms to be modified.[32] During the pandemic, the CARES Act *required* lenders to offer loan modifications that suspended payments for a time. Far fewer people needed help with their mortgage during the pandemic, partly because the expanded unemployment insurance benefits and Economic Impact Payments got money directly to people.

Going even further back, the economic decline in the first two quarters of the pandemic economy was similar to the decline in the Great Depression, which started in 1929. While it is hard to get accurate statistics going that far back, the available evidence suggests GDP fell by slightly more in the first two quarters of the pandemic than during the Great Depression and unemployment increased by slightly more in the pandemic.[33]

Yet policy mistakes during the Great Depression turned what might have been just a deep recession into a decade-long depression.[34] Economists still debate the relative importance of different contributing factors, but there is general agreement that policy mistakes in the Great Depression included the following:

- instituting bad monetary policy that decreased the money supply, caused deflation, and was a drag on economic activity for years[35]
- allowing waves of bank failures and bank runs[36]
- pulling back government spending to balance the budget
- not protecting the unemployed
- increasing tariffs and a trade war[37]

Many of the programs and policies that were so important during the pandemic have their roots in the Great Depression. Activist monetary policy during the pandemic vastly expanded the availability of credit, rather than actively harming the economy. The Federal Deposit Insurance Corporation was created in 1933 in response to the bank failures during the Depression. Deposit insurance means traditional bank runs are rare and were not a pandemic problem. Unlike in the Great Depression, the federal government did not try to balance its budget but instead spent rapidly and supported states and households, whose budgets do generally need to balance. Widespread unemployment insurance was created with the Social Security Act and accompanying state laws in 1935 in response to the Great Depression.[38] In contrast to the Great Depression, trade has mostly boomed during the pandemic, although supply chain difficulties and tariff policies made imports more difficult.

While there were certainly gaps in overall pandemic economic policies and inefficiencies from fraud and poorly directed spending, what stands out is how effective these policies were and how much we had learned compared with what could have been. Of course, as economists Carmen Reinhart and Kenneth Rogoff point out in their study of financial crises throughout history, memories are short and it has proved surprisingly difficult for policy lessons to stick.[39] This time was different. Perhaps next time will not be.

We Learned We Can't Keep Ignoring Affordable Housing and Child Care

Affordable housing and child care were problems before the pandemic, but the pandemic briefly showed how deep these problems run. As we saw in Chapter 3, housing is the largest expense for most people—about a third of total spending—and has only gotten more expensive. For families with young children, child care costs are often the second-largest expense.[40] And child care costs are sometimes hidden; rather than paying for child care outside the home, perhaps one parent stays home, giving up her income.

Many prepandemic financial problems come back to these huge costs in families' budgets. The more you spend on housing or child care, the less is available for everything else, leaving households more financially exposed to all the other shocks. And because there is often no easy way to reduce these costs, everything else in a household's budget revolves around them.

Housing became less affordable during the pandemic. Partly, with many people working from home, the demand for housing space went up, but the amount of space barely increased, so house prices rose rapidly. Rents, which had not increased much over 2020, started increasing in 2021 and increased rapidly in 2022.[41] Housing cost increases were a big part of the inflation in 2021 and 2022. Supply chain difficulties made it even harder and more costly to build in 2021 and 2022, so there was no building boom in response to the higher prices. And as the Federal Reserve started raising interest rates in 2022, mortgages became more expensive, making buying even less affordable and raising the costs of building. The pandemic briefly focused attention on the simmering eviction crisis but did nothing for the underlying affordable housing problems that the U.S. had ignored for too long.

When people think "affordable housing," they often think of government programs that build public housing, subsidize rents, or require developers to offer lower-cost housing. And such programs might be part of the solution. But the fundamental reason housing is costly is that more people want housing than there is housing available in a particular place. Subsidies or rent controls don't change that fundamental issue, they only redistribute the money to someone who needs it.

Instead, the problem is supply: we have stopped building in places where people want to live. What keeps that from happening? Mostly local zoning, regulations, and neighborhood opposition.[42] It's easy to see the effects if you look around. For example, in Washington, D.C., the metro system extends out into Virginia and Maryland. On the first stops after crossing the border, there are many apartment buildings. Many of the people who live in these buildings work in Washington (or used to before the pandemic). But Washington makes building densely expensive and prohibits tall buildings, so these buildings get pushed out to places where it is easier to build, increasing traffic, commutes, and housing costs. The economic and social costs to society are immense.[43]

The populations of the San Francisco and San Jose metro areas have increased more slowly, sometimes much more slowly, than the U.S. population over the last 20 years.[44] Economic growth in the Bay Area has been rapid, wages are high, and many people want to move and live there, if they could afford it. Why can't they? Because these cities and surrounding ones have not allowed much new building such as high-density apartment buildings or even multifamily townhouses. As a result, a substantial portion of those high Silicon Valley engineer salaries goes to housing, and the engineers have largely pushed out poorer residents, including Black and Hispanic residents. The displaced have either moved away entirely or taken on massive commutes. Is it any wonder that, during the pandemic, the populations of these prosperous metro areas fell by 3 percent when remote work broke many of these tech workers' needs to live close to their jobs?

The most productive cities and states have chosen to make it difficult to build and increase density. These choices protect rich, mostly white, incumbent homeowners from change. But they reduce economic growth. They make the nation poorer.[45] They perpetuate and increase racial inequities.[46] They trample property rights, keeping owners from developing their property, and keeping people from living how and where they want.[47] They create regional inequality. They harm the environment. And they push economic fragility to more and more people. The pandemic made all of these problems worse and pushed them to new places.

One important pandemic lesson is that solving one problem often solves others; by making housing more generally affordable, we would have fewer financial problems, and the worst problems, such as evictions and homelessness, would be less common. The good news is that, as more people and cities recognize the massive problem we have created by preventing building, perhaps momentum for change will build. Some cities and states are already taking important steps to allow greater density. The pandemic uprooted where many of us work and live and dramatically increased the cost of housing; perhaps it can help more of us say, "Yes in my backyard."

In the meantime, the pandemic showed that substantial rent assistance need not be expensive and mortgage foreclosures can be less common. One 2013 estimate suggests that providing rental assistance to households with incomes below 30 percent of the local median would cost about −$22.5 billion per year and short-term rental relief for families facing temporary difficulties would cost about $3 billion,[48] for a yearly total close to the yearly pandemic rental assistance. For context, in 2013 we spent about $118 billion subsidizing mostly high-income homeowners through mortgage interest tax deductions and other tax exemptions.[49] Similarly, the pandemic experience with mortgage forbearance suggests that it need not be hard or expensive to make foreclosure much less common.

The pandemic also showed how central child care is. Without it, parents cannot work. It's that simple. And when it is unreliable, parents are unreliable employees, if they can work at all. When child care and schools shut down in 2020, millions of mothers left the labor force. And many could not come back in 2021 because child care was often not available or unreliable. While the pandemic did not necessarily show how to make child care available and affordable, it showed we cannot continue to ignore it. Closing gender wage gaps. Economic growth. Labor force participation. Child care is central to all of them.

Yet the U.S. remains an outlier in how much the government helps with child care. Compared with parents in other high-income countries, which directly or indirectly pay for much or all of toddler child care (not to mention substantial parental leave), American parents are largely on their own.[50] We struggle to find child care, and when we find it, we often struggle to pay for it. While many proposals could help, the pandemic showed the high economic costs of ignoring child care.

We Learned Many of Us Can Work from Anywhere (and Maybe Many of Us Should)

As pandemic remote work dragged on from one year to two years, it became increasingly clear that much work could be done remotely. Chapter 8 examines some of remote work's benefits and costs. But we have likely only seen the first signs of a possible revolution. People make location decisions slowly, and relatively few people moved permanently because of pandemic remote work. But that will likely change. As one spouse gets a great job in a new city or needs to return to her hometown to take care of aging parents, rather than quit and look for a new job, the trailing spouse will ask to work remotely. Companies that previously would have said no because remote work was strange, scary, and unknown now understand the value of keeping an employee and how to integrate from afar. Companies may still say no, but the balance of evidence and power has shifted significantly. More and more companies moved to distributed work, with no single central location. By 2022, forcing an employee to move to an expensive city and come into the office was something companies had to negotiate over, not a fact of life.

It seems likely that Americans will work in more varied locations, although the change will be gradual. The big cities will continue to be draws, but smaller cities and rural areas, with more space, lower costs, and proximity to family, will no longer be places to escape from. They may become destinations again. Meanwhile, commercial real estate in big cities may go down in value or get repurposed. During the pandemic, former office buildings were converted to apartments, giving an entirely new meaning to work from home.[51]

The nature of inequality will change. Income and wealth are extremely concentrated in the big cities. Yet even before the pandemic there was a slow spread as those with very high income used the ability to work remotely to choose where to work. Before the pandemic, the most unequal place in the U.S. was Teton County, Wyoming.[52] A getaway destination for tech moguls, Teton County contains the Jackson Hole ski resort, the Grand Teton National Park, part of Yellowstone, a population of just over 20,000, and an economy heavily reliant on tourism. But ranches there were a hot commodity among the very wealthy, who could use it as a retreat yet still be connected to their business empires.

As more professionals realize they can choose where to live, more areas may come to resemble Teton County, although perhaps not quite as extreme. Real estate in Boise, Idaho, went through a boom during the pandemic as many newcomers moved there for its relatively affordable housing (compared with California) and location, pricing out many locals.[53] Even if employers are no longer willing to pay Bay Area wages to people not working in the Bay Area, the newcomers' wages will still likely be substantially higher than the local average. Local income and wealth inequality will increase. But it is important to remember that this inequality already existed; it's just that the high-income workers were geographically concentrated. Increasing remote work will increase inequality locally, but not necessarily change it nationally.

The new remote workers will also bring benefits. They will pay taxes. They will spend locally. They will tend to economically revitalize the places they move to. By breaking the stranglehold that location has for work, remote work can help flatten some of the growing geographic differences, spreading prosperity around more.

The new remote workers can also help bridge some of the great social divides that have developed. We have increasingly sorted ourselves into like-minded enclaves where almost everyone votes for the same political party, worships in the same churches (or not at all), and marries within the group.[54] Part of the sorting is by education, as many college educated moved to the big cities. Remote work lets the people who used to flow to the big cities return to their hometowns, exposing themselves, and their hometowns, to a broader world.

We Learned What Was Important to Us

On March 15, 2022, almost exactly two years after the first shutdowns, the Washington, D.C., public school system lifted its mask mandate. The Omicron surge, which had hit the D.C. region hard, had left D.C. schools cautious. But declining case counts and low within-school transmission meant it was time to start moving away from the pandemic's most visible protection measure. In a sign of how much had changed, when I talked with other parents, we weren't certain how to proceed. We wanted our kids to interact and learn maskless—to live in a world with only regular childhood worries—but we also wanted them to be safe and respectful of others. My wife and I asked our son what he wanted to do. He could barely remember a world without masks or virtual school, and he left it on until the end of the school year. As school mask mandates ended throughout the country that spring, many children now had to make yet another transition.[55]

Just as my son had to navigate a new world with new rules, as the virus receded, we all had to confront a new world. Many people had hardly altered their behavior and wondered what took everybody else so long. Others planned to continue social distancing and masking, appreciating the safety and social protection it afforded. In February 2022, close to 15 percent of respondents in one study of evolving workplace norms said they expected to continue social distancing even after the pandemic ended.[56] For these respondents, the pandemic had profoundly shaped their interactions with the world.

While I have focused on the pandemic's financial impacts, the pandemic forced many Americans to reevaluate what mattered. Fittingly, what mattered differed. For people working from home, it was often the realization that life is much better without a soul-crushing commute. Many decided that they were not interested in returning to the grind. For people who lost their jobs, it was often the forced realization that their job was not their life. Many decided they wanted to switch careers or stop working altogether. For many essential workers, it was the realization that their job was not worth their life. Many quit in search of better jobs.

Overall, these changes added up to a massive shift in views toward work and life. On average, the onset of the pandemic caused a 4.6 percent drop in the number of hours people wanted to work, which persisted through 2021.[57] Even as wages increased, many people, particularly those who could not work from home, decided that the pay was not worth it to bring them in. Much of the lower labor force participation that persisted into 2022, despite a tight job market, was because many people had reevaluated their priorities.

For others, it was the opportunity to start a new business and try something new. "I've been wanting to do it for years," Rose Galer told *Wired*.[58] She had quit a safe government job at the EPA to start zero-waste retail business Refill Exchange. "The pandemic made me think, you know what? If there's a time to do it, it's now." The better safety net and higher savings during the pandemic also provided many people the financial space to invest in themselves. By forcing many people to take a step back and reconsider, the pandemic let them see an opportunity. And by giving them the money to invest, pandemic policy helped them pursue it.

The pandemic helped show us what matters. Even as it stole more than a year of our lives, limited our choices, and killed many of our loved ones, it showed us we can take back control of our financial lives. It showed us we can have better social policy. It showed us that we can take on big problems, if we want to. It showed us we can work where we want to and take back control of how we work. It killed more than a million of us, but maybe it showed us a better way forward.

This book started with a terrifying economic collapse on top of the already precarious situation for many families. It ends more positively. While the pandemic was difficult, it briefly gave us a new economic freedom. While we failed in many ways to protect ourselves and each other from the virus, briefly and effectively, we protected ourselves and each other economically. We saved more. We made bipartisan agreements that positively affected our lives. We developed new programs that addressed long-standing needs.

Many of the programs we expanded or introduced during the pandemic, from better unemployment insurance, to rental relief, to mortgage forbearance, to the refundable child tax credits, could continue. And our pandemic experience suggests that with them unemployment would no longer be a financial disaster, jobs and pay might get better, fewer people would get evicted or lose their homes, child poverty would decline, and financial hardships and the difficult choices that accompany them would no longer be common. Without the pandemic rush to get money out the door, surely these or other programs could be even better. The pandemic policies did not reach everyone, and the big problems of housing affordability, child care, and wealth inequality linger. But while the pandemic caused great suffering, if we learn its lessons well, perhaps it can help us prevent suffering as well.

Epilogue

During the pandemic's first year, Sofia had not carried any credit card debt thanks to the expanded unemployment insurance benefits, Economic Impact Payments, and child tax credit, as we saw earlier in the book. In August 2021 she started carrying a balance again, around the same time many families like hers went back-to-school shopping. First her credit card debt passed $1,000 over the next several months, then $2,000; then, in spring 2022, she hit her card's limit of about $3,000, where her credit card debt stayed through the summer. A new medical debt showed up in collection on Sofia's credit record in fall 2021. Perhaps one of her kids had fallen ill. These trends suggest that Sofia was having some of the same difficulties making ends meet she'd experienced before the pandemic.

On average in October 2022, people were still better off financially than they had been before the pandemic. Checking account balances were higher, and credit card debt and defaults were still lower.[1] Employers struggled to enforce return-to-office mandates and the labor market remained tight, giving workers more power. But other aspects of life began to feel more like they had in 2019. For many, the pandemic's economic waves—higher savings, lower spending, and greater financial security—were fading away. Many people spent more on "revenge travel," catching up on missed vacations and buying fewer physical goods. Continuing high inflation and rising interest rates were squeezing others, and it was still too soon to tell whether it would take a recession to bring inflation down. Low-income renters were particularly hard hit as rents increased rapidly and housing became even less affordable.[2] The uncertainty and emerging financial threats left people feeling no better about their finances in 2022 than they had in 2019.[3] The pandemic paradox had not disappeared, but by October 2022 its direct financial impact was fading away.

The U.S. was returning to its prepandemic state in other ways as well. COVID-19 deaths fell by May 2022 to their lowest level since March 2020, averaging between 300 and 500 per day through September. These deaths were still tragic, but they had become comparable to other causes of death that were no longer shocking. Around 500 people died every day from accidents in 2019 and an average of 160 died every day from the flu and pneumonia.[4] COVID-19 had become one source of mortality among many. Yet this normalization misses how shockingly many were still dying from COVID-19 in the U.S. compared with other rich countries. Before the pandemic, life expectancy in the U.S. was already worse than that in other rich countries. The gap increased in 2020, and, as COVID-19 deaths continued, the gap increased again in 2021.[5]

Yet even as the U.S. moved on from treating COVID-19 as a pandemic, three significant new policies showed perhaps the high-water mark of the pandemic's policy waves. Partly responding to the pandemic's semiconductor shortages, an act to promote U.S. semiconductor manufacturing and create regional research hubs became law in August 2022. Then a massive act to fight climate change and fill health insurance gaps became law in August 2022. High inflation had continued through that summer, so the bill was named the Inflation Reduction Act, although its inflation impact was likely to be small. Finally, having given away $800 billion to mostly high-income small business owners through the Paycheck Protection Program, it became politically unpalatable to resume student loan payments without some sort of debt relief. So when the Department of Education announced it would extend the student loan payment pause through the end of the year for a final time in August 2022, it also announced it would forgive up to $10,000 in debt for borrowers who earned less than $125,000 a year and $20,000 for low-income Pell Grant recipients. If the debt forgiveness occurred and reached her, it is likely that Sofia would benefit. She had struggled with student loans from a degree she never finished. Tamira and Lisa, who struggled with loans they took out for their children, might also benefit.

Would these policies have been enacted without the pandemic? Perhaps. But supply chain issues brought greater attention to where things are made. Both the climate and semiconductor bills pushed for more U.S. manufacturing. The student loan payment freeze in the March 2020 CARES Act paved the way for outright debt relief in August 2022. And the climate change bill came from ambitious plans to "build back better" following the pandemic.

Even as the pandemic paradox's direct effects seemed to fade away, these policies and other proposals worked to ingrain it at a deeper level. The pandemic had showed the potential for ambitious government programs to transform society. We had seen the effects of rental assistance and eviction diversion programs, expanded unemployment insurance, and a stronger labor market. We had learned that it is still possible to do big things about systemic problems like climate change. After all, we had managed to protect each other financially from the biggest economic collapse since the Great Depression.

ACKNOWLEDGMENTS

THIS BOOK represents my own views, which are not necessarily the views of the Consumer Financial Protection Bureau (CFPB) or the United States. Parts of this book incorporate independent research I conducted while I was employed as an economist at the CFPB. Under the CFPB's independent research policy, the Assistant Director for the Office of Research reviewed these portions before their being made public. Following government ethics rules, as a government employee whose job includes research in consumer finance, I have not received any royalties for writing this book.

Thanks to Éva Nagypál, Erik Durbin, David Silberman, Phil Stoffel, Mark and Katherine Fulford, Susanto Basu, Christina Wang, Etan Ilfeld, and two anonymous reviewers whose comments improved the book. Thanks also to the editors and staff at Princeton University Press.

This book draws from the insights I gained explaining frequent economic changes in real time to a general audience within the CFPB. Thanks to Eric Wilson, Éva Nagypál, Leah Kazar, and Marie Rush, who contributed to these economics updates, and Jason Brown, who edited them.

Parts of this book draw from the CFPB's Making Ends Meet survey and reports written using the survey data. Many people helped contribute to developing the survey, including Jesse Leary, Cheryl Cooper, Lauren Taylor, Anita Chen, Marie Rush, Brian Bucks, and Mick Couper. Eric Wilson, Cortnie Shupe, and Marie Rush wrote reports with me using the survey. This book benefited from their work and thoughts on those reports. And thanks to the Americans who took time from their busy lives to respond to the survey. I hope I have fairly represented your financial ups and downs.

A great flowering of research occurred during the pandemic. Many organizations and researchers sought to better understand the pandemic's effects. This book benefits from this vibrant research and so much hard work. While it was a devastating time for the world, it was an exciting time to do research and to follow research. Often the best research comes from the worst of times. Economics is known as the "dismal science" for a reason.

Finally, thanks to my wife, who encouraged me to write this book and kept me from drifting too much into economese, the impenetrable language economists use to converse with each other.

I miss you, Sherwin. Thanks for sweating with us in the backyard in August 2020 and freezing in January 2021. I would have loved talking about this book with you.

NOTES

Chapter One

1. Jeff Cox, "Janet Yellen Says Second-Quarter GDP Could Decline by 30% and Unemployment Is Already at 12%–13%," CNBC, April 6, 2020, https://www.cnbc.com/2020/04/06/janet-yellen-says-second-quarter-gdp-could-decline-by-30percent-and-unemployment-is-already-at-12percent-13percent.html.

2. Heather Long and Andrew Van Dam, "U.S. Unemployment Rate Soars to 14.7 Percent, the Worst since the Depression Era," *Washington Post*, May 8, 2020, https://www.washingtonpost.com/business/2020/05/08/april-2020-jobs-report/.

3. Lucia Mutikani, "COVID-19 Crushes U.S. Economy in Second Quarter; Rising Virus Cases Loom over Recovery," Reuters, July 30, 2020, https://www.reuters.com/article/us-usa-economy-idUSKCN24V0FO.

4. This number is an approximation assuming Sofia earned $10,000 in the previous year and using the Texas Workforce Commission calculation that unemployment benefits are the "base period quarter with the highest wages" divided by 25. See Texas Workforce Commission, "Eligibility & Benefit Amounts," accessed June 22, 2022, https://www.twc.texas.gov/jobseekers/eligibility-benefit-amounts.

5. While the survey gives a rich picture, it is an incomplete one. The respondents' credit bureau records help give context for their financial situations and fill in some information. But financial cause and effect are not always clear, and no survey can capture the complete narrative of people's complicated and full lives. To help connect the narrative, I sometimes fill in supporting information that was not directly on the survey or suggest a possible cause for a financial decision. This supporting information does not change the overall financial story but gives it some coherence. I try to be transparent about what I know from the survey and which pieces I have filled in using other information. In addition, to protect respondents' privacy, I give only general locations and do not report exact numbers.

6. Consumer Financial Protection Bureau, "Building the CFPB: A Progress Report," July 18, 2011, https://www.consumerfinance.gov/data-research/research-reports/building-the-cfpb/.

7. Dodd-Frank Wall Street Reform and Consumer Protection Act, Public Law 111-203, 124 Stat. 1968 (2010), Section 1013(b)(1), https://www.govinfo.gov/content/pkg/STATUTE-124/pdf/STATUTE-124-Pg1376.pdf.

8. For two accounts more focused on the political deliberations of the early pandemic policies, see Nick Timiraos, *Trillion Dollar Triage*, Little, Brown, 2022; and Adam Tooze, *Shutdown*, Viking, 2021.

9. Estimates suggest that by February 2022, 58 percent had antibodies for infection. See Kristie E. N. Clarke, Jefferson M. Jones, . . . , and Adam MacNeil, "Seroprevalence of Infection-Induced SARS-CoV-2 Antibodies—United States, September 2021–February 2022," *Morbidity and Mortality Weekly Report*, April 26, 2022, http://dx.doi.org/10.15585/mmwr.mm7117e3. Later estimates suggest 82 percent of people in the U.S. had been infected at least once by July 11, 2022. See Institute for Health Metrics and Evaluation, "COVID-19 Results Briefing United States of America" July 18, 2022, https://www.healthdata.org/sites/default/files/Projects /COVID/2022/102_briefing_United_States_of_America_8.pdf.

Chapter Two

1. For some of the many things that happened that day, see Laurel Wamsley, "March 11, 2020: The Day Everything Changed," NPR, March 11, 2021, https://www.npr.org/2021/03/11 /975663437/march-11-2020-the-day-everything-changed.

2. World Health Organization, "WHO Director-General's Opening Remarks at the Media Briefing on COVID-19," March 11, 2020, https://www.who.int/director-general/speeches/detail /who-director-general-s-opening-remarks-at-the-media-briefing-on-covid-19---11-march -2020.

3. Bill Chappel, "Coronavirus: Over 1,000 Cases Now in U.S., and 'It's Going to Get Worse,' Fauci Says," NPR, March 11, 2020, https://www.npr.org/sections/health-shots/2020/03/11 /814460233/coronavirus-1-000-cases-now-in-u-s-and-it-s-going-to-get-worse-fauci-says.

4. Calculations based on S&P Dow Jones Indices LLC, S&P 500, retrieved from FRED, https://fred.stlouisfed.org/series/SP500.

5. Chappel, "Coronavirus."

6. Maura Judkis, "Who Were We and What Were We Thinking? A Return to Offices Frozen in Time," *Washington Post*, April 28, 2021, https://www.washingtonpost.com/lifestyle/style /returning-to-office-frozen-in-pre-pandemic-time/2021/04/27/281ce604-9959-11eb-b28d -bfa7bb5cb2a5_story.html.

7. Source: Author's calculations using Bureau of Labor Statistics, "Employment-Population Ratio—Black or African American" and "Employment-Population Ratio," retrieved from FRED, https://fred.stlouisfed.org/graph/?g=EcTo.

8. Paul Davidson, "It's Official: The US Is in a Recession, Ending Longest Expansion in History," *USA Today*, June 8, 2020, https://www.usatoday.com/story/money/2020/06/08 /recession-begins-us-ending-longest-expansion-history/5320335002/.

9. Katharine G. Abraham and Melissa S. Kearney, "Explaining the Decline in the US Employment-to-Population Ratio: A Review of the Evidence," *Journal of Economic Literature*, 2020, 58(3): 585–643.

10. Source: Author's calculations using Bureau of Labor Statistics, "Average Hourly Earnings of All Employees, Total Private" and "Consumer Price Index for All Urban Consumers: All Items," retrieved from FRED, https://fred.stlouisfed.org/graph/?g=EqVg.

11. Black employment does decline more in recessions, although it seems that historically it is not necessarily that Black applicants are the last to be hired, but that job losses for Black employees continue to be high for longer in a recession and the recovery. See Kenneth A. Couch

and Robert Fairlie, "Last Hired, First Fired? Black-White Unemployment and the Business Cycle," *Demography*, 2010, 47: 227–47, https://doi.org/10.1353/dem.0.0086.

12. Black employment fell from 59.4 percent in January 2007 to 52.0 percent in December 2009, a fall of 12.4 percent, while overall employment only fell from 63.3 percent to 58.3 percent, a fall of 7.9 percent.

13. Bureau of Labor Statistics, "Employment Situation Technical Note," last modified June 4, 2021, https://www.bls.gov/news.release/empsit.tn.htm.

14. Source: Author's calculations using Employment and Training Administration, "Initial Claims," retrieved from FRED, https://fred.stlouisfed.org/graph/?g=EI77.

15. Katia Dmitrieva, "U.S. Jobless Claims Soar to Once-Unthinkable Record 6.65 Million," *Bloomberg*, April 2, 2020, https://www.bloomberg.com/news/articles/2020-04-02/u-s-jobless-claims-doubled-to-record-6-65-million-last-week; Jim Zarroli and Avie Schneider, "3.3 Million File Unemployment Claims, Shattering Records," NPR, March 26, 2020, https://www.npr.org/2020/03/26/821580191/unemployment-claims-expected-to-shatter-records; Henry Olson, "Opinion: The Unemployment Numbers Are Terrifying. But We Ain't Seen Nothing Yet," *Washington Post*, April 2, 2020, https://www.washingtonpost.com/opinions/2020/04/02/unemployment-numbers-are-terrifying-we-aint-seen-nothing-yet/.

16. Department of Labor, "Unemployment Insurance Weekly Claims," April 2, 2020, https://oui.doleta.gov/press/2020/040220.pdf.

17. The problem is that the standard methodology multiplied the actual unemployment claim by a seasonal factor. When claims increased by more than 1,000 percent at the end of March, just when regular seasonal unemployment claims generally start to fall, the seasonal adjustment statistically created close to a million claims a week. Recognizing the problem, the BLS updated its approach starting with the September 3, 2020, release. After that, it added or subtracted some seasonal claims, rather than multiplying, which reduced the distortion and brought its "headline numbers" closer to reality. See Department of Labor, "Unemployment Insurance Weekly Claims," August 27, 2020, https://oui.doleta.gov/press/2020/082720.pdf.

18. For excellent discussions of two families' difficulties, see Jonathan Morduch and Rachel Schneider, "Spikes and Dips: How Income Uncertainty Affects Households," U.S. Financial Diaries, October 2013, https://www.usfinancialdiaries.org/issue1-spikes; and Jonathan Morduch and Rachel Schneider, *The Financial Diaries: How American Families Cope in a World of Uncertainty*, Princeton University Press, 2017.

19. Ben Casselman, "Why Unemployment Claims May Be Overcounted by Millions," *New York Times*, September 16, 2020, https://www.nytimes.com/2020/09/16/business/economy/unemployment-claims-numbers.html.

20. Bureau of Labor Statistics, "Employment Situation News Release," May 8, 2020, https://www.bls.gov/news.release/archives/empsit_05082020.htm.

21. See Heather Long, "A 'Misclassification Error' Made the May Unemployment Rate Look Better than It Is. Here's What Happened," *Washington Post*, June 6, 2020, https://www.washingtonpost.com/business/2020/06/05/may-2020-jobs-report-misclassification-error/; Bureau of Labor Statistics, "Employment Situation News Release," June 5, 2020, https://www.bls.gov/news.release/archives/empsit_06052020.htm; and Bureau of Labor Statistics, "Employment Situation News Release," May 8, 2020.

22. Employment and Training Administration, "Advisory: Unemployment Insurance Program Letter No. 14-05," Advisory System, February 18, 2005, https://oui.doleta.gov/dmstree/uipl/uipl2k5/uipl_1405.htm.

23. Tim Henderson, "Unemployment Payments Weeks Late in Nearly Every State," Stateline, December 2, 2020, https://www.pewtrusts.org/en/research-and-analysis/blogs/stateline/2020/12/02/unemployment-payments-weeks-late-in-nearly-every-state.

24. Source: Author's calculations from Employment and Training Administration, "Benefits: Timeliness and Quality Reports," https://oui.doleta.gov/unemploy/btq/btqrpt.asp.

25. Henderson, "Unemployment Payments."

26. Kif Leswing, "New Jersey Needs Volunteers Who Know COBOL, a 60-Year-Old Programming Language," CNBC, April 6, 2020, https://www.cnbc.com/2020/04/06/new-jersey-seeks-cobol-programmers-to-fix-unemployment-system.html.

27. Tim Henderson, "Fight against Fraud Slows Payments to Unemployed," Stateline, August 27, 2020, https://www.pewtrusts.org/en/research-and-analysis/blogs/stateline/2020/08/27/fight-against-fraud-slows-payments-to-unemployed.

28. Felix Salmon, "Half of the Pandemic's Unemployment Money May Have Been Stolen," Axios, June 10, 2021, https://www.axios.com/pandemic-unemployment-fraud-benefits-stolen-a937ad9d-0973-4aad-814f-4ca47b72f67f.html.

29. Henderson, "Fight against Fraud."

30. The term "Great Pause" was used in several places early in the pandemic. For example, see Bruno Maçães, "The Great Pause Was an Economic Revolution," Foreign Policy, June 22, 2020, https://foreignpolicy.com/2020/06/22/the-great-pause-was-an-economic-revolution%E2%80%A8/.

31. Sarah Mervosh, Denise Lu, and Vanessa Swales, "See Which States and Cities Have Told Residents to Stay at Home," New York Times, April 20, 2020, https://www.nytimes.com/interactive/2020/us/coronavirus-stay-at-home-order.html.

32. Bureau of Transportation Statistics, "Daily Travel during the COVID-19 Public Health Emergency," September 2, 2020, https://www.bts.gov/daily-travel.

33. Unacast, "Social Distancing Scoreboard," June 8, 2021, https://www.unacast.com/covid19/social-distancing-scoreboard#scoreboard.

34. Alexander W. Bartik, Marianne Bertrand, . . . and Matt Unrath, "Measuring the Labor Market at the Onset of the COVID-19 Crisis" (NBER Working Paper No. 27613, July 2020), 13, https://www.nber.org/papers/w27613.

35. Bartik, Bertrand, . . . and Unrath, "Measuring."

36. Éva Nagypál, Christa Gibbs, and Scott Fulford, "The Early Effects of the COVID-19 Pandemic on Credit Applications," CFPB Office of Research Special Issue Brief, April 2020, https://files.consumerfinance.gov/f/documents/cfpb_issue-brief_early-effects-covid-19-credit-applications_2020-04.pdf. Note that our publication preceded other evidence such as that of Opportunity Insights, which launched its excellent tracker on May 7.

37. Lauren Rosenblatt, "Car Dealerships Want Permission to Start Sales Again in Pennsylvania," Pittsburgh Post-Gazette, April 14, 2020, https://www.post-gazette.com/business/career-workplace/2020/04/14/car-dealerships-nonessential-non-life-sustaining-businesses-Pennsylvania-coronavirus-COVID19/stories/202004130113.

38. The Opportunity Insights team was led by Raj Chetty, John N. Friedman, Nathaniel Hendren, and Michael Stepner, and the tracker is available at https://tracktherecovery.org/. See the companion paper: Raj Chetty, John N. Friedman, . . . and the Opportunity Insights Team, "The Economic Impacts of COVID-19: Evidence from a New Public Database Built Using Private Sector Data" (working paper, November 2020), https://opportunityinsights.org/wp-content/uploads/2020/05/tracker_paper.pdf. We will discuss the insights from this work in greater detail in Chapter 4, as it helped understand the impact of the CARES Act and later relief bills.

39. These calculations are seasonally adjusted because we would normally expect a big increase in sales in the spring. For example, actual sales were about flat from February to March 2020, but we normally see a big increase in spending in the spring, so flat sales represents a big decline relative to what consumers and retailers normally do. Source: Census Bureau, "Monthly Retail Trade Report," https://www.census.gov/retail/index.html.

40. See Lucy Bayly, "Economy in Reverse: Initial Jobless Claims Rise for Second Week, GDP Falls by Record 33 Percent," NBC, July 30, 2020, https://www.nbcnews.com/business/economy/economy-reverse-initial-jobless-claims-rise-second-week-gdp-falls-n1235262; and Paul Davidson, "US Economy Contracted Record 32.9% in Q2 amid State Shutdowns, COVID-19 Contagion Fears," *USA Today*, July 30, 2020, https://www.usatoday.com/story/money/2020/07/30/economy-gdp-fell-annual-rate-32-9-q-2-amid-covid-19-crisis/5536647002/.

41. See Ben Casslman, "Why You'll See Two Figures for G.D.P. Decline: Very Big, and Huge," *New York Times*, July 29, 2020, https://www.nytimes.com/2020/07/29/business/economy/us-gdp-report.html, which kept the *New York Times* from incorrectly reporting. Similarly, the *Washington Post* reported the correct 9.5 percent contraction, warning that the annualized rate is "less useful this quarter because the economy is unlikely to experience another collapse like it did in the second quarter." See Rachel Siege and Andrew Van Dam, "U.S. Economy Contracted at Fastest Quarterly Rate on Record from April to June as Coronavirus Walloped Workers, Businesses," *Washington Post*, July 30, 2020, https://www.washingtonpost.com/business/2020/07/30/gdp-q2-coronavirus/.

42. David C. Wheelock, "Comparing the COVID-19 Recession with the Great Depression," *Economic Synopses*, August 2020, no. 39, Federal Reserve Bank of St. Louis, https://research.stlouisfed.org/publications/economic-synopses/2020/08/12/comparing-the-covid-19-recession-with-the-great-depression.

43. Source: Author's calculations from S&P Dow Jones Indices LLC, "S&P 500," retrieved from FRED, https://fred.stlouisfed.org/series/SP500.

44. Jeffrey Cheng, Tyler Powel, Dave Skidmore, and David Wessel, "What's the Fed Doing in Response to the COVID-19 Crisis? What More Could It Do?," Brookings, The Hutchins Center Explains, March 30, 2021, https://www.brookings.edu/research/fed-response-to-covid19/.

45. A decrease in prices causes the yield on a bond to increase, so the difference between corporate bonds and Treasury rates increased during this period. See Julian Kozlowski, Miguel Faria-e-Castro, and Mahdi Ebsim, "Credit Spreads during the Financial Crisis and COVID 19," *On the Economy* (blog), St. Louis Fed, February 8, 2021, https://www.stlouisfed.org/on-the-economy/2021/february/credit-spreads-financial-crisis-covid19.

46. Joseph G. Haubrich, "Stress, Contagion, and Transmission: 2020 Financial Stability Conference," Federal Reserve Bank of Cleveland, March 31, 2021, https://www.clevelandfed.org /en/newsroom-and-events/publications/economic-commentary/2021-economic -commentaries/ec-202107-financial-stability-conference-2020-summary.aspx.

47. Federal Reserve Board of Governors, "Federal Reserve Issues FOMC Statement," March 15, 2020, https://www.federalreserve.gov/newsevents/pressreleases/monetary20200315a.htm.

48. See Federal Reserve Statistical Release H.4.1, "Factors Affecting Reserve Balances," March 12, 2020, April 30, 2020, and December 31, 2020, https://www.federalreserve.gov/releases /h41/.

49. Federal Reserve Board of Governors, "Federal Reserve Board Announces Establishment of a Primary Dealer Credit Facility (PDCF) to Support the Credit Needs of Households and Businesses," March 17, 2020, https://www.federalreserve.gov/newsevents/pressreleases /monetary20200317b.htm.

50. Cheng, Powel, Skidmore, and Wessel, "What's the Fed Doing?" See also Federal Reserve Board of Governors, "Federal Reserve Board Broadens Program of Support for the Flow of Credit to Households and Businesses by Establishing a Money Market Mutual Fund Liquidity Facility (MMLF)," March 18, 2020, https://www.federalreserve.gov/newsevents/pressreleases /monetary20200318a.htm.

51. See Nick Timiraos, *Trillion Dollar Triage*, Little, Brown, 2022, 220–27.

52. Federal Reserve Board of Governors, "Primary Market Corporate Credit Facility," accessed June 11, 2010, https://www.federalreserve.gov/monetarypolicy/pmccf.htm.

53. Federal Reserve Board of Governors, "Transcript of Chair Powell's Press Conference," April 29, 2020, https://www.federalreserve.gov/mediacenter/files/FOMCpresconf20200429 .pdf.

54. For a discussion of some of the actions taken during this time, see Timiraos, *Trillion Dollar Triage*; and Adam Tooze, *Shutdown*, Viking, 2021, chap. 6.

55. Throughout the book, whenever I used exact numbers for an individual, the underlying number is actually within a range or is an approximation. I typically indicate this approximation by including "about." For example, the income Marcus reported on the survey was between $20,000 and $40,000. I round or alter numbers from the credit bureau in ways that do not change the conclusion to provide additional protections for respondents' privacy.

56. Chapter 3 discusses the financial well-being scale in greater detail. The distribution is fixed in 2016 so that we can see how the pandemic affected individuals compared with the prepandemic financial well-being distribution. Later chapters discuss how financial well-being changed on average during the pandemic. Sources: Making Ends Meet; Consumer Financial Protection Bureau, "National Financial Well-Being Survey," 2017, https://www.consumerfinance .gov/data-research/financial-well-being-survey-data/.

Chapter Three

1. This figure and other tables and figures in the chapter draw from Scott Fulford and Marie Rush, "Insights from the Making Ends Meet Survey," Consumer Financial Protection Bureau Office of Research, Research Brief No. 2020-1, July 2020, https://www.consumerfinance.gov /data-research/research-reports/insights-making-ends-meet-survey/.

2. For example, the Making Ends Meet survey benefits from the financial diaries approach described in Jonathan Morduch and Rachel Schneider, *The Financial Diaries: How American Families Cope in a World of Uncertainty*, Princeton University Press, 2017.

3. Bureau of Labor Statistics, "Consumer Expenditures Report 2019," December 2020, https://www.bls.gov/opub/reports/consumer-expenditures/2019/home.htm.

4. Source: Author's calculations from Census Bureau, "Median Household Income in the United States," and Department of Housing and Urban Development, "Median Sales Price of Houses Sold for the United States," retrieved from FRED, https://fred.stlouisfed.org/series /MSPUS. I linearly interpolate the annual releases for median income to compare with quarterly housing prices and project forward the 2020 median income (the last available as of writing) assuming it changes at the rate of inflation.

5. Sam Khater, "One of the Most Important Challenges Our Industry Will Face: The Significant Shortage of Starter Homes," Freddie Mac, April 15, 2021, http://www.freddiemac.com /perspectives/sam_khater/20210415_single_family_shortage.page.

6. Joint Center for Housing Studies of Harvard University, "The State of the Nation's Housing 2020," 2020, 34, https://www.jchs.harvard.edu/sites/default/files/reports/files/Harvard _JCHS_The_State_of_the_Nations_Housing_2020_Report_Revised_120720.pdf.

7. David S. Johnson, John M. Rogers, and Lucilla Tan, "A Century of Family Budgets in the United States," *Monthly Labor Review*, Bureau of Labor Statistics, May 2021, https://www.bls .gov/opub/mlr/2001/05/art3full.pdf.

8. Ryan Nunn, Jana Parsons, and Jay Shambaugh, "A Dozen Facts about the Economics of the US Health-Care System," Brookings Institution, The Hamilton Project, March 10, 2020, https://www.brookings.edu/research/a-dozen-facts-about-the-economics-of-the-u-s-health -care-system/.

9. Measuring the incidence of healthcare costs is hard, and estimates differ as to how much appears in lower wage growth, increased premium costs, lower benefits, or lower employment. One recent estimate suggests that changes from hospital consolidation (which tend to increase local healthcare prices) had the effect of reducing wages or benefits. See Daniel R. Arnold and Christopher M. Whaley, "Who Pays for Health Care Costs? The Effects of Health Care Prices on Wages" (RAND Working Paper WR-A621-2, July 2020), https://www.rand.org/pubs /working_papers/WRA621-2.html. Other studies find a wider range of effects. See the summary in Laurel Lucia and Ken Jacobs, "Increases in Health Care Costs Are Coming out of Workers' Pockets One Way or Another," UC Berkeley Labor Center, January 29, 2020, https:// laborcenter.berkeley.edu/employer-premium-contributions-and-wages/.

10. Julia Ticona, "Smartphones Are a New Tax on the Poor," *Wired*, December 16, 2021, https://www.wired.com/story/phones-connectivity-tax-policy/.

11. Elizabeth Kneebone and Natalie Holmes, "The Growing Distance between People and Jobs in Metropolitan America," Brookings Institution, Metropolitan Policy Program, July 2016, https://www.brookings.edu/wp-content/uploads/2016/07/srvy_jobsproximity .pdf.

12. Christof Spieler, "Racism Has Shaped Public Transit, and It's Riddled with Inequities," Rice University, Kinder Institute for Urban Research, August 24, 2020, https://kinder.rice.edu /urbanedge/2020/08/24/transportation-racism-has-shaped-public-transit-america -inequalities.

13. See Mikayla Bouchard, "Transportation Emerges as Crucial to Escaping Poverty," *New York Times*, May 7, 2015, https://www.nytimes.com/2015/05/07/upshot/transportation-emerges-as-crucial-to-escaping-poverty.html; and Kyle DeMaria, "Getting to Work on Time: Public Transit and Job Access in Northeastern Pennsylvania," Federal Reserve Bank of Philadelphia, January 2018, https://www.philadelphiafed.org/community-development/workforce-and-economic-development/getting-to-work-on-time.

14. Karen E. Dynan, Douglas W. Elmendorf, and Daniel E. Sichel, "The Evolution of Household Income Volatility," *B.E. Journal of Economic Analysis and Policy: Advances*, 2012, 12(2), https://doi.org/10.1515/1935-1682.3347.

15. For a discussion of many of these issues, see Katherine Guyot and Richard V. Reeves, "Unpredictable Work Hours and Volatile Incomes Are Long-Term Risks for American Workers," *Up Front* (blog), Brookings Institution, August 18, 2020, https://www.brookings.edu/blog/up-front/2020/08/18/unpredictable-work-hours-and-volatile-incomes-are-long-term-risks-for-american-workers/.

16. These statistics and some of this discussion are from Fulford and Rush, "Insights."

17. Jesse Bricker, Lisa J. Dettling, . . . and Richard A. Windle, "Changes in U.S. Family Finances from 2013 to 2016: Evidence from the Survey of Consumer Finances," *Federal Reserve Bulletin*, 2017, 103(3): 13, https://www.federalreserve.gov/publications/files/scf17.pdf.

18. Peter Ganong, Damon Jones, . . . and Chris Wheat, "Wealth, Race, and Consumption Smoothing of Typical Income Shocks" (NBER Working Paper No. 27552, July 2020), https://www.nber.org/papers/w27552.

19. For more on rollover and persistence of payday, auto title, and pawn loans, see Scott Fulford and Cortnie Shupe, "Consumer Use of Payday, Auto Title, and Pawn Loans: Insights from the Making Ends Meet Survey," Consumer Financial Protection Bureau Office of Research, Research Brief No. 2021-1, May 2021, https://www.consumerfinance.gov/data-research/research-reports/consumer-use-of-payday-auto-title-and-pawn-loans-insights-making-ends-meet-survey/; and Kathleen Burke, Jonathan Lanning, Jesse Leary, and Jialan Wang, "Payday Lending," Consumer Financial Protection Bureau Office of Research, Data Point, March 2014, https://files.consumerfinance.gov/f/201403_cfpb_report_payday-lending.pdf.

20. For a similar perspective asking why the poor in India, who are often borrowing at such high interest rates that any spending reduction has a spectacular return, still buy cups of tea, see Abhijit V. Banerjee and Esther Duflo, *Poor Economics: A Radical Rethinking of the Way to Fight Global Poverty*, PublicAffairs, 2012.

21. Daryl Collins, Jonathan Morduch, Stuart Rutherford, and Orlanda Ruthven, *The Portfolios of the Poor*, Princeton University Press, 2010.

22. Karen Berman and Joe Knight, "What Did Bernard Madoff Do?," *Harvard Business Review*, June 30, 2009, https://hbr.org/2009/06/what-did-bernard-madoff-do.

23. Financial Health Network, "FinHealth Score Toolkit," accessed December 1, 2021, https://finhealthnetwork.org/tools/financial-health-score/.

24. Consumer Financial Protection Bureau, "Financial Well-Being: The Goal of Financial Education," January 2015, https://files.consumerfinance.gov/f/201501_cfpb_report_financial-well-being.pdf.

25. If you want to answer these questions and find out your financial well-being score, go to https://www.consumerfinance.gov/consumer-tools/financial-well-being/.

26. This number is slightly different from the average financial well-being of all wave 1 respondents. The difference is whether the sample consists of people who responded to all three surveys or just one.

27. Scott L. Fulford, "The Surprisingly Low Importance of Income Uncertainty for Precaution," *European Economic Review*, 2015, 79: 151–71, https://doi.org/10.1016/j.euroecorev.2015.07.016.

28. For a discussion of some of these costs, see Barbara Ehrenreich, *Nickel and Dimed: On (Not) Getting by in America*, Picador, 2001.

29. Scott L. Fulford, "Demand for Emergency Savings Is Higher for Low-Income Households, but So Is the Cost of Shocks," *Empirical Economics*, 2020, 58(6): 3007–33, https://doi.org/10.1007/s00181-018-1590-9.

Chapter Four

1. Charles Dickens, *David Copperfield*, Project Gutenberg, 2016, https://www.gutenberg.org/files/766/766-h/766-h.htm.

2. Amounts are from Committee for a Responsible Federal Budget, "What's in the $2 Trillion Coronavirus Relief Package?," March 25, 2020, https://www.crfb.org/blogs/whats-2-trillion-coronavirus-relief-package.

3. Congressional Budget Office, "Re: Preliminary Estimate of the Effects of H.R. 748, the CARES Act, Public Law 116-136, Revised, with Corrections to the Revenue Effect of the Employee Retention Credit and to the Modification of a Limitation on Losses for Taxpayers Other than Corporations," April 27, 2020, https://www.cbo.gov/system/files/2020-04/hr748.pdf.

4. While processes evolved over time, mortgage servicers were particularly concerned because they were still obligated to make payments to investors for mortgages in forbearance. See Alan Rappeport, Matthew Goldstein, and Jeanna Smialek, "Excluded from Bailouts, Mortgage Servicers Face Cash Crunch," *New York Times*, April 20, 2020, https://www.nytimes.com/2020/04/20/us/politics/coronavirus-housing-mortgages.html.

5. Government Accountability Office, "Federal Reserve Lending Programs: Use of CARES Act-Supported Programs Has Been Limited and Flow of Credit Has Generally Improved," December 2020, GAO-21-180, https://www.gao.gov/assets/gao-21-180.pdf.

6. Heather Cagyle and Sarah Ferris, "House Passes $484 Billion Relief Package after Weeks of Partisan Battles," Politico, April 23, 2020, https://www.politico.com/news/2020/04/23/house-vote-pass-coronavirus-aid-package-203965.

7. Congressional Budget Office, "Estimate of the Effects of H.R. 748," 14.

8. For a discussion of this provision and how "accounting losses" are not always real losses, see Clint Wallace, "The Troubling Case of the Unlimited Pass-Through Deduction: Section 2304 of the CARES Act," *University of Chicago Law Review*, blog post, June 2020, https://lawreviewblog.uchicago.edu/2020/06/29/cares-2304-wallace/.

9. See a summary of the tax provisions in John Werlhof, "Tax Savings Opportunities from the CARES Act," Tax Adviser, July 1, 2020, https://www.thetaxadviser.com/issues/2020/jul/tax-savings-opportunities-coronavirus-cares-act.html.

10. Internal Revenue Service, "Questions and Answers about the First Economic Impact Payment—Topic A: Eligibility," updated March 9, 2021, https://www.irs.gov/newsroom/questions-and-answers-about-the-first-economic-impact-payment-topic-a-eligibility.

11. Internal Revenue Service, "Questions and Answers."

12. Migration Policy Institute, "Mixed-Status Families Ineligible for CARES Act Federal Pandemic Stimulus Checks," May 2020, https://www.migrationpolicy.org/content/mixed -status-families-ineligible-pandemic-stimulus-checks.

13. Dan Murphy, "Economic Impact Payments: Uses, Payment Methods, and Costs to Recipients," Economic Studies at Brookings, February 2021, https://www.brookings.edu/wp -content/uploads/2021/02/20210216_Murphy_ImpactPayments_Final-4.pdf.

14. Murphy, 10.

15. Elsa Augustine, Charles Davis, and Aparna Ramesh, "The Stimulus Gap: 2.2 Million Californians Could Miss $5.7 Billion in Federal Stimulus Payments," California Policy Lab, policy brief, April 6, 2021, https://www.capolicylab.org/wp-content/uploads/2021/04/The -Stimulus-Gap-in-California.pdf.

16. Michelle Singletary, "IRS Is Trying to Reach 9 Million People Who Haven't Collected Their Stimulus Payments," Washington Post, September 11, 2020, https://www.washingtonpost .com/business/2020/09/11/irs-stimulus-check-letter/.

17. For a summary of some of these challenges, see Murphy, Economic Impact Payments; and Government Accountability Office, "COVID-19 Federal Efforts Could Be Strengthened by Timely and Concerted Action," report to congressional committees, September 2020, GAO-20-701, https://www.gao.gov/assets/gao-20-701.pdf.

18. Federal Deposit Insurance Corporation, "How America Banks: Household Use of Banking and Financial Services, 2019 FDIC Survey," October 2020, https://www.fdic.gov/analysis /household-survey/2019report.pdf.

19. Murphy, "Economic Impact Payments," 17.

20. Interestingly, nearly half did not remember when the money arrived, suggesting that what may seem like a big deal to economists may not have been quite as important to many households who were not having financial problems.

21. Spending is the percent change from average spending in January 2020 and is seasonally adjusted. The drop around Thanksgiving in 2021 is an artifact of seasonal adjustment. Actual spending increased sharply starting on Black Friday but increased less sharply than in prior years, so relative to prior years, spending declined. Sources: Affinity Solutions; and Raj Chetty, John N. Friedman, . . . and the Opportunity Insights Team, "The Economic Impacts of COVID-19: Evidence from a New Public Database Built Using Private Sector Data" (working paper, November 2020), https://opportunityinsights.org/wp-content/uploads/2020/05 /tracker_paper.pdf.

22. Scott R. Baker, R. A. Farrokhnia, . . . and Constantine Yannelis, "Income, Liquidity, and the Consumption Response to the 2020 Economic Stimulus Payments" (NBER Working Paper No. 27097, September 2020), https://www.nber.org/papers/w27097.

23. Baker, Farrokhnia, . . . and Yannelis, 36, 41.

24. For the higher estimate, see Baker, Farrokhnia, . . . and Yannelis. For a lower estimate, see Jonathan A. Parker, Jake Schild, Laura Erhard, and David Johnson, "Household Spending Responses to the Economic Impact Payments of 2020: Evidence from the Consumer Expenditure Survey" (NBER Working Paper No. 29658, January 2022), https://www.nber.org/papers /w29648. For a careful comparison across estimates from different sources, see Michael Gelman

and Melvin Stephens Jr., "Lessons Learned from Economic Impact Payments during COVID-19," in *Recession Remedies*, ed. Wendy Edelberg, Louise Sheiner, and David Wessel, Brookings Institution, 2022, https://www.brookings.edu/essay/lessons-learned-from-economic-impact -payments-during-covid-19/.

25. Paul Krugman, "Notes on the Coronacoma (Wonkish): This Is Not a Conventional Recession, and G.D.P. Is Not the Target," *New York Times*, April 1, 2020, https://www.nytimes .com/2020/04/01/opinion/notes-on-the-coronacoma-wonkish.html.

26. Lawrence H. Summers, "Opinion: The Biden Stimulus Is Admirably Ambitious. But It Brings Some Big Risks, Too," *New York Times*, February 4, 2021, https://www.washingtonpost .com/opinions/2021/02/04/larry-summers-biden-covid-stimulus/.

27. Some estimates suggest the EIPs had similar impacts to previous stimulus payments (Baker, Farrokhnia, . . . and Yannelis, "Income, Liquidity"), while others find somewhat lower spending impact (Parker, Schild, Erhard, and Johnson, "Household Spending Responses").

28. Baker, Farrokhnia, . . . and Yannelis, "Income, Liquidity."

29. Center on Budget and Policy Priorities, "Policy Basics: Unemployment Insurance," March 15, 2021, https://www.cbpp.org/research/economy/unemployment-insurance.

30. Bureau of Labor Statistics, "Weekly and Hourly Earnings Data from the Current Population Survey," series ID LES1252881500, https://www.bls.gov/webapps/legacy/cpswktab1.htm.

31. Peter Ganong, Pascal J. Noel, and Joseph S. Vavra, "US Unemployment Insurance Replacement Rates during the Pandemic" (NBER Working Paper No. 27216, May 2020), https://www.nber.org/papers/w27216. In this calculation, they include nonwage compensation such as health insurance.

32. Department of Labor, "News Release: Statement by Secretary of Labor Eugene Scalia on Unemployment Insurance Claims," April 16, 2020, https://www.dol.gov/newsroom/releases /osec/osec20200416.

33. Scott Fulford and Cortnie Shupe, "Consumer Finances during the Pandemic: Insights from the Making Ends Meet Survey," Consumer Financial Protection Bureau Data Point No. 2021-3, December 2021, https://www.consumerfinance.gov/data-research/research-reports /consumer-finances-during-pandemic-insights-making-ends-meet-survey/.

34. See Fulford and Shupe.

35. Michael Karpman and Gregory Acs analyzed two Urban Institute surveys. Among families who had applied for unemployment insurance since March, they compared families who had received unemployment insurance by mid-May and those who had not. Food insecurity declined for the families who received unemployment insurance, and unmet needs for medical care increased among families who had not received it. See Michael Karpman and Gregory Acs, "Unemployment Insurance and Economic Impact Payments Associated with Reduced Hardship Following CARES Act," Urban Institute, June 2020, https://www.urban.org/sites/default /files/publication/102486/unemployment-insurance-and-economic-impact-payments -associated-with-reduced-hardship-following-cares-act.pdf.

36. Diana Farrell, Peter Ganong, . . . and Joseph Vavra, "The Unemployment Benefit Boost: Trends in Spending and Saving When the $600 Supplement Ended," JPMorgan Chase Institute Policy Brief, October 2020, https://www.jpmorganchase.com/content/dam/jpmc/jpmorgan -chase-and-co/institute/pdf/Institute-UI-Benefits-Boost-Policy-Brief_ADA.pdf.

37. Natalie Cox, Peter Ganong, . . . and Erica Deadman, "Initial Impacts of the Pandemic on Consumer Behavior: Evidence from Linked Income, Spending, and Savings Data," *Brookings Papers on Economic Activity*, Summer 2020, https://www.brookings.edu/wp-content/uploads/2020/06/SU20_S1_Cox-et-al._-final-paper.pdf.

38. Donald J. Trump, "Memorandum on Authorizing the Other Needs Assistance Program for Major Disaster Declarations Related to Coronavirus Disease 2019," Presidential Memorandum, August 8, 2020, https://trumpwhitehouse.archives.gov/presidential-actions/memorandum-authorizing-needs-assistance-program-major-disaster-declarations-related-coronavirus-disease-2019/.

39. Federal Emergency Management Agency, "Lost Wages Supplemental Payment Assistance Guidelines," last updated April 5, 2021, https://www.fema.gov/disasters/coronavirus/governments/supplemental-payments-lost-wages-guidelines.

40. Shahar Ziv, "FEMA Announces End of Extra $300 Lost Wages Assistance (LWA) Program for 7 States," *Forbes*, September 14, 2020, https://www.forbes.com/sites/shaharziv/2020/09/14/fema-announces-end-of-lost-wages-assistance-lwa-program-for-7-states-extra-300-uemployment/?sh=1a4ea4916ffb.

41. Federal Emergency Management Agency, "FEMA Supplemental Lost Wages Payments under Other Needs Assistance: Frequently Asked Questions," August 2020, https://www.fema.gov/sites/default/files/2020-10/fema_supplement-lost-wages-payments-under-other-needs-assistance_faq_09-30-20.pdf.

42. Greg Iacurci, "At Least 1 Million People May Not Get Trump's $400 Unemployment Boost," CNBC, August 11, 2020, https://www.cnbc.com/2020/08/11/at-least-1-million-people-may-not-get-trumps-400-unemployment-boost.html.

43. Andrew Stettner and Michelle Evermore, "Trump's Lost Wage Assistance Program No Substitute for Federal Unemployment Benefits," Century Foundation, August 20, 2020, https://tcf.org/content/commentary/trumps-lost-wage-assistance-program-no-substitute-federal-unemployment-benefits/.

44. JPMorgan Chase Institute, "Place Matters: Small Business Health in Urban Communities," September 2019, https://www.jpmorganchase.com/content/dam/jpmc/jpmorgan-chase-and-co/institute/pdf/institute-place-matters.pdf.

45. Alexander W. Bartik, Marianne Bertrand, . . . and Christopher T. Stanton, "How Are Small Businesses Adjusting to COVID-19? Early Evidence from a Survey" (NBER Working Paper No. 26989, April 2020), https://www.nber.org/papers/w26989.

46. Glenn Hubbard and Michael R. Strain, "Has the Paycheck Protection Program Succeeded?," *Brookings Papers on Economic Activity*, Conference Drafts, September 24, 2020, 8, https://www.brookings.edu/wp-content/uploads/2020/09/Hubbard-Strain-et-al-conference-draft.pdf.

47. Hubbard and Strain, 8.

48. Small Business Administration, "PPP Loan Forgiveness," accessed June 30, 2020, https://www.sba.gov/funding-programs/loans/covid-19-relief-options/paycheck-protection-program/ppp-loan-forgiveness.

49. Public Law No. 116-142, June 6, 2020, https://www.congress.gov/bill/116th-congress/house-bill/7010/text.

50. James M. Kane, James W. Morrissey, . . . and Mark C. Svalina, "It's Back: Paycheck Protection Program 2.0," *National Law Review*, January 1, 2021, https://www.natlawreview.com/article/it-s-back-paycheck-protection-program-20.

51. Small Business Administration, "Business Loan Program Temporary Changes; Paycheck Protection Program: A Rule by the Small Business Administration on 04/15/2020," *Federal Register*, April 15, 2020, 85 FR 20811, 20811–20817, https://www.federalregister.gov/documents/2020/04/15/2020-07672/business-loan-program-temporary-changes-paycheck-protection-program.

52. Larger loans had smaller fees: 3 percent for loans of more than $350,000 and less than $2,000,000, and 1 percent for loans of at least $2,000,000. See Small Business Administration, "Business Loan Program," 85 FR 20811.

53. Stephen Gandel, "Paycheck Protection Program Out of Money: Thousands of Small Businesses Shut Out," CBS News, April 16, 2020, https://www.cbsnews.com/news/paycheck-protection-program-out-of-money-small-businesses-shut-out/.

54. Stacy Cowley and Ella Koeze, "1 Percent of P.P.P. Borrowers Got over One-Quarter of the Loan Money," *New York Times*, December 2, 2020, https://www.nytimes.com/2020/12/02/business/paycheck-protection-program-coronavirus.html.

55. Source: Author's calculations from Small Business Administration, "PPP Data," as of June 30, 2021, https://www.sba.gov/funding-programs/loans/covid-19-relief-options/paycheck-protection-program/ppp-data.

56. Sifan Liu and Joseph Parilla, "New Data Shows Small Businesses in Communities of Color Had Unequal Access to Federal COVID-19 Relief," Brookings Institution, September 17, 2020, https://www.brookings.edu/research/new-data-shows-small-businesses-in-communities-of-color-had-unequal-access-to-federal-covid-19-relief/.

57. Jessica Battisto, Mels de Zeeuw, . . . and Ann Marie Wiersch, "Small Business Credit Survey: 2020 Report on Employer Firms," Federal Reserve Banks of Atlanta, Boston, Chicago, Cleveland, Dallas, Kansas City, Minneapolis, New York, Philadelphia, Richmond, St. Louis, San Francisco, 2020, 9, https://www.fedsmallbusiness.org/medialibrary/FedSmallBusiness/files/2020/2020-sbcs-employer-firms-report.

58. A research team had people apply for loans over the telephone in Washington, D.C., using identical profiles except for names that are typically associated with different racial groups and with racially recognizable voices. They found that in 43 percent of the tests, Black applicants were treated less favorably, and in about a quarter of tests Black applicants were actively discouraged from applying. See Anneliese Lederer, Sara Oros, . . . and Jerome Williams, "Lending Discrimination within the Paycheck Protection Program," National Community Reinvestment Coalition, 2020, https://www.ncrc.org/lending-discrimination-within-the-paycheck-protection-program/.

59. Isil Erel and Jack Liebersohn, "Does Fintech Substitute for Banks? Evidence from the Paycheck Protection Program" (NBER Working Paper No. 27659, December 2020), https://www.nber.org/system/files/working_papers/w27659/w27659.pdf.

60. Sabrina T. Howell, Theresa Kuchler, . . . and Jun Wong, "Automation and Racial Disparities in Small Business Lending: Evidence from the Paycheck Protection Program" (NBER Working Paper No. 29364, May 2022), https://www.nber.org/papers/w29364.

61. Under the new rules, 50 percent of loans below $50,000 could be earned in fees, up to a maximum of $2,500. While under the previous rules, a loan of $20,000 would earn the bank only $1,000, now the bank would earn $2,500 in fees. Loans as small as $5,000 would produce fees of $2,500. See Small Business Administration, "Business Loan Program Temporary Changes; Paycheck Protection Program as Amended by Economic Aid Act," *Federal Register*, January 14, 2021, 86 FR 3692, 3692–3712, https://www.federalregister.gov/d/2021-00451/p-402.

62. Stacy Cowley and Ella Koeze, "How Two Start-Ups Reaped Billions in Fees on Small Business Relief Loans," *New York Times*, June 27, 2021, https://www.nytimes.com/2021/06/27/business/ppp-relief-loans-blueacorn-womply.html.

63. David Autor, David Cho, . . . and Ahu Yildirmaz, "The $800 Billion Paycheck Protection Program: Where Did the Money Go and Why Did It Go There?" (NBER Working Paper No. 29669, January 2022), 7, http://www.nber.org/papers/w29669.

64. These loan and forgiveness numbers were reported on the SBA website: Small Business Administration, "PPP Data," accessed April 11, 2022, https://www.sba.gov/funding-programs/loans/covid-19-relief-options/paycheck-protection-program/ppp-data. The fees estimate is from taking the 5 percent of $800 billion to give $40 billion. Smaller loans in the December 2020 relief bill had a higher compensation rate, so the total paid is likely to be more than $40 billion.

65. Luke Pardu, "Small Business Experiences as the Paycheck Protection Program Ends: Evidence from Covered Period Expiration" (SSRN Working Paper 3753629, February 22, 2021), https://papers.ssrn.com/sol3/papers.cfm?abstract_id=3753629.

66. See Chetty, Friedman, . . . and the Opportunity Insights Team, "Economic Impacts of COVID-19"; Autor, Cho, . . . and Yildirmaz, "$800 Billion Paycheck Protection Program"; and Hubbard and Strain, "Has the Paycheck Protection Program Succeeded?"

67. Autor, Cho, . . . and Yildirmaz, "$800 Billion Paycheck Protection Program."

68. João Granja, Christos Makridis, Constantine Yannelis, and Eric Zwick, "Did the Paycheck Protection Program Hit the Target?" (NBER Working Paper No. 27095, November 2020), http://www.nber.org/papers/w27095.

69. Granja, Makridis, Yannelis, and Zwick, 13–21.

70. Cowley and Koeze, "1 Percent of P.P.P. Borrowers."

71. Gabriel Chodorow-Reich, Olivier Darmouni, Stephan Luck, and Matthew Plosser, "Bank Liquidity Provision across the Firm Size Distribution," *Journal of Financial Economics*, forthcoming.

72. For a detailed analysis of this argument, see Gabriel Chodorow-Reich, Ben Iverson, and Adi Sunderam, "Lessons Learned from Support to Business during COVID-19," in Edelberg, Sheiner, and Wessel, *Recession Remedies*, https://www.brookings.edu/essay/lessons-learned-from-support-to-business-during-covid-19/.

73. Hubbard and Strain, "Has the Paycheck Protection Program Succeeded?"

74. Sakai Ando, Ravi Balakrishnan, . . . and Alexandra Solovyeva, "European Labor Markets and the COVID-19 Pandemic" (IMF European Department Paper DP2022/04, March 2022), https://www.imf.org/-/media/Files/Publications/DP/2022/English/ELMCPFPAEA.ashx.

75. Hubbard and Strain, "Has the Paycheck Protection Program Succeeded?"

76. Granja, Makridis, Yannelis, and Zwick, "Did the Paycheck Protection Program?"

77. Ryan Sandler and Judith Ricks, "The Early Effects of the COVID-19 Pandemic on Consumer Credit," Consumer Financial Protection Bureau Office of Research Special Issue Brief, August 2020, https://files.consumerfinance.gov/f/documents/cfpb_early-effects-covid-19 -consumer-credit_issue-brief.pdf.

78. Source: Author's calculations using the Consumer Financial Protection Bureau Consumer Credit Panel. These figures follow the definitions in Sandler and Ricks, "Early Effects"; and the update in Corinne Candilis and Ryan Sandler, "Trends in Reported Assistance on Consumers' Credit Records," Consumer Financial Protection Bureau blog, July 13, 2021, https:// www.consumerfinance.gov/about-us/blog/trends-in-reported-assistance-consumers-credit -records/. Reporting of forbearance or assistance was inconsistent across lenders, so they developed a more comprehensive measure based on whether an open account had zero payment due but a positive balance.

79. The Department of Education did refund most of the money it incorrectly garnished but was unable to reach around 11,000 borrowers. See Danielle Douglas-Gabriel, "Thousands of Student Loan Borrowers Are Still Waiting for Refunds of Their Garnished Wages," *Washington Post*, August 19, 2021, https://www.washingtonpost.com/education/2021/08/19/wage -garnishment-refunds/.

80. U.S. Department of Education, "Biden-Harris Administration Announces Final Student Loan Pause Extension Through December 31 and Targeted Debt Cancellation to Smooth Transition to Repayment," August 24, 2022, https://www.ed.gov/news/press-releases/biden-harris -administration-announces-final-student-loan-pause-extension-through-december-31-and -targeted-debt-cancellation-smooth-transition-repayment.

81. See, for example, the discussion on money advice site Nerdwallet: Anna Helhoski, "Student Loans Are on Hold—Should You Pay Anyway?," Nerdwallet, August 6, 2021, https:// www.nerdwallet.com/article/loans/student-loans/you-can-pause-two-student-loan-payments -but-should-you.

82. See Susan Cherry, Erica Jiang, . . . and Amit Seru, "Government and Private Household Debt Relief during COVID-19," *Brookings Papers on Economic Activity*, September 9, 2021, https://www.brookings.edu/bpea-articles/government-and-private-household-debt-relief -during-covid-19/. This calculation takes $45 billion from March 2020 to May 2021 in table 2 and projects it forward to March 2022.

83. Fulford and Shupe, "Consumer Finances."

84. Cherry, Jiang, . . . and Seru, "Government and Private."

85. Fulford and Shupe, "Consumer Finances."

86. JPMorgan Chase Institute, "Is Mortgage Forbearance Reaching the Right Homeowners during the COVID-19 Pandemic?," policy brief, December 2020, https://www.jpmorganchase .com/content/dam/jpmc/jpmorgan-chase-and-co/institute/pdf/institute-covid-mortgage -forbearance-policy-brief-new.pdf.

87. JPMorgan Chase Institute, "Is Mortgage Forbearance Reaching?"

88. Xudong An, Larry Cordell, Liang Geng, and Keyoung Lee, "Inequality in the Time of COVID-19: Evidence from Mortgage Delinquency and Forbearance" (Federal Reserve Bank of Philadelphia Working Paper WP 21-09, February 2021), https://doi.org/10.21799/frbp.wp .2021.09.

89. Erik Durbin, Greta Li, David Low, and Judith Ricks, "Characteristics of Mortgage Borrowers during the COVID-19 Pandemic," Consumer Financial Protection Bureau Office of Research Special Issue Brief, May 2021, https://www.consumerfinance.gov/data-research/research-reports/characteristics-mortgage-borrowers-during-covid-19-pandemic/.

90. Carlos Garriga, Lowell R. Ricketts, and Don E. Schlagenhauf, "The Homeownership Experience of Minorities during the Great Recession," *Federal Reserve Bank of St. Louis Review*, First Quarter 2017, 99(1): 139–67, http://dx.doi.org/10.20955/r.2017.139-67.

91. See, for example, Jennifer Bjorhus and Patrick Kennedy, "CARES Act Tax Breaks a Jackpot for Huge Companies, Wealthy Business Owners," *Star Tribune*, June 2, 2020, https://www.startribune.com/minnesota-companies-cashing-in-on-cares-act-business-tax-breaks/570923132/.

92. See Allan Sloan, "The CARES Act Sent You a $1,200 Check but Gave Millionaires and Billionaires Far More," ProPublica, June 8, 2020, https://www.propublica.org/article/the-cares-act-sent-you-a-1-200-check-but-gave-millionaires-and-billionaires-far-more; and Jesse Drucker, interview by Terry Gross, "How the CARES Act Became a Tax-Break Bonanza for the Rich, Explained," *Fresh Air*, NPR, April 30, 2020, https://www.npr.org/2020/04/30/848321204/how-the-cares-act-became-a-tax-break-bonanza-for-the-rich-explained.

93. John Gallemore, Stephan Hollander, and Martin Jacob, "Who CARES? Evidence on the Corporate Tax Provisions of the Coronavirus Aid, Relief, and Economic Security Act from SEC Filings" (Becker Friedman Institute WP No. 2020-81, June 2020), https://bfi.uchicago.edu/wp-content/uploads/BFI_WP_202081.pdf.

94. "Fact Sheet: President Biden Announces Additional Steps to Help Americans Return to Work," White House Briefing Room, May 10, 2021, https://www.whitehouse.gov/briefing-room/statements-releases/2021/05/10/fact-sheet-president-biden-announces-additional-steps-to-help-americans-return-to-work/.

95. Sloan, "CARES Act."

96. Scott Fulford, Marie Rush, and Eric Wilson, "Changes in Consumer Financial Status during the Early Months of the Pandemic: Evidence from the Second Wave of the Making Ends Meet Survey," Consumer Financial Protection Bureau Data Point No. 2021-2, April 2021, https://www.consumerfinance.gov/data-research/research-reports/changes-in-consumer-financial-status-during-early-months-pandemic/.

97. Thea Garon, Andrew Dunn, Necati Celik, and Helen Robb, "US Financial Health Pulse: 2020 Trends Report," Financial Health Network, October 2020, https://s3.amazonaws.com/cfsi-innovation-files-2018/wp-content/uploads/2020/10/26135655/2020Pulse TrendsReport-Final-1016201.pdf. I used the month of the survey rather than the dating used in the report.

98. Cox, Ganong, . . . and Deadman, "Initial Impacts of the Pandemic."

99. Sandler and Ricks, "Early Effects."

100. Scott Fulford and Marie Rush, "Credit Card Debt Fell Even for Consumers Who Were Having Financial Difficulties before the Pandemic," Consumer Financial Protection Bureau blog, December 17, 2020, https://www.consumerfinance.gov/about-us/blog/credit-card-debt-fell-even-consumers-having-financial-difficulties-before-pandemic/.

101. The figure shows the average credit card debt from the Consumer Financial Protection Bureau Consumer Credit Panel adjusted for inflation among Making Ends Meet respondents

who could cover one month or less of expenses if their household lost its main source of income and respondents who could cover at least two months. Source: Author's calculations using Making Ends Meet and the Consumer Financial Protection Bureau Consumer Credit Panel, based on Fulford and Rush, "Credit Card Debt Fell."

102. Scott L. Fulford, "How Important Is Variability in Consumer Credit Limits?," *Journal of Monetary Economics*, 2015, 72: 42–63, https://doi.org/10.1016/j.jmoneco.2015.01.002.

103. I calculated these statistics from questions in the Wave 1 Making Ends Meet survey in June 2019.

104. Scott Fulford and Scott Schuh, "Credit Cards, Credit Utilization, and Consumption" (West Virginia University Economics Working Paper 19-07, 2019), https://researchrepository .wvu.edu/econ_working-papers/41/.

105. Limits did decline slightly for people with the highest credit scores who are rarely using much or any of their credit. For everyone else, limit growth slowed early in the pandemic but then started rising again in late 2020. See Corinne Candilis and Ryan Sandler, "Credit Card Limits Are Rising for Most Groups after Stagnating during the Pandemic," Consumer Financial Protection Bureau blog, August 11, 2021, https://www.consumerfinance.gov/about-us/blog /credit-card-limits-rising-for-most-groups-after-stagnating-during-pandemic/.

106. Sandler and Ricks, "Early Effects."

107. Emily Stewart, "It's Easy to Assume Pawnshops Are Doing Great in the Pandemic. It's Also Wrong," Vox, November 30, 2020, https://www.vox.com/the-goods/21611583/pawn-shop -covid-19-economy.

108. See Veritec Solutions, "Update: COVID-19 Impact Study on Small-Dollar Lending," June 18, 2021, https://www.veritecs.com/2021-update-covid-19-impact-study-on-small-dollar -lending/.

109. Allison Prang, "Overdraft Fees Fell in the Covid-19 Economy," *Wall Street Journal*, May 30, 2021, https://www.wsj.com/articles/overdraft-fees-fell-in-the-covid-19-economy -11622367000.

Chapter Five

1. Alyssa Rosenberg, "Opinion: 'Locked Down' Is Hard to Watch. It's a Reminder of How Wrong We Were at the Start of the Pandemic," *Washington Post*, January 27, 2021, https://www .washingtonpost.com/opinions/2021/01/27/locked-down-is-hard-watch-its-reminder-how -wrong-we-were-start-pandemic/.

2. Herb Scribner, "Does Anyone Else Feel Uncomfortable Watching Movies Now?," *Deseret News*, May 29, 2020, https://www.deseret.com/entertainment/2020/5/29/21272227/does -anyone-else-feel-uncomfortable-watching-movies-now.

3. See Berkeley Lovelace Jr., "CDC Quietly Releases Detailed Guidelines for Reopening America," CNBC, May 20, 2020, https://www.cnbc.com/2020/05/20/coronavirus-cdc-quietly -releases-detailed-guidelines-for-reopening-us.html; and Jeneen Interlandi, "Can the C.D.C. Be Fixed?," *New York Times Magazine*, June 16, 2021, https://www.nytimes.com/2021/06/16 /magazine/cdc-covid-response.html.

4. Bill Chappelle and Allison Aubrey, "CDC Advice on Surface Spread of COVID-19 'Has Not Changed,' Agency Says," NPR, May 22, 2020, https://www.npr.org/sections/coronavirus

-live-updates/2020/05/22/861193550/advice-on-surface-spread-of-covid-19-has-not
-changed-cdc-says.

5. Derek Thompson, "Hygiene Theater Is a Huge Waste of Time," *Atlantic*, July 27, 2020,
https://www.theatlantic.com/ideas/archive/2020/07/scourge-hygiene-theater/614599/.

6. Will Stone, "Deadly Mix: How Bars Are Fueling COVID-19 Outbreaks," Kaiser Health
News, August 21, 2020, https://khn.org/news/deadly-mix-how-bars-are-fueling-covid-19
-outbreaks/.

7. Jackie Reeve, "You Can Still Use Laundromats Safely during the Coronavirus Pandemic.
Just Take a Few Precautions First," Wirecutter, *New York Times*, April 23, 2020, https://www
.nytimes.com/wirecutter/blog/laundromats-during-coronavirus/.

8. Ariane de Vogue, "Supreme Embarrassment: The Flush Heard around the Country,"
CNN, May 6, 2020, https://www.cnn.com/2020/05/06/politics/toilet-flush-supreme-court
-oral-arguments/index.html.

9. Rachel Siegel and Andrew Van Dam, "U.S. Economy Recoups Two-Thirds of Ground Lost
in First Half of Year, but There Is Still Far to Go," *Washington Post*, October 29, 2020, https://
www.washingtonpost.com/business/2020/10/29/third-quarter-gdp-economy/.

10. NPR, Robert Wood Johnson Foundation, and Harvard Chan School of Public Health,
"The Impact of Coronavirus on Households in Major U.S. Cities," September 2020, https://
media.npr.org/assets/img/2020/09/08/cities-report-090920-final.pdf.

11. Steven H. Woolf, Derek A. Chapman, . . . and Latoya Hill, "Excess Deaths from COVID-
19 and Other Causes, March–April 2020," *Journal of the American Medical Association*, July 1,
2020, 324(5): 510–13, https://doi.org/10.1001/jama.2020.11787.

12. Dulce Gonzalez, Michael Karpman, Genevieve M. Kenney, and Stephen Zuckerman,
"Delayed and Forgone Health Care for Nonelderly Adults during the COVID-19 Pandemic,"
Urban Institute, February 2021, https://www.urban.org/sites/default/files/publication
/103651/delayed-and-forgone-health-care-for-nonelderly-adults-during-the-covid-19
-pandemic.pdf.

13. Harvey W. Kaufman, Zhen Chen, Justin Niles, and Yuri Fesko, "Changes in the Number
of US Patients with Newly Identified Cancer before and during the Coronavirus Disease 2019
(COVID-19) Pandemic," *JAMA Network Open*, August 4, 2020, 3(8): e2017267, https://doi.org
/10.1001/jamanetworkopen.2020.17267.

14. Bhavini Patel Murthy, Elizabeth Zell, . . . and Lynn Gibbs-Scharf, "Impact of the COVID-19
Pandemic on Administration of Selected Routine Childhood and Adolescent Vaccinations—10
U.S. Jurisdictions, March–September 2020," *CDC Morbidity and Mortality Weekly Report*, 2021,
70(23): 840–45, http://dx.doi.org/10.15585/mmwr.mm7023a2.

15. American Hospital Association, "Hospitals and Health Systems Face Unprecedented
Financial Pressures Due to COVID-19," May 2020, https://www.aha.org/guidesreports/2020
-05-05-hospitals-and-health-systems-face-unprecedented-financial-pressures-due.

16. Sylvie Douglis, "< 15 Million N95s without a Buyer," *The Indicator from Planet Money*,
NPR, March 30, 2021, https://www.npr.org/transcripts/982831448.

17. Marisa Iati, "More Experts Now Recommend Medical Masks. Good Ones Are Hard to
Find," *Washington Post*, February 2, 2021, https://www.washingtonpost.com/health/2021/02
/02/medical-mask-shortage/.

18. Colleen Long, "Government Investigating Massive Counterfeit N95 Mask Scam," AP News, February 10, 2021, https://apnews.com/article/government-investigation-n95-scam-16 94ed85d6ef99cdb6662f67d823c271.

19. Andrew Jacobs, "Counterfeit Covid Masks Are Still Sold Everywhere, Despite Misleading Claims," *New York Times*, November 30, 2021, https://www.nytimes.com/2021/11/30 /health/covid-masks-counterfeit-fake.html.

20. See, for example, this randomized trial of masking in Bangladesh: Jason Abaluck, Laura H. Kwong, . . . and Neeti Zaman, "The Impact of Community Masking on COVID-19: A Cluster-Randomized Trial in Bangladesh" (IPA Working Paper, September 2021), https://www .poverty-action.org/publication/impact-community-masking-covid-19-cluster-randomized -trial-bangladesh.

21. Tanya Albert Henry, "Can Telehealth Access Survive the Pandemic? These Policies Are Key," American Medical Association, January 28, 2021, https://www.ama-assn.org /practice-management/digital/can-telehealth-access-survive-pandemic-these-policies -are-key.

22. Shantanu Nundy, "A Surprising Pandemic Side Effect: It Has Improved Health Care," *Washington Post*, May 12, 2021, https://www.washingtonpost.com/outlook/health-care-covid -diabetes-home/2021/05/12/ae298558-b26e-11eb-ab43-bebddc5a0f65_story.html.

23. Nicole Friedman, "The Pandemic Ignited a Housing Boom—but It's Different from the Last One," *Wall Street Journal*, March 15, 2021, https://www.wsj.com/articles/the-pandemic -ignited-a-housing-boombut-its-different-from-the-last-one-11615824558.

24. Ana Durrani, "How the COVID-19 Pandemic Has Forever Changed the Process of Selling a House," Realtor.com, December 21, 2020, https://www.realtor.com/advice/sell/covid-19 -pandemic-changed-selling-a-house/.

25. Brandon Cornett, "Requirements for FHA Desktop and Exterior-Only Appraisals during COVID-19," FHA Handbook, July 2, 2020, http://www.fhahandbook.com/blog/desktop-and -exterior-only-appraisals-2020/.

26. Durrani, "How the COVID-19 Pandemic."

27. Andreas Fuster, Aurel Hizmo, . . . and Paul Willen, "How Resilient Is Mortgage Credit Supply? Evidence from the Covid-19 Pandemic" (CEPR Discussion Paper No. DP16110, July 2021), https://papers.ssrn.com/sol3/papers.cfm?abstract_id=3846222.

28. Fuster, Hizmo, . . . and Willen, 17.

29. Among other factors, mortgage licensing was more difficult because in-person testing and fingerprinting locations were closed. See Fuster, Hizmo, . . . and Willen, 28.

30. Dianne Gallagher and Pamela Kirkland, "Meat Processing Plants across the US Are Closing Due to the Pandemic. Will Consumers Feel the Impact?," CNN, April 27, 2020, https:// www.cnn.com/2020/04/26/business/meat-processing-plants-coronavirus/index.html.

31. Joseph Balagtas and Joseph Cooper, "The Impact of Coronavirus COVID-19 on U.S. Meat and Livestock Markets" (OCE Working Paper, Department of Agriculture, March 2021), https://www.usda.gov/sites/default/files/documents/covid-impact-livestock-markets.pdf.

32. Katie Shepherd, "'The Food Supply Chain Is Breaking': Tyson Foods Raises Coronavirus Alarm in Full-Page Ads, Defends Safety Efforts," *Washington Post*, April 27, 2020, https://www .washingtonpost.com/nation/2020/04/27/tyson-food-supply-coronavirus/.

33. Will Oremus, "What Everyone's Getting Wrong about the Toilet Paper Shortage: It Isn't Really about Hoarding. And There Isn't an Easy Fix," *Marker*, April 2, 2020, https://marker .medium.com/what-everyones-getting-wrong-about-the-toilet-paper-shortage-c812e1358fe0.

34. Marc Fisher, "Flushing out the True Cause of the Global Toilet Paper Shortage amid Coronavirus Pandemic," *Washington Post*, April 7, 2020, https://www.washingtonpost.com /national/coronavirus-toilet-paper-shortage-panic/2020/04/07/1fd30e92-75b5-11ea-87da -77a8136c1a6d_story.html.

35. Amelia Lucas, "Panera Bread Is Selling Groceries as Restaurant Sales Plummet," CNBC, April 8, 2020, https://www.cnbc.com/2020/04/08/panera-bread-is-selling-groceries-as -restaurant-sales-plummet.html.

36. Rick Chakraborti and Gavin Roberts, "Anti-gouging Laws, Shortages, and COVID-19: Insights from Consumer Searches," *Journal of Private Enterprise*, 2020, 35(4): 1–20, http://journal .apee.org/index.php?title=Parte1_2020_Journal_of_Private_Enterprise_Vol_35_No_4 _Winter.

37. Ryan Kath, "From Toilet Paper to PPE: A Closer Look at Price Gouging Complaints during Pandemic," NBC Boston, May 8, 2020, https://www.nbcboston.com/investigations /from-toilet-paper-to-ppe-a-closer-look-at-price-gouging-complaints-during-pandemic /2121272/.

38. Zawn Villines, "What Are the Best Alternatives to Toilet Paper?," Medical News Today, April 15, 2020, https://www.medicalnewstoday.com/articles/toilet-paper-alternatives.

39. Thomas Franck, "Got Change? There's a Coin Shortage Because of Coronavirus Stopping the Flow of Physical Currency," CNBC, June 17, 2020, https://www.cnbc.com/2020/06 /17/got-change-theres-a-coin-shortage-because-of-coronavirus-stopping-the-flow-of-physical -currency.html.

40. Nicolette Accardi, "The U.S. Is Experiencing a Coin Shortage. Here's How Stores Are Adjusting on the Fly," NJ.com, August 23, 2020, https://www.nj.com/business/2020/08/the -us-is-experiencing-a-coin-shortage-heres-how-stores-are-adjusting-on-the-fly.html.

41. Scott Fulford, Claire Greene, and William Murdock III, "U.S. Consumer Holdings and Use of $1 Bills," Research Data Reports No. 15-1, Federal Reserve Bank of Boston, January 2015, https://www.bostonfed.org/publications/research-data-report/2015/us-consumer-holdings -and-use-of-1-bills.aspx.

42. Amelia Lucas, "QR Codes Have Replaced Restaurant Menus. Industry Experts Say It Isn't a Fad," CNBC, August 21, 2021, https://www.cnbc.com/2021/08/21/qr-codes-have -replaced-restaurant-menus-industry-experts-say-it-isnt-a-fad.html.

43. Jacob Bunge and Jaewon Kang, "Meat Was Once in Short Supply amid Pandemic. Now, It's on Sale," *Wall Street Journal*, September 20, 2020, https://www.wsj.com/articles/meat-was -once-in-short-supply-amid-pandemic-now-its-on-sale-11600614000.

44. John Herrman, "The New Panic Buys: Kayaks, Pools, Tents and Trampolines," *New York Times*, August 4, 2020, https://www.nytimes.com/2020/08/04/style/outdoor-camping-gear -pools-backordered.html.

45. Julie Creswell, "Your Steak Is More Expensive, but Cattle Ranchers Are Missing Out," *New York Times*, June 23, 2021, https://www.nytimes.com/2021/06/23/business/beef-prices .html.

46. Raj Chetty, John N. Friedman, . . . and the Opportunity Insights Team, "The Economic Impacts of COVID-19: Evidence from a New Public Database Built Using Private Sector Data" (working paper, November 2020), https://opportunityinsights.org/wp-content/uploads/2020 /05/tracker_paper.pdf.

47. Lauren Kent, "Covid-19, Thanks for the Bad Hair Year," CNN, October 8, 2020, https:// www.cnn.com/2020/10/08/health/pandemic-hair-care-wellness/index.html.

48. Amanda Mull, "Americans Have Baked All the Flour Away," *Atlantic*, May 12, 2020, https://www.theatlantic.com/health/archive/2020/05/why-theres-no-flour-during -coronavirus/611527/.

49. Linni Kral, "The Pandemic Brought More Flavorful Flour into America's Kitchens," *Slate*, June 21, 2021, https://slate.com/human-interest/2021/06/micro-flour-pandemic-baking-boom -mills.html.

50. Laura Reiley, "Turkey Farmers Fear That, This Year, They've Bred Too Many Big Birds," *Washington Post*, October 19, 2020, https://www.washingtonpost.com/road-to-recovery/2020 /10/19/thanksgiving-turkey-shortage/?arc404=true.

51. Michael Sullivan, "How to Celebrate Thanksgiving during the Pandemic," Wirecutter, *New York Times*, November 12, 2020, https://www.nytimes.com/wirecutter/blog/celebrate -thanksgiving-coronavirus/.

52. A similar phenomenon may explain the drop in expenditure at retirement, as retirees spend significantly more time shopping and preparing food, so the quality and quantity of food does not decline, only the amount spent. In contrast, typically the unemployed cut both food expenditure and consumption to match long-term impact prospects. See Mark Aguiar and Erik Hurst, "Consumption versus Expenditure," *Journal of Political Economy*, 2005, 113(5): 919–48.

53. Gus Wezerek and Kristen R. Ghodsee, "Women's Unpaid Labor Is Worth $10,900,000,000,000," *New York Times*, March 5, 2020, https://www.nytimes.com/interactive /2020/03/04/opinion/women-unpaid-labor.html; the headline is the global unpaid labor value.

54. Tinder, "The Future of Dating Is Fluid: What the Last Year on Tinder Tells Us about the Next Decade of Dating," March 25, 2021, https://filecache.mediaroom.com/mr5mr_tinder /178656/Tinder_Future%20of%20Dating_3.24_FINAL.pdf.

55. Avery Hartmans and Allana Akhtar, "How Tinder and Hinge Owner Match Group Grew to Dominate the Country's Online Dating Market—but Let Bumble Get Away," Business Insider, February 3, 2021, https://www.businessinsider.com/what-is-match-group-history-of -tinder-parent-company-2021-1.

56. Match Group, "Letter to Shareholders Q1 2021," March 4, 2021, https://s22.q4cdn.com /279430125/files/doc_financials/2021/q1/Earnings-Letter-Q1-2021-vF_a.pdf.

57. Ashley Carman, "Virtual Dating Is Booming, but Daters Say It's Not Enough," Verge, July 15, 2020, https://www.theverge.com/21324221/tinder-bumble-video-virtual-dating-calls -feature-whyd-you-push-that-button-podcast.

58. Tinder, "Future of Dating," 4.

59. Ashley Carman, "Tinder Says It'll Allow People to Get Rid of Their Geography Filters Completely," Verge, May 21, 2020, https://www.theverge.com/2020/5/21/21265643/tinder -geography-global-mode-rollout-update-test-passport.

60. Ashley Carman, "Bumble Now Lets People Match with Anyone in Their Country," *Verge*, April 14, 2020, https://www.theverge.com/2020/4/14/21220574/bumble-location-virtual-dating-update-video-voice-call-donation.

61. Corinne Sullivan, "Bumble's New 'Social Distance' Dating Options Let You Ease Back into IRL Dates," *PopSugar*, June 9, 2020, https://www.popsugar.com/love/bumble-new-social-distance-dating-option-47537142.

62. Tinder, "Future of Dating," 5.

63. Lisa Bonos, "He's Cute. But Is He Swab-Worthy? How Rapid Testing Became a Dating Ritual," *Washington Post*, February 8, 2022, https://www.washingtonpost.com/lifestyle/2022/02/08/covid-test-dating/.

64. NYC Health Department, "Safer Sex and COVID-19," accessed December 17, 2021, https://www1.nyc.gov/assets/doh/downloads/pdf/imm/covid-sex-guidance.pdf.

65. See Lisa Bonos, "How Has the Pandemic Changed Dating? Here Are 7 Tips for Getting Back out There," *Washington Post*, July 20, 2021, https://www.washingtonpost.com/lifestyle/2021/07/20/dating-life-after-covid/; and Brenda K. Wiederhold, "How COVID Has Changed Online Dating—and What Lies Ahead," *Cyberpsychology, Behavior, and Social Networking*, July 2021, 25(7): 435–36, http://doi.org/10.1089/cyber.2021.29219.editorial.

66. Tinder, "Future of Dating, 5.

67. Brandon G. Wagner, Kate H. Choi, and Philip N. Cohen, "Decline in Marriage Associated with the COVID-19 Pandemic in the United States," *Socius*, December 29, 2020, https://doi.org/10.1177%2F2378023120980328.

68. Wendy D. Manning and Krista K. Payne, "Marriage and Divorce Decline during the COVID-19 Pandemic: A Case Study of Five States," *Socius*, April 5, 2021, https://doi.org/10.1177/23780231211006976; Krista K. Westrick-Payne, Wendy Manning, and Lisa Carlson, "Pandemic Shortfall in Marriages and Divorces in the U.S." SocArXiv, December 2021, https://doi.org/10.31235/osf.io/9tqvy.

69. Michelle M. Winner, "11 Ways the Pandemic Has Changed Wedding Traditions Forever," *Brides*, March 25, 2021, https://www.brides.com/ways-covid-19-pandemic-changed-weddings-5118315.

70. Rachel Wolfe, "The Wedding Is Rescheduled. You Didn't Make the New Guest List," *Wall Street Journal*, November 30, 2021, https://www.wsj.com/articles/dont-save-the-date-anymore-wedding-guests-get-uninvited-11638287789.

71. Rebecca Mead, *One Perfect Day: The Selling of the American Wedding*, 2008, Penguin Books.

72. Esther Lee, "This Was the Average Cost of a Wedding in 2020," *Knot*, February 11, 2021, https://www.theknot.com/content/average-wedding-cost.

73. Westrick-Payne, Manning, and Carlson, "Pandemic Shortfall."

74. For the U.K., see Maya Oppenheim, "Divorces Fell by 4.5% during Year Covid Hit," *Independent*, February 1, 2022, https://www.independent.co.uk/news/uk/home-news/divorce-rate-pandemic-statistics-ons-b2004967.html. For Canada, see Matthew Talbot, "Divorce Activity in Canada Hit 47-Year Low during Pandemic," CTV News, March 12, 2022, https://www.ctvnews.ca/canada/divorce-activity-in-canada-hit-47-year-low-during-pandemic-statcan-says-1.5816890.

75. Vincent M. Mallozzi, "Divorce Rates Are Now Dropping. Here Are Some Reasons Why," *New York Times*, March 24, 2021, https://www.nytimes.com/2021/03/24/style/divorce-rates-dropping.html.

76. Robert D. Putnam, *Bowling Alone*, Simon and Schuster, 2000.

77. For a lovely discussion of being single during the pandemic, see Belinda Luscombe, "Being Single Was Just a Part of Their Lives before the Pandemic. Then It Became the Defining One," *Time*, April 17, 2021, https://time.com/5955250/single-during-covid-19-pandemic/.

Chapter Six

1. Andrew Taylor, "$900B COVID Relief Bill Passed by Congress, Sent to Trump," AP News, December 22, 2020, https://apnews.com/article/congress-900-billion-coronavirus-bill-75389549d3eaf2f3828b16d45c9706e6.

2. Kevin Liptak, "Trump Chooses Chaos with Delayed Signature of Covid Relief Bill," CNN, December 28, 2020, https://www.cnn.com/2020/12/28/politics/donald-trump-covid-relief-bill/index.html.

3. Jennifer Liu, "Millions of Unemployed Americans Will Get a $300 per Week Federal UI Boost through March with New Stimulus Bill," CNBC, December 21, 2020, https://www.cnbc.com/2020/12/21/new-stimulus-provides-300-per-week-11-weeks-enhanced-unemployment.html.

4. Ellie Kaverman and Andrew Stettner, "Delay in Extending Unemployment Aid Has Short-changed Workers $17 Billion in January," Century Foundation, February 2, 2021, https://tcf.org/content/commentary/tardy-stimulus-action-causes-pandemic-unemployment-benefit-delays/.

5. Aimee Picchi, "Second Stimulus Check: Who Won't Be Getting a $600 Check?," CBS News, January 6, 2021, https://www.cbsnews.com/news/second-stimulus-check-600-dollars-eligibility-2021-01-06/.

6. Zach Montague, "A Look at What's in the Stimulus Package Trump Signed," *New York Times*, December 28, 2020, https://www.nytimes.com/2020/12/28/business/economy/second-stimulus-package.html.

7. Annie Nova, "National Eviction Ban Will Be Extended through January in Stimulus Deal," CNBC, December 21, 2020, https://www.cnbc.com/2020/12/21/stimulus-deal-extends-national-eviction-ban-through-january.html.

8. Montague, "Look."

9. Montague, "Look."

10. Julie Appleby, "Congress Acts to Spare Consumers from Costly Surprise Medical Bills," NPR, December 22, 2020, https://www.npr.org/sections/health-shots/2020/12/22/949047358/congress-acts-to-spare-consumers-from-costly-surprise-medical-bills.

11. Scott Fulford and Marie Rush, "Insights from the Making Ends Meet Survey," Consumer Financial Protection Bureau Office of Research, Research Brief No. 2020-1, July 2020, https://www.consumerfinance.gov/data-research/research-reports/insights-making-ends-meet-survey/.

12. Barbara Spunt, "Here's What's in the American Rescue Plan," NPR, March 11, 2021, https://www.npr.org/sections/coronavirus-live-updates/2021/03/09/974841565/heres-whats-in-the-american-rescue-plan-as-it-heads-toward-final-passage.

13. Michael Brice-Saddler, "D.C. Unemployment Recipients Who Have Missed Benefits since March Should Get Paid This Week," *Washington Post*, April 19, 2021, https://www.washingtonpost.com/local/dc-politics/dc-unemployment-payments-missed/2021/04/19/f2dafbc4-a147-11eb-a774-7b47ceb36ee8_story.html.

14. Tami Luhby and Katie Lobosco, "Stimulus Checks Could Come Quickly, but the Jobless May Have a Wait for Unemployment Benefits," CNN, March 10, 2021, https://www.cnn.com/2021/03/10/politics/stimulus-unemployment-benefits-checks/index.html.

15. Greg Iacurci, "24% of Unemployed Workers Have Been Jobless for Over a Year," CNBC, April 6, 2021, https://www.cnbc.com/2021/04/06/24percent-of-unemployed-workers-have-been-jobless-for-over-a-year.html.

16. The end of the unemployment benefit year typically means people must reapply for benefits and often marks the end of eligibility or a large reduction in benefits. Most states calculate the benefits someone is entitled to based on their earnings in the year three months before filing an unemployment claim. These calculations usually get reset at the end of the benefit year, leading to a drop in benefits. During normal times, most people reach the end of benefits eligibility before they reach the end of the benefit year, but pandemic policies had extended eligibility during the pandemic. See Brian Galle, Elizabeth Pancotti, and Andrew Stettner, "Expert Q&A about the Unemployment Provisions of the American Rescue Plan," Century Foundation, March 10, 2021, https://tcf.org/content/commentary/questions-answers-unemployment-provisions-america-rescue-plan-act/.

17. Mark Steber, "Top 3 Tax Tips for Unemployment Benefits," Jackson Hewitt, October 30, 2020, https://www.jacksonhewitt.com/tax-help/jh-tax-talk/top-3-tax-tips-for-unemployment-benefits/.

18. Megan Leonhardt, "Some Americans Owe Thousands in Taxes on Enhanced Unemployment Benefits: 'They Threw Us to the Fishes,'" CNBC Make It, March 2, 2021, https://www.cnbc.com/2021/03/02/some-states-didnt-withhold-taxes-from-enhanced-unemployment.html.

19. Alicia Adamczyk, "What You Need to Know about the Third Round of Stimulus Payments," CNBC Make It, March 10, 2021, https://www.cnbc.com/2021/03/10/what-you-need-to-know-about-third-stimulus-payment.html. This rapid phase-out implied a very high marginal tax rate for incomes between $75,000 and $80,000, because every additional $1,000 of income reduced the payment by $280. See Garrett Watson, "Senate Direct Payment Design Would Create High Implicit Marginal Tax Rates," Tax Foundation, March 5, 2021, https://taxfoundation.org/senate-american-rescue-plan-direct-payments/.

20. Mary Williams Walsh and Karl Russell, "Virus Did Not Bring Financial Rout That Many States Feared," *New York Times*, March 1, 2021, https://www.nytimes.com/2021/03/01/business/covid-state-tax-revenue.html.

21. Kate Davidson, "Covid-19's Hit to State and Local Revenues Is Smaller than Many Feared," *Wall Street Journal*, February 7, 202, https://www.wsj.com/articles/covid-19s-hit-to-state-and-local-revenues-is-smaller-than-many-feared-11612706030.

22. Alan Rappeport, "Empty Office Buildings Squeeze City Budgets as Property Values Fall," *New York Times*, March 3, 2021, https://www.nytimes.com/2021/03/03/business/pandemic-city-budgets.html.

23. Tamara Keith and Scott Horsley, "Not All COVID-19 Aid Is Spent. But Schools, Cities and States Say They Need More," NPR, February 24, 2021, https://www.npr.org/2021/02/24/970708820/not-all-covid-19-aid-is-spent-but-schools-cities-and-states-say-they-need-more.

24. Alan Berube and Eli Byerly-Duke, "Cities Are Taking It Slow with American Rescue Plan Funds," *The Avenue* (blog), Brookings Institution, September 7, 2021, https://www.brookings.edu/blog/the-avenue/2021/09/07/cities-are-taking-it-slow-with-american-rescue-plan-funds/.

25. Gabriel T. Rubin, "Stimulus Package Update: What's in the Covid-19 Relief Bill," *Wall Street Journal*, March 6, 2021, https://www.wsj.com/articles/stimulus-update-biden-covid-19-relief-package-11614095748.

26. Dylan Matthews, "Joe Biden Just Launched the Second War on Poverty," Vox, March 10, 2021, https://www.vox.com/policy-and-politics/22319572/joe-biden-american-rescue-plan-war-on-poverty.

27. More generally, what I describe here is the "headcount ratio" of poverty. There are other ways to measure poverty that avoid some of the problems I discuss, although all have some sort of threshold. My favorite is the poverty gap and the poverty gap index. The poverty gap measures how much money it would take to bring all families below the threshold up to the threshold and so eliminate "poverty." The poverty gap is surprisingly low, perhaps around $200 billion per year, which indicates why the refundable child tax credit is so effective at reducing poverty, although whether just giving the poor money would alleviate poverty in a broader sense is open to debate.

28. Gordon M. Fisher, "The Development of the Orshansky Poverty Thresholds and Their Subsequent History as the Official U.S. Poverty Measure" (working paper, Census Department, 1997), https://www.census.gov/library/working-papers/1997/demo/fisher-02.html.

29. Census Bureau, "How the Census Bureau Measures Poverty," accessed September 11, 2021, https://www.census.gov/topics/income-poverty/poverty/guidance/poverty-measures.html.

30. Mark Greenberg, "It's Time for a Better Poverty Measure," Center for American Progress, August 25, 2009, https://www.americanprogress.org/issues/poverty/reports/2009/08/25/6582/its-time-for-a-better-poverty-measure/.

31. Poverty here is the Supplemental Poverty Index, which includes most government benefits. See Liana Fox and Kalee Burns, "The Supplemental Poverty Measure: 2020," Census Bureau Report Number P60-275, September 14, 2021, https://www.census.gov/library/publications/2021/demo/p60-275.html.

32. Laura Wheaton, Sarah Minton, Linda Giannarelli, and Kelly Dwyer, "2021 Poverty Projections: Assessing Four American Rescue Plan Policies," Urban Institute, February 2021, https://www.urban.org/sites/default/files/publication/103656/2021-poverty-projections_1.pdf.

33. Zachary Parolin, Sophie Collyer, and Megan A. Curran, "Sixth Child Tax Credit Payment Kept 3.7 Million Children Out of Poverty in December," *Poverty and Social Policy Brief*, January 18, 2022, 6(1), https://static1.squarespace.com/static/610831a16c95260dbd68934a/t/61ea09926280d03df62aa31d/1642727841927/Monthly-poverty-December-2021-CPSP.pdf.

34. See Zachary Parolin, Elizabeth Ananat, . . . and Christopher Wimer, "The Initial Effects of the Expanded Child Tax Credit on Material Hardship" (NBER Working Paper No. 29285, September 2021), https://www.nber.org/papers/w29285. See also the thorough review in Amelia Thomson-DeVeaux, "Congress Found an Easy Way to Fix Child Poverty. Then It Walked Away," FiveThirtyEight, March 30, 2022, https://fivethirtyeight.com/features/congress-found-an-easy-way-to-fix-child-poverty-then-it-walked-away/.

35. See Chad Stone and William Chen, "Introduction to Unemployment Insurance," Center on Budget and Policy Priorities, July 30, 2014, https://www.cbpp.org/research/introduction-to-unemployment-insurance.

36. See Employment and Training Administration, "Comparison of State Unemployment Laws 2020," 3-10–3-14, accessed September 13, 2021, https://oui.doleta.gov/unemploy/comparison/2020-2029/comparison2020.asp. The "most common multiple used by states is 1/26 of the high-quarter" (3-10), which results in replacing half of the weekly high-quarter wages per week.

37. In these calculations, I assume that pandemic layoffs occurred in the third week of March 2020 and unemployment continued through 2021. Most people who were laid off early did find some employment during the pandemic, even if they were making less than before. But many found getting work difficult or experienced another round of layoffs in January 2021. By assuming the maximum unemployment duration, I am calculating close to the maximum benefit available in the average state. I include the December 2020 relief bill Economic Impact Payments in 2021.

38. Like many unemployment benefits eligibility requirements, figuring out whether a particular person is eligible is often complicated. See John Pallash, "Unemployment Insurance Program Letter No. 16-20," Employment and Training Administration Advisory System, U.S. Department of Labor, August 27, 2020, https://wdr.doleta.gov/directives/attach/UIPL/UIPL_16-20_Change_3_acc.pdf.

39. Scott Fulford and Cortnie Shupe, "Consumer Finances during the Pandemic: Insights from the Making Ends Meet Survey," Consumer Financial Protection Bureau Data Point No. 2021-3, December 2021, https://www.consumerfinance.gov/data-research/research-reports/consumer-finances-during-pandemic-insights-making-ends-meet-survey/.

40. Because of the sample size, the decline was only statistically significant for non-Hispanic white Americans and people with at least a college degree. We suspect that one reason for the larger standard errors is that the experiences of lower-income households may have been more varied. Some did very well relative to before the pandemic, buoyed by Economic Impact Payments and generous unemployment insurance. Others were left out from aid. High-income households, on the other hand, mostly avoided unemployment and cut their spending, so their experiences look fairly similar.

41. Source: Original calculations in Fulford and Shupe, "Consumer Finances."

42. Source: Author's calculations based on Fulford and Shupe.

43. Andrew Dunn, Thea Garon, Necati Celik, and Jess McKay, "Financial Health Pulse: 2021 U.S. Trends Report," Financial Health Network, 2021, https://fhn-finhealthnetwork-assets.s3.amazonaws.com/uploads/2021/10/2021_Pulse_Trends_Report.pdf.

44. Fiona Greig, Erica Deadman, and Tanya Sonthalia, "Household Cash Balance Pulse: Family Edition," JPMorgan Chase Institute, November 2021, https://www.jpmorganchase.com/institute/research/household-income-spending/household-cash-balance-pulse-families.

45. Fiona Greig, Chris Wheat, . . . and Shantanu Banerjee, "How Did the Distribution of Income Growth Change alongside the Hot Pre-pandemic Labor Market and Recent Fiscal Stimulus?," JPMorgan Chase Institute, September 2021, https://www.jpmorganchase.com/institute/research/household-income-spending/how-did-the-distribution-of-income-growth-change-alongside-the-hot-pre-pandemic-labor-market-and-recent-fiscal-stimulus.

46. Ryan Sandler, "Delinquencies on Credit Accounts Continue to Be Low Despite the Pandemic," Consumer Financial Protection Bureau blog, June 16, 2021, https://www.consumerfinance.gov/about-us/blog/delinquencies-on-credit-accounts-continue-to-be-low-despite-the-pandemic/.

47. Soma Biswas and Harriet Torry, "Coronavirus Was Supposed to Drive Bankruptcies Higher. The Opposite Happened," *Wall Street Journal*, March 29, 2021, https://www.wsj.com/articles/coronavirus-was-supposed-to-drive-bankruptcies-higher-the-opposite-happened-11617010201.

48. The source with confidence intervals is in Fulford and Shupe, "Consumer Finances."

49. Jeff Larrimore, Jacob Mortenson, and David Splinter, "Earnings Shocks and Stabilization during COVID-19," Federal Reserve Board Finance and Economics Discussion Series 2021-052, 2021, https://doi.org/10.17016/FEDS.2021.052.

50. For a more detailed breakdown and a full relationship matrix, see Fulford and Shupe, "Consumer Finances."

51. JPMorgan Chase Institute, "Is Mortgage Forbearance Reaching the Right Homeowners during the COVID-19 Pandemic?," policy brief, December 2020, https://www.jpmorganchase.com/institute/research/household-debt/report-did-mortgage-forbearance-reach-the-right-homeowners.

52. See Conference of State Bank Supervisors and Consumer Financial Protection Bureau, "CARES Act Forbearance & Foreclosure," May 2020, https://files.consumerfinance.gov/f/documents/cfpb_csbs_industry-forbearance-guide_2020-06.pdf.

53. Government Accountability Office, "COVID-19 Housing Protections: Mortgage Forbearance and Other Federal Efforts Have Reduced Default and Foreclosure Risks," July 2021, GAO-21-554, https://www.gao.gov/assets/gao-21-554.pdf.

54. 12 CFR 1024.39(a). Effective August 31, 2021, and until October 1, 2022, Consumer Financial Protection Bureau regulations also require that a servicer provide some delinquent borrowers with specific additional information about forbearance. Consumer Financial Protection Bureau, "Protections for Borrowers Affected by the COVID-19 Emergency under the Real Estate Settlement Procedures Act (RESPA), Regulation X," *Federal Register*, June 30, 2021, https://www.federalregister.gov/documents/2021/06/30/2021-13964/protections-for-borrowers-affected-by-the-covid-19-emergency-under-the-real-estate-settlement.

55. Xudong An, Larry Cordell, Liang Geng, and Keyoung Lee, "Inequality in the Time of COVID-19: Evidence from Mortgage Delinquency and Forbearance" (Federal Reserve Bank of Philadelphia Working Paper WP 21-09, February 2021), https://doi.org/10.21799/frbp.wp.2021.09.

Chapter Seven

1. John Scalzi, "Straight White Male: The Lowest Difficulty Setting There Is," *Whatever* (blog), May 15, 2012, https://whatever.scalzi.com/2012/05/15/straight-white-male-the-lowest -difficulty-setting-there-is/.

2. Carlos Garriga, Lowell R. Ricketts, and Don E. Schlagenhauf, "The Homeownership Experience of Minorities during the Great Recession," *Federal Reserve Bank of St. Louis Review*, First Quarter 2017, 99(1): 139–67, http://dx.doi.org/10.20955/r.2017.139-67.

3. Robert W. Fairlie, Kenneth Couch, and Huanan Xu, "The Impacts of COVID-19 on Minority Unemployment: First Evidence from April 2020 CPS Microdata" (NBER Working Paper No. 27246, May 2020), https://www.nber.org/papers/w27246.

4. Ella Koeze, "A Year Later, Who Is Back to Work and Who Is Not?," *New York Times*, March 9, 2021, https://www.nytimes.com/interactive/2021/03/09/business/economy/covid -employment-demographics.html.

5. Elise Gould and Jori Kandram, "Wages Grew in 2020 Because the Bottom Fell Out of the Low-Wage Labor Market," Economic Policy Institute, February 24, 2021, https://www.epi.org /publication/state-of-working-america-wages-in-2020/.

6. Amartya Sen, *Development as Freedom*, Anchor Books, 1999.

7. Milton Friedman and Rose Friedman, *Freedom to Choose*, Harcourt Brace, 1990, 132.

8. Other measures, such as consumption or income inequality, capture different aspects. Income inequality is often used because it is relatively easy to measure income and is often correlated with things we do care about. Consumption inequality is likely closer to measuring what we actually care about than income or wealth inequality. But consumption is more difficult to measure, particularly during the pandemic, and is rarely discussed except among economists and not even among all of those. To the extent that income inequality is a useful measure, it is because it gives us insights into consumption inequality and the kinds of choices people make when they are trying to make ends meet. For more on measuring consumption inequality, see Orazio P. Attanasio and Luigi Pistaferri, "Consumption Inequality," *Journal of Economic Perspectives*, 2016, 30(2): 3–28, https://pubs.aeaweb.org/doi/pdfplus/10 .1257/jep.30.2.3.

9. Source: Author's calculations using Federal Reserve Board, "Distributional Financial Accounts," https://www.federalreserve.gov/releases/z1/dataviz/dfa/. The series is adjusted for inflation using the Consumer Price Index for all Urban Consumers, with 2019 quarter 4 = 1.

10. Michael Batty, Jesse Bricker, . . . and Alice Henriques Volz, "The Distributional Financial Accounts of the United States," in *Measuring Distribution and Mobility of Income and Wealth*, ed. Raj Chetty, John N. Friedman, . . . and Arthur Kennickell, University of Chicago Press, December 2020, https://www.nber.org/books-and-chapters/measuring-distribution-and-mobility -income-and-wealth/distributional-financial-accounts-united-states.

11. Forbes Staff Leadership, "Press Release: Forbes 33rd Annual World's Billionaires Issue Reveals Number of Billionaires and Their Combined Wealth Have Decreased for the First Time Since 2016," *Forbes*, March 5, 2019, https://www.forbes.com/sites/forbespr/2019/03/05/press -release-forbes-33rd-annual-worlds-billionaires-issue-reveals-number-of-billionaires-and-their -combined-wealth-have-decreased-for-for-first-time-since-2016.

12. These estimates are based on known holding and share prices. See "Real Time Billion-aires," *Forbes*, November 21, 2021, https://www.forbes.com/real-time-billionaires/#40874c423d78.

13. JPMorgan Chase Institute, "Initial Impacts of the Pandemic Reflect That Families Changed Their Saving and Spending Behavior," June 2020, https://www.jpmorganchase.com/institute/research/household-income-spending/jpmorgan-chase-institute-take; Ryan Sandler and Judith Ricks, "The Early Effects of the COVID-19 Pandemic on Consumer Credit," CFPB Office of Research Special Issue Brief, August 2020, https://files.consumerfinance.gov/f/documents/cfpb_early-effects-covid-19-consumer-credit_issue-brief.pdf.

14. It is unclear from the documentation of the Distributional Financial Accounts whether their racial and ethnic categories are exclusive and how they define others. Hispanic as an ethnicity includes "white" as a race.

15. There is, of course, much debate on this connection. Yet, if money is speech, then wealth inequality is speech inequality. And wealth inequality has direct consequences for what policies get considered and enacted. Politicians are much more responsive to the views of the wealthy. See Martin Gilens and Benjamin I. Page, "Testing Theories of American Politics: Elites, Interest Groups, and Average Citizens," *Perspectives on Politics*, 2014, 12(3): 564–81. For two accounts, see Joseph E. Stiglitz, "Inequality and Economic Growth," *Political Quarterly*, 2015, 86: 134–55, https://doi.org/10.1111/1467-923X.12237; and Daron Acemoglu and James A. Robinson, *Why Nations Fail: The Origins of Power, Prosperity, and Poverty*, Crown Business, 2012.

16. Peter Ganong, Damon Jones, . . . and Chris Wheat, "Wealth, Race, and Consumption Smoothing of Typical Income Shocks" (NBER Working Paper No. 27552, July 2020), https://www.nber.org/papers/w27552.

17. Source: These estimates rely on several sources. While the 2020 numbers will likely not change much, the 2021 estimates are based on mortality tables that were still preliminary. For consistency, I use the numbers from 2019 and 2020, and preliminary estimates 2021 from Ryan K. Masters and Laudan Y. Aron, "Changes in Life Expectancy between 2019 and 2021: United States and 19 Peer Countries," medRxiv, April 5, 2022, https://doi.org/10.1101/2022.04.05.22273393. The 2019 and 2020 numbers closely match the estimates in Sherry L. Murphy, Kenneth D. Kochanek, Jiaquan Xu, and Elizabeth Arias, "Mortality in the United States, 2020," NCHS Data Brief No. 427, December 2021, https://www.cdc.gov/nchs/products/databriefs/db427.htm. Earlier years are from Internet Table I-15 in Elizabeth Arias, Betzaida Tejada-Vera, Farida Ahmad, and Kenneth D. Kochanek, "Provisional Life Expectancy Estimates for 2020," Vital Statistics Rapid Release, Report No. 015, CDC, July 2021, https://www.cdc.gov/nchs/data/vsrr/vsrr015-508.pdf.

18. Death estimates from National Center for Health Statistics, "COVID-19 Mortality Over-view," accessed August 24, 2021, https://www.cdc.gov/nchs/covid19/mortality-overview.htm.

19. David W. Smith and Benjamin S. Bradshaw, "Variation in Life Expectancy during the Twentieth Century in the United States," *Demography*, 2006, 43(4): 647–57, https://doi.org/10.1353/dem.2006.0039.

20. Centers for Disease Control and Prevention, "1918 Pandemic (H1N1 Virus)," March 20, 2019, https://www.cdc.gov/flu/pandemic-resources/1918-pandemic-h1n1.html.

21. See the summary in Kyriakos S. Markides and Karl Eschbach, "Hispanic Paradox in Adult Mortality in the United States," in *International Handbook of Adult Mortality*, ed. R. Rogers and E. Crimmins, Springer, 2011, 227–40, https://doi.org/10.1007/978-90-481-9996-9_11.

22. Steven H. Woolf, Ryan K. Masters, and Laudan Y. Aron, "Effect of the Covid-19 Pandemic in 2020 on Life Expectancy across Populations in the USA and Other High Income Countries: Simulations of Provisional Mortality Data," *BMJ*, 2021, 373: n1343, https://doi.org/10.1136/bmj.n1343.

23. Randall Akee and Sarah Reber, "American Indians and Alaska Natives Are Dying of COVID-19 at Shocking Rates," Brookings Institution, February 18, 2021, https://www.brookings.edu/research/american-indians-and-alaska-natives-are-dying-of-covid-19-at-shocking-rates/.

24. Centers for Disease Control and Prevention, "Risk for COVID-19 Infection, Hospitalization, and Death by Race/Ethnicity," July 16, 2021, https://www.cdc.gov/coronavirus/2019-ncov/covid-data/investigations-discovery/hospitalization-death-by-race-ethnicity.html.

25. Samantha Artiga, Latoya Hill, Kendal Orgera, and Anthony Damico, "Health Coverage by Race and Ethnicity," Kaiser Family Foundation, July 16, 2021, https://www.kff.org/racial-equity-and-health-policy/issue-brief/health-coverage-by-race-and-ethnicity/.

26. Soo Rin Kim, Matthew Vann, Laura Bronner, and Grace Manthey, "Which Cities Have the Biggest Racial Gaps in COVID-19 Testing Access?," FiveThirtyEight, July 22, 2020, https://fivethirtyeight.com/features/white-neighborhoods-have-more-access-to-covid-19-testing-sites/.

27. Amy Schoenfeld Walker, Anjali Singhvi, . . . and Yuriria Avila, "Pandemic's Racial Disparities Persist in Vaccine Rollout," *New York Times*, March 5, 2021, https://www.nytimes.com/interactive/2021/03/05/us/vaccine-racial-disparities.html.

28. Genevieve P. Kanter, Andrea G. Segal, and Peter W. Groeneveld, "Income Disparities in Access to Critical Care Services," *Health Affairs*, August 2020, 39(8), https://doi.org/10.1377/hlthaff.2020.00581.

29. Krutika Amin, Jared Ortaliza, . . . and Jennifer Kates, "COVID-19 Mortality Preventable by Vaccines," Peterson-KFF Health System Tracker, April 21, 2022, https://www.healthsystemtracker.org/brief/covid19-and-other-leading-causes-of-death-in-the-us/.

30. Woolf, Masters, and Aron, "Effect of the Covid-19 Pandemic." See also a similar calculation with similar results in Masters and Aron, "Changes in Life Expectancy."

31. Anne Case and Angus Deaton, *Deaths of Despair and the Future of Capitalism*, Princeton University Press, 2020, 193–202.

32. Thomas J. Bollyky, Erin N. Hulland, . . . and Joseph L. Dieleman, "Pandemic Preparedness and COVID-19: An Exploratory Analysis of Infection and Fatality Rates, and Contextual Factors Associated with Preparedness in 177 Countries, from Jan 1, 2020, to Sept 30, 2021," *Lancet*, February 1, 2022, https://doi.org/10.1016/S0140-6736(22)00172-6.

33. Case and Deaton, *Deaths of Despair*.

34. Anne Case, "Deaths of Despair Strike Women Too," Princeton University Press, March 1, 2020, https://press.princeton.edu/ideas/deaths-of-despair-strike-women-too.

35. Debbie Cenziper and Karin Brulliard, "People in Addiction Treatment Are Losing Crucial Support during Coronavirus Pandemic," *Washington Post*, March 27, 2020, https://www.washingtonpost.com/health/people-in-addiction-treatment-are-losing-crucial-support-during-coronavirus-pandemic/2020/03/26/5698eae0-6ac6-11ea-abef-020f086a3fab_story.html.

36. See Centers for Disease Control and Prevention, "Provisional Drug Overdose Death Counts," accessed December 18, 2021, https://www.cdc.gov/nchs/nvss/vsrr/drug-overdose -data.htm.

37. Betsy McKay, "U.S. Drug-Overdose Deaths Soared Nearly 30% in 2020, Driven by Synthetic Opioids," *Wall Street Journal*, July 14, 2021, https://www.wsj.com/articles/u-s-drug -overdose-deaths-soared-nearly-30-in-2020-11626271200?mod=hp_lead_pos10.

38. Bryan Walsh, "America's Deepening Drinking Habit," Axios, July 7, 2021, https://www.axios .com/americans-drinking-alcohol-pandemic-29ee70d7-40ae-4e71-807a-3f4ad2ee19b8.html.

39. Michael S. Pollard, Joan S. Tucker, and Harold D. Green Jr., "Changes in Adult Alcohol Use and Consequences during the COVID-19 Pandemic in the US," *JAMA Network Open*, September 29, 2020, 3(9): e2022942, https://jamanetwork.com/journals/jamanetworkopen /fullarticle/2770975.

40. NielsenIQ, "Rebalancing the 'COVID-19 Effect' on Alcohol Sales," May 7, 2020, https:// nielseniq.com/global/en/insights/analysis/2020/rebalancing-the-covid-19-effect-on-alcohol -sales/.

41. For example, see MentalHelp.net, "5 Signs That You May Have a Drinking Problem," accessed July 14, 2021, https://www.mentalhelp.net/substance-abuse/alcohol/5-signs-drinking -problem/.

42. Elyse R. Grossman, Sara E. Benjamin-Neelon, and Susan Sonnenschein, "Alcohol Consumption during the COVID-19 Pandemic: A Cross-Sectional Survey of US Adults," *International Journal of Environmental Research and Public Health*, 2020, 17(24): 9189, https://doi.org /10.3390/ijerph17249189.

43. Hartford Health Care, "Binge Drinking up 41 Percent among Women since COVID-19," October 1, 2020, https://hartfordhealthcare.org/about-us/news-press/news-detail?articleId =29111&publicid=471.

44. Aaron M. White, "Gender Differences in the Epidemiology of Alcohol Use and Related Harms in the United States," *Alcohol Research Current Reviews*, October 29, 2020, 40(2), https:// doi.org/10.35946/arcr.v40.2.01.

45. Aneri Pattani, "Women Now Drink as Much as Men—Not So Much for Pleasure, but to Cope," NPR, June 9, 2021, https://www.npr.org/sections/health-shots/2021/06/09 /1003980966/women-now-drink-as-much-as-men-and-suffer-health-effects-more -quickly.

46. Kim Tingley, "How Bad Is Our Pandemic Drinking Problem?," *New York Times Magazine*, April 21, 2021, https://www.nytimes.com/2021/04/21/magazine/covid-drinking-alcohol -health.html.

47. Sally C. Curtin, Holly Hedegaard, and Farida B. Ahmad, "Provisional Numbers and Rates of Suicide by Month and Demographic Characteristics: United States, 2020," Vital Statistics Rapid Release, Report No. 16, CDC, November 2021, https://www.cdc.gov/nchs/data/vsrr /VSRR016.pdf.

48. Jane Pirkis, Ann John, . . . and Matthew J. Spittal, "Suicide Trends in the Early Months of the COVID-19 Pandemic: An Interrupted Time-Series Analysis of Preliminary Data from 21 Countries," *Lancet Psychiatry*, 2021, 8: 579–88, https://doi.org/10.1016/S2215-0366(21) 00091-2.

49. Joel Achenbach, "Coronavirus Is Harming the Mental Health of Tens of Millions of People in U.S., New Poll Finds," *Washington Post*, April 2, 2020, https://www.washingtonpost .com/health/coronavirus-is-harming-the-mental-health-of-tens-of-millions-of-people-in-us -new-poll-finds/2020/04/02/565e6744-74ee-11ea-85cb-8670579b863d_story.html.

50. Mark É. Czeisler, Rashon I. Lane, . . . and Shantha M. W. Rajaratnam, "Mental Health, Substance Use, and Suicidal Ideation during the COVID-19 Pandemic—United States, June 24–30, 2020," *Morbidity and Mortality Weekly Report*, August 2020, 69(3): 1049–57, http://dx.doi.org/10 .15585/mmwr.mm6932a1.

51. Maddy Savage, "Coronavirus: The Possible Long-Term Mental Health Impacts," BBC, October 28, 2020, https://www.bbc.com/worklife/article/20201021-coronavirus-the-possible -long-term-mental-health-impacts.

52. Brad Boserup, Mark McKenney, and Adel Elkbuli, "Alarming Trends in US Domestic Violence during the COVID-19 Pandemic," *American Journal of Emergency Medicine*, December 1, 2020, 38(12): 2753–55, https://doi.org/10.1016/j.ajem.2020.04.077.

53. Clare E. B. Cannon, Regardt Ferreira, Frederick Buttell, and Jennifer First, "COVID-19, Intimate Partner Violence, and Communication Ecologies," *American Behavioral Scientist*, February 6, 2021, 65(7): 992–1013, https://doi.org/10.1177%2F0002764221992826.

54. Heather M. Foran and K. Daniel O'Leary, "Alcohol and Intimate Partner Violence: A Meta-analytic Review," *Clinical Psychology Review*, 2008, 28(7): 1222–34, https://doi.org/10 .1016/j.cpr.2008.05.001.

55. UN Women, "The Shadow Pandemic: Violence against Women during COVID-19," accessed July 30, 2020, https://www.unwomen.org/en/news/in-focus/in-focus-gender-equality -in-covid-19-response/violence-against-women-during-covid-19; Jeffrey Kluger, "Domestic Violence Is a Pandemic within the COVID-19 Pandemic," *Time*, February 3, 2021, https://time .com/5928539/domestic-violence-covid-19/.

56. See Esther Arenas-Arroyo, Daniel Fernandez-Kranz, and Natalia Nollenberger, "Intimate Partner Violence under Forced Cohabitation and Economic Stress: Evidence from the COVID-19 Pandemic," *Journal of Public Economics*, 2021, 194: 104350, https://doi.org/10.1016/j.jpubeco .2020.104350; and Jorge M. Agüero, "COVID-19 and the Rise of Intimate Partner Violence," *World Development*, 2021, 137: 105217, https://doi.org/10.1016/j.worlddev.2020.105217.

57. See Giulia Lausi, Alessandra Pizzo, . . . and Emanuela Mari, "Intimate Partner Violence during the COVID-19 Pandemic: A Review of the Phenomenon from Victims' and Help Professionals' Perspectives," *International Journal of Environmental Research and Public Health*, June 2021, 18(12): 6204, https://doi.org/10.3390/ijerph18126204; and Heather X. Rhodes, Kirklen Petersen, Laura Lunsford, and Saptarshi Biswas, "COVID-19 Resilience for Survival: Occurrence of Domestic Violence during Lockdown at a Rural American College of Surgeons Verified Level One Trauma Center," *Cureus*, August 2020, 12(8): e10059, https://dx .doi.org/10.7759%2Fcureus.10059.

58. Babina Gosangi, Hyesun Park, . . . and Bharti Khurana, "Exacerbation of Physical Intimate Partner Violence during COVID-19 Pandemic," *Radiology*, 2021, 298(1): E38–E45, https:// doi.org/10.1148/radiol.2020202866.

59. Jaewon Kang and Sharon Terlep, "Retailers Phase Out Coronavirus Hazard Pay for Essential Workers," *Wall Street Journal*, May 19, 2020, https://www.wsj.com/articles/retailers -phase-out-coronavirus-hazard-pay-for-essential-workers-11589915679.

60. Suresh Naidu, "'Essential' Workers Are Just Forced Laborers," *Washington Post*, May 21, 2020, https://www.washingtonpost.com/outlook/2020/05/21/essential-workers-pay-wages -safety-unemployment/.

61. Pallavi Gogoi, "$600 a Week: Poverty Remedy or Job Slayer?," NPR, July 27, 2020, https://www.npr.org/2020/07/27/895674685/-600-a-week-poverty-remedy-or-job -slayer.

62. Molly Kinder, Laura Stateler, and Julia Du, "The COVID-19 Hazard Continues, but the Hazard Pay Does Not: Why America's Essential Workers Need a Raise," Brookings Institution, October 29, 2020, https://www.brookings.edu/research/the-covid-19-hazard-continues-but -the-hazard-pay-does-not-why-americas-frontline-workers-need-a-raise/.

63. Department of the Treasury, "Fact Sheet: The Coronavirus State and Local Fiscal Recovery Funds Will Deliver $350 Billion for State, Local, Territorial, and Tribal Governments to Respond to the COVID-19 Emergency and Bring Back Jobs," May 10, 2021, https://home .treasury.gov/system/files/136/SLFRP-Fact-Sheet-FINAL1-508A.pdf.

64. Susan Haigh, "Who's a Hero? Some States, Cities Still Debating Hazard Pay," *PBS News Hour*, November 25, 2021, https://www.pbs.org/newshour/economy/whos-a-hero-some-states -cities-still-debating-hazard-pay.

65. Jennifer Cohen and Yana van der Meulen Rodgers, "Contributing Factors to Personal Protective Equipment Shortages during the COVID-19 Pandemic," *Preventive Medicine*, December 2020, 141: 106263, https://doi.org/10.1016/j.ypmed.2020.106263.

66. Sophia Ankel, "Photos Show How Shortages Are Forcing Doctors and Nurses to Improvise Coronavirus PPE from Snorkel Masks, Pool Noodles, and Trash Bags," Business Insider, April 23, 2020, https://www.businessinsider.com/photos-show-doctors-nurses-improvising -due-to-lack-of-ppe-2020-4.

67. J. David McSwane, "'Those of Us Who Don't Die Are Going to Quit': A Crush of Patients, Dwindling Supplies and the Nurse Who Lost Hope," ProPublica, December 30, 2020, https://www.propublica.org/article/those-of-us-who-dont-die-are-going-to-quit-a-crush-of -patients-dwindling-supplies-and-the-nurse-who-lost-hope.

68. Eric Lee, Will Loh, Ivy Ang, and Yanni Tan, "Plastic Bags as Personal Protective Equipment during the COVID-19 Pandemic: Between the Devil and the Deep Blue Sea," *Journal of Emergency Medicine*, April 13, 2020, 58(5): 821–23, https://doi.org/10.1016/j.jemermed.2020 .04.016.

69. See, for example, Dhruv Khullar, "Treating the Unvaccinated," *New Yorker*, July 16, 2021, https://www.newyorker.com/science/medical-dispatch/treating-the-unvaccinated; and Chavi Eve Karkowsky, "Vaccine Refusers Risk Compassion Fatigue," *Atlantic*, August 11, 2021, https:// www.theatlantic.com/ideas/archive/2021/08/health-care-workers-compassion-fatigue -vaccine-refusers/619716/.

70. Eviction Lab, "National Estimates: Eviction in America," Princeton University, May 11, 2018, https://evictionlab.org/national-estimates/.

71. CoreLogic, "United States Residential Foreclosure Crisis: Ten Years Later," March 2017, https://www.corelogic.com/wp-content/uploads/sites/4/research/foreclosure-report /national-foreclosure-report-10-year.pdf.

72. See Eviction Lab, "National Estimates"; and CoreLogic, "United States Residential Foreclosure Crisis."

73. Ashley Gromis and Matthew Desmond, "Estimating the Prevalence of Eviction in the United States: New Data from the 2017 American Housing Survey," *Cityscape*, 2021, 23(2): 279–90, https://www.jstor.org/stable/27039963.

74. Alexandra Dobre, Marie Rush, and Eric Wilson, "Financial Conditions for Renters before and during the COVID-19 Pandemic," Consumer Financial Protection Bureau Office of Research, Brief No. 2021-9, September 2021, https://www.consumerfinance.gov/data-research/research-reports/financial-conditions-for-renters-before-and-during-covid-19-pandemic/.

75. Matthew Desmond, *Evicted: Poverty and Profit in the American City*, Penguin Random House, 2017, 74–73 and endnotes.

76. Joint Center for Housing Studies of Harvard University, "The State of the Nation's Housing 2020," 2020, https://www.jchs.harvard.edu/sites/default/files/reports/files/Harvard_JCHS_The_State_of_the_Nations_Housing_2020_Report_Revised_120720.pdf.

77. Jerusalem Demsas, "California Is Ending a Rule That Helped Cause Its Housing Crisis," Vox, September 17, 2021, https://www.vox.com/2021/9/17/22679358/california-newsom-duplex-single-family-zoning.

78. JPMorgan Chase Institute, "Renters vs. Homeowners," March 2021, https://www.jpmorganchase.com/institute/research/household-debt/renters-homeowners-income-and-liquid-asset-trends-during-covid-19.

79. Dobre, Rush, and Wilson, "Financial Conditions for Renters."

80. The lines are four-week moving averages calculated as the difference from the yearly average number of evictions. Source: Author's calculations from Peter Hepburn, Renee Louis, and Matthew Desmond, "Eviction Tracking System: Version 1.0," 2020, https://evictionlab.org/eviction-tracking/get-the-data/.

81. Laurie Goodman, Karan Kaul, and Michael Neal, "The CARES Act Eviction Moratorium Covers All Federally Financed Rentals—That's One in Four US Rental Units," *Urban Wire* (blog), Urban Institute, April 2, 2020, https://www.urban.org/urban-wire/cares-act-eviction-moratorium-covers-all-federally-financed-rentals-thats-one-four-us-rental-units.

82. Dartunorro Clark, "'Eviction Crisis': Housing Advocates Fear Waves of Homelessness as Moratoriums Expire," NBC News, July 4, 2020, https://www.nbcnews.com/politics/politics-news/eviction-crisis-housing-advocates-fear-waves-homelessness-moratoriums-expire-n1232846.

83. Centers for Disease Control and Prevention, "Temporary Halt in Residential Evictions to Prevent the Further Spread of COVID-19," *Federal Register*, September 4, 2020, 85 FR 55292, https://www.federalregister.gov/documents/2020/09/04/2020-19654/temporary-halt-in-residential-evictions-to-prevent-the-further-spread-of-covid-19.

84. Maggie McCarty, David H. Carpenter, and Libby Perl, "The CDC's Federal Eviction Moratorium," Congressional Research Service, IN11673, updated August 31, 2021, https://crsreports.congress.gov/product/pdf/IN/IN11673.

85. Adam Liptak and Glenn Thrush, "Supreme Court Ends Biden's Eviction Moratorium," *New York Times*, August 26, 2021, https://www.nytimes.com/2021/08/26/us/eviction-moratorium-ends.html.

86. See the analysis in Government Accountability Office, "COVID-19 Housing Protections," GAO-21-370, March 2021, https://www.gao.gov/assets/gao-21-370.pdf. The Government

Accountability Office analysis is an update of research originally conducted by Rebecca Cowin, Hal Martin, and Clare Stevens, "Measuring Evictions during the COVID-19 Crisis," Federal Reserve Bank of Cleveland, July 17, 2020, https://doi.org/10.26509/frbc-cd-20200717.

87. Annie Gowen, "She Wanted to Stay. Her Landlord Wanted Her Out," *Washington Post*, June 28, 2021, https://www.washingtonpost.com/nation/interactive/2021/eviction -moratorium-lifts/.

88. Based on Eviction Lab estimates, there were an average of 918,000 evictions yearly from 2012 through 2016. Taking this number as a baseline, a fall in evictions by about 50 percent over two years results in about 900,000 fewer evictions. Other estimates appear to project what would have happened given the pandemic, but absent any policy intervention, which is a different and more difficult baseline to estimate. For example, an Eviction Lab post seems to suggest that 2.5 million fewer eviction filings occurred from March 2020 through July 2021 but does not explain how it came to this number, which is more than the evictions that would have occurred absent the pandemic, or how it calculated a baseline. See Jasmine Rangel, Jacob Haas, . . . and Peter Hepburn, "Preliminary Analysis: 11 Months of the CDC Moratorium," Eviction Lab, August 21, 2021, https://evictionlab.org/eleven-months-cdc/. For baseline eviction numbers, see Eviction Lab, "National Estimates: Eviction in America," May 11, 2018, https://evictionlab .org/national-estimates/.

89. See the analysis in Government Accountability Office, "COVID-19 Housing Protections." The Government Accountability Office analysis is an update of research originally conducted by Cowin, Martin, and Stevens, "Measuring Evictions."

90. There is limited evidence that suggests a small shift to informal evictions. See Matthew Fowle and Rachel Fyall, "The Impact of the COVID-19 Pandemic on Low-Income Tenants' Housing Security in Washington State," University of Washington, Evans School of Public Policy and Governance, June 30, 2021, https://evans.uw.edu/wp-content/uploads/2020/09 /Tenants-Union_Research-Report-Formatted-Fowle-Fyall-v7.19.21.pdf.

91. For example, "Our results show that policies enacted to replace lost income for workers losing jobs during the COVID-19 pandemic, particularly the enhanced UI provided by the CARES Act, have been highly effective at keeping renter households out of debt for those households that received these benefits." Davin Reed and Eileen Divringi, "Household Rental Debt during COVID-19," Federal Reserve Bank of Philadelphia, October 2020, https://www .philadelphiafed.org/-/media/frbp/assets/community-development/reports/household -rental-debt-during-covid-19.pdf.

92. For further evidence, and a discussion of the data problems, see Jung Hyun Choi, Laurie Goodman, and Daniel Pang, "Navigating Rental Payment and Eviction Data during the Pandemic," Urban Institute, February 2022, https://www.urban.org/sites/default/files/2022-02 /navigating-rental-payment-and-eviction-data-during-the-pandemic.pdf.

93. Source: Author's calculations from National Multifamily Housing Council, "NMHC Rent Payment Tracker," https://www.nmhc.org/research-insight/nmhc-rent-payment-tracker/.

94. The National Multifamily Housing Council discontinued this series at the end of 2021, explaining that "the consistency of the data month to month demonstrated that the multifamily industry was stable, eliminating the need for continued monitoring." National Multifamily Housing Council, "NMHC Rent Payment Tracker."

95. Fiona Greig, Chen Zhao, and Alexandra Lefevre, "How Did Landlords Fare during COVID?," JPMorgan Chase Institute, October 2021, https://www.jpmorganchase.com/institute/research/household-debt/how-did-landlords-fare-during-covid.

96. The forbearance did come with some additional requirements that renters could not be evicted for nonpayment of rent. See Natalie Campisi, "Fannie Mae Extends Covid-19 Landlord and Renter Protection," *Forbes*, June 3, 2021, https://www.forbes.com/advisor/mortgages/fannie-mae-extends-covid-19-landlord-renter-protection/.

97. Marin Scott, "Landlords and Renters Have Hope for Financial Revival as COVID-19 Pandemic Subsides," Avail Research, February 8, 2022, https://www.avail.co/blog/landlords-and-renters-have-hope-for-financial-revival-as-covid-19-pandemic-subsides.

98. Scott, "Landlords and Renters."

99. Laurie Goodman and Jung Hyun Choi, "Black and Hispanic Landlords Are Facing Great Financial Struggles Because of the COVID-19 Pandemic. They Also Support Their Tenants at Higher Rates," *Urban Wire* (blog), Urban Institute, September 4, 2020, https://www.urban.org/urban-wire/black-and-hispanic-landlords-are-facing-great-financial-struggles-because-covid-19-pandemic-they-also-support-their-tenants-higher-rates.

100. Source: Author's calculations from Department of Treasury, "Emergency Rental Assistance Program Interim Report," accessed June 15, 2022, https://home.treasury.gov/policy-issues/coronavirus/assistance-for-state-local-and-tribal-governments/emergency-rental-assistance-program.

101. Almost any jurisdiction representing at least 200,000 people could apply for funds. For ERA2 funds, 410 states, counties, and cities set up programs, according to the Treasury's funds distribution as of April 2022. Source: Author's calculations from Department of Treasury, "Emergency Rental Assistance Program."

102. Andrew Giambrone, "Why Isn't New York Offering Paper Applications for COVID Rent Relief?," *New York Focus*, September 2, 2021, https://www.nysfocus.com/2021/09/02/rent-relief-paper-applications/.

103. For some of New York's Problems, see Peter Hepburn, "Why the Delay for Those Needing Federal Rental Assistance?," interview by Leila Fadel, *NPR Morning Edition*, August 26, 2021, https://www.npr.org/2021/08/26/1031193152/why-the-delay-for-those-needing-federal-rental-assistance; and Eric Lach, "Andrew Cuomo Left Behind a Rent-Relief Debacle," *New Yorker*, September 4, 2021, https://www.newyorker.com/news/our-local-correspondents/andrew-cuomo-left-behind-a-rent-relief-debacle.

104. Annie Nova, "With Eviction Ban Expiring in 14 Days, Many States Have Given out under 5% of Rental Assistance," CNBC, June 15, 2021, https://www.cnbc.com/2021/06/15/many-states-have-given-out-under-5percent-of-rental-assistance-.html.

105. See, for example, Steve Sbraccia, "Frustration Mounting among Landlords Who Say Wake County Rental Assistance Program Is Taking Too Long," CBS 17, October 25, 2021, https://www.cbs17.com/news/investigators/frustration-mounting-among-landlords-who-say-wake-county-rental-assistance-program-is-taking-too-long/; and Julia James, "Mississippi Leaders Scramble to Get Rental Assistance into the Right Hands after a Slow Start," *Mississippi Today*, October 20, 2021, https://mississippitoday.org/2021/10/20/mississippi-rental-assistance-fixes-after-slow-start/.

106. Department of the Treasury, "Treasury Announces Seven Additional Policies to Encourage State and Local Governments to Expedite Emergency Rental Assistance," August 25, 2021, https://home.treasury.gov/news/press-releases/jy0333.

107. Scott Fulford and Cortnie Shupe, "Consumer Finances during the Pandemic: Insights from the Making Ends Meet Survey," Consumer Financial Protection Bureau Data Point No. 2021-3, December 2021, 38, https://www.consumerfinance.gov/data-research/research-reports/consumer-finances-during-pandemic-insights-making-ends-meet-survey/.

108. Will Parker, "Why Some Landlords Don't Want Any of the $50 Billion in Rent Assistance," *Wall Street Journal*, March 19, 2021, https://www.wsj.com/articles/why-some-landlords-dont-want-any-of-the-50-billion-in-rent-assistance-11616155203.

109. Department of the Treasury, "Fact Sheet: The Biden-Harris Administration Announces Enhanced Efforts to Prevent Evictions and Provide Emergency Assistance to Renters," May 7, 2021, https://home.treasury.gov/system/files/136/FACT_SHEET-Emergency-Rental-Assistance-Program_May2021.pdf.

110. Michaelle Bond, "Philly's Program for Preventing Evictions Is a National Model. Lawmakers Want to Make It Permanent," *Philadelphia Inquirer*, December 8, 2021, https://www.inquirer.com/real-estate/housing/rental-assistance-philadelphia-eviction-diversion-program-20211208.html.

111. For examples, see Melissa Alonso and Susannah Cullinane, "Thousands of Cars Form Lines to Collect Food in Texas," CNN, November 16, 2020, https://www.cnn.com/2020/11/15/us/dallas-texas-food-bank-coronavirus/index.html; Nicholas Kulish, "'Never Seen Anything like It': Cars Line Up for Miles at Food Banks," *New York Times*, April 8, 2020, https://www.nytimes.com/2020/04/08/business/economy/coronavirus-food-banks.html; and Maria Arias, "In Photos: Americans Wait at Food Banks before Thanksgiving," Axios, November 22, 2020, https://www.axios.com/coronavirus-thanksgiving-food-bank-6b278831-5ac9-4183-9f1a-d108c07815a3.html.

112. Sharon Cohen, "Millions of Hungry Americans Turn to Food Banks for 1st Time," Associated Press, December 7, 2020, https://apnews.com/article/race-and-ethnicity-hunger-coronavirus-pandemic-4c7f1705c6d8ef5bac241e6cc8e331bb.

113. See Department of Housing and Urban Development, "PIT and HIC Guides, Tools, and Webinars," accessed November 21, 2021, https://www.hudexchange.info/programs/hdx/guides/pit-hic/#hic-guides-and-tools; and Audubon Society, "About the Great Backyard Bird Count," accessed November 21, 2021, https://www.audubon.org/conservation/about-great-backyard-bird-count.

114. Jennifer A. Kingson, "Big Cities Call Off 2021 Homeless Counts Due to Pandemic Safety," Axios, January 8, 2021, https://www.axios.com/homeless-counts-cities-hud-housing-1face65a-b3c0-4601-b6f2-1b9d0a15662b.html.

115. Internal Revenue Service, "Those Experiencing Homelessness Can Get Economic Impact Payments and Other Tax Benefits; Permanent Address Not Required," April 15, 2021, IR-2021-87, https://www.irs.gov/newsroom/those-experiencing-homelessness-can-get-economic-impact-payments-and-other-tax-benefits-permanent-address-not-required.

116. In the Making Ends Meet survey, 15 percent of respondents reported their household had a large income fall from unemployment but did not receive unemployment insurance

themselves, about 18 million households. Several approximations could make this number possibly too big or too small as a measure of people missed by policy. First, people who do not return a survey may be more likely to have trouble. The survey's association with credit bureau data also means that people without a credit record never receive a survey. People without credit records may be more likely to be missed by pandemic policies. On the other hand, the questions asked whether the survey respondent had received unemployment insurance and whether the household experienced a significant drop in household income from unemployment. Some people may not have been unemployed themselves and so did not receive unemployment insurance, even though someone else in their household did. Others may not have had a significant income loss from unemployment because of unemployment insurance.

Chapter Eight

1. Lydia Dishman, "No, Remote Work Isn't a 'New' Perk—It's Been Around for about 1.4 Million Years," *Fast Company*, April 16, 2019, https://www.fastcompany.com/90330393/the-surprising-history-of-working-from-home.

2. For an examination of the price of light over time, and the complexity of measuring it and why it matters, see William D. Nordhaus, "Do Real-Output and Real-Wage Measures Capture Reality? The History of Lighting Suggests Not," in *The Economics of New Goods*, ed. Timothy F. Bresnahan and Robert J. Gordon, University of Chicago Press, 1996, 27–70, http://www.nber.org/books/bres96-1.

3. See Jose Maria Barrero, Nicholas Bloom, and Steven J. Davis, "Why Working from Home Will Stick" (Becker Friedman Institute Working Paper No. 2020-174, April 2021), https://bfi.uchicago.edu/wp-content/uploads/2020/12/BFI_WP_2020174.pdf.

4. For example, one paper found that about 35 percent of those who had been employed switched from commuting to remote work by May 2020. Erik Brynjolfsson, John J. Horton, . . . and Hong-Yi TuYe, "COVID-19 and Remote Work: An Early Look at US Data" (NBER Working Paper No. 27344, June 2020), https://www.nber.org/papers/w27344.

5. Source: Author's calculations using Bureau of Labor Statistics Current Population Survey data: Sarah Flood, Miriam King, . . . and Michael Westberry, "Integrated Public Use Microdata Series, Current Population Survey: Version 9.0," 2021, https://doi.org/10.18128/D030.V9.0.

6. Lydia Saad and Jeffrey M. Jones, "Seven in 10 U.S. White-Collar Workers Still Working Remotely," Gallup, May 17, 2021, https://news.gallup.com/poll/348743/seven-u.s.-white-collar-workers-still-working-remotely.aspx.

7. Lydia Saad and Ben Wigert, "Remote Work Persisting and Trending Permanent," Gallup, October 13, 2021, https://news.gallup.com/poll/355907/remote-work-persisting-trending-permanent.aspx.

8. Kim Parker, Juliana Horowitz, and Rachel Minkin, "COVID-19 Pandemic Continues to Reshape Work in America," Pew Research Center, February 16, 2022, https://www.pewresearch.org/social-trends/2022/02/16/covid-19-pandemic-continues-to-reshape-work-in-america/.

9. Simon Kennedy, "The Return to Office Is More Slog than Stampede," Bloomberg, March 31, 2022, https://www.bloomberg.com/news/newsletters/2022-03-31/what-s-happening-in-the-world-economy-the-return-to-office-is-peaking.

10. Bureau of Labor Statistics, "Job Flexibilities and Work Schedules—2017–2018: Data from the American Time Use Survey," September 24, 2019, https://www.bls.gov/news.release/pdf/flex2.pdf.

11. Kim Parker, Juliana Menasce Horowitz, and Rachel Minkin, "How the Coronavirus Outbreak Has—and Hasn't—Changed the Way Americans Work," Pew Research Center, December 9, 2020, https://www.pewresearch.org/social-trends/2020/12/09/how-the-coronavirus-outbreak-has-and-hasnt-changed-the-way-americans-work/.

12. Saad and Wigert, "Remote Work Persisting."

13. Barrero, Bloom, and Davis, "Why Working from Home."

14. Rachel Lerman, "The Hunt for a Work-from-Home Webcam: A Story of Broken Supply Chains, 'Sold-Out' Messages and Refreshing Online Carts," *Washington Post*, May 21, 2020, https://www.washingtonpost.com/technology/2020/05/21/webcam-backorder-coronavirus-pandemic/.

15. Kiet Do, "'Desks Are the New Toilet Paper'; Needed Furniture for Makeshift Home Classrooms, Offices Sold Out," CBS SF Bay Area, September 15, 2020, https://sanfrancisco.cbslocal.com/2020/09/15/desks-new-toilet-paper-needed-furniture-makeshift-home-classrooms-offices-sold-out/.

16. Monica Humphries, "A Mom Turned Her Bathroom into a Home Office, Where She's Worked for over a Year above a Toilet," Insider, May 24, 2021, https://www.insider.com/mom-transformed-bathroom-into-home-office-photos-2021-5.

17. Monica Torres, "12 of the Most Clever Work-from-Home Spaces Created in Quarantine So Far," HuffPost, April 14, 2020, https://www.huffpost.com/entry/clever-work-from-home-spaces-quarantine_l_5e90de76c5b6ad719f27b923.

18. Michael Gibbs, Friederike Mengel, and Christoph Siemroth, "Work from Home & Productivity: Evidence from Personnel & Analytics Data on IT Professionals" (Becker Friedman Institute Working Paper No. 2021-56, July 2021), https://bfi.uchicago.edu/wp-content/uploads/2021/05/BFI_WP_2021-56.pdf.

19. Evan DeFilippis, Stephen Michael Impink, . . . and Raffaella Sadun, "Collaborating during Coronavirus: The Impact of COVID-19 on the Nature of Work" (NBER Working Paper No. 27612, July 2020), https://www.nber.org/papers/w27612.

20. Microsoft, "The Rise of the Triple Peak Day," accessed April 14, 2022, https://www.microsoft.com/en-us/worklab/triple-peak-day.

21. See Barrero, Bloom, and Davis, "Why Working from Home"; and Julian Birkinshaw, Jordan Cohen, and Pawel Stach, "Research: Knowledge Workers Are More Productive from Home," *Harvard Business Review*, August 31, 2020, https://hbr.org/2020/08/research-knowledge-workers-are-more-productive-from-home.

22. Roy Maurer, "Study Finds Productivity Not Deterred by Shift to Remote Work," Society for Human Resource Management, September 16, 2020, https://www.shrm.org/hr-today/news/hr-news/pages/study-productivity-shift-remote-work-covid-coronavirus.aspx.

23. Phillip Molnar, "Are Americans Actually More Productive Working from Home?," *San Diego Union-Tribune*, November 6, 2020, https://www.sandiegouniontribune.com/business/story/2020-11-06/are-americans-actually-more-productive-working-from-home.

24. Jose Maria Barrero, Nick Bloom, and Steven J. Davis, "60 Million Fewer Commuting Hours Per Day: How Americans Use Time Saved by Working from Home" (Becker Friedman Institute Working Paper No. 2020-132, September 2020), https://bfi.uchicago.edu/wp-content/uploads/2020/09/BFI_WP_2020132.pdf.

25. Daniel Kahneman and Alan B. Krueger, "Developments in the Measurement of Subjective Well-Being," *Journal of Economic Perspectives*, 2006, 20(1): 3–24, https://doi.org/10.1257/089533006776526030.

26. Barrio, Bloom, and Davis, "60 Million Fewer Commuting Hours."

27. Birkinshaw, Cohen, and Stach, "Research."

28. Ed Zitron, "Why Managers Fear a Remote-Work Future," *Atlantic*, July 29, 2021, https://www.theatlantic.com/ideas/archive/2021/07/work-from-home-benefits/619597/.

29. Alison Green, "All the Intrusive and Insulting Ways Bosses Are Smothering Their Remote Workers," *Slate*, August 10, 2020, https://slate.com/human-interest/2020/08/work-from-home-remote-managers-micromanaging.html.

30. Aaron Mak, "The Exploding Market for Devices That Help You Evade Corporate Productivity Trackers," *Slate*, December 3, 2021, https://slate.com/technology/2021/12/mouse-movers-market-corporate-productivity-tracking.html.

31. Longqi Yang, David Holtz, . . . and Jaime Teevan, "The Effects of Remote Work on Collaboration among Information Workers," *Nature Human Behaviour*, 2021, 6: 43–54, https://doi.org/10.1038/s41562-021-01196-4.

32. Jeremy Howells and John Bessant, "Introduction: Innovation and Economic Geography: A Review and Analysis," *Journal of Economic Geography*, 2012, 12(5): 929–42, https://doi.org/10.1093/jeg/lbs029.

33. Melanie S. Brucks and Jonathan Levav, "Virtual Communication Curbs Creative Idea Generation," *Nature*, 2022, 605: 108–12, https://doi.org/10.1038/s41586-022-04643-y.

34. Jack Kelly, "Apple CEO Tim Cook Exemplifies the Current Trend of Cautiously Balancing Working Remotely versus Returning to the Office," *Forbes*, September 22, 2020, https://www.forbes.com/sites/jackkelly/2020/09/22/apple-ceo-tim-cook-exemplifies-the-current-trend-of-cautiously-balancing-working-remotely-versus-returning-to-the-office/?sh=4b6215e14901.

35. Annabelle Williams, "JPMorgan CEO Says That Working Remotely 'Does Not Work' for Young People and Those Who Want to 'hustle,'" Business Insider, May 4, 2021, https://www.businessinsider.com/jpmorgan-ceo-jamie-dimon-remote-work-downsides-young-people-hustlers-2021-5.

36. Amanda Mull, "Generation Work-from-Home May Never Recover," *Atlantic*, October 2020, https://www.theatlantic.com/magazine/archive/2020/10/career-costs-working-from-home/615472/.

37. Camille Lloyd, "Black Women in the Workplace," Gallup, March 5, 2021, https://www.gallup.com/workplace/333194/black-women-workplace.aspx.

38. The survey defined "knowledge worker" as "anyone who handled information for a living." See Angelica Puzio, "Why Post-pandemic Offices Could Be Whiter and More Male," FiveThirtyEight, August 11, 2021, https://fivethirtyeight.com/features/why-post-pandemic-offices-could-be-whiter-and-more-male/.

39. Natachi Onwuamaegbu, "Many Black Women Felt Relieved to Work from Home, Free from Microaggressions. Now They're Told to Come Back," *Washington Post*, July 24, 2021, https://www.washingtonpost.com/lifestyle/2021/07/24/black-women-office-work-home/.

40. Chip Cutter and Kathryn Dill, "Remote Work Is the New Signing Bonus," *Wall Street Journal*, June 26, 2021, https://www.wsj.com/articles/remote-work-is-the-new-signing-bonus-11624680029.

41. Jamie Dimon, "Chairman and CEO Letter to Shareholders," JPMorgan Chase, April 4, 2022, https://reports.jpmorganchase.com/investor-relations/2021/ar-ceo-letters.htm.

42. Matthew Boyle, "Return-to-Office Plans Unravel as Workers Rebel in Tight Job Market," Bloomberg, May 11, 2022, https://www.bloomberg.com/news/articles/2022-05-11/wall-street-silicon-valley-return-to-office-plans-unravel-in-hot-job-market.

43. Barrero, Bloom, and Davis, "Why Working from Home."

44. Gianni De Fraja, Jesse Matheson, and James Rockey, "Zoomshock: The Geography and Local Labor Market Consequences of Working from Home," *Covid Economics*, January 2021, 64(13): 1–42, https://cepr.org/file/10211/download?token=ZZzuKAeJ.

45. Barrero, Bloom, and Davis, "Why Working from Home."

46. Lukas Althoff, Fabian Eckert, Sharat Ganapati, and Conor Walsh, "The Geography of Remote Work" (NBER Working Paper No. 29181, August 2021), http://www.nber.org/papers/w29181.

47. Kim Lyons, "Oracle Moves Its HQ from California to Texas," Verge, December 13, 2020, https://www.theverge.com/2020/12/13/22172610/oracle-moves-headquarters-california-texas-hewlett-packard-tesla.

48. Paul Roberts and Katherine Anne Long, "REI to Sell Its Never-Used Bellevue Headquarters and Shift Office Work to Multiple Seattle-Area Sites," *Seattle Times*, August 12, 2020, https://www.seattletimes.com/business/local-business/rei-to-sell-its-new-bellevue-headquarters-and-shift-office-work-to-multiple-seattle-sites/.

49. Heather Kelly and Rachel Lerman, "The Pandemic Is Making People Reconsider City Living, Trading Traffic for Chickens," *Washington Post*, June 1, 2020, https://www.washingtonpost.com/technology/2020/06/01/city-relocate-pandemic/.

50. Matt Grossman, "Rising Interest in Recreational Vehicles Helps Rental Platform Secure Investment," *Wall Street Journal*, October 21, 2020, https://www.wsj.com/articles/rising-interest-in-recreational-vehicles-helps-rental-platform-secure-investment-11603242402.

51. Nellie Bowles, "The #Vanlife Business Is Booming," *New York Times*, July 3, 2020, https://www.nytimes.com/2020/07/03/technology/the-vanlife-business-is-booming.html.

52. See, for example, Charu Suri, "Why Work from Home When You Can Work from Barbados, Bermuda or . . . Estonia?," *New York Times*, August 19, 2020, https://www.nytimes.com/2020/08/19/travel/remote-worker-visa.html; and Carrie Kahn, "Costa Rica Jumps into the Global Competition for Remote Workers," NPR, December 28, 2021, https://www.npr.org/2021/12/28/1068430174/costa-rica-jumps-into-the-global-competition-for-remote-workers.

53. Charlie Wells and Ivan Levingston, "Dreams of Working from a Beach Risk Turning into a Tax Nightmare," Bloomberg Wealth, June 15, 2021, https://www.bloomberg.com/news/articles/2021-06-15/remote-work-jobs-tax-filing-nightmare-threatens-dream-of-beach-home-office.

54. Arian Campo-Flores, Paul Overberg, Joseph De Avila, and Elizabeth Findell, "The Pandemic Changed Where Americans Live," *Wall Street Journal*, April 27, 2021, https://www.wsj.com/articles/pandemic-supercharged-changes-in-where-americans-live-11619536399.

55. Kirk Siegler, "Homebuyers Squeezed as Western States See Prices Double or More in Last Decade," NPR, May 28, 2021, https://www.npr.org/2021/05/28/1000879058/homebuyers-squeezed-as-western-states-see-prices-double-or-more-in-last-decade.

56. Scott L. Fulford, "How Important Are Banks for Development? National Banks in the United States, 1870–1900," *Review of Economics and Statistics*, December 2015, 97(5): 921–38, https://doi.org/10.1162/REST_a_00546.

57. Enrico Moretti, *The New Geography of Jobs*, First Mariner Books, 2013.

58. Chang-Tai Hsieh and Enrico Moretti, "Housing Constraints and Spatial Misallocation," *American Economic Journal: Macroeconomics*, 2019, 11(2): 1–39, https://doi.org/10.1257/mac.20170388.

59. See one argument to this effect: Austan Goolsbee, "The Battles to Come over the Benefits of Working from Home," *New York Times*, July 20, 2021, https://www.nytimes.com/2021/07/20/business/remote-work-pay-bonus.html/.

60. Konrad Putzier, "Dreaded Commute to the City Is Keeping Offices Mostly Empty," *Wall Street Journal*, May 31, 2022, https://www.wsj.com/articles/dreaded-commute-to-the-city-is-keeping-offices-mostly-empty-11653989581.

61. Amy reported they had moved in the previous year in the June 2020 survey. Her credit card debt spiked in February 2020, suggesting that was when the move occurred.

Chapter Nine

1. For one short history, see Sarah Gibbens, "Hurricane Katrina, Explained," *National Geographic*, January 16, 2019, https://www.nationalgeographic.com/environment/article/hurricane-katrina.

2. The rise of G.I. Joe and how Hasbro and Marvel turned it into a media tie-in juggernaut in which comic books, cartoons, and movies helped toy sales, and the reverse, presages modern media empires. See, for example, Rob Lammle, "A History of G.I. Joe: A Real American Hero," *Mental Floss*, July 4, 2015, https://www.mentalfloss.com/article/62636/history-gi-joe-real-american-hero.

3. Nelson D. Schwartz and Coral Murphy Marcos, "They Didn't Expect to Retire Early. The Pandemic Changed Their Plans," *New York Times*, July 2, 2021, https://www.nytimes.com/2021/07/02/business/economy/retire-early-pandemic-social-security.html.

4. Bridget Fisher, Teresa Ghilarducci, and Siavash Radpour, "The Pandemic Retirement Surge Increased Retirement Inequality," New School Equity Retirement Lab, June 2021, https://www.economicpolicyresearch.org/images/Retirement_Project/status_of_older_workers_reports/Q2_OWAG_2021_V6.pdf.

5. Richard W. Johnson and Barbara Butrica, "Age Disparities in Unemployment and Reemployment during the Great Recession and Recovery," Urban Institute Brief #3, May 2012, https://www.urban.org/research/publication/age-disparities-unemployment-and-reemployment-during-great-recession-and-recovery.

6. Source: Author's calculations using Bureau of Labor Statistics Current Population Survey data, available from the Integrated Public Use Microdata Series, Current Population Survey.

7. Fisher, Ghilarducci, and Radpour, Pandemic Retirement Surge.

8. Juliette Cubanski, Wyatt Koma, Anthony Damico, and Tricia Neuman, "How Many Seniors Live in Poverty?," Kaiser Family Foundation, November 19, 2018, https://www.kff.org /medicare/issue-brief/how-many-seniors-live-in-poverty/.

9. Fisher, Ghilarducci, and Radpour, Pandemic Retirement Surge.

10. Paul Sullivan, "For Some People, Working from Home Sped Up Their Decision to Retire," *New York Times*, July 9, 2021, https://www.nytimes.com/2021/07/09/your-money /pandemic-working-from-home-retire.html.

11. For example, see Laura Santhanam, "'This Is Not Working.' Parents Juggling Jobs and Child Care under COVID-19 See No Good Solutions," *PBS News Hour*, July 23, 2020, https:// www.pbs.org/newshour/health/this-is-not-working-parents-juggling-jobs-and-child-care -under-covid-19-see-no-good-solutions.

12. Claudia Goldin, "Understanding the Economic Impact of COVID-19 on Women" (Brookings Papers on Economic Activity, March 24–25, 2002), https://www.brookings.edu/wp -content/uploads/2022/03/SP22_BPEA_Goldin_conf-draft.pdf.

13. Misty L. Heggeness, "Estimating the Immediate Impact of the COVID-19 Shock on Parental Attachment to the Labor Market and the Double Bind of Mothers," *Review of Economics of the Household*, 2020, 18: 1053, https://doi.org/10.1007/s11150-020-09514-x.

14. Caitlyn Collins, Liana Christin Landivar, Leah Ruppanner, and William J. Scarborough, "COVID-19 and the Gender Gap in Work Hours," *Gender, Work, and Organization*, 2021 28(S1): 549–60, https://doi.org/10.1111/gwao.12506.

15. Jessica Grose, "'They Go to Mommy First': How the Pandemic Is Disproportionately Disrupting Mothers' Careers," *New York Times*, July 15, 2020, https://www.nytimes.com/2020 /07/15/parenting/working-moms-coronavirus.html.

16. See, for example, Da Ke, "Who Wears the Pants? Gender Identity Norms and Intrahousehold Financial Decision-Making," *Journal of Finance*, 2021, 76: 1389–425, https://doi.org/10.1111 /jofi.13002.

17. Lauren Weber, "As Schools Plan to Reopen, Single Parents Have Few Child-Care Options," *Wall Street Journal*, August 2, 2020, https://www.wsj.com/articles/as-schools-plan-to-reopen -single-parents-have-few-child-care-options-11596381796.

18. Dani Blum, "For Grandparents, Filling in for Child Care Can Be 'Wonderful and Exhausting,'" *New York Times*, May 12, 2020, https://www.nytimes.com/2020/05/12/parenting /coronavirus-grandparents-childcare.html.

19. Kathryn A. Edwards, "Women Are Leaving the Labor Force in Record Numbers," *RAND Blog*, November 24, 2020, https://www.rand.org/blog/2020/11/women-are-leaving-the-labor -force-in-record-numbers.html.

20. Source: Author's calculations using Bureau of Labor Statistics Current Population Survey data, available from the Integrated Public Use Microdata Series, Current Population Survey.

21. What comparison is the right counterfactual is difficult to determine. See Goldin, "Understanding the Economic Impact," for more on the comparison.

22. Tyler Boesch, Rob Grunewald, Ryan Nunn, and Vanessa Palmer, "Pandemic Pushes Mothers of Young Children out of the Labor Force," Federal Reserve Bank of Minneapolis, February 2, 2021, https://www.minneapolisfed.org/article/2021/pandemic-pushes-mothers-of -young-children-out-of-the-labor-force.

23. Stephanie Aaronson and Francisca Alba, "The Relationship between School Closures and Female Labor Force Participation during the Pandemic," Brookings Institution, November 3, 2021, https://www.brookings.edu/research/the-relationship-between-school-closures -and-female-labor-force-participation-during-the-pandemic/.

24. Goldin, "Understanding the Economic Impact."

25. Anna Saavedra, Amie Rapaport, and Dan Silver, "Why Some Parents Are Sticking with Remote Learning—Even as Schools Reopen," *Brown Center Chalkboard* (blog), Brookings Institution, June 8, 2021, https://www.brookings.edu/blog/brown-center-chalkboard/2021/06 /08/why-some-parents-are-sticking-with-remote-learning-even-as-schools-reopen/.

26. Associated Press, "Indications Emerge That Some Parents Who Tested Out Homeschooling Earlier in the Pandemic Are Planning to Stick with It," MarketWatch, August 5, 2021, https://www.marketwatch.com/story/indications-emerge-that-some-parents-who-tested-out -homeschooling-earlier-in-the-pandemic-are-planning-to-stick-with-it-01628198159.

27. Claudia Goldin, "A Grand Gender Convergence: Its Last Chapter," *American Economic Review*, 2014, 104(4): 1091–119, http://dx.doi.org/10.1257/aer.104.4.1091.

28. The term comes from sociologist Lewis Coser, who defined "greedy institutions" as ones that "seek exclusive and undivided loyalty," including Leninism and the priesthood. It was explored in Claire Cain Miller, "Women Did Everything Right. Then Work Got 'Greedy,'" *New York Times*, April 26, 2019, https://www.nytimes.com/2019/04/26/upshot/women-long-hours -greedy-professions.html.

29. Ellen Wulfhorst, "Gender Pay Gap Is Dramatic among Top U.S. Lawyers, Survey Finds," Reuters, December 6, 2018, https://www.reuters.com/article/us-usa-women-pay/gender-pay -gap-is-dramatic-among-top-u-s-lawyers-survey-finds-idUSKBN1O52JL.

30. Stephanie Francis Ward, "Women Outnumber Men in Law Schools for First Time, Newly Updated Data Show," *ABA Journal*, December 19, 2016, https://www.abajournal.com /news/article/women_outnumber_men_in_law_schools_for_first_time_newly_updated _data_show.

31. Kim Elsesser, "Female Lawyers Face Widespread Gender Bias, According to New Study," *Forbes*, October 1, 2018, https://www.forbes.com/sites/kimelsesser/2018/10/01/female -lawyers-face-widespread-gender-bias-according-to-new-study/?sh=2f7720fc4b55.

32. Miller, "Women Did Everything Right."

33. Claudia Goldin and Lawrence K. Katz, "A Most Egalitarian Profession: Pharmacy and the Evolution of a Family Friendly Occupation," *Journal of Labor Economics*, 2016, 34(3): 705–45, https://scholar.harvard.edu/files/goldin/files/pharm_cg.pdf.

34. Titan Alon, Matthias Doepke, Jane Olmstead-Rumsey, and Michèle Tertilt, "This Time It's Different: The Role of Women's Employment in a Pandemic Recession" (NBER Working Paper No. 27660, August 2020), https://www.nber.org/papers/w27660.

35. Rakesh Kochhar, "Women's Lead in Skills and Education Is Helping Narrow the Gender Wage Gap," Pew Research Center, January 30, 2020, https://www.pewresearch.org/social-trends/2020/01/30/womens-lead-in-skills-and-education-is-helping-narrow-the-gender-wage-gap/.

36. Kathryn A. Edwards, "Women Are Leaving the Labor Force in Record Numbers," *RAND Blog*, November 24, 2020, https://www.rand.org/blog/2020/11/women-are-leaving-the-labor-force-in-record-numbers.html.

37. Source: Bureau of Labor Statistics, "Of Total Unemployed, Percent Unemployed 27 Weeks & Over," retrieved from FRED, https://fred.stlouisfed.org/series/LNU03025703.

38. Wiji Arulampalam, Paul Gregg, and Mary Gregory, "Introduction: Unemployment Scarring," *Economic Journal*, 2001, 111(475): F577–F84, http://www.jstor.org/stable/798306.

39. See Austin Nichols, Josh Mitchell, and Stephan Lindner, "Consequences of Long-Term Unemployment," Urban Institute, July 2013, https://www.urban.org/sites/default/files/publication/23921/412887-Consequences-of-Long-Term-Unemployment.PDF.

40. The exact number is hard to pin down confidently. For one analysis, see Lou Adler, "New Survey Reveals 85% of All Jobs Are Filled via Networking," LinkedIn, February 29, 2016, https://www.linkedin.com/pulse/new-survey-reveals-85-all-jobs-filled-via-networking-lou-adler.

41. Derek Thompson, "The Unluckiest Generation: What Will Become of Millennials?," *Atlantic*, April 26, 2013, https://www.theatlantic.com/business/archive/2013/04/the-unluckiest-generation-what-will-become-of-millennials/275336/.

42. Tom Brokaw, *The Greatest Generation*, Random House, 2004.

43. Pew Research Center, "The Whys and Hows of Generation Research," September 3, 2015, https://www.pewresearch.org/politics/2015/09/03/the-whys-and-hows-of-generations-research/.

44. Philip Oreopoulos, Till von Wachter, and Andrew Heisz, "The Short- and Long-Term Career Effects of Graduating in a Recession," *American Economic Journal: Applied Economics*, 2012, 4(1): 1–29, https://doi.org/10.1257/app.4.1.1.

45. Hannes Schwandt, "Recession Graduates: The Long-Lasting Effects of an Unlucky Draw," SIEPR Policy Brief, April 2019, https://siepr.stanford.edu/research/publications/recession-graduates-effects-unlucky.

46. Lisa B. Kahn, "The Long-Term Labor Market Consequences of Graduating from College in a Bad Economy," *Labour Economics*, 2010, 17(2): 303–16, https://doi.org/10.1016/j.labeco.2009.09.002.

47. See Jesse Rothstein, "The Lost Generation? Labor Market Outcomes for Post Great Recession Entrants" (working paper, May 2020), https://eml.berkeley.edu/~jrothst/workingpapers/rothstein_lostgeneration_may2020.pdf; and Kevin Rinz, "Did Timing Matter? Life Cycle Differences in Effects of Exposure to the Great Recession" (Census Bureau Working Paper Number CES-19-25, September 2019), https://www.census.gov/library/working-papers/2019/adrm/ces-wp-19-25.html.

48. On average, someone entering the workforce at the end of 2009 (unemployment rate about 10 percent) would earn about 38 percent less initially and would still be earning 14 percent less after 15 years compared with someone entering the workforce in 2007 (unemployment rate about 4.5 percent). While more complicated life-cycle growth models could account for more

complex dynamics, taking the personal income per capita in 2019 of $56,500, the dollar value of earnings lost would be more than $200,000.

49. Andrew Van Dam, "The Unluckiest Generation in U.S. History," *Washington Post*, June 5, 2020, https://www.washingtonpost.com/business/2020/05/27/millennial-recession -covid/.

50. David Pogue, "How to Make Your Virtual Jam Session Sound—and Look—Good," *Wired*, June 4, 2020, https://www.wired.com/story/zoom-music-video-coronavirus-tips/.

51. For example, see Doug Young, "Virtual Jamming: The Latest Tools for Playing Together in Real Time," *Acoustic Guitar*, August 9, 2021, https://acousticguitar.com/virtual-jamming-the -latest-tools-for-playing-together-in-real-time/.

52. Deborah A. Phillips, Mark W. Lipsey, . . . and Christina Weiland, "The Current State of Scientific Knowledge on Pre-kindergarten Effects," Brookings Institution, 2017, 23, https://www .brookings.edu/wp-content/uploads/2017/04/duke_prekstudy_final_4-4-17_hires.pdf.

53. Emma Dorn, Bryan Hancock, Jimmy Sarakatsannis, and Ellen Viruleg, "COVID-19 and Education: The Lingering Effects of Unfinished Learning," McKinsey & Company, July 27, 2021, https://www.mckinsey.com/industries/public-and-social-sector/our-insights/covid-19-and -education-the-lingering-effects-of-unfinished-learning.

54. Karyn Lewis, Megan Kuhfeld, Erik Ruzek, and Andrew McEachin, "Learning during COVID-19: Reading and Math Achievement in the 2020–21 School Year," NWEA Center for School and Student Progress Research Brief, July 2021, https://www.nwea.org/content/uploads /2021/07/Learning-during-COVID-19-Reading-and-math-achievement-in-the-2020-2021 -school-year.research-brief-1.pdf.

55. Dan Goldhaber, Thomas J. Kane, . . . and Douglas O. Staiger, "The Consequences of Remote and Hybrid Instruction during the Pandemic" (NBER Working Paper No. 30010, May 2022), https://www.nber.org/papers/w30010.

56. For evidence using test scores, see Curriculum Associates, "Academic Achievement at the End of the 2020–2021 School Year," Curriculum Associates Research Brief, June 2021, https:/ /www.curriculumassociates.com/-/media/mainsite/files/i-ready/iready-understanding -student-needs-paper-spring-results-2021.pdf. For estimates that students in the Netherlands made no progress learning from home, see Per Engzell, Arun Frey, and Mark D. Verhagen, "Learning Loss due to School Closures during the COVID-19 Pandemic," *Proceedings of the National Academy of Sciences*, April 27, 2021, 118(17): e2022376118, https://doi.org/10.1073/pnas .2022376118. For projections based on lost school days, see Center for Research on Education Outcomes, "A Meta-Analysis of Simulations of 2020 Achievement Assessments in 19 States," Stanford University, October 2020, https://credo.stanford.edu/wp-content/uploads/2021/12 /covid_sim_meta_analysis_final_v.3.pdf.

57. Laura Meckler and Hannah Natanson, "'A Lost Generation': Surge of Research Reveals Students Sliding Backward, Most Vulnerable Worst Affected," *Washington Post*, December 6, 2020, https://www.washingtonpost.com/education/students-falling-behind/2020/12/06 /88d7157a-3665-11eb-8d38-6aea1adb3839_story.html.

58. Eric A. Hanushek and Ludger Woessmann, The Economic Impacts of Learning Losses, Organisation for Economic Co-operation and Development, September 2020, https://www .oecd.org/education/The-economic-impacts-of-coronavirus-covid-19-learning-losses.pdf.

59. See Michèle Belot and Dinand Webbink, "Do Teacher Strikes Harm Educational Attainment of Students?," *Labour*, 2010, 24(4): 391–406; David Jaume and Alexander Willén, "The Long-Run Effects of Teacher Strikes: Evidence from Argentina," *Journal of Labor Economics*, 2019, 37(4): 1097–139; and Michael Baker, "Industrial Actions in Schools: Strikes and Student Achievement," *Canadian Journal of Economics*, 2013, 46(3): 1014–36.

60. Kamila Cygan-Rehm, "Is Additional Schooling Worthless? Revising Zero Returns to Compulsory Schooling in Germany" (CESifo Working Paper No. 7191, 2018), https://www .cesifo.org/en/publikationen/2018/working-paper/additional-schooling-worthless-revising -zero-returns-compulsory. Other analysis has found little to no effect of the episode. See Jörn-Steffen Pischke, "The Impact of Length of the School Year on Student Performance and Earnings: Evidence from the German Short School Years," *Economic Journal*, 2007, 117(523): 1216–42, https://doi.org/10.1111/j.1468-0297.2007.02080.x.

61. I reached the $2.2 million number by taking $1.7 million and adjusting for inflation from January 2008 to December 2021 using the Consumer Price Index. In calculating lifetime earnings, the authors adjusted for inflation but did not discount future earnings. Median lifetime earnings are from Anthony P. Carnevale, Stephen J. Rose, and Ban Cheah, The College Payoff: Education, Occupations, Lifetime Earnings, Georgetown University Center on Education and the Workforce, 2014, https://cew.georgetown.edu/wp-content/uploads/2014/11/collegepayoff -complete.pdf.

62. This calculation has many assumptions. It is the presented discounted value of the economic loss projected over the working lives of the affected cohort. The calculation is thus very sensitive to the 3 percent discount rate used. For a discussion of their methodology, see annex B in Hanushek and Woessmann, Economic Impacts of Learning Losses.

63. Dorn, Hancock, Sarakatsannis, and Viruleg, "COVID-19 and Education."

64. Lewis, Kuhfeld, Ruzek, and McEachin, "Learning during COVID-19."

65. Even worse, it is possible that the effect of each lost month of school is larger for more disadvantaged students because they end up with less education total. If so, the earnings impact from the lost education will be even larger than these estimated education gaps—more months lost at a greater impact per month. Because they are also likely to learn less, the welfare loss is likely even larger. It is difficult to measure whether returns to education are the same across groups. But the available evidence suggests that an extra month of education increases earnings by about the same amount across racial, ethnic, and income groups. See Lisa Barrow and Cecilia Elena Rouse, "Do Returns to Schooling Differ by Race and Ethnicity?," *American Economic Review: Papers and Proceedings*, 2005, 95(2): 83–87, https://www.jstor.org/stable/4132795.

66. Joelle Goldstein, "More Kids than Ever Are Expected at Summer School—and Some Teachers Are Getting Bonuses to Help," *People*, June 7, 2021, https://people.com/human -interest/more-kids-than-ever-heading-to-summer-school-teachers-getting-bonuses-to-help -pandemic/.

67. Jennifer Calfas and Kristina Peterson, "School Districts Tackle 'Learning Loss,' School Safety with Covid-19 Aid," *Wall Street Journal*, March 26, 2021, https://www.wsj.com/articles /school-districts-tackle-learning-loss-school-safety-with-covid-19-aid-11616781121.

68. Andrew Bacher-Hicks, Joshua Goodman, and Christine Mulhern, "Inequality in Household Adaptation to Schooling Shocks: Covid-Induced Online Learning Engagement in Real

Time" (NBER Working Paper No. 27555, November 2020), https://www.nber.org/papers/w27555.

Chapter Ten

1. NBER Business Cycle Dating Committee, "Determination of the April 2020 Trough in US Economic Activity," July 19, 2021, https://www.nber.org/news/business-cycle-dating-committee-announcement-july-19-2021.

2. Jeanne Whalen, "John Deere Workers Vote Today on Whether to End Their First Strike since 1986," *Washington Post*, November 16, 2021, https://www.washingtonpost.com/us-policy/2021/11/16/deere-strike-labor-shortage/.

3. United Auto Workers, "John Deer UAW Members Ratify a 6-Year Agreement with Substantial Gains," November 17, 2021, https://uaw.org/john-deere-uaw-members-ratify-6-year-agreement-substantial-gains/.

4. David Levine, "U.S. Faces Crisis of Burned-Out Health Care Workers," *U.S. News and World Report*, November 15, 2021, https://www.usnews.com/news/health-news/articles/2021-11-15/us-faces-crisis-of-burned-out-health-care-workers.

5. Katie Johnston, "Workers Are Resisting Being Called Back to the Office—and Some Employers Are Scrapping Their Plans," *Boston Globe*, November 18, 2021, https://www.bostonglobe.com/2021/11/18/business/workers-are-resisting-being-called-back-office-some-employers-are-scrapping-their-plans/.

6. The Reddit r/antiwork (https://www.reddit.com/r/antiwork/) had a particular moment exploding in popularity. See one description in Farhad Manjoo, "Even with a Dream Job, You Can Be Antiwork," *New York Times*, October 22, 2021, https://www.nytimes.com/2021/10/22/opinion/work-resignations-covid.html.

7. Emily Stewart, "America's Cruel Unemployment Experiment," Vox, June 7, 2021, https://www.vox.com/policy-and-politics/2021/6/3/22465160/states-ending-unemployment-labor-shortage-texas.

8. The *Wall Street Journal*, comparing the change in nonfarm payroll from April to July 2021 without controlling for anything except the change in benefits, found employment growth was slower in the early cutoff states. See Sarah Chaney Cambon and Danny Dougherty, "States That Cut Unemployment Benefits Saw Limited Impact on Job Growth," *Wall Street Journal*, September 1, 2021, https://www.wsj.com/articles/states-that-cut-unemployment-benefits-saw-limited-impact-on-job-growth-11630488601. Alternatively, a different research group used the CPS to study flows into employment and found a small increase in employment, but also a large increase in financial stress. See Harry J. Holzer, R. Glenn Hubbard, and Michael R. Strain, "Did Pandemic Unemployment Benefits Reduce Employment? Evidence from Early State-Level Expirations in June 2021" (NBER Working Paper No. 29575, December 2021), https://www.nber.org/papers/w29575.

9. Joseph Briggs and Ronnie Walker, "Back to Work When Benefits End," Goldman Sachs, US Economics Analyst, August 21, 2021, https://www.gspublishing.com/content/research/en/reports/2021/08/21/80a7093f-b7a9-4a05-84e3-a28ac2adab70.html.

10. Kyle Coombs, Arindrajit Dube, . . . and Michael Stepner, "Early Withdrawal of Pandemic Unemployment Insurance: Effects on Earnings, Employment and Consumption" (working paper, August 20, 2021), https://files.michaelstepner.com/pandemicUIexpiration-paper.pdf.

11. Adam Liptak and Glenn Thrush, "Supreme Court Ends Biden's Eviction Moratorium," *New York Times*, August 26, 2021, https://www.nytimes.com/2021/08/26/us/eviction-moratorium-ends.html.

12. Yangling Mayer, "More than 1.2 Million Loans to Exit Forbearance in the Coming Wave of Plan Terminations," CoreLogic, September 30, 2021, https://www.corelogic.com/intelligence/more-than-1-2-million-loans-to-exit-forbearance-in-the-coming-wave-of-plan-terminations/.

13. Katie Rogers and Tara Siegel Bernard, "The White House Will Freeze Federal Student Loan Repayments until May 1," *New York Times*, December 22, 2021, https://www.nytimes.com/2021/12/22/your-money/student-loan-pause.html.

14. See Federal Student Aid, "The Biden-Harris Administration's Student Debt Relief Plan Explained," accessed August 25, 2022, https://studentaid.gov/debt-relief-announcement/. The plan provided $10,000 of debt cancellation for loans held by the Department of Education (most, but not all student loans) and up to $20,000 of debt cancellation for Pell Grant recipients. The debt cancellation was limited to individuals earning $125,000 or less.

15. Around five million borrowers in March 2020 had risk factors that suggested that resuming payments might be a problem. See Thomas Conkling, Christa Gibbs, and Vanessa Jimenez-Read, "Student Loan Borrowers Potentially At-Risk When Payment Suspension Ends," Consumer Financial Protection Bureau Office of Research Special Issue Brief, April 2022, https://www.consumerfinance.gov/data-research/research-reports/student-loan-borrowers-potentially-at-risk-payment-suspension-ends/.

16. Source: Author's calculations from Bureau of Labor Statistics, "Employed Full Time: Median Usual Weekly Real Earnings: Wage and Salary Workers: 16 Years and Over"; Bureau of Economic Analysis, "Real Gross Domestic Product per Capita"; and Department of Labor, "Federal Minimum Hourly Wage for Nonfarm Workers for the United States," adjusted using Consumer Price Index All Urban; retrieved from FRED, https://fred.stlouisfed.org/graph/?g=KCmq.

17. In National Income and Product Accounts, GDP is equal to gross domestic income, so I use income here intentionally rather than GDP. There is some complication with prices: GDP is "deflated" using a GDP deflator, while earnings use the Consumer Price Index. Comparing prices over time is always a bit perilous. But the two inflation indexes largely track each other, so while the exact numbers are sensitive to how we adjust for inflation, the qualitative conclusions are not.

18. The labor share is sensitive to how it is defined. The difficulty comes less from measuring employee compensation than from measuring all of the other things, in particular, how much of a proprietor's income is compensation for her labor (paid to herself) and how much is compensation for owning a business. For different approaches, see Michael D. Giandrea and Shawn Sprague, "Estimating the U.S. Labor Share," *Monthly Labor Review*, February 2017, https://doi.org/10.21916/mlr.2017.7; Michael W. L. Elsby, Bart Hobijn, and Aysegul Sahin, "The Decline of the U.S. Labor Share," *Brookings Papers on Economic Activity*, Fall 2013, https://www.brookings

.edu/bpea-articles/the-decline-of-the-u-s-labor-share/; and Josh Bivens, "The Fed Shouldn't Give Up on Restoring Labor's Share of Income—and Measure It Correctly," *Working Economics Blog*, Economic Policy Institute, January 30, 2019, https://www.epi.org/blog/the-fed-shouldnt -give-up-on-restoring-labors-share-of-income-and-measure-it-correctly/. Figure source: Author's calculations from Bureau of Labor Statistics, "Nonfarm Business Sector: Labor Share for All Employed Persons," retrieved from FRED, https://fred.stlouisfed.org/graph/?g=Jjik. The value for the first quarter of 2016 is set to 57.9 percent based on Giandrea and Sprague, "Estimating the U.S. Labor Share."

19. Tips plus wages must add up to the federal minimum wage of $7.25. So tips first go to the restaurant, not the server, until the federal minimum wage is met. See Department of Labor, "Minimum Wages for Tipped Employees," September 30, 2021, https://www.dol.gov/agencies /whd/state/minimum-wage/tipped.

20. Source: Bureau of Labor Statistics, "Quits: Total Private" and "Layoffs and Discharges," retrieved from FRED, https://fred.stlouisfed.org/series/JTU1000QUL.

21. Arianne Cohen, "How to Quit Your Job in the Great Post-pandemic Resignation Boom," *Bloomberg Businessweek*, May 10, 2021, https://www.bloomberg.com/news/articles/2021-05-10 /quit-your-job-how-to-resign-after-covid-pandemic.

22. Kathryn Hymes, "'The Great Resignation' Misses the Point," *Wired*, November 1, 2021, https://www.wired.com/story/great-resignation-misses-the-point/.

23. Mary Hanbury and Dominick Reuter, "WE ALL QUIT: A Photo of a Burger King Sign Went Viral after Workers Protested Long Hours, Low Pay, and Kitchen Temperatures That Reached 97 Degrees," Business Insider, July 13, 2021, https://www.businessinsider.com/burger -king-we-all-quit-sign-viral-workers-labor-shortage-2021-7.

24. Hanbury and Reuter, "WE ALL QUIT."

25. Cindy Lange-Kubick, "We All (Still) Quit: Lincoln Burger King Workers Who Walked Got Better Gigs During the 'Great Resignation,'" Flatwater Free Press, December 3, 2021, https://flatwaterfreepress.org/we-all-still-quit-lincoln-burger-king-workers-who-walked-got -better-gigs-during-great-resignation/.

26. Source: Bureau of Labor Statistics, "Quits: Total Private" and "Layoffs and Discharges," retrieved from FRED, https://fred.stlouisfed.org/series/JTU1000QUL.

27. There are some other requirements as well. To count, a job opening must meet three conditions:

> JOLTS [the Job Openings and Labor Turnover Survey] defines Job Openings as all positions that are open (not filled) on the last business day of the month. A job is "open" only if it meets all three of the following conditions:
>
> 1. A specific position exists and there is work available for that position. The position can be full-time or part-time, and it can be permanent, short-term, or seasonal, and
> 2. The job could start within 30 days, whether or not the establishment finds a suitable candidate during that time, and
> 3. There is active recruiting for workers from outside the establishment location that has the opening.

Bureau of Labor Statistics, "Job Openings and Labor Turnover Survey: Data Definitions," accessed January 1, 2022, https://www.bls.gov/jlt/jltdef.htm.

28. For example, see Laura Entis, "When Quitting Your Job Feels like the Only Option," *Vox*, September 21, 2021, https://www.vox.com/the-highlight/22666665/jobs-recovery-covid-economy-workers-quit.

29. See, for example, Catalyst, "The Great Work/Life Divide (Report)," Catalyst-CNBC, October 19, 2021, https://www.catalyst.org/research/flexibility-demand-future-of-work/.

30. Beth Ann Bovino, Satyam Panday, Shruti Galwankar, and Debabrata Das, "Economic Research: Labor Force Exit Has the U.S. Economy in a Bind," S&P Global, November 22, 2021, https://www.spglobal.com/ratings/en/research/articles/211122-economic-research-labor-force-exit-has-the-u-s-economy-in-a-bind-12192055.

31. The estimates for the number of people affected by long COVID vary but even the lowest estimates suggest a substantial reduction in work hours due to continuing symptoms. See Katie Bach, "New Data Shows Long Covid Is Keeping as Many as 4 Million People Out of Work," Brookings Institution, August 2022, https://www.brookings.edu/research/new-data-shows-long-covid-is-keeping-as-many-as-4-million-people-out-of-work; and Dasom I. Ham, "Long-Haulers and Labor Market Outcomes," Federal Reserve Bank of Minneapolis, Opportunity and Growth Institute Working Paper No. 60, July 2022, https://doi.org/10.21034/iwp.60.

32. Maggie Koerth, "Would You Manage 70 Children and a 15-Ton Vehicle for $18 an Hour?," FiveThirtyEight, November 11, 2021, https://fivethirtyeight.com/features/would-you-manage-70-children-and-a-15-ton-vehicle-for-18-an-hour/.

33. Economists debate the relative importance of these different impacts. For a recent review and discussion of CARES Act benefits, see Jason Faberman and Ali Haider Ismail, "How Do Unemployment Benefits Relate to Job Search Behavior?," Federal Reserve Bank of Chicago, Chicago Fed Letter No. 441, June 2020, https://www.chicagofed.org/publications/chicago-fed-letter/2020/441.

34. Gwynn Guilford, "The Other Reason the Labor Force Is Shrunken: Fear of Covid-19," *Wall Street Journal*, April 11, 2021, https://www.wsj.com/articles/the-other-reason-the-labor-force-is-shrunken-fear-of-covid-19-11618163017.

35. Arindrajit Dube, Twitter thread, November 6, 2021, https://twitter.com/arindube/status/1457156787828891657?s=21.

36. See, for example, Alison Green, "Companies Are Desperate for Workers. Why Aren't They Doing the One Thing That Will Attract Them?," *Slate*, January 24, 2022, https://slate.com/human-interest/2022/01/job-market-vacancies-hiring-desperate-no-workers-why.html.

37. Neil Irwin, "Worker Shortage Unleashes a Forever Jobs Crisis," Axios, January 21, 2021, https://www.axios.com/workers-labor-market-hiring-f64c1d75-9405-4c12-8273-20c442162b89.html.

38. See also Conor Sen, "Why Companies Might Learn to Love Unions," Bloomberg, December 3, 2021, https://www.bloomberg.com/opinion/articles/2021-12-03/the-great-resignation-may-teach-companies-to-love-unions.

39. Source: Affinity Solutions; Raj Chetty, John N. Friedman, . . . and the Opportunity Insights Team, "The Economic Impacts of COVID-19: Evidence from a New Public Database Built Using Private Sector Data" (working paper, November 2020), https://opportunityinsights.org/wp-content/uploads/2020/05/tracker_paper.pdf.

40. Roni Caryn Rabin, "C.D.C. Traces Covid Outbreaks in Gyms, Urging Stricter Precautions," *New York Times*, February 24, 2021, https://www.nytimes.com/2021/02/24/health/coronavirus-gyms-outbreaks.html.

41. Anders Melin and Jack Pitcher, "Peloton Moves into Breakaway Mode to Secure Its Sudden Dominance," *Bloomberg Businessweek*, January 22, 2021, https://www.bloomberg.com/news/articles/2021-01-22/peloton-pton-looks-to-keep-growing-after-coronavirus-pandemic.

42. Claudia Assis, "Peloton's IPO Documents Show Steep Losses for Maker of High-End Exercise Bikes," MarketWatch, August 27, 2019, https://www.marketwatch.com/story/pelotons-ipo-documents-show-steep-losses-for-maker-of-high-end-exercise-bikes-2019-08-27.

43. Robert Annis, "Bike Shortages Will Likely Last Until Next Year, and Possibly into 2022," *Bicycling*, November 6, 2020, https://www.bicycling.com/news/a34587945/coronavirus-bike-shortage/.

44. Soumya Karlamangla, "The Busiest Port in the U.S.," *New York Times*, October 18, 2021, https://www.nytimes.com/2021/10/18/us/port-of-los-angeles-supply-chain.html.

45. Anna Nagurney, "The $14 Trillion Reason You Should Care about the Shipping Container Shortage," *Fast Company*, September 28, 2021, https://www.fastcompany.com/90678954/the-14-trillion-reason-you-should-care-about-the-shipping-container-shortage.

46. Arthur Donovan, "The Impact of Containerization: From Adam Smith to the 21st Century," *Review of Business*, 2004, 25(3): 10–15.

47. Costamare, "Container Facts," accessed October 24, 2021, https://www.costamare.com/industry_containerisation.

48. Raunek, "The Ultimate Guide to Ship Sizes," Marine Insight, December 9, 2021, https://www.marineinsight.com/types-of-ships/the-ultimate-guide-to-ship-sizes/.

49. Chris Isidore, "Everything You're Waiting for Is in These Containers," CNN, October 23, 2021, https://www.cnn.com/2021/10/20/business/la-long-beach-port-congestion-problem-national-impact/index.html.

50. Paul Berger, "California Port's 24-Hour Operation Is Going Unused," *Wall Street Journal*, September 30, 2021, https://www.wsj.com/articles/california-ports-24-hour-operation-is-going-unused-11633018532.

51. See, for example, Vanessa Yurkevich, "Wanted: 80,000 Truck Drivers to Help Fix the Supply Chain," CNN, October 19, 202, https://www.cnn.com/2021/10/19/economy/trucking-short-drivers/index.html; or for a more nuanced look, Madeleine Ngo and Ana Swanson, "The Biggest Kink in America's Supply Chain: Not Enough Truckers," *New York Times*, November 9, 2021, https://www.nytimes.com/2021/11/09/us/politics/trucker-shortage-supply-chain.html.

52. Pamela N. Danziger, "Unclogging the Ports Will Not Fix the Supply Chain's Even Bigger Trucking Crisis," *Forbes*, October 15, 2020, https://www.forbes.com/sites/pamdanziger/2021/10/15/unclogging-the-ports-will-not-fix—the-supply-chains-even-bigger-trucking-crisis/?sh=6ba62637124f.

53. Stephen V. Burks and Kristen Monaco, "Is the U.S. Labor Market for Truck Drivers Broken?," *Monthly Labor Review*, March 2019, https://www.bls.gov/opub/mlr/2019/article/is-the-us-labor-market-for-truck-drivers-broken.htm.

54. Nicolas Rivero, "There Is No Shortage of US Truck Drivers," *Quartz*, November 10, 2021, https://qz.com/2086977/there-is-no-truck-driver-shortage-in-the-us/.

55. Ryan Johnson, "I'm a Twenty Year Truck Driver, I Will Tell You Why America's 'Shipping Crisis' Will Not End," Medium, October 27, 2021, https://medium.com/@ryan79z28/im-a -twenty-year-truck-driver-i-will-tell-you-why-america-s-shipping-crisis-will-not-end -bbe0ebac6a91.

56. Grace Kay, "Truckers at Backlogged Ports Say They've Waited in Miles-Long Lines for up to 8 Hours without Pay," Business Insider, November 4, 2021, https://www.businessinsider .com/truckers-wait-outside-backlogged-ports-8-hours-without-pay-2021-11.

57. James Manyika, Jan Mischke, . . . and Samuel Cudre, "A New Look at the Declining Labor Share of Income in the United States," McKinsey & Company Discussion Paper, May 22, 2019, https://www.mckinsey.com/featured-insights/employment-and-growth/a-new-look-at-the -declining-labor-share-of-income-in-the-united-states.

58. Jeff Desjardins, "The 100 Tallest Buildings in New York City," Visual Capitalist, April 26, 2019, https://www.visualcapitalist.com/100-tallest-buildings-in-new-york-city/.

59. CBSLA Staff, "As Many as Half a Million Shipping Containers Could Be Waiting Off Ports of LA, Long Beach," CBS Los Angeles, October 4, 2021, https://losangeles.cbslocal.com /2021/10/04/shipping-containers-waiting-ports-los-angeles-long-beach/; Matt Egan, "$24 Billion in Goods Is Floating Outside California's Biggest Ports," CNN Business, October 25, 2021, https://www.cnn.com/2021/10/25/business/supply-chain-ports-inflation/index.html.

60. Isidore, "Everything You're Waiting For."

61. Will Knight, "Why the Chip Shortage Drags On and On . . . and On," Wired, November 12, 2021, https://www.wired.com/story/why-chip-shortage-drags-on/.

62. Willy Shih, "Why the Global Chip Shortage Is Making It So Hard to Buy a PS5," interview by Nilay Patel, Verge, August 31, 2021, https://www.theverge.com/2021/8/31/22648372/willy -shih-chip-shortage-tsmc-samsung-ps5-decoder-interview.

63. Ina Fried, "Huawei Sanctions Snarled Chip Supply Chains," Axios, December 3, 2021, https://www.axios.com/huawei-sanctions-chips-supply-chains-30d86353-9585-45a9-9249 -b088cea9250d.html.

64. Neal E. Boudette, "G.M. Will Idle More Factories This Month as a Chip Shortage Drags On," New York Times, September 2, 2021, https://www.nytimes.com/2021/09/02/business/gm -chip-shortage.html.

65. Peter Coy, "How to Soften the Bullwhip Effect," New York Times, December 15, 2021, https://www.nytimes.com/2021/12/15/opinion/inflation-shortages-overordering.html.

66. Derek Thompson, "What's behind America's Shocking Baby-Formula Shortage?," Atlantic, May 12, 2022, https://www.theatlantic.com/ideas/archive/2022/05/baby-formula-shortage -abbott-recall/629828/.

67. Patti Domm, "Gasoline Demand Improves as States Reopen and Drivers Hit the Road, but It's Still Down 30%," CNBC, May 13, 2020, https://www.cnbc.com/2020/05/13/gasoline -demand-improves-as-states-reopen-and-drivers-hit-the-road-but-its-still-down-30percent .html.

68. Neil Irwin, "What the Negative Price of Oil Is Telling Us," New York Times, April 21, 2020, https://www.nytimes.com/2020/04/21/upshot/negative-oil-price.html.

69. Source: Author's calculations from Bureau of Labor Statistics, "Consumer Price Index for All Urban Consumers: Used Cars and Trucks in U.S. City Average," "Consumer Price Index

for All Urban Consumers: All Items in U.S. City Average," and "Consumer Price Index for All Urban Consumers: Energy in U.S. City Average," retrieved from FRED, https://fred.stlouisfed .org/graph/?g=JkqJ.

70. Amara Omeokwe, "U.S. June Consumer Prices Rose Sharply as Reopenings Prompted More Buying," *Wall Street Journal*, July 14, 2020, https://www.wsj.com/articles/u-s-june -consumer-prices-rose-sharply-as-reopenings-prompted-more-buying-11594731052.

71. Simon Workman and Steven Jessen-Howard, "The True Cost of Providing Safe Child Care during the Coronavirus Pandemic," Center for American Progress, May 2020, https:// americanprogress.org/article/true-cost-providing-safe-child-care-coronavirus-pandemic/.

72. To be fair, the Bureau of Labor Statistics, which calculates the CPI, was aware of the is- sues. For example, it posted a cryptic note on weight updates that would not make sense without the preceding discussion: "Starting in January 2022, weights for the Consumer Price Index will be calculated based on consumer expenditure data from 2019–2020. The Bureau of Labor Sta- tistics considered interventions, but decided to maintain normal procedures." Bureau of Labor Statistics, "Consumer Price Index: January 2022 CPI Weight Update," accessed January 1, 2021, https://www.bls.gov/cpi/notices/2021/2022-weight-update.htm.

73. See a good summary in Chris Isidore, "Here's Why Car Prices Are So High, and Why That Matters," CNN Business, July 8, 2021, https://www.cnn.com/2021/07/08/business/car -prices-inflation/index.html.

74. Nicole Friedman, "Supply-Chain Issues Leave New Homes without Garage Doors and Gutters," *Wall Street Journal*, January 9, 2022, https://www.wsj.com/articles/supply-chain-issues -leave-new-homes-without-garage-doors-and-gutters-11641724201.

75. Marisa Iati, "Supply-Chain Issues and a Cyberattack: Why Your Bagel's Cream Cheese Might Be Spread a Little Thin," *Washington Post*, December 16, 2021, https://www.washingtonpost .com/food/2021/12/16/cream-cheese-shortage-2021/.

76. Ramishah Maruf, "The Surprising Reason You Can't Find Cream Cheese Anywhere," CNN, December 18, 2021, https://www.cnn.com/2021/12/18/business/cream-cheese -cyberattack-schreiber-foods/index.html.

77. For different perspectives, see initial predictions in Francesco Bianchi, Jonas D. M. Fisher, and Leonardo Melosi, "Some Inflation Scenarios for the American Rescue Plan Act of 2021," Chicago Fed Letter No. 453, April 2021, https://www.chicagofed.org/publications /chicago-fed-letter/2021/453; later estimates in Òscar Jordà, Celeste Liu, Fernanda Nechio, and Fabián Rivera-Reyes, "Why Is U.S. Inflation Higher than in Other Countries?," Federal Reserve Bank of San Francisco Economic Letter 2022-07, March 28, 2022, https://www.frbsf.org /economic-research/publications/economic-letter/2022/march/why-is-us-inflation-higher -than-in-other-countries/; and Menzie Chinn, "Four Questions and Four Answers: US and Euro Area Core Inflation," *Econbrowser* (blog), April 25, 2022, http://econbrowser.com/archives /2022/04/four-questions-and-four-answers-us-and-euro-area-core-inflation.

78. I was on "team transitory," as it came to be called, of those who thought inflation was temporary, as was the Federal Reserve in public statements. See, for example, Rachel Siegel, "The Fed's Inflation Challenge: Getting the Policy and the Messaging Right," *Washington Post*, December 13, 2021, https://www.washingtonpost.com/business/2021/12/09/inflation-fed -transitory-powell/.

79. For a discussion of this point, see Paul R. Krugman, *The Age of Diminished Expectations: U.S. Economic Policy in the 1990s*, MIT Press, 1997, 56–62.

80. Associated Press, "Turkey Launches New Currency," NBC News, January 1, 2005, https://www.nbcnews.com/id/wbna6776071.

81. For example, "Why the Federal Reserve Has Made a Historic Mistake on Inflation," *Economist*, April 23, 2022.

82. Raphael Bostic, "The Current Inflation Episode: Have We Met Our FAIT?," speech to the Peterson Institute for International Economics, October 21, 2021, https://www.atlantafed.org/news/speeches/2021/10/12/bostic-the-current-inflation-episode.

83. Jerome H. Powell, "Testimony before the Select Subcommittee on the Coronavirus Crisis," U.S. House of Representatives, June 22, 2021, https://www.federalreserve.gov/newsevents/testimony/powell20210622a.htm.

84. See Olivier Coibion, Yuriy Gorodnichenko, Lorenz Kueng, and John Silvia, "Innocent Bystanders? Monetary Policy and Inequality in the U.S." (NBER Working Paper No. 18170, June 2012), https://www.nber.org/papers/w18170. Monetary policy's effect on wealth inequality and racial wealth inequality is more complicated because wealth is concentrated among white households. See Alina K. Bartscher, Moritz Kuhn, Moritz Schularick, and Paul Wachtel, "Monetary Policy and Racial Inequality," Federal Reserve Bank of New York Staff Report No. 959, March 2022, https://www.newyorkfed.org/research/staff_reports/sr959.html.

85. Stephanie R. Aaronson, Mary C. Daly, William Wascher, and David W. Wilcox, "Okun Revisited: Who Benefits Most from a Strong Economy?," *Brookings Papers on Economic Activity*, Spring 2019, https://www.brookings.edu/bpea-articles/okun-revisited-who-benefits-most-from-a-strong-economy/.

86. Source: Author's calculations from Census Bureau, "Business Applications: Total for All NAICS in the United States" and "High-Propensity Business Applications: Total for All NAICS in the United States," retrieved from FRED, https://fred.stlouisfed.org/graph/?g=KNwA.

87. Census Bureau, "Business Formation Statistics: Methodology," accessed December 6, 2021, https://www.census.gov/econ/bfs/methodology.html.

88. John C. Haltiwanger, "Entrepreneurship during the COVID-19 Pandemic: Evidence from the Business Formation Statistics" (NBER Working Paper No. 28912, June 2021), https://www.nber.org/papers/w28912.

89. Author's calculations from Census Bureau, "Business Dynamics Statistics," Center for Economic Studies, 2019, https://bds.explorer.ces.census.gov/. See also Ben Casselman, "A Start-Up Slump Is a Drag on the Economy. Big Business May Be to Blame," *New York Times*, September 20, 2017, https://www.nytimes.com/2017/09/20/business/economy/startup-business.html.

90. Ian Hathaway and Robert E. Litan, "Declining Business Dynamism in the United States: A Look at States and Metros," Brookings Institution, May 2014, https://www.brookings.edu/wp-content/uploads/2016/06/declining_business_dynamism_hathaway_litan.pdf.

91. Daniel Garcia-Macia, Chang-Tai Hsieh, and Peter J. Klenow, "How Destructive Is Innovation?," *Econometrica*, 2019, 87(5): 1507–41, https://doi.org/10.3982/ECTA14930.

92. Erik Hurst and Benjamin Wild Pugsley, "What Do Small Businesses Do?" *Brookings Papers on Economic Activity*, Fall 2011, 73, https://www.brookings.edu/wp-content/uploads/2011/09/2011b_bpea_hurst.pdf.

93. John Haltiwanger, Ron S. Jarmin, and Javier Miranda, "Who Creates Jobs? Small versus Large versus Young," *Review of Economics and Statistics*, 2013, 95(2): 347–61, https://doi.org/10.1162/REST_a_00288.

94. Haltiwanger, "Entrepreneurship during the COVID-19 Pandemic."

95. Catherine E. Fazio, Jorge Guzman, Yupeng Liu, and Scott Stern, "How Is COVID Changing the Geography of Entrepreneurship? Evidence from the Startup Cartography Project" (NBER Working Paper No. 28787, May 2021), https://www.nber.org/papers/w28787.

96. Robert Fairlie, "Racial Inequality in Business Ownership and Income," *Oxford Review of Economic Policy*, Winter 2018, 34(4): 597–614, https://doi.org/10.1093/oxrep/gry019.

97. Robert W. Fairlie, Alicia Robb, and David T. Robinson, "Black and White: Access to Capital among Minority-Owned Startups" (NBER Working Paper No. 28154, November 2020), https://www.nber.org/papers/w28154.

98. Alana Semuels, "Why Does Sweden Have So Many Start-Ups?," *Atlantic*, September 28, 2017, https://www.theatlantic.com/business/archive/2017/09/sweden-startups/541413/.

99. Robert Fairlie, "The Impact of COVID-19 on Small Business Owners: Evidence from the First Three Months after Widespread Social-Distancing Restrictions," *Journal of Economics and Management Strategy*, Winter 2020, 29(4): 727–40, https://doi.org/10.1111/jems.12400.

100. Source: Author's calculations from Bureau of Labor Statistics series "Employment Level—All Industries Self-Employed, Unincorporated (LNU02027714)" and "Employment Level—Total Wage and Salary, Incorporated Self Employed (LNU02048984)," accessed using FRED, Federal Reserve Bank of St. Louis, May 24, 2022. Thanks to Susan Woodward, whose analysis and private discussions pointed out that business registrations had mostly not turned into self-employment or new small business employment.

101. Karen Weise and Noam Scheiber, "Amazon Workers on Staten Island Vote to Unionize in Landmark Win for Labor," *New York Times*, April 1, 2022, https://www.nytimes.com/2022/04/01/technology/amazon-union-staten-island.html.

102. Jodi Kantor and Karen Weise, "How Two Best Friends Beat Amazon," *New York Times*, April 4, 2022, https://www.nytimes.com/2022/04/02/business/amazon-union-christian-smalls.html.

103. Part of the reason for closing in-store butcheries was that technology allowed Walmart to use prepackaged meats more readily. But it was also a clear signal: unions beware. Ann Zimmerman, "Pro-union Butchers at Wal-Mart Win a Battle, but Lose the War," *Wall Street Journal*, April 11, 2000, https://www.wsj.com/articles/SB955407680495911513.

104. Richard Curtin, "March 2022 Survey Results," University of Michigan Surveys of Consumers, March 25, 2022, https://data.sca.isr.umich.edu/fetchdoc.php?docid=69756.

Chapter Eleven

1. Scott L. Fulford, "The Surprisingly Low Importance of Income Uncertainty for Precaution," *European Economic Review*, 2015, 79: 151–71, https://doi.org/10.1016/j.euroecorev.2015.07.016.

2. Scott L. Fulford, "Demand for Emergency Savings Is Higher for Low-Income Households, but So Is the Cost of Shocks," *Empirical Economics*, 2020, 58(6): 3007–33, https://doi.org/10.1007/s00181-018-1590-9.

3. A broad economics literature considers why savings might have declined. At least one reason may be the expansion of credit, which both provides the ability to buy durable goods (like houses and cars) without as much prior savings and provides emergency funds in case of need. For an explanation of some of the complexities of measuring savings rates, see Rudolph G. Penner, "Measuring Personal Saving: A Tale of American Profligacy," Urban Institute Brief Series No. 21, May 2008, https://www.urban.org/sites/default/files/publication/31726/411671 -Measuring-Personal-Saving-A-Tale-of-American-Profligacy.PDF; and William G. Gale and John Sabelhaus, "Perspectives on the Household Saving Rate" (Brookings Institution Working Paper, 1999), https://www.brookings.edu/wp-content/uploads/2016/06/19991.pdf.

4. Source: Bureau of Economic Analysis, "Personal Saving Rate," retrieved from FRED, https://fred.stlouisfed.org/graph/?g=Ka5D.

5. Because it measures total savings divided by total income, rather than the average or the savings rate across households, the personal savings rate is most affected by the choices of high-income households; they have a lot more money. We might be more interested in the average savings rate, which takes each household's savings divided by its income and then takes the average. But the aggregate personal savings rate can be measured for decades, while the average of each household's savings rates is much harder to measure.

6. These figures are technically the Household Savings Rate calculated by the OECD, so use a slightly different definition, but are largely comparable. See Organization for Economic Cooperation and Development, "Household Savings," accessed December 27, 2021, https://data .oecd.org/hha/household-savings.htm. China's "excess savings" are an important economic question in their own right.

7. Fiona Greig, Erica Deadman, and Tanya Sonthalia, "Household Cash Balance Pulse: Family Edition," JPMorgan Chase Institute, November 2021, HYPERLINK "https://www .jpmorganchase.com/institute/research/household-income-spending/household-cash-balance -pulse-families" https://www.jpmorganchase.com/institute/research/household-income -spending/household-cash-balance-pulse-families.

8. For a series of examples, see Amanda Mull, "The Rise of Coffee Shaming," Atlantic, July 2019, https://www.theatlantic.com/health/archive/2019/07/coffee-financial-advice/594244/.

9. Suze Orman, "Suze Orman: If You Waste Money on Coffee, It's like 'Peeing $1 Million down the Drain,'" interview by Emmie Martin, CNBC Make It, March 28, 2019, https://www .cnbc.com/2019/03/28/suze-orman-spending-money-on-coffee-is-like-throwing-1-million -down-the-drain.html.

10. Donna R. Gabaccia, We Are What We Eat: Ethnic Food and the Making of Americans, Harvard University Press, 1998. See in particular chap. 12.

11. Avocado toast as an indulgence was a much-ridiculed internet meme after a rich property mogul in Australia asserted it was why millennials could not buy houses. See Maura Judkis, "Don't Mess with Millennials' Avocado Toast: The Internet Fires Back at a Millionaire," Washington Post, May 15, 2017, https://www.washingtonpost.com/news/food/wp/2017/05/15/dont -mess-with-millennials-avocado-toast-the-internet-fires-back-at-a-millionaire/.

12. Convenience Store News, "At-Home Coffee Consumption Climbs to 81% amidst Pandemic," July 29, 2021, https://www.csnews.com/home-coffee-consumption-climbs-81-amidst -pandemic.

13. Nick Kostov, "At-Home Coffee Boom during Pandemic Powers Sales at Nestlé," *Wall Street Journal*, April 22, 2021, https://www.wsj.com/articles/at-home-coffee-boom-during -pandemic-powers-sales-at-nestle-11619090637.

14. Comunicaffe International, "Half of Americans Have Become At-Home Baristas during the Pandemic," October 7, 2020, https://www.comunicaffe.com/half-of-americans-have -become-at-home-baristas-during-the-pandemic/.

15. See, for example, Discover, "60% of Americans Say the Pandemic Has Made Them Realize How Little They Have Saved," July 28, 2021, https://investorrelations.discover.com /newsroom/press-releases/press-release-details/2021/60-Of-Americans-Say-the-Pandemic -Has-Made-Them-Realize-How-Little-They-Have-Saved/default.aspx; and Capital One, "Reimagining Digital Banking for the Post-pandemic World," November 10, 2021, https://www .capitalone.com/about/newsroom/digital-banking-post-pandemic/.

16. In one survey, 51 percent said "having an emergency fund is higher priority" because of COVID-19. See Alicia Castro, "What Does the Average American Need to Feel Financially Healthy?," Empower Retirement and Personal Capital, July 28, 2021, https://www.personalcapital .com/blog/whitepapers/what-americans-need-to-feel-financially-healthy/.

17. This range comes from two sources: Raj Chetty, "Moral Hazard versus Liquidity and Optimal Unemployment Insurance," *Journal of Political Economy*, 2008, 116(2): 173–234, https:// doi.org/10.1086/588585; and Ioana Marinescu and Daphné Skandalis, "Unemployment Insurance and Job Search Behavior," *Quarterly Journal of Economics*, 2021, 136(2): 887–931, https://doi .org/10.1093/qje/qjaa037.

18. See the evidence discussed in Chapter 10 on the end of unemployment insurance and Jesse Rothstein, "Unemployment Insurance and Job Search in the Great Recession," *Brookings Papers on Economic Activity*, Fall 2011, https://www.brookings.edu/bpea-articles/unemployment -insurance-and-job-search-in-the-great-recession/.

19. See, for example, the questions by Senator Ron Wyden to Labor Secretary Eugene Scalia: Committee on Finance, United States Senate, "Unemployment Insurance during COVID-19: The CARES Act and the Role of Unemployment Insurance during the Pandemic," June 9, 2022, 10–12, https://www.finance.senate.gov/imo/media/doc/458081.pdf.

20. Indeed, there is good reason to go even further. Unemployment insurance replaces too little income in most states, so raising it to above 50 percent would be good policy with or without a recession. It might make sense to make it even more generous, such as by extending eligibility, during recessions. During a recession, because it is harder to find a job, unemployment insurance likely diminishes the incentives to look for a job even less, while it protects families even more. For more, see Gabriel Chodorow-Reich and John Coglianese, "Unemployment Insurance and Macroeconomic Stabilization," in *Recession Ready: Fiscal Policies to Stabilize the American Economy*, ed. Heather Boushey, Ryan Nunn, and Jay Shambaugh, Brookings Institution, 2019, https://equitablegrowth.org/recession-ready-2/.

21. Neta C. Crawford, "The U.S. Budgetary Costs of the Post-9/11 Wars," Brown University Costs of War Project, September 1, 2021, https://watson.brown.edu/costsofwar/files/cow/imce /papers/2021/Costs%20of%20War_U.S.%20Budgetary%20Costs%20of%20Post-9%20 11%20Wars_9.1.21.pdf.

22. See Joseph E. Stiglitz and Linda J. Bilmes, *The Three Trillion Dollar War: The True Cost of the Iraq Conflict*, W. W. Norton, 2008; and Joseph E. Stiglitz and Linda J. Bilmes, "The True Cost of the Iraq War: $3 Trillion and Beyond," *Washington Post*, September 5, 2010, https://www.washingtonpost.com/wp-dyn/content/article/2010/09/03/AR2010090302200.html.

23. Throughout this section and for the figure, I use a single source, the Committee for a Responsible Budget, for these numbers so that they are comparable to each other. The numbers may not compare exactly to the amounts discussed in the individual bills, which generally used the amounts "allowed" under the statute. The numbers are amounts committed or disbursed as of May 2022. Source: Committee for a Responsible Budget, "COVID Money Tracker," accessed May 9, 2022, https://www.covidmoneytracker.org/.

24. See Gabriel Chodorow-Reich, Ben Iverson, and Adi Sunderam, "Lessons Learned from Support to Business during COVID-19," in *Recession Remedies*, ed. Wendy Edelberg, Louise Sheiner, and David Wessel, Brookings Institution, https://www.brookings.edu/essay/lessons-learned-from-support-to-business-during-covid-19/.

25. Tracy Gordon, "State and Local Budgets and the Great Recession," Brookings Institution, December 31, 2012, https://www.brookings.edu/articles/state-and-local-budgets-and-the-great-recession/.

26. On some of the waste, see J. David McSwane, *Pandemic, Inc.: Chasing the Capitalists and Thieves Who Got Rich While We Got Sick*, Atria, 2022.

27. Which is not to argue that the AIG bailout was not necessary even if it left many feeling disgusted. As Federal Reserve chairman Ben Bernanke testified to the Senate Budget Committee in 2009, "I think if there is a single episode in this entire 18 months that has made me more angry, I cannot think of one than AIG. . . . We were then forced—we had no choice but to try to stabilize the system because of the implications that the failure would have had for the broad economic system." Ben Bernanke, in *Economic and Budget Challenges for the Short and Long Term: Hearing before the Committee on the Budget, United States Senate, March 3, 2009*, U.S. Government Printing Office, 2010, 19, https://www.govinfo.gov/content/pkg/CHRG-111shrg70993/pdf/CHRG-111shrg70993.pdf.

28. Mortgage problems during and following the financial crisis were much larger than during the pandemic when prices were generally rising, making mortgage modifications easier. Yet there is wide agreement that the two biggest programs, the Home Affordable Modification Program and Home Affordable Refinance Program, were largely inadequate. They reached relatively few homeowners compared with the scale of the problem, often did not effectively help many of the owners they reached because of the way the programs were designed, and often took too long to reach homeowners needing help. For a comparison of policies during the pandemic and following the financial crisis, see Ronel Elul and Natalie Newton, "Helping Struggling Homeowners during Two Crises," Federal Reserve Bank of Philadelphia, 2021, https://www.philadelphiafed.org/-/media/frbp/assets/economy/articles/economic-insights/2021/q4/eiq421-helping-struggling-homeowners-during-two-crises.pdf. For a different viewpoint, see Dan Immergluck, "Too Little, Too Late, and Too Timid: The Federal Response to the Foreclosure Crisis at the Five-Year Mark," *Housing Policy Debate*, 2013, 23(1): 199–232, https://doi.org/10.1080/10511482.2012.749933.

29. The quotation is from Mario Draghi, then president of the European Central Bank, in 2012 during the biggest of several follow-up crises to the 2008 financial crisis. His speech is widely credited with helping save the euro by committing to strong policy, thereby preventing the crisis from worsening; his famous phrase became the standard for a central bank that is believed to have identified the problem and is prepared to solve it and that, by winning credibility, reduces the size of the problem and makes it more remediable. See, for example, Andrew Walker, "Mario Draghi: His Legacy after Eight Tumultuous Years at the ECB," BBC, October 24, 2019, https://www.bbc.com/news/business-50020948.

30. See, for example, the review in Alan S. Blinder and Mark Zandi, "The Financial Crisis: Lessons for the Next One," Center on Budget and Policy Priorities, October 15, 2015, https://www.cbpp.org/research/economy/the-financial-crisis-lessons-for-the-next-one.

31. The American Recovery and Reinvestment Act of 2009 was the most important bill. Several other programs would have provided benefits including a one-time payment to Social Security recipients and an expansion of child tax credits. For a comparison of ARRA and the CARES Act, see Kimberly Amadeo, "ARRA, Its Details, with Pros and Cons," Balance, November 17, 2020, https://www.thebalance.com/arra-details-3306299#arra-compared-to-cares-act.

32. The details are complicated and full of acronyms. Many at the time argued that not helping borrowers while bailing out banks was problematic, notably Federal Deposit Insurance Corporation chair Sheila Bair. See Paul Kiel, "The Great American Foreclosure Story: The Struggle for Justice and a Place to Call Home," ProPublica, April 10, 2012, https://www.propublica.org/article/the-great-american-foreclosure-story-the-struggle-for-justice-and-a-place-t.

33. David C. Wheelock, "Comparing the COVID-19 Recession with the Great Depression," Economic Synopses, August 2020, no. 39, Federal Reserve Bank of St. Louis, https://research.stlouisfed.org/publications/economic-synopses/2020/08/12/comparing-the-covid-19-recession-with-the-great-depression.

34. For a summary of some of these mistakes see Gary Richardson, "The Great Depression," Federal Reserve History, November 22, 2013, https://www.federalreservehistory.org/essays/great-depression.

35. See the speech: Ben Bernanke, "Remarks by Governor Ben S. Bernanke at the Conference to Honor Milton Friedman," Federal Reserve Board, November 8, 2002, https://www.federalreserve.gov/boarddocs/speeches/2002/20021108/default.htm. The importance of the money supply for economic activity is most associated with economists Milton Friedman and Anna J. Schwartz although more recent work has emphasized other monetary policies. Milton Friedman and Anna J. Schwartz, A Monetary History of the United States, Princeton University Press, 1963.

36. Price V. Fishback, "U.S. Monetary and Fiscal Policy in the 1930s," Oxford Review of Economic Policy, 2010, 26(3): 385–413, https://doi.org/10.1093/oxrep/grq029.

37. Jakob B. Madsen, "Trade Barriers and the Collapse of World Trade during the Great Depression," Southern Economic Journal, 2001, 67(4): 848–68, https://doi.org/10.2307/1061574.

38. Daniel N. Price, "Unemployment Insurance, Then and Now, 1935–85," Social Security Bulletin, 1985, 48(10): 22–32, https://www.ssa.gov/policy/docs/ssb/v48n10/v48n10p22.pdf.

39. Carmen M. Reinhart and Kenneth S. Rogoff, *This Time Is Different: Eight Centuries of Financial Folly*, Princeton University Press, 2009.

40. For families with working mothers who paid for child care, the expenses averaged 17 percent of the average mother's earnings. See Elizabeth U. Cascio, "Public Investments in Child Care," in *The 51%: Driving Growth through Women's Economic Participation*, ed. Diane Whitmore Schanzenbach and Ryan Nunn, Brookings Institution, October 2017, https://www .brookings.edu/wp-content/uploads/2017/10/THP_The51__Cascio_0419.pdf.

41. Abha Bhattarai, "Rents Are Up More than 30 Percent in Some Cities, Forcing Millions to Find Another Place to Live," *Washington Post*, January 30, 2020, https://www.washingtonpost .com/business/2022/01/30/rent-inflation-housing/.

42. See, for example, the recent discussion in Jenny Schuetz, *Fixer-Upper: How to Repair American's Broken Housing Systems*, Brookings Institution Press, 2022; and M. Nolan Gray, *Arbitrary Lines: How Zoning Broke the American City and How to Fix It*, Island Press, 2022. For a summary, see Jenny Schuetz, "To Improve Housing Affordability, We Need Better Alignment of Zoning, Taxes, and Subsidies," Brookings Institution, January 2020, https://www.brookings .edu/wp-content/uploads/2019/12/Schuetz_Policy2020_BigIdea_Improving-Housing -Afforability.pdf.

43. See, for example, Matt Yglesias, "Legalize Skyscrapers," *Slate*, April 18, 2012, https://slate .com/business/2012/04/d-c-s-height-restrictions-on-buildings-are-hurting-america.html.

44. Author's calculations from Census Bureau, "Annual Estimates of the Population of Metropolitan and Micropolitan Statistical Areas," retrieved from FRED, https://fred.stlouisfed.org /graph/?g=QM0y.

45. Chang-Tai Hsieh and Enrico Moretti, "Housing Constraints and Spatial Misallocation," *American Economic Journal: Macroeconomics*, 2019, 11(2): 1–39, https://doi.org/10.1257/mac .20170388.

46. Schuetz, *Fixer-Upper*.

47. For one argument along these lines, see Matthew Yglesias, *The Rent Is Too Damn High*, Simon and Schuster, 2012.

48. Bipartisan Policy Center, "Housing America's Future: New Directions for National Policy," February 2013, https://bipartisanpolicy.org/wp-content/uploads/2019/03/BPC _Housing-Report_web_0.pdf.

49. Changes to the tax code in 2017 reduced the amount spent on the mortgage interest tax deduction by about half. For the rent and mortgage subsidies calculations, see Bipartisan Policy Center, "Housing America's Future."

50. Claire Cain Miller, "How Other Nations Pay for Child Care. The U.S. Is an Outlier," *New York Times*, October, 6, 2021, https://www.nytimes.com/2021/10/06/upshot/child-care-biden .html.

51. Roger K. Lewis, "Following Pandemic, Converting Office Buildings into Housing May Become New 'Normal,'" *Washington Post*, April 3, 2021, https://www.washingtonpost.com /realestate/following-pandemic-converting-office-buildings-into-housing-may-become-new -normal/2021/03/31/2fec400e-8820-11eb-8a8b-5cf82c3dffe4_story.html.

52. Estelle Sommeiller and Mark Price, "The New Gilded Age: Income Inequality in the U.S. by State, Metropolitan Area, and County," Economic Policy Institute Report, July 19, 2018,

https://www.epi.org/publication/the-new-gilded-age-income-inequality-in-the-u-s-by-state
-metropolitan-area-and-county/.

53. Mark Strassmann, "The Least Affordable Housing Market in the U.S.? Boise," CBS News,
December 3, 2021, https://www.cbsnews.com/news/housing-market-boise-idaho-least
-affordable/.

54. Bill Bishop and Robert G. Cushing, *The Big Sort: Why the Clustering of Like-Minded
America Is Tearing Us Apart*, Houghton Mifflin, 2008.

55. Some children struggled, others welcomed the change. See Lesley McClurg, "Some Kids
Are Happy to Ditch the Mask at School, Others Struggle with the Transition," NPR, March 27,
2022, https://www.npr.org/sections/health-shots/2022/03/27/1082633794/some-kids-are
-happy-to-ditch-the-mask-at-school-others-struggle-with-the-transit.

56. See Jose Maria Barrero, Nicholas Bloom, and Steven J. Davis, "SWAA March 2022 Updates," March 2022, https://wfhresearch.com/wp-content/uploads/2022/03/WFHResearch
_updates_March2022.pdf; an update to Jose Maria Barrero, Nicholas Bloom, and Steven J.
Davis, "Why Working from Home Will Stick" (Becker Friedman Institute Working Paper
No. 2020-174, April 2021), https://bfi.uchicago.edu/wp-content/uploads/2020/12/BFI_WP
_2020174.pdf.

57. R. Jason Faberman, Andreas I. Mueller, and Ayşegül Şahin, "Has the Willingness to Work
Fallen during the Covid Pandemic?" (NBER Working Paper No. 29784, February 2022), http://
www.nber.org/papers/w29784.

58. Arielle Pardes, "Everyone Wants to Be an Entrepreneur," *Wired*, January 24, 2022, https://
www.wired.com/story/everyone-wants-be-entrepreneur/.

Epilogue

1. Chris Wheat and Erica Deadman, "Household Pulse through June 2022: Gains for Most,
but Not All," JPMorgan Chase Institute, September 2022, https://www.jpmorganchase.com
/institute/research/household-income-spending/household-pulse-cash-balances-through
-june-2022.

2. Scott Fulford, "Office of Research Blog: Housing Inflation Is Hitting Low-Income Renters," Consumer Financial Protection Bureau blog, July 27, 2022, https://www.consumerfinance
.gov/about-us/blog/office-of-research-blog-housing-inflation-is-hitting-low-income-renters/.

3. Andrew Dunn, Andrew Warren, Necati Celik, and Wanjira Chege, "Financial Health Pulse
2022 U.S. Trends Report: Landmark Changes in Americans' Financial Health," Financial Health
Network, September 2022, https://finhealthnetwork.org/research/financial-health-pulse-2022
-u-s-trends-report/.

4. Melonie Heron, "Deaths: Leading Causes for 2019," *National Vital Statistics Report*, 2021,
70(9), https://www.cdc.gov/nchs/data/nvsr/nvsr70/nvsr70-09-508.pdf.

5. The latest research shows a stunning drop in life expectancy in 2021, even after vaccines
became widely available. In almost all other rich countries, life expectancy increased in 2021.
See Ryan K. Masters, Laudan Y. Aron, and Steven H. Woolf, "Changes in Life Expectancy between 2019 and 2021 in the United States and 21 Peer Countries," medRxiv preprint, June 2022,
https://doi.org/10.1101/2022.04.05.22273393.

INDEX

activity stoppages, 5, 27–28. *See also under* employment; shutdowns

adaptations to pandemic, 99–120; case example of, 117–20; cleaning protocols as, 99–100; comparative advantage changes and, 110–13; dating, marriage, divorce, and friend interaction changes as, 113–16; delayed or forgone medical care as, 101–4; home vs. market production as, 109–13, 246–47, 272–73, 321n52; house purchases/sales and, 104–6, 319n29; overview of, 99–101; social contact changes as, 100, 109, 111–12, 113–16; spending changes as, 102, 107, 245–47, 271–74, 321n52; supply chain shortages necessitating, 106–9; work from home as, 100, 104–5 (*see also* work from home)

Affordable Care Act, 128, 159

African American families. *See* Black families

age: COVID-19 risks with, 209; financial well-being and, 136. *See also specific age groups*

agglomeration effects, 199–200

AIG, bailout of, 284, 359n27

Akerlof, George, 103

alcohol consumption. *See* substance use/abuse

Amazon, 263

American Recovery and Reinvestment Act (2009), 360n31

American Rescue Plan Act (March 2021), 125–30; background of, 121–22, 125; child tax credits in, 128, 130, 325n27; Economic Impact Payments in, 121, 126, 255, 281; educational support in, 225; effects of, 12, 122, 128; health-related provisions in, 128; Paycheck Protection Program funding in, 79, 121; poverty measures and, 128–30, 325n27; provisions of, 125–30; renter and homelessness assistance in, 127–28, 175–76, 178; SNAP increase extension in, 128; state and local government relief in, 126–27, 165, 282; unemployment insurance benefits in, 121, 123, 125–26, 156, 234–35, 324n16

Asian Americans, death toll from COVID among, 159

automobiles: auto title loans, 53; CARES Act benefits toward loans for, 86, 87; eligibility for relief from loans for, 144; inflationary prices of, 254, 255; spending decline on, 29; state laws hampering online sales of, 29; supply chain issues for, 251–52, 254; unexpected expenses for, 45, 46, 48, 54. *See also* travel and transportation

baby formula, 251

Bank of Japan, 33

bankruptcies, 138

banks and financial institutions: borrowing from, 52–53; CARES Act administration by, 67, 79–82, 83–84, 314n61; deposit insurance in, 287; Federal Reserve programs for, 32–34, 66–67; as Paycheck Protection Program intermediaries, 79–81, 314nn61,64; 2008 financial crisis and, 27, 286, 359n27, 360n32

spent on, 42, 254; CARES Act provisions
on, 66, 69; employment issues in, 28, 243,
249–50, 254–55; initial pandemic decline
in, 5, 27–28; oil and gas prices and, 252–53;
"revenge travel," 296; school bus drivers
in, 243; shipping (or transshipping) for,
247–48, 250, 252; spending changes in,
245–46, 254; supply chain backups tied to,
247–50, 252, 254–55; trucking in, 248–50;
unexpected expenses for, 45, 46, 48; work
from home omitting, 187, 192, 201–2.
See also automobiles; commute
Treasury, U.S. Department of the, 33–34, 65,
70, 177, 283
Treasury securities, 32–33, 279, 305n45
2008 financial crisis and Great Recession:
credit cards debt in, 92; economic conditions in, 4, 19–20, 22, 27, 126; economic
growth following, 19; food insecurity in,
178; government policies and relief in, 4,
5, 32–33, 72, 144, 284–86, 359–60nn27–29,
31–32; housing foreclosures in, 5, 13,
88, 144, 167, 286, 359n28; inequality of
effects of, 151, 154; millennials impacted by,
218–21, 345–46n48; new business decline
during, 260; older workers's experiences
after, 208; savings following, 271; unemployment in, 4, 22, 217, 218, 220–21,
276, 286
Tyson Foods, 106

unemployment: definition and measurement
of, 20–21; employee reevaluation of
acceptable work after, 232–33; European
coverage of, 84–85; inequality of risks of,
151–52; initial pandemic surge of, 3, 17–18,
21–27, 28, 239, 286, 326n37; insurance
benefits for (*see* unemployment insurance); long-term, 216–18; of millennials,
218–21, 345–46n48; new business formation following, 262; of older workers's,
208–9; prepandemic, 20–21; quitting vs.,
239 (*see also* quitting); scarring from,

216–18; seasonal adjustments in, 23, 303n17;
spending decreases with, 28–29, 321n52;
substance abuse and suicide increase
with, 161; tight labor market and lower,
242; 2008 financial crisis and, 4, 22, 217,
218, 220–21, 276, 286; unexpected income
reduction with, 46–47
unemployment insurance: American
Rescue Plan Act on, 121, 123, 125–26, 156,
234–35, 324n16; as automatic stabilizer,
276–77; CARES Act on, 4, 5, 66, 68,
73–76, 121, 123, 126, 156, 274–77, 335n91; case
examples of effects of, 131–34, 326nn37–38,
40; costs of expanded, 280; December
2020 relief bill on, 121, 122–23, 156, 324n16;
eligibility for, 165, 179–80, 324n16, 326n38,
337–38n16; end of pandemic benefits,
234–35; essential workers not eligible for,
165, 276; financial well-being improvements with, 138–40, 274–77, 280, 358n20;
fraudulent claims, 26, 141–42; Great
Depression-era creation of, 287; inequality
of access to, 179–80, 276, 337–38n116;
initial pandemic claims for, 21–27; lesson
learned on benefits of, 274–77, 280, 358n20;
new business formation using, 262; older
adult benefits of, 209; Paycheck Protection Program vs., 82–85; poverty measures
and, 130; regular state benefits for, 130,
275–77; seasonal adjustments in claims
for, 23, 303n17; $600 supplement to, 4,
66, 68, 73–75, 121, 123, 126, 139, 165, 276;
spending changes in relation to, 29, 75,
235; state system administration of,
23–24, 25–27, 74, 76, 123, 125, 130, 142,
234–35, 276; taxes on, 125–26; $300
supplement to, 123, 125, 234–35; timing
of payments of, 25–27, 74–75, 123, 142,
276–77, 311n35; 2008 financial crisis claims
for, 22, 276, 286
unions, 232, 245, 263, 356n103
UPS, 244–45
Urban Institute, 130, 175, 311n35

www.ingramcontent.com/pod-product-compliance
Lightning Source LLC
Jackson TN
JSHW082014120125
76987JS00002B/3